REBEL MEXICO

REBEL MEXICO

Student Unrest and Authoritarian
Political Culture During the Long Sixties

Jaime M. Pensado

STANFORD UNIVERSITY PRESS
Stanford, California

This book is made possible in part by support from the Institute for Scholarship in the Liberal Arts, College of Arts and Letters, University of Notre Dame

Stanford University Press
Stanford, California

Printed in the United States of America on acid-free, archival-quality paper

Library of Congress Cataloging-in-Publication Data

Pensado, Jaime M., author

   Rebel Mexico : student unrest and authoritarian political culture during the long sixties / Jaime M. Pensado.

   pages cm.

Includes bibliographical references and index.

ISBN 978-0-8047-8653-9 (cloth : alk. paper) — ISBN 978-0-8047-9725-2 (pbk. : alk. paper)

1. Students—Political activity—Mexico—History—20th century. 2. Student movements—Mexico—History—20th century. 3. Political culture—Mexico—History—20th century. 4. Mexico—Politics and government—1946–1970. I. Title

LA428.7.P44 2013

378.1'981097209046—DC23   2013010531

ISBN 978-0-8047-8729-1 (electronic)

Typeset at Stanford University Press in 10/14 Minion

Para mi papá, Jenny, Andrés y Maité
que siempre han estado presentes

Contents

Tables, Figures, and Illustrations

Tables

Figures

Illustrations

Key Acronyms

CEU	University Student Council
CIDOC	International Documentation Center
CJM	Federation of Mexican Young People
CONCAMIN	Confederation of Chambers of Manufacturing
CME	Center of Mexican Writers
CNED	National Central of Democratic Students
CNH	National Strike Council
CTM	Confederation of Mexican Workers
CU	University City
CUEC	University Center of Film Studies
DDC	Directorate of Cultural Diffusion
DDF	Department of the Federal District
DFS	Office of Federal Security
ENP	National Preparatory School
FCMAR	Mexican Civic Front of Revolutionary Affirmation
FEU	University Student Federation
FNET	National Front of Technical Students
FUA	University Anticommunist Front
FUSA	University Federation of Student Societies
GCE	Grand Student Commission
INJM	National Institute of Mexican Youth

IPN	National Polytechnic Institute
IPS	General Directorate of Political and Social Investigations
JCM	Mexican Communist Youth
MLN	National Liberation Movement
MURO	University Movement of Renovational Orientation
PAN	National Action Party
PEFI	Student Party of Integrated Forces
PCM	Mexican Communist Party
PNR	National Revolutionary Party
PP	Popular Party
PRI	Institutional Revolutionary Party
SEP	Ministry of Public Education
UI	University Iberoamericana
UNAM	National Autonomous University of Mexico

Acknowledgments

I AM GRATEFUL TO the many people who shared with me their stories and experiences for this project. Many of them preferred not to have their names used. I have chosen to respect their wishes by using the nicknames they gave me or by referring to them with pseudonyms. This history of the long sixties would have been simply impossible to write without the enjoyable conversations and valuable insights shared, among many others, by "El Chaparro," "El Negro," Nicandro Mendoza, "El Gato," Jorge "Oso" Oceguera, Camilo, René Rivas, Celia Ramírez, Rodolfo Echeverría, "El Barbas," "El Mamado," "El Chapulin," Arturo Martínez, Jesus Flores Palafox, "El Chuiquilin," Salvador Ruiz Villegas, Carmen Guitán, Jorge Maza Reducindo, Carlos Ortiz Tejeda, Enrique Semo, and Carlos Monsiváis (1938–2010). I wish especially to thank Oscar González and Luis "Palillo" Rodríguez. Sadly, they have both recently passed away. In a variety of ways, and unlike any other published study, they opened my eyes to the intricacies and realities of student politics in Mexico. The same is true of "El Angel," who taught me a great deal about contemporary history and politics. I am particularly thankful to him and to his friends for their willingness to share with me their experiences with student politics, some as agents provocateurs and intermediaries, others as activists, and still others as self-identified "witnesses." I met with Oscar, Palillo, and El Angel on numerous occasions over long hours of the day at bars and in their homes, and I am extremely grateful to all of them for sharing their experiences with humor, nostalgia, pain, great detail, and, above all, honesty.

The research for my book depended on the assistance of several people. I thank the archivists and librarians who made retrieving the documents much easier. I am also grateful to those who helped me with different stages of my research and to those who generously shared their private archives with me. In particular, I am thankful to the staff at the Archives of the Dirección Federal de Seguridad, the Dirección General de Investigacions Políticas y Sociales, the Fondo Histórico "Genaro Estrada," the Fondo Histórico del Politécnico, CESU, and the Fondo Histórico de la UNAM, including, among many others, Gerardo, Miguel, Vicente Capello, and Luis Olivera. I thank *Excélsior*, *El Universal*, *Siempre!*, the Dirección General de Asuntos Diplomáticos at the Archivo Histórico Genaro Estrada, and the Fondos Enrique Díaz and Hermanos Mayo at the Archivo General de la Nación, for granting me permission for the reproduction of cartoons and photographs. Many thanks also go to Larissa Lomintz, David Vega, and, especially, Hugo Sánchez Gudiño and José Enrique Pérez Cruz. They played instrumental roles in helping me identify key documents. They also introduced me to various people that I interviewed for this project and generously shared with me their personal collections of documents, old stacks of newspapers, and notes. I thank them greatly for their valuable insight and generosity. I also wish to thank the two undergraduate students who helped me with some of the research at the Hesburgh Library, Robyn Grant and Joseph VanderZee.

I began this project in graduate school at the University of Chicago. I owe a great deal to my dissertation chairs, Emilio Kourí and Claudio Lomnitz, for their encouragement, patience, and valuable advice. Emilio's friendship and unconditional support made my graduate studies more enjoyable than I would have thought possible. Together with Claudio, he pushed me to be a more critical thinker, reader, and writer. I am also grateful to Dain Borges, who encouraged me to pursue this project the very first semester I enrolled in his seminar. He is a great teacher and a wonderful mentor.

My interest in Mexican history and social movements originated in an undergraduate class at California State University in Los Angeles taught by Professor Enrique Ochoa. Enrique's genuine commitment to his students, to his family, and to a more democratic university has been truly inspirational. He has played an instrumental role in my academic career and personal life. I thank him for all the advice and encouragement he has offered me over the last fifteen years. At Cal-State, I also thank William Bollinger, Charyl Koos, Pete Sigel, and Donald and Marjorie Bray, for introducing me to Latin American Studies and encouraging me to apply to graduate school.

Many people have given me their insight and help along the way through discussion or written comments on various parts of my manuscript. I am especially indebted to my friend José Angel Hernández, who read early, very rough, and multiple versions of my project. I value his friendship and work ethic tremendously. Many thanks go as well to my friends, colleagues, and teachers for their support at Chicago, Lehigh, and Notre Dame, including, Friedrich Katz (1929–2010), Pablo Ben, Romina Robles Ruvalcaba, Julia Young, John Flores, Anne Schneider, Dora Sánchez, Patrick Iber, Mikael Wolfe, Jessica Graham, Antonio Prieto, Sharon Schierling, and Sabine MacCormack (1941–2012). At Notre Dame, special thanks are due to my colleagues in the History Department, the Kellogg Institute for International Studies, and the Institute for Latino Studies. In particular, I thank Ted Beatty and Allert Brown-Gort for their integrity, generosity, professionalism, and, above all, friendship. The workshops and conferences at Chicago, Harvard, Yale, the Oaxaca Institute, Michigan State, St. John's University, UMASS, San Diego, Los Angeles, Lehigh, Notre Dame, Washington DC, Montreal, Queen's University, and the Congreso Internacional in Chile have left an indelible intellectual stamp on this project, and I am thankful to those who commented and offered valuable critiques. At San Francisco, I am also thankful to Ramón Solorzano. His keen eye, patience, careful listening, and copyediting skills played key roles in the transformation of this manuscript into a book. Eric Zolov and Bill French offered me critical comments and valuable suggestions for improvement on separate versions of my manuscript. I thank them both for their time and generosity. At Stanford University Press, I thank Norris Pope, Emma S. Harper, John Feneron, Martin Hanft, and Mary Mortensen.

Funding and institutional support for the development of this project came from a number of institutions. I am particularly thankful to the Mellon Foundation at the University of Chicago, the Latin American Studies Program at Lehigh University, and the Kellogg Institute for International Studies and the Institute for Scholarship in the Liberal Arts (ISLA) at the University of Notre Dame.

I want also to acknowledge several people for their ongoing support and love. I am especially grateful to my mom, Marina Valero, for the many sacrifices she made for my education and for emphasizing the value of hard work, respect for others, and the pleasure of learning. I am also thankful to my sister in Mexico, Maricarmen. Her lessons about perseverance, as passed along by our parents, have oriented my life and work. I also thank those who gave me a great foundation during an earlier period of my life, including my grandmother (*la viejita*), Tito, Marina, Jessica, Giovanni, and *tia* Eva. My mother- and father-in-law, Toni and Mario Morales, have provided unconditional love and support for me and my family over many distant, at times, difficult, but always exciting years. I will forever be in debt for their immeasurable love.

The greatest debt I owe is to my wife, two children, and dad. They have had the most influence on my life. I dedicate this book to them for all they have given to me since we first left Los Angeles in 2001. Jenny's unconditional support and love are beyond measure. To my delight, my love and debt to her continue to grow every day. Without her beautiful smiles and her immense love for our family, this book simply would not be. I thank our two children, Maité and Andrés. With them, the appreciation of everyday life is a joyous one. I hope that when they are old enough to read this book, they will find some value, if not in its content, at the very least in the long process that we all shared with great joy during its production. I thank my dad, Manuel Pensado, for remaining present with all of us all of these years. I thank him for watching over the safety of our family in Chicago, Mexico, Bethlehem, Puerto Rico, Spain, and South Bend.

—*Jaime Pensado*
September 2012

REBEL MEXICO

Introduction

ON THE NIGHT OF SEPTEMBER 18, 1968, Mexican president
Gustavo Díaz Ordaz (1964–1970) ordered the Federal Army to
take over the University City. His goal was to put an unqualified end to a two-
month-old student strike led by *revoltosos* ("troublemakers") that had threatened to spoil Mexico's hosting of the 1968 Olympic Games. The following day,
the president received a telegram of support from an appreciative citizen with
the following message: "My eleven children, wife, and I congratulate you for
this latest action taken against the communist plot." Hundreds of comparable letters continued to arrive to the presidential office in the following days
stressing that agents provocateurs sponsored by "foreign elements" had "infiltrated" Mexico. A man stated, "[As] a [true] Mexican, I celebrate the fact that
the University has been rescued by the Army." Others similarly wrote:

> This is an appropriate measure, *Señor [Presidente.]*
> I applaud you for the intervention.
> The unrest of the bad Mexicans [will finally be] crushed.
> Accept my modest support for your highly patriotic conduct.
> I am at your marching orders.
> The reign of prosperity, justice, and integrity is the flag of our
> government.
> Mexico needs order.

Analogous letters continued to arrive at the office of Díaz Ordaz after October
2, 1968, the day when an undetermined number of young students (estimated

in the hundreds) were ambushed and brutally killed or arrested by government authorities in the Plaza of Tlatelolco. A citizen expressing his indebtedness to Díaz Ordaz wrote to the president a day after the student massacre: "The true Mexican people congratulate you for having exercised, at last, the authority [of our government]." Three months later, another citizen wrote "[*Señor Presidente,*] do not let anything get in the way of putting an end to the *revoltosos.*"[1]

The excerpts highlighted above not only complicate the historiography on student politics in Mexico, which tends to overstate public support for the 1968 student movement, but also echo similar sentiments of disapproval regarding revoltosos and *porros* ("thugs" for hire/"agents provocateurs") previously voiced in Mexico for more than a decade; such sentiments continued to be heard after the student massacre in Tlatelolco. This book traces the rise of Mexico's "student problem," reaching its zenith in the '68 movement, by examining the political and social factors that led to a consolidation of *porrismo* ("student thuggery/provocation") and *charrismo estudiantil* ("student clientelism") in the postwar period. These authoritarian processes are understood by closely analyzing Mexican student politics and culture, as well as reactions to them on the part of school authorities, government officials, competing political powerbrokers, divergent voices of the Right, and the print media, particularly during the long sixties. Examining student unrest and response in the forms of sponsored student thuggery, provocation, clientelism, and *relajo* ("fun") during this period offers insight into larger issues of state formation and hegemony. Further, it helps provide an explanation for the irrefutable longevity of the Partido Revolucionario Institucional (PRI).[2]

Porros and Revoltosos

Young man, you seem to be wasting your time. I don't know who pointed you to our archives; but apparently, you have been misinformed. Here, you will never find legitimate sources on the so-called porros. Frankly, I am not sure why a historian working at an American university would be interested in such a fictional topic. Obviously I am not in a position of telling you what to do, but I strongly recommend that you reconsider your theme of investigation. Student violence in Mexico is a messy topic. In fact, the phenomenon of porrismo that you are inquiring about is nothing but a myth. It was invented by the enemies of our nation with the sole purpose of discrediting our precious institutions.

The skeptical words quoted above were uttered by an influential director from the Instituto Politécnico Nacional (National Polytechnic Institute, IPN) upon my visiting his office.[3] I responded by stating that my interests in the archives were not constrained to porrismo. Rather, I insisted that I was also seeking information pertinent to student activism inside the Politécnico during the 1950s that had been minimized in the secondary literature. In a more irritated voice he then asked me, "Is that it? Did you really come to Mexico to write a book on revoltosos and porros? Plenty of books have been written on the 1968 student movement and the so-called Tlatelolco massacre. Why write another one?"[4]

The director's attitude reflects the general wisdom within the historiography of modern Mexico, which insists on limiting the rich history of the student movement to the massacre in Tlatelolco on of October 2. Further, it speaks to a conservative voice that not only arose in support of the administration of Díaz Ordaz but also went so far as to raise doubts regarding the number of people killed on that night in 1968. Attempting to provide a broader history of student activism and divergent conservative reactions, this book examines the origins, growth, and consequences of Mexico's "student problem" by exploring student culture, political patronage, and Cold War violence in the nation's capital after the 1940s, with particular attention to the "long sixties" (1956–ca.1971). In so doing, it draws attention to the shifting notion of "youth" in Cold War Mexico, revises the historiography of the 1968 student movement by examining key antecedents of the movement and its immediate aftermath, and demonstrates how deviating authorities inside and outside the government structure responded differently to the various student revolts.

As a backdrop to this critical history of student unrest and response, this book takes up two historical questions that have not been addressed in the historiography of post-1940 Mexico: (1) What were the social, cultural, and political factors that caused porrismo to proliferate in Mexico during this period?; and (2) What does porrismo tell us about Mexican politics during the nation's "economic miracle" in general, and about the impact of the Cold War in student politics in particular?[5] The answer to these questions has much to say about the authoritarian culture of the governing elite, the conservative reactions to political dissent, the competition among local powerbrokers for control of the schools, and the defiant student activism so prominent in the nation's capital during the long sixties. The argument here stresses that porrismo, simultaneously defined as a mechanism of control and mediation, was effectively consolidated as an extralegal tool of repression and conciliation by the government and rival political elites inside the secondary schools and universities during this period. Its purpose was both to crush and to negotiate with what authorities in various positions of power saw throughout this confrontational era of the Cold War as the "rise" of "radical" student political forces.

In recent years a number of books on student culture, Cold War violence, and political patronage in Mexico have been published. In the work on student uprisings, memoirs of former student leaders, chronicles, and photographic testimonies are the most common.[6] While insightful, they are often impressionistic. With a few exceptions, this literature tends to overstate the idiosyncrasies of the 1968 student movement, lacks a rigorous examination of the importance of earlier student uprisings, falls short in explaining the social and political factors that contributed to the escalation of student factionalism that characterized this period, and fails to consider the incongruities of the student movement, including the students' readiness to invoke the legitimacy of violence in the name of democracy.[7] To offer a more comprehensive history of student activism, this book employs the term "the long sixties" to denote an era in student politics characterized by a new culture of more aggressive public protest and political violence. In dialogue with the historiography of the global sixties, this book argues that the political activism of the era did not take place in a vacuum. Instead, it was characterized by an international language of dissent in which students assumed the role of central protagonists of "revolutionary" and/or "democratic" changes who embraced innovative strategies of defiance and opened new spaces of contestation.[8] The book contends that in Mexico, the crucial—yet hitherto overlooked—1956 strike at the Instituto Politécnico Nacional was the opening salvo of this period's student activism, and both the 1956–1959 workers' movements against charrismo ("labor union bossism") and the Cuban Revolution of 1959 greatly influenced the direction of student political and cultural activity in subsequent years.

The military occupation of the IPN in 1956, the regular use of the riot police, and the imprisonment of students, labor leaders, and intellectuals thereafter sparked the birth of a "New Left." As conceived of by a new generation of students and intellectuals (and recently brought to our attention by a few historians), this New Left denounced the authoritarian nature of the "revolutionary" state, the "anachronistic" language in defense of "traditional values" endorsed by older parents and school authorities, and what many began to see as the incompetence of an "old" generation of leftists.[9] After the 1968 uprising, a small yet significant segment of the otherwise moderate New Left was further radicalized by the student massacre carried out by the military in the Plaza of Tlatelolco. Moreover, as others have demonstrated, the positive image that Mexico had come to enjoy in the international arena as a stable and relatively democratic nation was tarnished by this violent outcome.

The state took major steps throughout the long sixties to shore up its political authority inside the schools and restore its image abroad. After 1956, it made a deliberate effort to distinguish itself from other Latin American countries by reducing the role of the military in politics.[10] In moving away from the use of overt force, Mexico invested tremendous resources in extralegal mechanisms of control and mediation, which included the use of agents provocateurs and charismatic intermediaries (*porristas,* or "male cheerleaders") inside the schools and the installation of corrupt leaders (*charros*) in the student organizations (and labor unions). To complement these mechanisms and to transfer power to a civilian government, the state also expanded its riot police force (the *granaderos*), and with the financial support of the U.S. Intelligence Services, it transformed the Office of Federal Security (Dirección Federal de Seguridad, DFS) into a powerful and efficient machine of repression and surveillance.[11] In the aftermath of the Cuban Revolution the state went to great lengths to carry out a series of populist reforms and institute a more aggressive form of porrismo. To elaborate this point, this book engages in dialogue with the few studies that have examined this uniquely Mexican phenomenon.[12] But distinctively, it argues that these combined efforts were, on the one hand, directed toward the repression and co-opting of the moderate activists, responsible for the student activism of the long sixties and served, on the other hand, as a cover for the surgical government repression launched against the more radical activists of this period. Furthermore, unlike the few studies that have examined porrismo, the book argues that the politics of "fun," or relajo, also constituted a vital aspect of this mechanism of control and mediation, which school and national authorities manipulated to both accentuate the crisis of youth and to "manage" student politics.[13]

The long sixties also witnessed what students of the New Left themselves interpreted as the creation of and participation in new (and more democratic) spaces of contestation inside the schools. This book argues that such spaces, which included a renovated radio station, countercultural and academic journals, and movie houses (*cineclubs*) as well as innovative student assemblies and independent student organizations and newspapers, allowed for the articulation of demands that were largely identical to those put forth by the student activists in 1968. The print media and divergent voices of the Right, concerned with the students' readiness to invoke the legitimacy of violence in these new spaces of contestation, joined authorities in painting these demands as "subversive threats" to the centrist position promoted by the state. The democratic as well as violent actions by the students were met with public outrage in the nation's most influential newspapers and magazines (*Excélsior*, *El Universal*, and *Tiempo*), as the growing "student problem" represented one of several anxieties that came to the fore at this time. Taking their cues from the changing perceptions of youth in other countries, Mexican journalists, government authorities, and key intellectuals referred to students who engaged in politics, relajo, and violence as "rebels without a cause," "revoltosos," and eventually "porros" whose hedonistic subculture and infatuation with vandalism imperiled Mexico's traditional values.[14] Drawing from key texts in Youth Studies, this book argues that school and national authorities fanned the flames of public fears by lumping together "the rising student problem" with the "threatening" images of the Cold War, such as reactionary politics and especially communism.[15] The divergent voices published in the media, echoing the sentiments expressed by the state, argued that "foreign ideologies," or worse yet, *manos extrañas* ("foreign hands") endangered national unity, social stability, and economic progress. They made persistent demands that the ruling authorities in the PRI do something about them, using force if necessary.

Many of the most important scholarly works dealing with the PRI make evident that the state indeed responded to popular protests (although not always "successfully") with wide-scale repression during this period.[16] On the one hand, the postwar era, traditionally celebrated in the historiography for its political stability, rapid economic growth, and the consolidation of the middle class, simultaneously witnessed a steady progression of social unrest.[17] On the other hand, the PRI did not have a monopoly on the repression of such unrest, as scholars frequently assume.[18] Key figures representing competing ideological positions within the PRI, but also from oppositional parties as well as from the private sector, also became involved in promoting porrismo in the context of the Cold War.

Historians recently have expanded debates about the impact of the Cold War in Latin America in three significant ways.[19] First, they have shifted away from a focus on the Cold War as strictly a bipolar conflict, and so have made it clear that the presence of the "superpowers" in Latin America was not as monolithic as the historiography often assumes. Second, they have demonstrated that key decision-making power during the Cold War was not always confined to Latin American states. Finally, by stressing the political nature of culture, authors have reminded us that political power does not only flow from above in the form of laws and institutional intervention, but also from below, "through language and symbolic systems and manifests itself in identities and everyday practices."[20] Engaging with these three assertions, this book shows that a variety of figures inside and outside of the government (or the *priísta* structure) developed porrismo into an effective mechanism of control and mediation during this period in order to both subdue and negotiate with a new generation of increasingly militant, yet emphatically factionalized, "rebellious" students. In making this argument, the book draws on the work of a variety of authors who have demonstrated that political power in Mexico has historically been negotiated between diverse corporate groups through a complex social and political network of *camarillas* ("political cliques") and clientelism.[21] But distinctively, by taking a close look at the role *padrinos del relajo* played in student politics, it joins the relatively few scholars who have explored the interconnections between cultural expressions of fun and the realm of politics.[22]

Further, in examining the role that agents provocateurs played in fomenting student factionalism, the book also addresses the demographic, social, cultural, and political components that contributed to the lack of unification in the student body. The dominant historiography suggests that the state had successfully unified its citizens by the 1950s under the umbrella of "revolutionary nationalism."[23] By contrast, this book demonstrates how incredibly faction-ridden the population of the nation's capital was, particularly young people who repeatedly challenged the state's patrimonial authority, not in 1968 for the first time, as the scholarship tends to suggest, but throughout the postwar period (and especially in the aftermath of the Cuban Revolution). Powerful, even violent, distinctions were made between "good" and "bad" Mexicans, "patriots" and "sell-outs," not only by the conservative representatives of the state but also by the Left, the Right, the students themselves, and the public, in general, which grew increasingly intolerant of the "undemocratic" nature of student culture, as evident in the destruction of property, the occupation of public spaces, and the defamation of "sacred," "religious," "national," and/or "revolutionary" symbols and traditional values.

Finally, tracing the development and consequences of porrismo, this book draws a parallel between porrismo and a similar mechanism, charrismo. This form of institutionalized union cronyism was characterized by a kind of *caciquismo* ("bossism") that took advantage of the networks that developed among corrupt union leaders, business interests, and government authorities.[24] In the 1940s and 1950s charrismo served government elites quite well as a means of thwarting and controlling labor unions. This book argues that projects dedicated to modernization, national unity, centralization, revolutionary progress, and bureaucratization—present in the National Autonomous University of Mexico (UNAM), the Politécnico (IPN), and their secondary schools (*preparatorias* and *vocacionales*, respectively)—not only failed to eliminate caciquismo but rather nationalized it in the forms of porrismo and charrismo estudiantil.[25]

Sources and Methodology

The book relies on interviews and a variety of documents from Mexican and U.S. archives. The majority of the interviews developed from casual conversations with former students enrolled in the Politécnico and UNAM during the 1950s and early 1960s.[26] Some of these interviewees, such as Luis "Palillo" Rodriguez, Jorge "El Oso" Oceguera, and Oscar González, served as key intermediaries between cultural activities and politics.[27] Others, such as Nicandro Mendoza and Carlos Ortiz Tejeda, had leading roles in the student protests of 1956 and 1958, respectively.[28] Not all of the interviewees were prominent figures, but their testimony was valuable nonetheless—some former provocateurs, such as "El Angel," "El Negro," and "El Gato," provided candid accounts of their activities.[29] With very few exceptions, none of the people interviewed played a significant role in the 1968 student movement.[30] And because the overwhelming majority of students who engaged in public activism, provocation, violence, and *desmadre* (a more aggressive culture of youth defiance) were young men, these and similar voices referenced here speak primarily to a male perspective. As Elaine Carey (among others) has demonstrated, these hegemonic voices were challenged throughout the long sixties, but only became louder in 1968 when thousands of young female students took over the streets to engage "in a two-front gender battle." Carey explains, "They subverted gender roles and social and political constructs of their elders by becoming public, but they also struggled with their male comrades in the movement who continued to view their female peers through a traditional lens."[31] Earlier parallels to the 1956 student uprising emphasized here suggest that when female students engaged in public protest, they too acquired the otherwise masculine label of revoltoso.[32]

Interviewing people who served as leading lights in student politics during the 1950s and early 1960s was a conscious decision on the part of the author. The goal was to move away from what has developed into an "official" narrative of student activism in Mexico, an account that continues to dominate the historiography. Ignoring important antecedents that took place in the 1940s, 1950s, and early 1960s, this "official history," Herbert Braun explains, "reside[s] at the core of a broad set of ideas held mainly by a small and vocal group of seasoned student militants, university professors, teachers, and intellectuals who were initially at the forefront of the [1968 student] movement," such as Gilberto Guevara Niebla, Raúl Alvarez Garín, Luis González de Alba, Elena Poniatowska, Carlos Monsiváis, Daniel Cazés, and Marcelino Perelló.[33] These authors, political activists, and intellectuals as well as the scholars who continue to rely on their interpretations, have failed to locate important historical events within a local context of repeated postrevolutionary mobilizations, such as the 1942, 1950, and (especially) the 1956 strikes organized in the IPN or the protest launched by *universitarios* (UNAM students) in 1958.[34] In doing so, they fail to recognize events that crystallized a higher level of engagement on the part of a new generation of intellectuals and student activists who began to decry the degeneration of the Mexican Revolution.

Political cartoons published in the nation's most influential newspapers, photographs, and films were particularly important in documenting the rise of a national "student problem" during the Cold War. As historian Elisa Servín has argued, besides involving military threats and "geopolitical containments" on an international level, the Cold War also entailed an ideological "war of words." Propaganda was orchestrated by the two conflicting powers for a common objective: to manipulate information in order to "inflict fear" and "create new monsters and heroes."[35] Mexico's mainstream media was not immune to this ideological war. Besides "words," it also became invested in the manipulation of "images," in which photographers, filmmakers, and cartoonists in the nation's leading newspapers, *El Universal* and *Excélsior*, played a crucial role in swaying public opinion in favor of the "discreet" yet highly "authoritarian" anticommunist stance preferred by the "centrist" Mexican state during the most volatile years of the Cold War.[36] For instance, with the financial and political support from the U.S. and Mexican governments, the cartoonists Andrés Audiffred, Arias Bernal, and Rafael Freyre (repeatedly referenced in the book) not only were involved in creating an atmosphere that made it easy for the Mexican public to accept the 1954 CIA-sponsored overthrow of the democratically elected Guatemalan government of Arbenz, but, echoing the institutionalized rhetoric of the state, they also portrayed the Mexican Revolution as "incomplete," yet one that was very much alive and still reliant on a strong presidential leader.[37] Promoting this paternalistic view of Mexico, the three cartoonists argued that postwar Mexico was experiencing some sort of "youth crisis" that threatened "national unity," *mexicanidad* (national identity promoted by the state), the "family," "traditional" gender roles, and "revolutionary progress." In particular, echoing the words of others, they worried that if left without institutional guidance, UNAM and IPN students could be led astray by foreign ideologies, such as "youthful rebelliousness without a cause," or worse yet, communism. Nonetheless, the Cuban Revolution and the countercultural turn associated with the global youthful unrest of the 1960s would have a significant impact on a new generation of political cartoonists. Largely represented in the book by Eduardo del Río (Rius), this new generation of cartoonists would open new and more independent spaces of contestation to argue that little had changed since the Mexican Revolution, and they demanded that more radical measures needed to be taken. Further, unlike the critical yet more conservative cartoonists of the 1950s, they would redefine students as "active agents" of society capable of bringing real revolutionary changes to Mexico.[38]

Equally important in the effort to depart from the "official history" of the student movement was the consultation of student manifestoes, pamphlets, propaganda, and school newspapers produced during the 1940s, 1950s, and early 1960s. The same is true of newspaper accounts representing a broad range of perspectives from the Left, the center, and the Right; reports relating to cultural, athletic, and political matters that were sent to the university rector's office; U.S. government documents produced primarily by the U.S. embassy in Mexico; diplomatic telegrams and detailed reports received by the Ministry of Interior (Gobernación) from multiple Mexican embassies stationed in different countries of Europe, Asia and the Americas; and thousands of Mexican government reports written by agents of the Office of Federal Security (DFS) and the General Directorate of Political and Social Investigations (Dirección General de Investigaciones Políticas y Sociales, hereafter IPS).[39]

President Vicente Fox ordered Gobernación in November 2001 to make these documents available to the public, so as to bring to light information related to past human rights abuses.[40] In June 2002 Gobernación, following the president's directive, compiled "some eighty million documents that were deposited in the National Archive." One of the goals of the Fox administration was to find "evidence" that would detail the authoritarianism of the PRI. Nonetheless, as the present work concludes from the use of these same archives, the PRI never consolidated a monopoly on political violence, as testimonies by student activists often assume. Influential *panistas* (PAN members), as well as key members from oppositional parties and the Right, also relied on the use of agents provocateurs and intermediaries inside the schools.

Research for this book suggests that documents out of the DFS and related agencies pertaining to *problemas estudiantiles* ("student problems," as they were called) became more frequent in the early 1950s, and there was a noticeable increase following the 1956 student protest at the IPN.[41] When Colonel Manuel Rangel Escamilla became director of the DFS (a post he held from 1958 to 1964), the flow of documents from the agency became a torrent, and the documents themselves became more detailed. These and other sources show that, following the outbreak of the Cuban Revolution, the DFS and IPS managed to infiltrate the leading educational institutions of Mexico, particularly those where leftist students had achieved the greatest degree of prominence (the Law, Economics, Political Science, and Philosophy and Letters schools), as well as Preparatorias #2 and #5, where porros held sway. The goal of the DFS and the IPS, as the straightforward language of these reports makes plain (especially in the case of the DFS under Fernando Gutiérrez Barrios [1964–1970]), was to prevent the spread of both communism and ultraconservative ideology inside the schools. To accomplish this goal, training programs on espionage, information gathering, and social behavior underwent significant improvements.[42] But by the mid-1960s secret agents of the DFS and the IPS had come to rely on porros as informants (*orejas*) and provocateurs. Moreover, these documents include ample evidence confirming that school officials, national authorities, the police, and secret agents were aware of the activities, political networks, and specific crimes committed by porros. Yet the government seemed to have prosecuted only the "provocateurs," "delinquents," or "criminals" (as they called them) when they were no longer useful, or, as El Angel (a porro leader at Preparatoria #2 in the mid-1960s) angrily lamented during an interview, "when we made the mistake of messing with the wrong padrinos." He explained:

> We frequently worked together with agents of the DFS and the police. We
> sold them information. Some of us even bought their bullshit (*chingaderas*),
> you know? We really thought that communism was taking over Mexico and,
> as the guardians of order that we were, we intervened in student politics
> to stop the radicals from importing foreign revolutionary models into our
> nation. Other porros were much savvier that I ever was. They collaborated
> with the DFS, school authorities, important políticos, and the police, but
> for personal ambitions. Accordingly, these porros ended up as full time
> agents of the DFS, as members of the judicial police, as school directors, or
> as "respectable" politicians. I, like many other porros, by contrast, ended
> up in prison. Others were not so lucky. They ended up with drug problems
> or dead. We were all victims of an authoritarian system. The powerful
> prevailed. Those who wanted to make Mexico a more democratic nation are
> still struggling. We all learned in the process.[43]

But porros were not the only actors who served as "guardians of order"
inside the schools or as key intermediaries between school and government
authorities and students. DFS and IPS documents give ample evidence that
athletes, as well as bona fide student leaders and charros, also played key roles
in the political management of student activists. Many of these actors, such
as El Angel, became victims of an authoritarian system. Others excelled;
took advantage of their direct and/or indirect role in the consolidation of
charrismo estudiantil and porrismo; and became key authorities within the
schools, the government, oppositional parties, and the private sector. One of
the intermediaries who became a successful politician was the IPN director
noted at the beginning of the introduction. His career began as an influential
charro leader at the IPN during the 1950s. His networks of political patronage
expanded in the aftermath of the 1956 student protest. And despite his insistence that porrismo was nothing but a "myth," provocateurs as well as former
student leaders later testified that this influential IPN director became a chief
promoter of porrismo in subsequent decades.[44]

Structure of the Book

Divided into three parts, the book first traces the socioeconomic, demographic, political, and cultural changes emerging during the postwar period
that compelled key authorities and intellectuals to view politicized students

as potential threats to "national unity" and "revolutionary progress." Chapter 1 gives a broad overview of the structural changes that developed during the heyday of Mexico's "economic miracle," as differently perceived by middle class universitarios and working-class *politécnicos* (IPN students). Chapter 2 specifically analyzes the cultural and political significance of *relajo* and traces its links to desmadre. It asserts that authorities responded to the growing political awareness and defiance of students inside and outside the school setting by framing them as a population "in a transitional moment of crisis" in need of governmental control. School and national authorities would eventually sponsor and manipulate with some success both these practices throughout the long sixties to accentuate the so-called crisis of youth, covertly undermining the growth of student activism.

Part II examines the rise of Mexico's "student problem" and state response in the form of the consolidation of charrismo estudiantil during the early part of the long sixties. The 1956 student strike in the Politécnico is the focus of Chapter 3. This chapter argues that, more than any other national student protest, this very significant yet understudied strike signaled the end of an era in student activism and the beginning of a new one. On the one hand, the 1956 protest was the last in a series of student demonstrations demanding a return to cardenista "popular politics." On the other, this important episode represents the first massive student strike of the long sixties to challenge notions of power and authority in public by bringing an incipient concept of democracy and new strategies of struggle into the streets. In so doing, young students came to be seen as a "subversive threat to the nation" manipulated by manos extrañas. Chapter 4 examines both putatively legal and extralegal mechanisms of control employed by government authorities and competing political powerbrokers to repress, co-opt, and/or negotiate with students of the Politécnico during the 1956 student protest. As a key point of comparison, this chapter also examines the consolidation of charrismo estudiantil inside UNAM during the university's "Golden Years." Occurring during the administrations of Nabor Carrillo Flores (1953–1961), this period tends to be described in the historiography as one of economic prosperity and social stability, as evidenced by the founding of Ciudad Universitaria (University City, or CU), an increase in federal funding, and no massive student protests (with the exception of 1958). However, for an emerging generation of students claiming to transform UNAM into a truly autonomous and democratic space, the emergence of charrismo estudiantil during the rectorship of Nabor Carrillo also marked a dark period in the history of this institution. Chapter 5 reviews the significance of the 1958 student strike organized by universitarios in support of striking bus drivers. It argues that, despite the protest's short duration (August 22 to September 4), this event should be interpreted as one of the most important student actions of postrevolutionary Mexico, which would partly influence the rise of Mexico's New Left. Following the 1958 strike, students began to see themselves as a unifying front—*el estudiantado*—a "movement" that could challenge the institutionalized barriers of class differences that had traditionally kept students from different institutions apart. In particular, this chapter argues that the uprisings of 1958 emerged to a large extent as a direct response to the consolidation of charrismo as a mechanism of control across the domains of labor and education.

Part III examines student unrest and government response in the aftermath of the Cuban Revolution. Chapter 6 explores the impact of this defining international event on the leftist student political landscape at UNAM, as evident in at least four significant ways: the radicalization of students throughout the 1960s in response to the proliferation of charrismo estudiantil; the revaluation of the importance of ideology by this new generation of politicized students (and intellectuals); the creation of innovative spaces of contestation; and the rise of reactionary politics and political violence. The chapter argues that the internationalist spirit of the 1960s gave rise to a new culture of political violence and protest inside UNAM. It illustrates the characteristics of Mexico's "New Left" by focusing on several intellectuals who were influential inside UNAM and who decried the degeneration of the Mexican Revolution in their prime vehicles of expression: the political cartoonist Rius, the participants of the university cineclubs, the collaborators of Radio Universidad, and the writers of *El Espectador, Revista de la Universidad,* and *El Corno Emplumado.* Chapter 7 lays out the different ways in which the administration of Díaz Ordaz and competing political powerbrokers responded to the "radicalization" of students during the 1960s, with particular attention to the financial support of "porra gangs" and pseudo-student organizations. The so-called international threat imposed on Mexico during the 1968 student movement is the subject of analysis in Chapter 8. Unlike previous studies of this important event, this concluding chapter examines the divergent conservative reactions that came in support of President Díaz Ordaz. It argues that '68 renovated the language of the Right and brought the different factions together, which—once unified—played an important role in minimizing the popular support of the movement and in defending the repressive reaction of the government. The conclusion illustrates the particularly violent environment that emerged inside the schools during Luis Echeverría's so-called democratic aperture, offers a brief critique of the *Memorial del 68* (opened in the Plaza of Tlatelolco in 2007–2008 to commemorate the fortieth anniversary of the 1968 student movement), and raises a number of historical inquiries that remain unaddressed in the scholarship.

PART I

Prelude to the Sixties: Youth Unrest
and Resistance to Postwar "National Identity"

1 Conflicting Interpretations of Mexico's "Economic Miracle"

B EGINNING IN 1938 and continuing during the presidential administrations of Manuel Ávila Camacho (1940–1946), Miguel Alemán (1946–1952), and Adolfo Ruiz Cortines (1952–1958), Mexico experienced a period of dramatic changes. The new Import Substitution Industrialization (ISI) economic model was created and ideologically promoted under revolutionary nationalism. As understood throughout the continent, the idea of ISI was that, by investing in its own national industries, Latin America would minimize the historical dependency on European and North American manufacturing and agricultural goods and, thus, become more integrated and self-sufficient, particularly, during difficult worldwide economic recessions.[1] With this goal in mind, the patriotic banner of "national unity" served as the impetus for ISI, whose effect was felt primarily in the nation's capital. In time, these economic changes came to be equated with rapid urban industrialization, an influx of entrepreneurs and technocrats into the government, the centralization of state power, and a more harmonious relationship with the private sector.[2]

This period was commonly hailed as Mexico's "economic miracle." It was widely reported, for example, that between 1940 and 1966, the Mexican GDP grew 368 percent. In addition, the press, governmental reports, and scholars also noted that the average annual growth-rate of GDP for the same period was larger than 6 percent.[3] Other indications of this tremendous growth included significant advances in manufacturing, an unprecedented low inflation, and a steady foreign exchange rate.[4] Furthermore, the economic miracle represented a moment when a number of important technological advances in the energy, communications, and transportation systems were realized, and increases in production, tourism, and the availability of consumer goods stimulated mass consumption for a burgeoning middle class. This was especially true following the presidential administration of Ávila Camacho, when dozens of new industries dramatically transformed the economic and social landscapes of Mexico.[5]

However, a closer look at other forms of statistical data reveals that this economic boom came with a high price. For example, while this period saw substantial economic growth as measured in GDP, dependency on foreign capital in the form of direct foreign investment (mostly from the United States) grew more than 700 percent between 1940 and 1957, primarily because of the state's failure to finance itself from domestic resources.[6] As a result of this investment, the economic and cultural roles of the United States in Mexico during this period grew significantly important. U.S. government officials, advertising agencies, and business executives regained ownership of production properties and dominated bilateral trade and high technology.[7] Moreover, they brought with them new capitalists beliefs that primarily benefited the rising middle class in the urban sector as represented in the celebrations of upward social mobility, material prosperity, and what historian Julio Moreno calls "a form of democracy through consumption."[8] Concurrently, the economic miracle did not necessarily benefit all sectors of society equally. Economist Roger Hansen noted, for example, that economic growth during this period did not imply a reduction of social and economic inequalities. He concluded, in fact, that the cost of living index for Mexico City's working class increased significantly from 21.3 in 1940 to 75.3 in 1950 (1954=100). Yet real wages plummeted by as much as 30 percent between 1940 and 1950.[9] The situation did not improve during the next decade for the bottom 30 percent of families, as they experienced a decline in their monthly incomes from an average monthly salary of 302 pesos in 1950 to 241 in 1963.[10] The top 30 percent of families, in contrast, saw an average increase in their monthly incomes from 1,132 pesos in 1950 to 2,156 in 1963.[11]

Economic disparities had an important impact on the composition of schools. More than 80 percent of *politécnicos* (students enrolled in the National Polytechnic Institute, IPN) during the late 1930s came from parents of the lower class, particularly the working, public, and peasant sectors (see Table

TABLE 1.1. Social Background of Politécnicos, 1936

Type of school	Total students enrolled	Occupation of head of household								
		A	B	C	D	E	F	G	H	I
Prevocacional & vocacionales	6,527	327	1,583	2,646	1,064	454	298	75	8	72
Superiores	4,662	78	1,401	1,452	548	616	189	278	14	86
Total	11,189	405	2,984	4,098	1,612	1,070	487	353	22	158
Percent	100%	3.6	26.7	36.6	14.4	9.5	4.7	3.1	—	1.4

Key: A, Domestic workers, etc.; B, Workers, peasants, and artisans; C, Government employees, including members of the police and the military, etc.; D, Small commerce and agricultural workers; E, Female housekeepers; F, Shopkeepers and small entrepeneurs; G, Self-sufficient students; H, Students who depend on Boarding Schools; I, Not classified.
Source: Data from IPN, *50 años*, 63.

1.1). Only a small fraction of them (4.7 percent) came from households in which their parents held a professional career.[12] Unfortunately there are no reliable statistics on the social background of politécnicos during the 1940s and early 1950s. Jorge "Oso" Oceguera (head of the cheerleading team of the IPN, 1950–1957) remembered during an interview, "[T]he fact that we were students certainly put us in a privileged position. But in reality, the over-whelming majority of politécnicos were from the working class or what could broadly be described as a lower middle class on the verge of upward social mobility."[13]

Nicandro Mendoza (principal leader of the 1956 student protest) gave a similar description:

Prior to the [1956] strike, the majority of us came from humble origins. This was evident in the clothes we wore, in the neighborhoods where we lived, and especially, in the nature of the demands that we raised during our student protests. The majority of students enrolled in the Politécnico came from parents of the lower classes. Many politécnicos certainly witnessed a gradual improvement in their lives during the 1940s and 1950s, but judging from the frustration expressed in many of the political rallies organized during these two decades, you could conclude that a large majority of students felt that they had been excluded from the economic boom.[14]

The socioeconomic circumstances of the politécnicos differed from the overwhelming majority of *universitarios* (students enrolled at the National Autonomous University of Mexico, UNAM) during the growth of Mexico's economic boom. The first census taken at UNAM in 1949, for example, indicated that from a total of twenty-three thousand students, 29 percent came

TABLE 1.2. Social Description of Universitarios, 1958–1965

	ENP students (total %)		UNAM students (total %)	
	1958–1960	1965	1958–1960	1965
Age:				
18 yrs old or less in 1st grade	81.2	72.5		—
21 yrs old or less in 1st grade	—	—	81	n/a
Single (marital status)	96	98.7	87.5	92.5
Depend for income on parents	81.3	85.8	76.7	79.5
Profession of the person supporting the student:				
Professional	31.7	25.1	23.2	17.6
White collar	52	59.3	52.4	56.1
Blue collar and peasant	16.3	15.6	24.4	26.3
Monthly Income of Parents (in 1965 pesos):				
Less than 1,000 (minimum salary = 656.75)	—	7.6	—	3.9
1,001–2,000	—	26.4	—	17.1
2,001–3,000	—	23.3	—	18.7
3,001–5,000	—	25.6	—	27.9
5,001–7,000	—	10.3	—	16.9
7,001–12,000 (or more)	—	4.8	—	15.5
Students who work (part-time and/or full time)				
First graders	21.2	17.7	26.9	23.3
All grades	25.4	22.6	34.3	36.6
Born in the Federal District	n/a	70.8	n/a	60.8

Source: Data from Covo, "La composición social."

from parents that were described as *comerciantes* (merchants), 20.64 percent as *empleados* (public employees), and 10.58 percent as *profesionistas* (professionals). In other words, unlike the majority of working-class politécnicos, a total of 70 percent of all students enrolled at UNAM in the late 1940s could be broadly defined as members of the middle class. The remaining 30 percent were from the lower- and upper-class sectors.[15] Historian David E. Lorey noted that little had changed over a decade later.[16]

Data compiled from a study by Milena Covo (see Table 1.2) supports Lorey's major findings. It also offers a more detailed description of the social composition of most universitarios during the late 1950s and early 1960s. Nearly all students enrolled at UNAM during this period were between the ages of eighteen and twenty-five. At least one-third of all universitarios were born outside the Federal District. Only a small fraction of the total number of students were married. By and large, their education was paid for by their parents, who generally held a professional or white-collar job.[17] An average of one-fifth of all universitarios held a part-time or a full-time job to supplement their income. In short, as Lorey similarly noted in his study, a significant number of students enrolled at UNAM came from the middle- and upper-class sectors, which witnessed the greatest benefits of the economic boom.

The class distinctions between politécnicos and universitarios would influence the distinct political trajectories that these two groups of students would take during the 1940s and 1950s. Because the postrevolutionary state proceeded to transform UNAM into the most important educational institution in Mexico's pursuit of modern industrial capitalism, universitarios overwhelmingly fared much better as a result of the restructuring of the economic and political systems during this period than did the politécnicos. For the latter, the "shift to the Right" in politics and the state projects of "modernization" and "national unity" meant a gradual abandonment of the cardenista policies, including what they deemed as an "attack" on popular education and a deterioration of their schools. For universitarios, on the other hand, these two decades brought unprecedented economic opportunities celebrated with the creation of Ciudad Universitaria and a new attitude of middle-class consumption. For both, this period of extraordinary economic expansion also marked the rise of a unique environment of corporatism and nationalist anticommunism, as well as an unprecedented growth in student population. A further examination of the impact these socioeconomic, demographic, and political changes had on the student population lays the groundwork for the so-called student problem that emerged during the long sixties and the perceived need on the part of authorities to control it. But first, a brief historical sketch of the founding of UNAM and the IPN and the successful efforts to extend state corporatism into the domains of these major centers of higher education is in order.

Conflicting Origins of UNAM and the Politécnico

UNAM has its roots in the Royal and Pontifical University of Mexico, which was founded in 1551 and officially inaugurated in 1553 as the oldest North American university in the Western tradition. For two centuries it would serve as one of the principal institutions of colonial culture and authority. Its time-honored elite status repeatedly expressed itself in a conservatism, a resistance to change from without, and an uneasy, see-saw relationship with the state. For example, in 1821 the university refused to accept the new independent nation, and it sheltered those who fought in favor of retaining colonial rule. The conservative university was viewed as a threat to the new nation by

influential liberals like José María Luis Mora, who declared it "useless, pernicious, and irreformable."[18] Following the war of independence, the university
was forced to close its doors several times.[19]

After closing the university in 1867, President Benito Juárez opened the
Escuela Nacional Preparatoria (National Preparatory School, or ENP) in
the colonial building of San Ildefonso. Located at the center of what became
known as the *barrio estudiantil* (student neighborhood), the ENP served as
the most prestigious institution since its creation in 1867 until September of
1910, when the National University reopened its doors as part of the centen-
nial celebration of independence. Two months later, the Mexican Revolution
erupted, and once again the university served as a refuge for those who found
themselves in opposition to the insurgents.[20] Tension between the university
and the state continued to grow following the violent phase of the revolution
(1910–1917). The subordination of the university to the Ministry of Public Education (SEP) in 1923, and the creation of the *secundarias* (Secondary Schools)
two years later, further worsened the relationship.[21] The tension came to a
head in a 1929 student protest that resulted in important concessions. The
protest forced the state to grant the university its autonomy; it gave the school
the legal rights to administer its resources, make academic decisions, and
appoint its own administrators. By incorporating the Federación Estudiantil
Universitaria (University Student Federation, FEU) into the University Council, students were represented as a unified body.[22]

Relations between the university and the state would turn bitter once again
in the early 1930s during a debate over the role that socialist ideas should have
in the schools. Student strikers had raised the issue of a specifically socialist
approach to education during a 1929 strike, and the 1933 University Congress
in Puebla provided a forum for opposing sides on this issue to meet.[23] One
camp of students and school authorities was represented by Vicente Lombardo Toledano, a teacher, union leader, political activist, and a director of the
ENP at the time. While praising the university for its "affirmation of spiritual
values and human dignity," Lombardo Toledano believed that only a radical
redistribution of wealth on the part of the state and a socialist educational
campaign carried out with the help of universitarios could incorporate the
poor into the revolutionary project to create a truly just society.[24] Strongly
disagreeing with this position was a second and larger faction. It was composed of old liberals, conservatives with close affiliations to the church, and
leftists, broadly represented by the man of letters and former university rec-

tor Antonio Caso. For Caso and his followers, academic freedom could be guaranteed only with institutional neutrality and, thus, a legally sanctioned socialist pedagogy placed this in jeopardy. For those who agreed with Caso, politics had no place inside the schools. Rather, they envisioned the universities as cultural communities exclusively concerned with research and teaching.[25] Key players inside the university—including José Vasconcelos (rector of the university in 1920 and first Secretary of Public Education, 1920–1925), Rodolfo Brito Foucher (director of the Law School), and Alejandro Gómez Arias (leader of the 1929 student strike)—sided with the Caso position. In retaliation, the state announced the New Organic Law of 1933, stating that the government would no longer subsidize the university. Consequently, the university obtained complete autonomy from the state and thus lost its "national character." Now students were allowed to participate directly in the school's governance, and they gained a hand in designating school authorities. At this point the National University became the Autonomous University of Mexico (UAM). But over time autonomy in the name of liberty had the de facto effect of creating a more favorable climate for conservatives.[26]

The historical roots and aspirations of the IPN varied significantly from those celebrated by the founders of UNAM. The Politécnico was created in 1937. Originally conceived within a "pragmatic" Marxist framework, the main goal of the IPN was to serve the nation by educating the children of the working class in the latest technological advances.[27] Responding to the worldwide depression and crisis that began in 1929, the founders of the IPN deemed that in order to eliminate dependence on foreign suppliers, Mexico, first, had to invest in technical education and, then, develop its own industries.[28] It was therefore necessary for the nation to distance itself from the idea, widely accepted in the past, that the technical professions were beneath the cultural level of the so-called liberal professions of UNAM, primarily law and medicine.[29]

As expressed in a proposal presented to the Ministry of Education by Juan de Dios Bátiz, head of the Department of Vocational Education, "the Revolutionary Government had the obligation to offer Mexico's youth—especially to the children of the working class—new professions that would take advantage of natural resources." These new professions, to be created by the state, he further argued, would foster a new social state, one that was more humane and just.[30] The popular and nationalistic emphases presented in Bátiz's proposal and championed by President Lázaro Cárdenas (1934–1940) envisioned the IPN as a genuine project of the Mexican Revolution. As such, it was to enjoy an official relationship with the state that precluded institutional autonomy. Its directors were to be designated by the government according to a vertical relation of power, and its budget was to be drawn up with the exclusive goal of meeting the nation's greatest needs.

This particular affiliation of the IPN and the state tended to relegate the students to a subordinate position vis-à-vis the government, much like the paternalistic relationship. For its part, *Papá Gobierno* (Papa Government) was to ensure that the schools were equipped with the latest technology, and that students received practical training that would help meet the needs of the people. The government was also charged with guaranteeing an education for all members of the popular sectors of society through the provision of a number of benefits, including full and partial scholarships, subsidized meals, dormitories, and free publications. Its social mission was designed into a decidedly practical and communitarian curriculum and pedagogy. To this end, Rural Medicine replaced the traditional curriculum of Medicine, the program of Commerce made cooperatives in poor neighborhoods a central priority, and the Engineering and Electricity schools were tailored to nationalized industries. The government also committed to budget increases that would support the growing student population.[31]

During the administration of Lázaro Cárdenas, the relationship between the state and IPN students was understood as a kind of contract based on a modern vision of the revolution. Young people were not only expected to embrace the revolutionary proposals and commit themselves to the same social causes championed by the government, but also to embark on the "spiritual journey of peaceful transition" to development that cardenismo was allegedly trying to implement.[32] Further, with a new technical education, the thousands of students who migrated to the capital to enroll in the Politécnico were expected to leave behind their "Indian" or "provincial" identities and become "Mexicans" and thus accept the state as the supreme representative of the nation.[33] Young politécnicos enthusiastically embraced the cause of social justice, indifference to religion, and anti-imperialism.[34] The IPN, they believed, would serve to train the once-marginalized sons and daughters of the pueblo so that they could break Mexico's economic dependency on foreign capitalist influences. With time, however, both politécnicos and universitarios would grow increasingly frustrated with the state and become particularly critical of the corporatist and authoritarian model of schooling at their respective institutions.

The Establishment of the Corporatist Structure

An authoritarian hierarchical political coalition, originally created under the Plutarco Calles (1924–1928) presidency, was well established by 1940 under Lázaro Cárdenas (1934–1940). It grew in response to social pressures from below in tandem with political crises that originated outside Mexico.[35] It became fully consolidated under the National Revolutionary Party (PNR). At the top was the office of the president, which had accrued an immense amount of political power to itself by 1940. Uniting under the broad banner of the Mexican Revolution were workers, as represented by the Confederation of Mexican Workers (CTM); peasants, as represented by the National Peasants Confederation (CNC); and the popular sector, represented by the National Confederation of Popular Organizations (CNOP). Since the 1920s a vertically oriented political system that shared PNR party loyalty was present in the parallel organization of student groups at UNAM and the IPN (as shown in Figure 1.1).

After a consolidation of the technical schools in 1936–1937, the cardenista government encouraged all student federations associated with the tech-

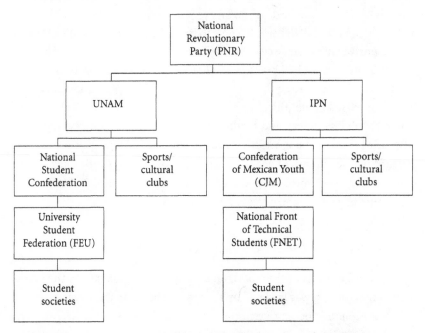

FIG. 1.1. Corporatist Structure inside the Schools, 1930s. (Data from IPN, *50 años*; and Covo, "La composición social.")

nical schools to unite into a single umbrella organization representing all IPN students. In 1937 this coalition took the name of Federación Nacional de Estudiantes Técnicos (National Federation of Technical Students, FNET). Two years later, FNET became part of the Confederación de Jóvenes Mexicanos (Federation of Mexican Young People, CJM), or the youth wing of the PRN, and later an unofficial student wing of the (Institutional Revolutionary Party) PRI. By the late 1930s, student leaders with affiliation to the PNR were similarly ensconced in the parallel student umbrella group at UNAM, the FEU.

The various organizations under the influence of the PRN exhibited a structure known as "corporatist"—that is, a noncompetitive and hierarchical system in which the constituent units, including their representative and bargaining power, are recognized and licensed exclusively by the state.[36] When the masses resist such tutelage, and negotiation and co-opting on the part of the authorities prove ineffective, the use of force and provocation then become "necessary" mechanisms for repression.[37] FNET would remain part of the corporatist apparatus of the state throughout the 1940s and the early 1950s. Yet, unlike the student organizations at UNAM, it would also become a bastion of support for cardenismo and popular education. As such, the most radical members of FNET would come to be seen as a threat to national unity by the postrevolutionary state. Nonetheless, as a number of historians have correctly pointed out in recent years, the structural changes that took place in the political realm during this time should not be interpreted as if they were strictly imposed monolithically by the governing party. The PNR changed its name to the PRI in 1946 and further strengthened its corporatist apparatus afterward. Yet it did not act in a perfectly vertical fashion upon passive and disenfranchised groups of people. Rather, the conservative authoritarian corporatist structure evolved within the broader context of historical influences, new shifts in politics, and demographic changes.

Student Population Growth and Campus Construction

As in other parts of the world, an unprecedented increase in the rate of population growth was initiated by a surge in labor demand triggered by the postwar economic boom that in the case of Mexico was particularly evident in the nation's capital. Responding to the employment opportunities offered by the growth of industrial investment in the urban center, an accelerating

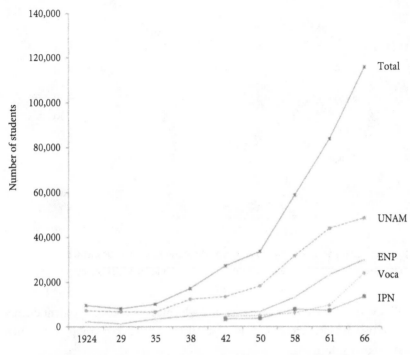

FIG. 1.2. Growth of Student Population: Mexico City, 1929–1966. (Data from Covo, "La composición social"; Mendoza Rojas, *Los conflictos*, 25–26; IPN, *50 años*, 161; and Sánchez Hidalgo B., *Trazos y mitos*, 190.)

number of people from the *provincia* (outside Mexico City) moved to the capital in search of upward social mobility.

As illustrated in Figure 1.2, the first considerable increase in the student population occurred after 1940 (just as the general population of the nation's capital began to grow steadily at a 6 percent annual rate from 1.6 million in 1940 to 5.2 million in 1960).[38] In addition, the figure shows that the number of students enrolled at UNAM and its affiliated preparatory schools (ENPs) increased significantly from 19,033 in 1942 to 78,094 in 1966. The growth was also noticeable inside the IPN, as the number of students grew from 8,026 in 1942 to 37,429 in 1966. Particularly significant was the accelerating growth in the middle schools of the IPN (*vocacionales*), where the number of students grew from 4,666 in 1942 to 23,889 in 1966. Overall, the figure further shows that the student population of Mexico City quadrupled in twenty-four years, from 27,059 in 1942 to 115,523 in 1966.

A comparison of the numbers of female and male students enrolled at

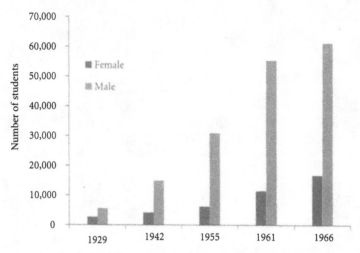

FIG. 1.3. Comparative View of Female/Male Student Population Growth, 1929–1966. (Data from González Cosío, *Historia Estadística*, Cuadro XXIII, 72, opp. page.)

UNAM reveals that the experience and advantages of being a student during these two decades largely accrued to an already privileged group, young men (see Figure 1.3).[39]

In 1929 about 32 percent of the entire student population in Mexico City were young women. By 1961, not only had the percentage not increased but, in fact, it had declined, so that women made up a mere fifth of the entire student population. Five years later the enrollment of female students grew slightly, as the total numbers increased from 11,444 in 1961 to 16, 766 in 1966.[40] The relatively low number of female students would have a tremendous impact on both the construction of Mexico's postwar youth and the articulation of student politics throughout the long sixties. As stressed in subsequent chapters, the two most important public celebrations emphasizing the changing understanding of Mexico's youth—the *novatadas* (hazing rituals) and cheerleading—would be performed exclusively by young men. This would begin to change in the latter part of the long sixties. By the end of this period, for example, cheerleading would be almost exclusively performed by young female students; more important, following the 1956 strike at the Politécnico and especially the 1968 student movement, politécnicas and universitarias would begin to adopt a more "active role" in the streets and, in this process, to expand the category of the "revoltoso."[41]

TABLE 1.3. Schools Built in CU, 1952–1958

		Number of students	
School	Year built in CU	1960	1965
Escuela Nacional de Arquitectura	1956	3,504	3,284
Facultad de Economía	1954	1,642	2,499
Facultad de Odontología	1954	925	1,388
Facultad de Ciencias Políticas y Sociales	1958	505	1,038
Facultad de Ciencias	1952	948	1,943
Facultad de Derecho	1953	6,194	7,138
Facultad de Filosofía y Letras	1953	1,583	3,086
Facultad de Ingeniería	1954	6,440	6,889
Facultad de Medicina	1956	7,642	8,243
Facultad de Química	1954	2,669	2,683

Source: Data from García Barragán, ed., *La Ciudad Universitaria*, 175–176; and Covo, "La composición social."

To accommodate the accelerating growth in the student population, the state made substantial investments in the expansion of UNAM and the IPN. Particularly noteworthy was the construction of Ciudad Universitaria (CU). As shown in Table 1.3, the new campus included a large number of students from all of the major schools of the university.[42]

The location of newly built college facilities has much to say about the way the new construction both reinforced old divisions and created new meanings for the growing student body. The CU was built in the southern and more affluent part of the city during the late 1940s and early 1950s. Built in the Coyoacán borough at a time when large segments of this part of the city were covered with volcanic rock, and public transportation was virtually nonexistent, CU covered an impressive eighteen hundred acres of land.

Ciudad Universitaria was situated approximately eight miles south from the old barrio estudiantil in Mexico City. The old barrio estudiantil was located in the heart of downtown, near the Zócalo, the central plaza and locus of Mexican political and religious leadership dating back to pre-Columbian times. The barrio was made up of all of the major schools and institutions that had composed the social, cultural, and political life of the university during the 1920s, 1930s, 1940s, and early 1950s, including movie theaters, bars, bookstores, libraries, cafes, art galleries, and billiard parlors. Also located within walking distance in the barrio estudiantil were the buildings of San Ildefonso, where the Escuela Nacional Preparatoria was founded (ENP #1), the Palacios de Mineria and Inquisición, the Colegios de San Pedro and San Pablo, and the Academy of San Carlos.[43] By the mid to late 1950s, the construction of Ciudad Universitaria had been completed, and the old barrio estudiantil gradually ceased to be the most important center of political and cultural activism among students. The new campus included the University Olympic Stadium, which offered universitarios a space where they would engage in numerous rivalries with politécnicos during American football games throughout the decade (see Chapter 2). The Escuelas Preparatorias saw dramatic expansion. This set of schools grew from three in the 1940s to nine in the mid-1960s. The first three preparatorias (#s 1, 2, and 3) were located in the old barrio estudiantil, while the new preparatorias were built throughout the city: in Coyoacán (#4), in Coapa (#5), in Tacubaya (#6), in Calzada de la Viga (#7), in Mixcoac (#8), and in Lindavista (#9).

The Politécnico would also experience tremendous changes in its schools. As noted earlier, the IPN was founded in 1937 with the conglomeration of the existing technological and vocational schools, including six *prevocacionales*, four *vocacionales*, and seven professional schools.[44] That same year, the IPN built its principal campus in what used to be the Hacienda of Santo Tomás, approximately three miles northeast from the Zócalo. In the late 1940s, the IPN acquired additional lands from the Plutarco Calles Park by the government to expand its new campus. With the acquisition of the new lands, the campus grew from a couple of isolated buildings to an area measuring 325,000 square meters (meek in comparison to the eighteen hundred acres of CU).[45] By 1952, the "Casco de Santo Tomás" stood as the center of Ciudad Politécnica. It was surrounded by a total of seven vocacionales. The area surrounding the IPN included neighborhoods for many of the city's lower-income residents, and the idea that IPN was a second-tier institution for working-class students became an enduring legacy. But following more than a decade of student strikes that included among their demands the construction of more efficient IPN buildings, government authorities expropriated additional lands from the *ejidos* (communal lands) of San Pedro Zacatenco and Santa María Ticoman in the late 1950s to begin construction of a second and more modern campus. In 1959, President Adolfo López Mateos inaugurated the new campus of the IPN, which became known as Unidad Profesional Zacatenco (UPZ). Constructed farther north of the city in a land covering 633 acres (about a seventh of the size of CU), UPZ was located approximately five miles north of the Zócalo and twelve miles northeast of CU. Equipped with modern laboratories and athletic facilities, designed with new buildings for the schools of Mechanical and Electrical Engineering (ESIME) and Architecture (ESIA), and reorganized with new graduate programs, UPZ had a closer resemblance to the schools of UNAM during this period than to the schools that were consolidated in the late 1930s to create the IPN.

In short, UNAM and the Politécnico experienced significant transformations in their schools during the span of Mexico's economic boom. Both of these schools expanded their campuses during this period to accommodate the accelerating growth in their student populations. The social differences that contrasted these institutions in earlier decades would fade significantly by the late 1960s but would not completely disappear.

Favoritism toward UNAM

At UNAM, the 1940s were framed as the beginning of a new era of prosperity, political opportunity, modernity, and middle-class consumerism. This moment of optimism was made possible in part via a conscious effort to transform UNAM into the most important educational institution of modern Mexico. It was here that middle-class consumption was meant to transform Mexico into a more "democratic" nation. The governing elite intended to make UNAM the flagship of Mexico's system of higher education. In turn, as illustrated in Figure 1.4, the university began to receive an unprecedented amount of financial support in the mid-1940s.

But this state investment in modernity came at the expense of the cardeni-

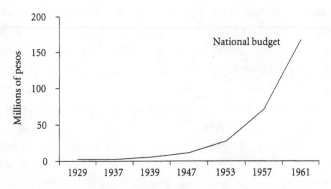

FIG. 1.4. Investment Growth: UNAM, 1929–1961. (Data from González Cosío, *Historia Estadística*, Cuadro XVII, 66–68.)

sta-inspired educational programs in other parts of the higher education system. Cardenista educational institutes (Rural, Normal, and Technical schools) and other schools that promoted popular education, such as the University of Michoacán, suffered financially and politically.[46] The postrevolutionary state conceived of liberal education as the most efficient springboard for individual social transformation.[47] In particular, the governing elite argued that the future economists, politicians, and bureaucrats that the nation so desperately needed in order to transform Mexico into a fully developed and modern nation would emerge from UNAM.

The arguments projecting UNAM as the incubator of Mexico's future leaders, whether self-fulfilling or not, did bear fruit, particularly with respect to politicians. As Roderic Camp has noted, over 80 percent of the young men with college degrees who held influential positions in the government graduated from one single institution, UNAM. Of this astonishingly high number, more than 60 percent graduated from one single school within the National Autonomous University, the School of Law.[48] Unlike the politécnicos, who symbolized the popular base of workers and peasants, the universitarios during the 1940s and 1950s were closely linked with economic prosperity and national unity. "They were part of the social 'estate' of 'university men,'" as historian Enrique Krauze once wrote, "destined to gain growing access to power until they became the dominant force in Mexican public life."[49] In short, by the late 1940s UNAM had become the most important space for upward social and political mobility for young people. What was more, UNAM had evolved into a space of national pride, middle-class consumption, and modernity.

The most important symbol of national pride in education was Ciudad Universitaria (CU). Like other accomplishments of this era, such as the port of Acapulco and the national highways, this "crown jewel of Mexican state nationalism," as anthropologist Claudio Lomnitz once referred to CU, was "predicated on the teaching of the Mexican Revolution."[50] Thus, it is highly significant that President Miguel Alemán chose November 20 (anniversary of the Revolution), 1952, as the day on which to inaugurate Ciudad Universitaria (even though the project remained largely unfinished for another two years).[51] The analogy, which Miguel Alemán drew during his inauguration speech between CU and the national flag, on this symbolic date, exemplifies such revolutionary nationalism. Further, it embodies the paternalistic relationship he sought to establish between himself (the state) and the students during this period. He addressed the universitarios as follows:

> Today . . . in this anniversary of the Mexican Revolution, I give all
> universitarios of Mexico the insignia of our nation. This flag symbolizes the
> effort of the liberty of our [beloved] pueblo of which all of us Mexicans have
> been in debt since 1910. [With this flag] we should all abandon all the possible
> differences that could keep us divided. In front of such a symbol of the
> Law, we should all recognize our common citizenship and human equality.
> Our greatest heroes died defending her: She is a symbol of sacrifice and an
> icon of honor. We should all live to defend such heroism in the name of our
> nation by extolling her dignity and maintaining her integrity in times of
> peace and in times of war. For all universitarios this flag should gives us the
> encouragement that we need to exalt our culture and wisdom for the benefit
> of our nation. Let us all sacrifice [our differences] to prove that we are all
> worthy of her.[52]

With these words, President Miguel Alemán presented Ciudad Universitaria
as a personal gift to the students, who were thus obliged to respect everything
that the new city represented. This paternalistic relationship was concret-
ized with a gigantic statue of Miguel Alemán erected inside CU adjacent to
the building of Rectoría, which, in part, was decorated by a series of three-
dimensional murals painted by David Alfaro Siqueiros that further encouraged Mexico's youth to embrace the goals of the revolution.[53] The monument
was strategically located in the main entrance of the university and portrayed
Alemán in a toga and holding a book of law with his left hand. Universitarios
were to abide by the laws of the university and to respect Ciudad Universitaria. The new campus, it was believed, was a neutral space of progress, modernity, and national unity free of the ideological differences that in the past had
threatened the autonomous status of the university.

Claiming to express the gratitude of all universitarios, the representative
leaders of the FEU publicly thanked President Alemán on numerous occasions, asked him to "have confidence in [Mexico's] youth," and assured him
that the students would come together from then on to serve the nation and
the university with pride and respect.[54] However, the postrevolutionary state
was not entirely ready to trust its youth. One of the principal reasons Ciudad
Universitaria had been founded, after all, was to remove students from the
old barrio estudiantil.[55] Moreover, in an attempt to further depoliticize the
universitarios the state would encourage a climate of corrupt student politics.
Further, it would subsidize a number of cultural festivals and rituals and pass

new laws that would drastically limit the autonomy of the university. These and similar measures also adopted at the Politécnico were part of a rising wave of authoritarian rule that in conjunction with the benefits of the economic boom simultaneously characterized the 1940s and 1950s.

The Authoritarian Side of the Miracle

The corporatist structure that matured by the 1940s ushered in a period of authoritarianism, an ideological shift to the Right in Mexican politics, and an unprecedented level of political corruption.[56] Historian Stephen Niblo explains that high government officials offered lucrative rewards to individuals "as incentives for jettisoning the idealistic elements of the cardenista project."[57] In this burgeoning environment of the Cold War, conservative housecleaning meant that influential leftist leaders and intellectuals were expelled from the government, independent labor unions were consolidated within conservative circles of the state, cardenista policies in agriculture and the popular educational sector were dismantled, and what Lorenzo Meyer has called the rise of a "discreet" official "nationalist anticommunism" took hold.[58]

However, the paternalism inherent in such power did not go uncontested. The creation of the IPN, for example, was the result of the combined efforts of a variety of actors inside as well as outside the government who often responded to local pressures from below. The same would be true in subsequent decades. The PRI would be forced to negotiate with disgruntled workers, peasants, and students who refused to be incorporated into the corporate apparatus of the state as well as with a variety of individuals outside the party on numerous occasions in order to resolve grievances and protests. In these efforts, extralegal and legal changes would serve as both reactions to, and catalysts for, social unrest. In this history of student politics, the consolidation of charrismo in the labor sector, the implementation of the Social Dissolution and Caso Laws, and the creation of the granaderos and the Dirección Federal de Seguridad (Office of Federal Security, or DFS) particularly stand out. Although originally promulgated to ensure national security in the face of the threat of fascism during World War II, these mechanisms of control were used by subsequent administrations to imprison, threaten, and harass all individuals who were perceived as "threats" to the nation.

Charrismo

The 1950s witnessed the rise of a new wave of more aggressive social protests that would radicalize dissatisfied sectors of society thereafter. The most prominent examples of these social and political ruptures included the massive strikes organized at the end of the decade across the nation by teachers as well as by telegraph and railroad workers. These were sectors of the working class that, despite their long history of political activism dating back to the Porfiriato (1876–1911), had been largely pacified by the state's corporatist apparatus throughout much of the twentieth century.[59] Scholars who have studied the 1958 strikes agree that, in all of them, workers shared at least three basic demands: (1) an increase in salaries for a more dignified life; (2) the removal of corrupt union representatives in favor of more democratic leaders; and (3) a complete reorganization of the administration of the labor sector, free of corruption and irregularities.[60] Unlike previous social uprisings, this latest wave of political activism was distinguished for having been organized without the blessing of the leadership of the state-sponsored unions. Many of these massive protests, in fact, were originally carried out in clandestine fashion—after work or during lunch meetings—so as to bypass the corrupt leadership of the official unions.

Open dissatisfaction with union leadership had existed since the 1940s, and progressive sectors of the labor unions began to apply the reproachful label "charros" to many union leaders. The term has its origins in Mexican politics in connection with a corrupt leader of the Railway Workers' Union (STFRM) named Jesús Díaz de Léon, also known as "el charro" because of his fondness for cowboy gear. During his leadership, real wages as well as working conditions rapidly deteriorated. Yet his economic and political life improved significantly.[61] Over time, charros came to symbolize all corrupt union leaders supported economically and politically by the government to control, intimidate, repress, negotiate with, and/or co-opt disgruntled workers who threatened to break away from the corporatist structure of the state.

Charrismo was instituted by the governing elite as a means of controlling the labor unions (or inhibiting the formation of independent unions in the first place) through a kind of syndicate politics reminiscent of the mafia. Two innovations enabled the consolidation of charrismo into effective mechanisms of control and mediation: (1) the employment of goons, informants, provocateurs, and scabs by strong local bosses; and (2) the installation of corrupt leaders (charros) and/or charismatic intermediaries inside the labor unions who claimed to represent their constituents by various means, including offering bribes and employing leftist propaganda and rhetoric (usually in reference to anti-imperialism). Failing this, charros intimidated and disciplined workers through violence. These mechanisms of control were particularly effective during the election of union leaders. Carlos Monsiváis notes that everyone knew that "union leaders had historically been handpicked from above." But with the sophistication of charrismo in the late 1940s and 1950s, the degree of corruption reached unprecedented levels. He explains, for example, that under charro control

> the results of the elections were no longer made available to the workers; [social and political] rights were instantly suspended to those workers who participated in rebellious acts; all workers who had worked in the same company for more than ten years were immediately fired; the local stations of union members were constantly ransacked; the job contracts were rewritten.[62]

In effect, charrismo established a "patron clientism," to use Judith A. Teichman's term, that organized labor groups into mafialike syndicates.[63] The outlines of collective agreements, rights to government contracts, housing, loans, and scholarships were all potentially under their purview and control. Elevated to material and symbolic heights, charros could bestow these benefits to a pacified following as long as the charros could in term meet their obligations ultimately to deliver political loyalty to the government and, more specifically, the PRI.

By the 1950s it was evident that these individuals sprung from rural Mexico had become crucial urban sector intermediaries of the corporate structure of the postrevolutionary state. More so than previous union leaders, they wielded an enormous amount of political power, and often enjoyed the unconditional support of the national security agency (DFS), a dependable team of lawyers, a sympathetic reporter at the newspaper, and a group of thugs (*golpeadores*) and strikebreakers led by a feared (though charismatic) lower boss.[64] In an insightful analysis, historian Ilán Semo has referred to charrismo as a kind of urban caciquismo. He states: "The metaphor could not have been less ambiguous: the 'charro' is the modern version of the cacique"; better yet, "the sugarcoated image of the cacique." He then goes on to say that charrismo is the fusion of Mexico's two worlds: the urban and the rural; the campesino culture and the proletarian culture, and further that "the central political feature [of charrismo] is its conjunction between corporatism and nationalism." For its existence, its supporters rely on a "strange yet effective combination between the law and despotism."[65]

In short, charrismo translated the deeply historical, cultural, economic, and political aspects of caciquismo into the Mexican government's vision for retaining its authority in the contemporary context. The term "charro," in turn, came to represent corrupt, self-serving, and relatively powerful union leaders who used their often charismatic personalities to exert a network-supported authority via legal, propagandistic, extralegal, and, if necessary, illicitly forceful means. Eventually the meaning of charro and charrismo broadened such that it became simply synonymous with violence, corruption, anticommunism, and antidemocracy. As Joe Foweraker has noted, the internal contradictions of charrismo often in time became apparent to workers and fueled local and potentially wider resistance.[66] The activism of workers during the late forties and fifties found sympathies with the growing and changing student population in Mexico. Even as students began to highlight the contradictions of traditional charrismo in the labor sector, its utility as a mechanism of government mediation and control found expression in the educational sphere itself. Charrismo would find its analogue in the student leaders, intermediaries, and bosses that became entrenched in higher education at the time. It arose as a significant threat to the potential of a labor-youth show of solidarity. Porrismo, as a form of charrismo estudiantil, would emerge as yet another color of the chameleon-like mechanism though which caciquismo would be nationalized in modernizing Mexico. As usual, it was accompanied at all times with the threat and reality of force when consent to its wishes was not granted voluntarily (see Chapter 4).

The Weight of the Law

To act against political activists and complement charrismo, authorities relied repeatedly on the infamous granaderos, the modernization of the secret service, and the revived catchall Law of Social Dissolution. Under the suggestions of Othón León Lobato, the chief of police in Mexico City, and the training of American colonel Rex Applegate, the granaderos were created in the late 1940s to replace the fire department hitherto used to control mass protests, but which lacked the equipment and training to deal with the escalating number of confrontational riots that characterized the postrevolutionary period. In addition to assisting the granaderos, Rex Applegate also played a key role in the training of Mexico's secret agents.[67]

Mexico established its first modern intelligence agency in 1918 with the creation of the Servicios Confidenciales (Secret Service). As this organization advanced its technical skills in the 1930s and their leaders gave greater attention to political activism, its name was changed to the Departamento de Investigaciones Políticas y Sociales (Department of Political and Social Investigation) in 1939, and later to the Dirección General de Investigaciones Políticas y Sociales (General Directorate of Political and Social Investigation, or IPS) in the late 1940s. This period also saw the establishment of the DFS in 1947, aided greatly by an unprecedented increase in funding from the federal government as well as training of personnel by the U.S. Federal Bureau of Investigation (FBI).[68] But unlike the IPS and similar institutions that were linked to the Ministry of Interior, the DFS was directly managed from the office of the president. This meant that the DFS was put in charge of guaranteeing the security of Mexico while its leaders were given an opportunity to establish close ties with the leading figures of the priísta apparatus.[69]

President Ávila Camacho first promulgated the Law of Social Dissolution in 1941 under Article 145 of the constitution in response to the international threat of fascism posed by the Axis powers during World War II. According to Article145, the law was to apply to:

> any foreigner or Mexican national who in speech or in writing, or by any other means, carries on political propaganda among foreigners or Mexican nationals, spreading ideas, programs, or forms of action of any foreign government which disturb the public order or affect the sovereignty of the Mexican State.[70]

By "disturbing public order," Article 145 meant any act that was intended "to produce rebellion, sedition, riot, or mutiny." In addition, the law was to be used to punish all individuals who carried out "acts of sabotage," or those who threatened to "subvert the institutional life of the country" by carrying out "acts of provocation" or "invasion of territory." In short, the goal of this intentionally vague law was to protect "national sovereignty" from all of those persons labeled as "subversives." In the 1950s, the law was tailored to the new international political climate in the wake of the Cold War. Its elasticity enabled the perceived threat of communism to stand in for the older discourse about fascism. The scope of the law was expanded in 1950 following an amendment sent to Congress by President Miguel Alemán (Art. 145-bis). In particular, the statute broadened the term of imprisonment from three to six years, as it had originally stated, to two to twelve years. Fascism no longer represented a threat, yet those who supported the amendment did so by identifying communism as the new threat.[71]

Throughout the long sixties the government would use the same Law of Social Dissolution to intimidate, repress, and imprison a variety of left-wing reformers, revolutionary dissidents, and independent labor activists. During the railroad workers' strike, for example, several leaders were arrested and charged under the sabotage clause of the Law of Social Dissolution—that is, once the strike had been labeled "illegal." More famously, labor leader Demetrio Vallejo and Valentín Campa were indicted using this law, and they would remain imprisoned for more than a decade, as they were denied parole on numerous occasions. Other important labor leaders charged with social dissolution included the organizers of the Revolutionary Movement of Teachers (MRM), Otón Salazar, J. Encarnación Pérez Rivero, Nicolás García Abadand, and Venancio Zamudio Cruz. In 1960 the famous muralist David Alfaro Siqueiros and the journalist Filomeno Mata would suffer the same fate. Four years later the leaders of the doctors' strike faced imprisonment under the same law. Many others would be arrested, and they too could be wrongfully accused of attempting to overthrow the government with force.[72]

But by no means was imprisonment under the law of social dissolution limited to important labor leaders and famous activists. By 1959, the newspaper *El Popular* reported that Mexico was holding approximately 800 political prisoners, and of that number, it was estimated that 150 had been imprisoned simply because they had been labeled "communists."[73] During one student demonstration in support of the strike organized by the normalistas in 1958, the Student Society from the School of Philosophy at UNAM demanded the immediate deletion of Article 145 and 145-bis from the constitution. The following year student activists from the Law School voiced the same demands as they organized various demonstrations in support of the teachers' strike. The number of individuals jailed for political reasons would continue to grow throughout the 1960s, giving rise to an increasing number of demonstrations advocating removal of the Law of Social Dissolution from the Penal Code. Between 1960 and 1967, the National Liberation Movement (MLN) and the National Central of Democratic Students (CNED) organized a number of demonstrations protesting this law and demanding that it be repealed. After years of repeated calls along these lines, that repeal of the Law of Social Dissolution was enacted in December of 1970.

From Socialist to Nationalist Education

In the educational sector, conservatives established an important milestone in 1940, when President Ávila Camacho announced the annulment of Article 3 of the constitution, which had declared in 1934 that all elementary schools should follow a socialist pedagogical plan.[74] The change to the constitution, ratified in 1946, stated that education would be scientific, secular, democratic, compulsory, and national. Moreover, as part of what would be an ongoing effort to depoliticize students, it declared that education would be free of any political bias.[75] The original announcement in 1940 was immediately followed by the removal of all key proponents of popular education, including Luis Sánchez Pontón, the minister of education, and his undersecretary, Enrique Arreguín. Once these leftists were removed from power, Ávila Camacho was then able to appoint the more reactionary figure of Octavio Véjar Vázquez as the new minister of education.[76]

The attacks against "reds" in the IPN gained support in the business sector through influential members of the Confederation of Chambers of Manufacturing (CONCAMIN). This organization consisted mostly of wealthy industrialists who had maintained close ties to the government since its foundation in 1917. Their relationship with the governing elite grew even stronger during the 1940s, when they signed a pact of mutual cooperation with the principal labor unions. Their hope was to weaken public seats of power in the Politécnico in order eventually to privatize it. Taking the Technological School of Monterrey as a model, CONCAMIN concluded that to progress Mexico needed to privatize its technological schools fully.[77] The administrations of Ávila Camacho (1940–1946), Miguel Alemán (1946–1952), and Adolfo Ruiz Cortinez (1952–1958) would eventually agree with CONCAMIN. Control and management of the IPN had to be taken out of the hands of the state. To this end, government and school authorities put pressure on the IPN by various means, including the application of new reforms that would abolish social benefits and investments in infrastructure that politécnicos had enjoyed since the 1930s. By contrast, at UNAM, the principal strategy to depoliticize students included the imposition of the Caso Law of 1945.

UNAM had gained autonomous status after the passage of the New Organic Law of 1933, but a number of measures had weakened that autonomy, the most significant of which was the Caso Law. After asking Brito Foucher, the conservative rector, to tender his resignation on July 28, 1944, Camacho put wheels in motion that resulted in the selection of Alfonso Caso as the new rector. Caso was a respected archaeologist who, in the name of academic freedom, had opposed the imposition of a socialist educational philosophy on UNAM.[78] Because of these credentials, Caso's supporters believed that he was the best man to rescue the university from the political crisis in which it had become embroiled since losing its independence at the hands of conservative forces (1933–1944).[79] Without necessarily embracing the task, Caso assumed the post with confidence. Alfonso Caso was one of the first intellectuals to put forward the idea that "foreign" political ideologies (outgrowths of the two world wars) had a pernicious effect within the university, especially on the minds of young students. In particular, he noted that Mexico had not been exempt from *causas externas* ("foreign ideologies") and argued that while the modern world had engaged in ideological battles and conflicting interests, it had become evident that the spread of foreign ideas had influenced the disorganization of the university.[80]

Caso also argued uniquely that young students should no longer be envisioned as a simple metaphor for national progress. After all, in his opinion student protesters had displayed poor judgment and, being young, were especially vulnerable to being manipulated by politicians as "political instruments."[81] According to this renowned archaeologist, the university had been in great peril for more than a decade as a direct result of ideological battles between irresponsible radicals from the Left and equally irresponsible reactionaries from the Right. He declared, "Since students gained university autonomy in 1933, it has become evident that young Mexicans have not been able to direct themselves!" He went on to ask: "What should our country expect from the future if our best men have not been able to govern themselves?"[82] What young Mexicans needed in these difficult moments of crisis, Caso proposed, was a profound re-evaluation of the Mexican reality that would lead them to embrace "true patriotism" and reveal student complaints as relatively inconsequential.[83] For Caso the solution to the unrest that had taken hold on campuses seemed clear. There needed to be a serious re-evaluation of the original mission of the university. The university was first and foremost a technical (read academic) institution, and not a political one. For him, it had to be understood as a public corporation capable of maintaining its own judicial power and one that, by definition, had the obligation to deliver practical and professional higher education for Mexico's future. In addition, he argued that the university had to function as a community, one in which teacher and student were not adversaries but participants in a process of teaching and learning, respectively.[84]

Caso also cited irresponsibility on the part of school authorities and politicians as a root cause of the chaos that had come to characterize the university. Authorities, he charged, had transformed the university into an ideological "trench" by promoting foreign ideologies in the form of socialist education, communism, and ultraconservative politics.[85] Emphasizing the need to restructure the hierarchical nature of power within the university, Caso argued in favor of creating a new board of trustees composed of a group of trusted individuals not aligned with political interests. This board would be the centerpiece of his efforts to depoliticize students. In response to Ávila Camacho's call for national unity, Caso hoped that the creation of the Junta de Gobierno would preserve the autonomy of the university by "eliminating the politicking around the designation of directors and Rector."[86] As such, the Caso Law in 1945 placed the University Council at the top of this redefined pyramidal structure. This important group selected the rector, who, in turn, was designated the official spokesman for the university. Below the rector stood the *Patronato*. This was designed as an independent body of trustees in charge of the administration of the university endowment. Below the Patronato were the directors of faculties, school, and institutes. Finally, at the base of the pyramidal structure were located the *Consejos Tecnicos*, or Technical Councils.[87]

In name, the Caso Law gave back to the university the national character that it had lost during the 1933 student protest.[88] Furthermore, it recognized the university as an autonomous, public institution, and it specified that the university would receive an annual budget from the state. In addition, the law asserted that the board of trustees would be responsible for appointing the rector and the directors of all faculties and institutes.[89] Finally, with the new pyramidal structure, the *Academias* of schools and faculties were replaced by the Consejos. As historian Donald Mabry has documented, the Academias that came into being inside the university following the student protest for university autonomy in 1929 had opened a real political space of contestation and negotiation for both professors and students.[90] The replacement of the

Academias constituted a significant step backward for students in terms of their representational power to negotiate. The Caso Law, therefore, returned Mexico's university to its pre-1929 status. In other words, the legislation transformed the university once again into yet another subservient agency of the government that made the national president, who sat at the top of the pyramid, the most important figure in the university system.[91]

Once school authorities sympathetic to the government were placed in influential positions of power on the board, the hegemony that conservatives had once enjoyed within the university during the 1930s and early 1940s was broken. In fact, Brito Foucher (1942–1944) was the last conservative rector to administer the university. With time, formerly influential *panistas* (members of the conservative opposition, the National Action Party, or PAN) became less relevant in student politics.[92] Furthermore, with the new authorities in power, the government was able to regain a strong political grip on the FEU, and the Student Societies under its structure, by removing conservative students from important political positions and replacing them with leaders who were more closely aligned with the PRI. On the surface, Caso's goals were temporarily realized. To begin with, following the implementation of the Caso Law, it appears that an overwhelming number of universitarios took advantage of the many opportunities afforded by the university to secure jobs in politics, the government bureaucracy, or the private sector following graduation. It is also true that no massive student protests were organized after the Caso Law inside the university until 1958. In fact, the political environment that gradually developed between 1948 and 1961 appeared so promising that many scholars have enthusiastically described this period as the "Golden Years" of the university.[93] To emphasize the progressive nature of this moment scholars have stressed a wide range of factors that indeed give the impression of greater internal peace and social prosperity. For example, it is often mentioned that between 1932 and 1948 eleven rectors administered UNAM—many of whom were forced to resign as a consequence of political pressure and student unrest. In contrast, during the 1950s UNAM had only two rectors: Luis Garrido, who served a full term from 1948 to 1953, and Nabor Carrillo, who was unanimously re-elected in 1957 for a second term (1953–1957 and 1957–1961). Moreover, during the administration of these two rectors, Ciudad Universitaria was founded, the annual budget from the federal government grew significantly, student protests directed against the government were reduced to only a minimum (mostly by conservative students), and a close relationship between the state and the university was reestablished. Yet a closer examination of this supposed period of peace and prosperity reveals that there was important organized student resistance at UNAM during this time (see Chapters 4 and 5). This unrest followed on the heels of even more marked resistance at the IPN, a subject we turn to next.

Student Resistance to the Shift

Politécnicos did not take long to resist the conservative policies that were put in place in the 1940s. The first signs of massive student discontent appeared inside the IPN during March of 1942. At the time a major Organic Law, supported by wealthy industrialists of the CONCAMIN group and governmental authorities, was announced by the Politécnico. If passed, this law would have divided the IPN into trade schools. Other proposals included the elimination of all scholarships and subsidized meals, as proposed by Véjar Vázquez and by Gustavo Baz, the secretary of the Department of Health, respectively.[94] To many, this law would in effect take away the professional status that the IPN had gained in 1937, and the trade schools would have the sole purpose of serving the interests of their investors.

In reaction to this perceived political crisis, representatives of FNET sent a list of demands to the president that included a New Organic Law which would safeguard the professional status of the Politécnico and would reincorporate all the prevocational schools in the IPN. In addition, FNET demanded greater investment on the part of the government in the infrastructure of the IPN and a guaranteed budget that would secure the scholarships of all students.[95] In response, Ávila Camacho promised to negotiate with the politécnicos after meeting with the representatives of FNET. But as the students started to grow more impatient, tensions began to build up outside the main schools of the Politécnico. In desperation, the politécnicos organized a march from the Casco de Santo Tomás toward the Zócalo to talk to the president. En route, however, the students were confronted by the fire department, which had been sent by the government. What resulted was a violent street battle. Afterward, tragically, twenty people were injured and six people died, including four students, an innocent bystander, and a police sergeant.[96] For the politécnicos, the message was clear: "reactionary elements" within the government wanted to "destroy the Politécnico" by promoting violence. In a student corrido, for example, politécnicos specifically pointed to the new minister of education, Véjar Vázquez, as the principal enemy of public education:

[1] With my heart saddened/and [with] my virile word,/I come here to sing the corrido/of the student strike.

[2] To remain silent/would make me an accomplice./This is why, with energy/ I tell the pueblo the truth.

[3] The Masters of Education, /with great premeditation, /want to see the Politécnico destroyed.

[4] To accomplish their objectives/they dictated some accords,/that only breed grief/ inside the Institute.

[5] The students protested/with sufficient reason,/but their demands were crushed/by the "kings" of Education.

[6] There, the students spilled their blood,/there, they lost their lives./ With great Pain, they sealed off/ what they failed to obtain while they were still alive.

[7] Vejár Vázquez, Assassin! [/] Condemned by the pueblo, [/] a perverse man who needs to be . . . judged.

[8] Vejár Vázquez, impotent man! [/] with a wicked heart. [/] You have to, Señor Presidente [/] remove him from Education.

[9] The Nation demands it [/] with a potent and virile voice [/] because such a despicable brain [/] is not worthy of Education.

[10] [Señor Presidente], [/] you have to allow all Mexicans, [/] without despotism or pride, to demand what belongs to all of us.[97]

But Véjar Vázquez was not removed from office by the Señor Presidente as the politécnicos wished.[98] Nevertheless, under pressure from influential cardenistas, Ávila Camacho did attempt to negotiate with the students during a public meeting, saying that he would make sure that a "great part of the educational budget" would address the most urgent demands of the students.[99] In response, FNET representatives called the strike off—just nine days after it was announced. However, student discontent continued to grow during the remaining years of the 1940s and 1950s, partly as a result of the physical deterioration of the schools of the IPN. This disgruntlement, which forced several directors of the IPN to resign, was due in part to a gradual abandonment of the IPN by the government and to the socioeconomic inequalities that existed between the politécnicos and the universitarios.[100]

In April of 1950 student unhappiness coalesced into a strike once again when President Miguel Alemán and Secretary of Interior Adolfo Ruiz Cortines tried to weaken the IPN further by threatening to deprive it of its vocational schools through another Organic Law. This time, however, the student demonstration garnered a great deal of support from the people, who, according to one participant, "had demonstrated their solidarity to our cause" with "food, work, and moral support." He further explains, "[M]en and women, primarily from humble origins, marched with us towards the Casco de Santo Tomás to help us in this shared struggle against the anti-popular regime that had distanced itself from the principles of the Mexican Revolution."[101] It is difficult to determine how deep or helpful the support of the pueblo actually was. Nonetheless, on May 26, just a month after the strike commenced, the government indicated its willingness to negotiate with the students. The state granted disgruntled students a series of benefits, including an increase of five pesos in the students' scholarships and an additional thousand subsidized meals. In addition, the state asked Alejandro Guillot, the director of the IPN, to step down, declared that all students arrested during the strike were to be released, and promised the creation of a new *internado* (or dormitory).[102] The efforts on the part of the government were enough for the student leaders to end the strike. Nevertheless, the students' frustrations would continue to mount throughout the early 1950s as the government persisted in its attempt to roll back the cardenista policies that had made the founding of the Politécnico possible.

In what might have been the first public demonstration in which a group of students directly challenged the figure of the Señor Presidente, Miguel Alemán was booed and insulted during his speech at the inauguration of the new buildings of the Casco de Santo Tomás in 1952. The students' hostility, as one politécnico who was present at this rally remembers, grew out of their awareness that the alemanistas were devoting scant resources to the Ciudad Politécnica, whereas the "glorious" Ciudad Universitaria was the recipient of substantial governmental assistance.[103] This obvious distinction between universitarios and politécnicos served to confirm the latter's belief that the economic miracle of which the state was so proud did not extend to them. Political grievances and socioeconomic frustrations among politécnicos would reach a boiling point during the 1956 protest. Following this critical event, the IPN would witness a gradual transformation in its student-body, as greater numbers of students entering higher education would help to create an increase in upward social mobility. This transformation, from a working-class institution in the 1940s and early 1950s, to a more middle-class institution in the late 1950s and 1960s, would coincide with physical improvements of the schools of the IPN and a change in politécnicos' demands. In the earlier period, they asked for basic needs such as the creation of dormitories inside their schools, and the construction of communal cafeterias with subsidized meals. Later their requests became more directly political and sweeping, as, for example, they increasingly called for freedom for all political prisoners and greater participatory democracy in the schools and the labor unions (see Chapter 3).

Conclusion: Uneven Development in Modern Mexico

The socioeconomic, demographic, and political changes that emerged during the 1940s and 1950s compelled key authorities and intellectuals to view politicized students as potential threats to national unity and economic progress. The student population grew rapidly during this period, and new schools were created to accommodate such an unprecedented increase in the student population. In general, this growth was segmented in terms of the socioeconomic background and gender, and it affected the two major schools of higher education, UNAM and IPN, differently.

Traditionally, the scholarship has indiscriminately described this period as the defining decades of a "golden age." According to these interpretations, an unprecedented growth in Mexico's economy, evident in its modern urban centers and infrastructure, successfully consolidated the nation state and, in so doing, allowed the PRI to represent itself as the legitimate leader of the revolution and the sole guarantor of the nation's pursuit of modern industrial capitalism. However, as has been emphasized here, there was also a "darker side" of the miracle, which failed to incorporate a large segment of the population into the nation-state.[104] This uneven development was not evident only in the economic marginalization of a significant segment of the population but also in the rise of a new generation of activists who questioned the economic, social, cultural, and political contradictions that accompanied such prosperity. In the case of Mexico City, young politécnicos, whose lives scarcely improved (in comparison with those of the universitarios) with the economic miracle, were at the forefront of this protest, but so was a new generation of intellectuals whose academic essays, novels, and films would openly (or indirectly) question the PRI's trajectory of repression and express a critical stance toward the outcome and legacy of the Mexican Revolution.[105]

2 Fun and Politics in Postwar Mexico

The two World Wars that we have witnessed in this half century,
while dismantling the moral structure of contemporary humanity,
have intensified the worldwide crisis of youth.

—Celestino Porte Petit, professor of penal law and
strong supporter of President Miguel Alemán (1946–1952)[1]

T HE 1940S AND 1950S WITNESSED a dramatic shift in the con-
ceptualization of Mexico's youth that stemmed largely from the
structural changes that came with the "economic miracle," including an unprecedented growth in student population in the nation's capital and an expansion of state corporatism. Key figures within the government as well as
school authorities, journalists, and prominent intellectuals feared that, in the
absence of institutional support and direction, Mexico's youth would develop
into a "risk group to social order."[2] As in other parts of the world, authorities
in Mexico raised concerns about the growing numbers of rebellious youth
imagined as reincarnations of the infamous "rebels without a cause" portrayed in American films.[3]

Of particular concern to the postwar elite were a set of extremely popular student cultural practices that have been largely overlooked by historians.
These included hazing rituals (novatadas) and new customs associated with
the adoption of American football, such as the burning of mascots in effigy.
This chapter examines the cultural and political significance of these student
activities and traces their links to a more aggressive culture of defiance (desmadre). By focusing on the interconnected relationship between "fun" (relajo) and politics, it argues that school and national authorities sponsored and
manipulated these cultural practices as well as the social rivalry that devel-

oped between *universitarios* and *politécnicos* with some success to accentuate
the so-called emerging crisis of youth with the covert intention of undermining the growth of student activism. In addition, it contends that the symbolic
rituals of relajo associated with Mexico's emerging youth subcultures simultaneously opened new opportunities for students to publicly embrace and
resist the Cold War–influenced models of Mexican citizenship and modernity
advanced by the state.

Student Hazing and the Paseo de los Perros

Student hazing has a long historical tradition dating back to the Middle
Ages. At their core, such practices have consisted of acts of subordination and
submission. These are often performed in public or semipublic settings, and
they exact some physical and/or psychological cost. A leading scholar on the
subject points out that a practice known as fagging became a common hazing
ritual at Oxford and eventually made its way to other European, Canadian,
and American universities during the seventeenth, eighteenth, and nineteenth
centuries. Senior students forced new students, called fags, to act as their ser-
vants.[4] The fag did the "master's" chores, ran errands, cleaned his shoes, made
his bed, "and anything else that came into the senior student's mind," including, at times, sexual acts of subordination.[5]

The practice of student hazing in the Iberian Peninsula holds particular
interest given Spain's role in Mexican colonial history. There, hazing rituals
in schools were called *novatadas*, and, in one form, the practice was given the
descriptive name *dar matracas* ("hitting with a rattle"). Such rituals consisted
of collective beatings that occurred once a student was identified as a *novato*,
or newcomer. Another form of novatada commonly practiced in Spain well
into the nineteenth century was a form of fagging called *el patente*, or "the
tax." During this practice, the novato was obligated to pay his seniors a "fee"
in the form of a dinner, money, or a particular service. If the novato refused to
pay his tax, he would then be subjugated to a number of punishments including collective beatings, forced drinking, public humiliations, or a variety of
other pranks.[6]

In nineteenth-century Mexico, the assignment of an *apodo* (nickname)
developed into an important application in the ritualized induction of students into college life. A colorful reference to this common custom in Mexican mocking culture came in the autobiographical *Mangy Parrot* by well-

known writer and journalist José Joaquín Fernández de Lizardi. His main protagonist was nicknamed by his schoolmates Periquillo Sarniento ("Little Parrot Sarniento"):

> At my school, we forgot our own given names because we only called ourselves by the insulting ones that we made up for each other. One boy was known as Squinty, another was Hunchback; this one was Sleepy, the other was Wasted. There was one who happily answered to Crazy, another to Donkey, a third to Turkey, and so on down the line. With so many godparents around, I could not escape my christening. When I went off to school, I wore a green waistcoat and yellow pants. These colors, and the fact that my teacher sometimes affectionately called me not Pedro but Pedrillo, furnished my friends with my nickname: *Periquillo*, or Little Parrot. But I still needed some kind of adjective to distinguish me from another Parrot we already had. This adjective or surname was not long in coming: I came down with a case of *saran*, or mange, and the boys had no sooner noticed it than they remembered my true surname, Sarmiento, and turned it into the resounding title of *Sarniento*, Mangy. So here you have me, known not just at school and as a child, but full-grown and far and wide, as Periquillo Sarniento, the Mangy Parrot.[7]

The signature effect of nicknaming in the student hazing tradition also comes through in the memoirs of one of Mexico's most prolific writers and journalists, Alejandro Villaseñor. As he describes, the first days of middle school have historically represented a defining moment in the academic lives of most Mexican students. They represented a moment when *perros* ("dogs," or first-year students) were "baptized" with a nickname that would often last beyond their academic careers. The writer did not need to wait long for such a moment. He recalled being beaten by a group of older students the very first night he arrived at the National Preparatory School (ENP) in 1875 without any intervention by school authorities. He notes, "In order to be respected," it soon became obvious, "one had to know how to use his fists, as they usually came in handy."[8] For the toughest, craftiest, and most charismatic perros, early testing marked an opportunity to gain respect from, and authority over, their peers.[9] Thus some ENP students earned nicknames that were given as a sign of respect. Alejandro Villaseñor remembers, for instance, that a student was nicknamed El Perro Amador ("Lovable Dog"), sarcastically alluding to his admired toughness when it came to fighting.

But the unwelcome labels assigned to the weakest and less fortunate students condemned them to enduring *bromas pesadas* (harsh jokes or pranks) for the rest of the year. Nicknames were commonly used to make fun of a student's physical appearance, birth defect, or perceived odd behavior. Some examples include: La Molécula ("The Molecule") because of the student's short stature, El Chante Molina because of the student's dark complexion,[10] and El Aerolito ("The Meteorite"), a nickname given to the famous novelist Federico Gamboa presumably because of his relatively large head. Nicknaming was often spontaneous, arbitrary, and opportunistic. Villaseñor recalled that all it took was a silly comment on the part of El Chante Molina (or other students resembling his dark complexion), for other students to laugh out loud or engage in mockery.[11] As scholar Nancy Vogeley notes, the common practice of giving nicknames to students "reproduced the frequent use of language for vilification and humiliation" inherited from the colonial period. She explains:

> Over centuries Mexicans had learned habits of abuse by their Spanish overlords, and so they turned the ugly, destructive language (the only one they knew) against one another. Indeed, Lizardi thought that the Mexican taste for familiar joking really disguised the anger and self-hatred they had learned as colonials.[12]

Baptizing novatos with nicknames (whether a brutal practice inherited by the colonialists or not) as well as the collective beatings, pranks, and mockery remained an important part of student culture with the basic purpose of installing a particular sense of maturity, identity, and belonging throughout the twentieth century.

During the 1940s and 1950s, the new school year was marked by a set of flamboyant public parades known as the *paseo de los perros* ("the parade of the dogs"), where first-year students would participate in a kind of open-air public hazing, celebration, and mockery. These fagging rituals were organized by older students with the intention of initiating the novatos. They varied year by year according to the characteristics and ingenuity of each class. In general, these annual parades featured humiliating and ridiculous displays, such as shaving of young novatos' heads in public, forcing them to dress in diapers or other outlandish outfits, making them crawl like animals, or forcing them to ride a tricycle sucking a pacifier or drinking from a gigantic baby bottle. In time older students and the assembled pubic would take the opportunity to throw water, mud, paint, confetti, and even rotten eggs at the young novatos.

In addition, the older students would require that these young students be pulled along on all fours wearing a dog collar and a leash.

The noisiest and most famous novatadas were those organized in the principal streets of the *barrio estudiantil* by students enrolled in the School of Architecture of the National Autonomous University of Mexico (UNAM). Typically, these parades began at the famous Art School of San Carlos, made their way to Cinco de Mayo Avenue, turned right to Correo Mayor, and circled back to San Carlos through Cinco de Mayo Avenue.[13] But unlike the variety of hazing rituals that took place inside the schools, these annual possessions of an important section of the city could only be possible with the consent of city officials and the financial support of school and government authorities. Former student leader of the National Polytechnic Institute (IPN), Nicandro Mendoza, remembered during an interview that "school and key government authorities always supported novatadas and all other activities that students found amusing." He then went on to explain that he personally witnessed several times how public functionaries gave students money and even free boxes of eggs to throw at the novatos so that students would engage in relajo instead of getting involved in politics.[14] UNAM's most famous cheerleader, Palillo, offered a similar interpretation regarding the closely interconnected relationship between fun and politics that characterized this period. He noted during an interview:

> During the 1940s and 1950s I engaged in joyous yet fierce competition with other student leaders to see who would win in organizing the most outrageous paseos de los perros. This was not an easy endeavor. From above I had to obtain the blessing of our *padrinos* [financial and political patrons]. From below I had to attract as many young participants as possible by making sure that the themes we selected for our parades addressed the needs and concerns of our students. These conflicting interests required a certain degree of sensitivity on my part. Our padrinos expected harsh pranks, even the mockery of public figures, but they were not very happy when the novatadas got out of control and drew too much attention in the media.[15]

Indeed, novatadas not only involved the collaboration between students and authority figures but they also frequently grabbed the attention of journalists and photographers who often captured the complex purposes served by these outlandish performances.

Judging from the students' smiles and elaborate floats depicted in Illustration 2.1, for example, it becomes evident that many newcomers willing-

ILLUS. 2.1. Novatos Dressed as Romans, c. 1940s. (Reproduced with permission of the Archivo General de la Nación, Fondo Enrique Díaz, No. 68/30 [n.d.].)

ly participated in these rituals, which celebrated a cosmopolitan notion of youth through a temporary appropriation of the streets. For many students, the "conquered territories" also gave them the necessary space and time to celebrate the beginning of their new life as students.[16] A regular participant of the paseo de los perros, Francisco Javier Arenas, would later write in his memoirs, "There is no indignation here." Novatadas, he insisted, gave students the opportunity to tell everyone in a loud voice: "I am a dog! I am a dog! I am now part of this school! No one will get in the way of my [upward social] mobility! The future is in my hands! I am a dog; I am a dog and this is my baptism!"[17]

This celebratory attitude toward youth and the university was also evident in the careful work, time, and energy that young novatos put into the creation of the elaborate floats that they used during the paseos. Students

ILLUS. 2.2. Novatos Dressed as women, c. 1940s. (Reproduced with permission from the Archivo General de la Nación, Fondo Hermanos Mayo, No. 5930 [n.d.].)

proudly paraded in the principal streets of Mexico City dressed not only as noble Romans but also as Aztec goddesses, Hindu leaders, African chiefs, ballerinas, and firemen. After all, one of the principal points of the novatadas, as Elizondo Alceraz writes in his memoirs, was to suspend—at least momentarily—the dreadfulness of adult life and to enjoy the moment of youth that the school and the parades offered students. He writes: "[D]ressed as witches in roller skates, with long artificial hair and wearing enormous noses covered with pimples, the students armed themselves with brooms that they used to hit everyone who got in front of their way." Then he adds: "[T]he parade was a reflection of an extraordinary moment in people's lives in which the vitality of [youth] burst open into the heart of Mexico City."[18]

In addition to being a great deal of fun and celebrating a universal notion of youth, the paseo de los perros also offered students an opportunity to mock everything that the nation considered appropriate, including traditional and newly acquired values, institutions, authorities, and modernity itself. As depicted in Illustration 2.2, for example, students who participated in these novatadas often dressed as women to ridicule traditional gender roles. Other students preferred to dress as Romans to mock Western civilization and values. Still others dressed as politicians, bureaucrats, and school authorities with outrageous outfits to challenge the official history they had learned as elementary and secondary students, as well as patriarchy, patronage, and authoritarian strictness by making fun of them and the institutions they represented.

In sum, the celebration of novatadas had several purposes. For one, these annual parades served as a way of teaching precedence to newcomers, many of whom were seen as "savages" who had just migrated to the city and needed to undergo hardships to prove themselves worthy of admission into the modern urban schools.[19] Public humiliation during the paseo de los perros forced novatos to break with their childhood and helped the *provincianos* (students who had arrived at the capital from other cities) who engaged in these rituals break with their rural past and outdated values. The nicknames, pranks, and mockery of these parades gave students a new sense of belonging, and hence a new sense of identity as universitarios or politécnicos. Similarly, the symbolic occupation of streets on the part of the novatos opened up a space in which students experienced youth as a collective behavior. In addition, the paseos allowed newcomers to demonstrate that they possessed the courage to survive the symbolic ordeals necessary to live in the emerging metropolis of Mexico

City.[20] For youth at this time, these included achieving sexual maturity in the urban space, becoming acquainted with new institutional norms, being worthy of embracing a cosmopolitan notion of youth, and dealing with a new type of peer pressure that revolved around struggling with the fast pace of modernity and urbanization that characterized the 1940s and 1950s. Therefore, novatadas should also be interpreted as public tests of masculinity in which strength, courage, and determination established leadership and respect, while signs of weakness indicated who was unworthy of living in the new metropolis. Finally, the paseo de los perros gave male students a moment to invert social norms and institutional values by engaging in a state of relajo or festive disorder in which—like a carnival—"the forbidden was permitted and social and sexual roles became interchangeable."[21] Similarly, American football also offered an opportunity for students to engage in relajo and celebrate middle-class consumption. Further, it opened a space for school and government authorities to intervene in the social and political lives of students.

American Football and School Spirit

It would perhaps come as a surprise to many that the favorite sport of universitarios and politécnicos in the 1950s was not *fútbol* (soccer), boxing, or even basketball, but American football. Over time, this sport became a vehicle of relajo whereby team loyalty was promoted as a surrogate for national pride, to secure an American consumerist vision of modernity, and to advocate Pan-Americanism. As historian Julio Moreno has argued, regardless of their ideological positions nearly all Mexicans rejected the imperialist attitude of U.S. investors residing in Mexico, but they welcomed the capitalist cultural traits that they brought with them, including American sports.[22]

According to the few scholars who have studied the history of American football in Mexico, the first game ever played with this "odd-looking ball" took place among a small group of U.S. Marines in Xalapa, Veracruz, in 1890.[23] The game of American football began to become popular with Mexico's youth in the 1930s. At this time a number of public and private schools across the nation began to include the sport in their physical education curriculum, parks and small stadiums were built to host games, and new sport institutions (such as the Mexican Association of American Football) assumed formal control over diversions.[24] The increased interest in American football was spurred on by the governing elite, often in conjunction with a growing number of American and Mexican entrepreneurs who promoted the civic importance of sports and invested in the creation of the Confederation of Mexican Sports (CDM). New state-supported football teams sprang up in sporting clubs, such as the Young Men's Christian Association (YMCA), the Mexican Athletic Center (CAM), and the Swiss Sporting Club.[25]

The promotion of football led to measures that extended the influence of the United States in Mexican society, even as nationalist rhetoric framed Americans as competitors and opponents. Mexican teams began to hire coaches from U.S. colleges, sent their best players and managers to train in the United States, and invited North American teams to play in Mexico. Opportunities to play against North American college and high school teams were welcomed. After all, as one fan of the game put it during an interview, "[W]hat a better way to beat the gringos than at their own game?"[26] These measures facilitated the creation of more competitive teams and helped to regulate the sport with uniform guidelines.

For entrepreneurs who supported the proliferation of the game, American football had become a potential revenue-producing activity. New forms of mass media were created, including new sporting newspapers (*Tribuna Deportiva* and *Deporte Gráfico*) and radio stations that specifically targeted young fans of the game (*Radio XENK 620*). At the same time, private entrepreneurs took advantage of these media outlets to advertise a variety of new and old products to be consumed by a cosmopolitan young market. These ranged from tangible products such as soda pop, chewing gum, and collegiate sweaters, to entertainment like Afro-Cuban rhythms and North American films. By financing organized games, Mexican politicians and foreign capitalists residing in Mexico agreed that the game (and the consumption of its culture) would instill in the middle class proper—more Americanized—attitudes. Traits such as ambition, dedication, competition, and a concern for health were necessary to support economic development in Mexico and thus contribute to democracy.[27] They agreed that the proliferation of sports was a fundamental necessity to encourage Mexico's youth to abandon the social "vices" and "lazy attitude" that kept the nation from moving forward toward modernity.[28]

But unlike earlier notions of progress endorsed by the state, which intended to "liberate the masses" from its own ignorance—as Carlos Monsiváis once noted—the notions of progress and modernity that evolved in the postrevolutionary period were expressed rather "objectively" to benefit a select group of people.[29] Higher education, in its capacity as a means to economic success, made politécnicos and (especially) universitarios suitable representatives of this consumerist notion of progress and modernity. Constructed on a monumental scale to serve this purpose, Ciudad Universitaria and the University Olympic Stadium instantly helped to transform sports like American football into youth spectacles, and to shape students into middle-class consumers. With the adoption of American football came new outward expressions and customs that fused school spirit and relajo. Students adopted American-styled sports clothing and paraphernalia that contributed to the environment of team loyalty. Schools imported American collegiate sweaters, flags, and mascots, chosen to match the respective school colors. Worn in public and celebrated in the new spaces of consumption, such as the football stadiums, these new icons endowed young students with a privileged status. Like the novatos who proudly proclaimed, "I am a dog," students who wore sweaters bearing the "U" of UNAM (or to a lesser extent the "P" of the IPN), might have conveyed with great joy the sentiment "I am a universitario. I am a universitario!" After all, unlike his father, who had to go to work, he had the luxury of playing, the privilege of enjoying leisure, and the space to engage in relajo.[30]

On the political front, football provided a vehicle during the World War II era for nationalist revolutionary slogans and patriotic forewarnings of the potential threat of the devastating war in Europe.[31] Thus American football was fostered as a fusion of individual, institutional, and national concern. It became a national commodity where pride in one's team meant loyalty to the modern nation. With the national anthem sung before each game, loyalty to the team was then translated into loyalty to the state, and by extension, to the nation. The two would merge symbolically with the singing of the Mexican national anthem before each football game, and more visibly when the president himself would provide the initial kick-off for the most important games. In these ways team loyalty was advanced specifically as dedication to the party in power, the Institutional Revolutionary Party, or PRI.

In contrast to the revolutionary nationalism of earlier periods, the nationalism of the 1940s and 1950s promoted sports with the hope that it would give young people "something to do other than politics."[32] This new attitude toward sports was particularly common among government authorities close to President Miguel Alemán. In 1950, for example, the National Institute of Mexican Youth (INJM) was founded as a Cold War mechanism of indoctrinating youth and distracting them from radical politics.[33] In a speech given at UNAM in 1952, for example, Alemán warned the students: "[Today you are being exposed] to new schools of thought that have brought upon us a new environment of restlessness and contradictions." He went on to tell those students interested in "conquering and maintaining peace, prosperity, culture, and liberty for the Mexican pueblo" that it was vital for them to "behave with strength, determination, courage, [and above all], prudence, sagacity . . . and political disinterest."[34]

This paternalistic attitude toward youth was also manifested in specific cultural practices that revolved around American football and school spirit. Many school and national authorities began to manipulate the football rivalry that developed between politécnicos (white donkeys) and universitarios (pumas), precisely in an effort to depoliticize students. Simultaneously, the relajo associated with novatadas and American football served as an opportunity for students to embrace and or resist such state-sponsored cultural activities as well as the multiple programs of modernity advanced by the state. The following case study illustrates how this emphasis on student rivalry championed by charismatic cheerleaders, and the relajo that often accompanied it, buttressed the commonly held conception of the so-called youth crisis of postwar Mexico.

Porristas, the Burning of Effigies, and Social Rivalry

Porristas, or cheerleaders, were instrumental figures in the celebration of relajo. The main responsibility of the porristas was to encourage crowd participation in songs and anthems and organizing a variety of dances, acrobatic acts, and stunts to entertain and excite the crowd during football games. Similar to their counterparts in the United States during this period, porristas served as important icons "of youthful prestige, wholesome attractiveness, peer leadership . . . mindless enthusiasm, [and] shallow boosterism" in the schools.[35]

Initially, cheerleading was understood as a strictly male activity in Mexico and the United States. Female students were perceived as physically inferior to young men and therefore incapable of displaying leadership and performing difficult acrobatic exercises seen as necessary to "fire up" the crowd.[36] With time, female cheerleaders would replace male cheerleaders in both countries. In the United States this began in a small way in the 1920s but became much more widespread during World War II when many young students temporarily left their schools to join the military.[37] In Mexico, this transition took longer to occur, taking place two decades later during the mid-to-late 1960s. Prior to this time, the majority of female students involved in the Mexican football scene engaged in activities deemed suitable, in the patriarchal logic of the time, for delicate and demure women, such as beauty pageants and dance competitions.[38] Since superiority could be expressed in part through standards of female beauty, rival porristas from UNAM and the IPN engaged in a jovial contest to see which school could showcase the most beautiful female students, who waved to the fans as they paraded around the football fields in convertible cars prior to the game.[39] Porristas also competed to see who could convince the most famous actress to endorse their teams as symbolic *madrinas* (god-mothers).[40] Thus, in contrast to the passive engagement of female figureheads, male porristas competed fiercely to see who could come up with the loudest *porras* ("cheers"), the most outrageous stunts, and wildest public celebrations.[41]

One of the most popular celebrations that developed around American football was the burning in effigy of the opposite team's mascot.[42] In the context of the promotion of festive disorder, the effigies twinkling in the eyes of students helped to keep their focus on each other rather than on political matters. Like novatadas, the burnings of the "white donkey" (the politécnicos' mascot) and the puma (the universitarios' mascot) took place as public events via the temporary appropriation of the streets. The celebration of these rituals usually began outside the doors of the old school of San Ildefonso the evening before a "classic" matchup between UNAM and the IPN. After gathering in the tradition-laden barrio estudiantil, the students set off on a long and joyous walk during which they carried a coffin containing the opposite team's mascot, sang their team's anthem, and repeatedly screamed their cheers prior to the burnings. At times followed by a caravan of convertibles and school buses adorned with their school colors and icons, the students also took advantage of this moment to insult the weakness of the opposite team.[43] Universitarios would typically mock the lower social background of the politécnicos, who were labeled *mantenidos* ("freeloaders," in reference to support received by the populist state), *boleros* ("shoe-shiners," in reference to their working-class background), or *rojillos* ("little red ones," in reference to the students' politicized reputation). For their part, politécnicos called universitarios *juniors* (in reference to their privileged class status guaranteed by their daddy's money) and *hijos de Alemán* ("children of President Alemán," in reference to blind allegiance to the head of state). Once the young rivals reached their final destination, usually outside the stadium or close to a publishing house of an important newspaper, students took the opposite team's mascot out of the coffin and proceeded to beat and insult it. The festivities ended with the effigy burning followed by loud cheers, including the *Goya* cheer of UNAM and the *Huélum* cheer of the IPN.[44] As with the novatadas, these communal roasts of the opposition could only be possible with the financial support of padrinos and institutional sanction. A regular organizer of the rituals later explained, "All of us who participated in the organization of novatadas and the burning of the donkeys perfectly understood that if the rector and the city's regent both failed to give us their financial and political blessing, we simply could not afford to organize these events."[45] A closer look at the motives behind these *padrinos del relajo* (patrons of diversion) gives a clearer picture of the political culture of the schools during this period.

Student Leaders as Intermediaries

Scholars who have studied patron-client relationships in Mexico have contributed to our understanding of the various social networks of power that developed in marginal societies. By and large, this field has been dominated by specific case studies of clientelism, *caciquismo* (bossism), and *compadrazgo* (parenthood) that aim to explain how marginal societies have taken advantage of these social networks to guarantee material exchange and economic security.[46] For instance, anthropologists and sociologists who have studied the contractual system of fictive kinship known throughout the Hispanic world as compadrazgo have described in great detail how baptisms, confirmations, and first communions have been used by marginal sectors of society to improve their economic situations.[47] However, few scholars have applied models of informal economic and political relations to the political postwar kinship that developed within the universities during this period. Yet, as already noted, ritualized student diversions such as novatadas, hazing practices, effigy rallies, graduation ceremonies, and so on could not have been organized without financial and social support. Novel kinshiplike social and political networks led by padrinos del relajo, facilitated by *intermediantes del relajo* (diversion-focused intermediaries), crystallized to provide such support.

Roderic Camp has demonstrated the important role teachers, public officers, and national politicians have played in establishing social networks for
political recruitment inside UNAM and its preparatory schools. He describes
"these networks as *camarillas* and Mexican politics as a whole as a series of
interlocking pyramidal camarillas that culminate in the president and his
political clique." Camp further points out that "camarillas crosscut ideological, social, and sectoral barriers and are welded together by personal loyalties."[48] Similarly, sociologist Larissa Lomnitz has documented at length the
struggle that takes place for political hegemony in each of the multilayered
bases of the pyramidal structure of power that has characterized the university. She explains, for instance, how in each of the political levels (of the pyramid) an intermediary (or "broker") creates (i) a horizontal social network that
allows him to build legitimacy with the people he represents; and (ii) a vertical political network with the people that support him (the "padrino").[49]

The metaphor of the pyramid serves as a useful starting point to describe
the political structure of UNAM. The qualification "starting point" is apt
because such a metaphor might suggest a rigid hierarchical form of organization, but, in the sense used here, the pyramid does not preclude competition,
negotiation, and resistance.[50] A network of social relations distinct from formal political lines of hierarchical authority makes this capillarity possible.
Such was the case with the way in which UNAM was organized during the
postwar period. Larissa Lomnitz describes the internal structure of power of
UNAM as follows:

> At the top there is a leader who generates loyalty. Immediately below there
> is an inner circle of trusted assistants or leading activists, followed by a
> second level, and so on. Social proximity to the leader is the main factor
> for individual ranking and for social solidarity with the group. The entire
> student body, and indeed the university itself, may be thought of as a
> conglomerate of pyramidal structures (some formal and others informal),
> which includes faculty, unions, research groups, and even delinquent gangs,
> all competing for resources, jobs, status, and power with the larger pyramid
> of the university structure.[51]

In this form of organization, the role of the "intermediary" becomes critical for maintaining cohesion and capillarity.[52] Echoing Lomnitz's and Camp's
main arguments, Wil Pansters demonstrates that power within this large
structure is "negotiated among corporate groups," or internal "hierarchical'
pyramids" that are held together or reinforced through "clientelistic exchange,

reciprocity, and loyalty." The effective operation of a hierarchical structure depends on the glue of "collective (corporatist) and unanimous support," and this is a prime function of the charismatic intermediaries.[53] To borrow from Eric Wolf's classic essay, the charismatic intermediaries played the role of "buffers between groups" whose

> basic function [was] to relate community oriented individuals who want[ed] to stabilize or improve their life chances, but who [otherwise] lack[ed] . . . political connections with nation-oriented individuals who operate[d] primarily in terms of the complex cultural forms standardized as national institutions.[54]

Within the particular context of UNAM during this postrevolutionary period, the role of the intermediary was indebted to two significant changes in the formal organization of the university.[55] The first took place during the 1920s when the emerging corporatist state extended its support to the creation of the University Student Federation (FEU). During this period the presidents and leading representatives of the student societies and the FEU emerged as the most important official intermediaries in serving as the brokers between the university community and the emerging corporatist state. Student leaders represented the multiple interests of groups competing at the community as well as the national level, and, thus, resolved the conflicts raised by the collision of these interests.[56] These brokers became instrumental figures in strengthening the institutional life of the university. On one side, universitarios took advantage of the student societies and the FEU to redefine their political position during student protests. On the other, individuals in important positions of power within the government also took advantage of these brokers to negotiate with disgruntled students and the new conservative patrons who gradually took control of the university.

The second significant change within the hierarchical structure of the university occurred following the implementation of the Caso Law in the mid-1940s, a move that made the state an integral and leading figure in the university's formal organization. The law also severely reduced the representative power of universitarios by excluding their representative bodies, the Academias, from the new and powerful Governing Board (see Chapter 1). As a consequence, representative student leaders lost a space in which to discuss academic policies and their ability to influence the appointment of professors and directors. Instead of bringing to a halt student political activity, the law in time merely shifted the intermediary function from a place within the formal UNAM structure to the exploding number of student organizations that sprang up at the time by taking advantage of the cultural and recreational sponsorship clause of the Caso Law. This clause allowed political authorities to invest, both politically and economically, in student politics. In particular, the clause stated that students had "the freedom to organize societies that they found convenient." In turn, the school authorities had "the right to establish a cooperative relationship" with the new student organizations "as long as these maintained a cultural, athletic, or social" character.[57]

The original purpose of this clause was to encourage students to abandon the radical and reactionary internal political organizations that Caso had seen as a threat. But because student organizations began to receive generous support from a number of political figures outside of the university structure—such as patrons of graduating classes and sponsors of sporting and cultural events (what I call padrinos del relajo)—the student organizations became more and more politicized after the Caso Law. Thus, despite Caso's intention to depoliticize the university, cultural and sporting organizations, such as the *porras* (cheerleading teams), were quickly transformed into political arenas in which control of the student body was up for grabs. In this struggle charismatic cheerleaders, such as the highly influential "Palillo," played a vital role.

Palillo y Sus Padrinos

According to Larissa Lomnitz, in the structure of UNAM at least four careers can be identified: the academics, the professionals, the politicians, and the fighting gangs. She explains:

> "Academics" are members of the university community who develop a preference for research and teaching as a way of life. . . . The "professionals" represent a life career which is clearly oriented toward a role outside the university proper. . . . The "politicians" are members of the academic community who have shown an active interest in political affairs from their student days.

Examples of the latter include student activists, lobbyists, representatives of the student societies, and so on. The fourth career group, as defined by Lomnitz, includes the "fighting gangs." The best examples of these are the porro squads led by charismatic student charro leaders (see Chapter 7). As she correctly points out, these "individuals hire[d] themselves out occasionally to pressure groups that provide[d] the slogan and resources for their activities."[58] To the list of careers described above, I would add intermediaries of relajo, such as the fashionable male cheerleaders of the 1940s and 1950s. They, like the gangs mentioned by Lomnitz, also hired themselves out occasionally. But unlike the gangs, the advocates of relajo generally avoided violence. As noted earlier, popularity with the students, a charismatic personality, and perceived leadership abilities were the three most important factors that determined who became the captain of the cheerleading team.

By the mid-1950s, porras had been officially organized in nearly all schools of UNAM, the IPN, and their preparatory and vocational schools. A handful of male cheerleaders had emerged as some of the most influential and charismatic figures (read intermediaries) within these schools. For an impressive period that lasted close to three decades (1937–1964), Luis Rodriguez, better known as Palillo ("Toothpick"), was the most popular porrista at UNAM.[59] At the peak of Palillo's career as a student, entertainer, and advocate of relajo, he was in charge of more than five thousand cheerleaders and was capable of moving thousands when instructed by his padrinos (or when he, himself, saw it appropriate). Many later remembered that this popular Peter Pan–like leader was able to influence more students than "all political student organizations and societies combined."[60]

Luis Rodriguez was born in San Sebastián, Jalisco.[61] In the mid-1930s, his parents first enrolled the young Luis in the ENP. After enrolling in the university in the late 1940s, Palillo quickly became the foremost student leader. His slender frame served as an immediately recognizable icon in the flourishing industries of show business and student spectacles, a fact that was well noted in important political circles of power.[62] Carlos Ortiz Tejeda, an influential student leader at the time, later recalled that "when the authorities took notice of the popularity of Palillo and his potential gift to unite so many students vis-à-vis the sports and relajo, the authorities quickly looked for the best way to take advantage of [him.]"[63] On the surface, his achievements included reinventing old cheers, composing inane school anthems and songs, dancing in public places, creating student magazines (such as *Goya* and *Touch Down*), and surrounding himself with beautiful female students.[64] Echoing the voices of many, Oscar González, also one of the most influential student leaders of the 1950s, remembered during an interview that students liked to hang around with Palillo because "he always organized the most outrageous parties (*reven-*

tones), craziest *novatadas*, most delightful beauty pageants, wildest burnings of the white donkeys, and most memorable *pintas*."[65] Many others agreed: "Student organizations endorsed by the FEU were boring to many of us." A young *preparatoriano* recalled:

> Instead we found Palillo's *porra* to be a much more exciting adventure. If you made it to his circle of friends (and this was not very hard to do), you had access to a life of excitement. He gave us a taste of what the presidents always promised in their speeches. He took us to the movies, billiards, and bars and we never had to pay. He took us to the football games and we had the opportunity to meet the most beautiful girls in the schools and in the movie industry. Oh, that Palillo; he always made us laugh with his crazy sense of humor and wild stunts.[66]

In one of his most memorable stunts, Palillo convinced the secretary of communication to lend him the services of a helicopter from the American embassy. The helicopter appeared out of nowhere and landed inside the football stadium during a game between UNAM and the IPN. "From the sky," Palillo humorously later recalled, "I organized the most original Goya. The guys would not stop talking about it for weeks."[67] People also remembered fondly the time Palillo parachuted into a stadium, "but on the wrong side of the field. You know, where the *porra* of the Politécnico organized their [Huélum] cheers."[68] Testimonies also make reference to when Palillo collected money to arrange a dance competition of mambo and cha-cha-chá inside the prestigious Palace of Fine Arts (Palacio de Bellas Artes). Above all, Palillo is remembered by his famous saying:

> If you want to have some glee
> then Palillo you must see
> And to leave your studies behind
> Palillo you must find.[69]

Yet, after several unperturbed years moving from major to major, Palillo was "asked" to leave the country in 1964 on a guaranteed research scholarship in psychology, by the administration of Díaz Ordaz. He remembered this day as follows:

> One day I was approached by two *guaruras* (bodyguards) straight out of a gangster movie—you know—wearing sun glasses and a pistol for everyone to see, and they kindly told me [that] "our new boss has given you two

options: you leave for Paris by the end of this week or you leave your beloved university for good." I told them to send my gratitude (*mis mercies*) to their *patrón* (boss) and told them that I would take advantage of this opportunity to pursue my degree in psychology in French.

Palillo recalled that "the political atmosphere had changed . . . and I knew that it was time to step down."[70] His departure was swift, leaving only treasured memories by admirers who only understood him as a master of relajo. To better understand why the administration of Díaz Ordaz saw such a move as necessary requires a closer look at the intermediary function of porristas like Palillo and the forms of sponsorship provided to them by padrinos.

The popularity of porristas derived not only from the entertainment provided at the parties they organized but also by the way these parties channeled requests for a variety of academic and social favors. Such favors were given in exchange for various demonstrations of loyalty to a given political group. Loyalty to a porrista would make possible finding a place to sleep in the dormitories, free meals, guest passes to local events, free school paraphernalia, upward adjustments to grades, and ultimately entrees into political posts after graduation. A principal cheerleader of the IPN, Jorge "El Oso" Ocegera, later noted that students who came to Mexico City to attend the Politécnico but lacked a place to sleep (the so-called *gaviotas*, or "gulls") often took advantage of these parties to ask him for social assistance. He explained during an interview, "[T]he gaviotas always came to me during our parties; you know to ask me for some kind of favor. In return, I asked them to accompany me to the games. You know, just in case things got out of hand with the universitarios. In exchange, I gave the Secretary of Public Education a list of students who needed a place inside the dormitories."[71] Other students came to these parties to ask porristas for help with their academic careers. A student who preferred to remain anonymous recalled an academic favor granted via the intercession of the porrista Palillo at a party:

> We all knew that if we were failing a course either because of our own ineptitude or because of an injustice on the part of one professor, we could always count on Palillo. All we had to do was ask: "Palillo, I will not be able to graduate because professor such and such will not let me pass his class." He would then reply, "Don't worry. I will talk to him tomorrow. This is a party and we are here to have fun. Grab a drink!" . . . The next month I received my diploma.[72]

Oscar González López, a frequent guest of the parties funded by rector Nabor Carrillo and organized by Palillo, nostalgically recalled during a conversation with the author that these events were sometimes thrown in luxurious hotels and brothels where the "real politics" of the university took place. Often, their allure capitalized on the more opportunistic impulses of students who would leave their ideological ambitions at the door. He explained:

> The France Hotel, the most enjoyable [bar the] Wai-ki-ki, and other less famous places were where politics actually took place during this time. I remember that the famous Palillo was in charge of inviting the prettiest girls [to the parties]—for the entertainment. Others were in charge of bringing the alcohol, which brought us closer together with the rector and his secretary. Of course, only those that were politically close to the rector's group could attend these parties. But when we bragged about these wild parties to the rest of the guys in the school, nearly all of them left their ideologies to the side and tried to see how they could penetrate this circle of power. Once intoxicated with alcohol and relajo, these respected authorities would tell us who we had to harass politically and who we had to leave in peace, or support in any case.[73]

To be sure, students attended these parties, novatadas, and football games organized by porristas primarily with the intention of having fun. The drinks, beauty pageants, music, free tickets to the games, and complimentary college sweaters that accompanied these events supported such relajo. But at the same time that they enabled porristas like Palillo to build a horizontal social network, they also helped to construct an informal political base for padrino sponsors. Many later remembered that Palillo, in fact, had more control over the students than any political activist during this time.[74] During the rectorship of Nabor Carrillo (1952–1961), Palillo came into his own as a successful intermediary. At the zenith of his power during his long career as an intermediary, Palillo even managed to befriend President Miguel Alemán. When asked to comment on a photograph published in a student newspaper in which Palillo appears standing next to Miguel Alemán at the National Palace waving to a crowd, the charismatic leader explained his "friendship" with the president with the following words:

> The President was a generous man. Several times I went to the National Palace to ask him for resources; you know, *para el cotorreo de los chavos* (to have fun with the guys). He would always tell me: "You, again Palillo! What

do you need this time?" On one occasion I told him, "Just a couple of bucks to buy 20 sweaters for the porra." I would never forget his response. He told me, "Well, here's enough to buy 200 sweaters. Make sure to spend it wisely."[75]

Thus, in a manner strikingly reminiscent of a local union boss, Palillo had become a Janus-like figure who "specialized in accommodating and monopolizing upward and downward linkages" by operating at various levels of the political system.[76] However, such a system cannot be attributed solely to the relationship that he developed with one man. Besides Miguel Alemán, the patronage network that supported Palillo inside the university also included the rector, Nabor Carrillo, and his general secretary, Efrén del Pozo. This is the same general secretary who became infamous for maintaining a close relationship with student leaders with unpleasant reputations, such as known provocateurs. Other important political figures with whom Palillo developed relationships outside the university included President Ruiz Cortines; the private secretary of Miguel Alemán and future president, Adolfo López Mateos; head of the federal district, Ernesto Peralta Uruchurtu;[77] and Humberto Romero Pérez.[78]

The systemic nature of Palillo's network of exchange was well represented in the official "vouchers" he parlayed in his numerous dealings with his associates. Without the need for actual cash as his universal means of exchange, these slips were his licenses to attend to the business of relajo both inside and outside the university, as he later described to the author:

> Most of the times, they gave me [some sort of] voucher or a signed slip of paper. I would then take these signatures to the Department [of Physical Education], to the secretaries of the rector, or to the office of an important *licenciado* so that they would give me tickets to the games, sweaters for the boys, or jackets for the captains [of the porra]. The same would happen in other social spheres: I would take my voucher to the Liris or Goya cinema, and the people in charge would give me tickets for the boys. I would go to the billiards and they would let us play for free. I would take them to the bar and they would let us drink for free. I would take them to the brothels and well you know . . . . We could say that in those days I had some sort of *licencia para echar relajo* (permit to organize fun).[79]

Official documents by the DFS do not undermine the validity of Palillo's claims, or those who benefited from the relationship with him. These government documents testify to the fact that the political influence of Palillo was felt not only at football games but also during student elections, political rallies, and in a variety of informal social gatherings.[80]

The nonstop cavalcade of fun Palillo and other porristas orchestrated helped to keep universitarios' eyes fixed on the football and away from the student activism occurring at the IPN in 1956 (see Chapter 3). In this, Palillo served the depoliticizing ends of authorities magnificently. During the 1958 movement, however, Palillo collaborated with activists. With the blessing of the university rector Nabor Carrillo (who sympathized with the strike), Palillo organized an important student torchlight march to the Zócalo from Ciudad Universitaria involving more than 100,000 students in support of the public transportation strike (see Chapter 5). Apparently the same mechanisms that could amass hundreds and thousands of students to show school spirit at school events could be put to work just as easily in opposition to official policies that came down from above. Football rallies could be replaced by political protest rallies, and cheerleaders transformed into protest leaders. And if students insisted on resisting authority, then it would be their very own organizations, or facsimiles thereof, that might lead them to self-destruct. To bring this about, relajo could transfigure into "rogue defiance" or desmadre. Herein lay the potential danger of Palillo and the porristas, and thus the necessity for authorities to either oust such leaders or somehow stem such a tidal shift through cooptation.

Desmadre and the Simmering of a "Youth Crisis"

As the culture of public student hazing and festive disorder developed in Mexico in the late 1940s and 1950s, it contributed to a print media–led alarm regarding a "crisis of youth" that went hand in hand with a "crisis of authority." Even though the verbal and symbolic duels that characterized student hazing and football culture rarely culminated in violent clashes with authority, a single incident would be all that was necessary to generate demands for disciplinary action. For instance, the letters of ordinary citizens were frequently sent to President Adolfo Ruiz Cortines and would often make their way into the pages of *Excélsior, El Universal, Tiempo, La Prensa,* and *La Nación.* In one example, Guadalupe Plascencia chose an occasion when a group of dueling students splashed innocent bystanders with water to complain more generally about student behavior: "It is deplorable to see the Mexican masculine youth, the future of a better Nation, has relaxed its customs." At the beginning of each academic year, she added, "they throw paint and shave off the hair of the 'dogs.' Perhaps this is world-wide tradition, but the bad thing is that innocent people including ladies . . . are bathed publicly in this uproar." Echoing the voices found in numerous editorial pages, Guadalupe went to demand sterner disciplinary action on the part of authorities by proposing to the "Sr. President" that all students who have proven to be "disrespectful" be "FORCED TO DO MILITARY SERVICE." Only this, and other "drastic" measures, she added, would "correct . . . the bad behavior" of Mexico's youth and, thus, return "progress" to the nation. The time has come, she further told the president regarding the *revoltosos*, for them "to learn to honor their MOTHER COUNTRY, their HOMES, AND THEIR PARENTS."[81]

For a large number of people, particularly those of the older generation (such as Guadalupe Plascencia), novatadas and other forms of relajo represented a "barbaric tradition" at odds with a number of values. These included values of modesty and gendered behavior. Many people appeared to have been especially surprised and upset, for example, by all the skin exposed during the novatadas. Young men wearing women's clothing in public—even for fun— was simply at odds with traditional Mexican values.[82] Standards of morality were thought to be compromised as small store owners complained that students took advantage of novatadas and effigies to steal from stores and harass their female customers.[83] The public argued that the "barbaric practices" of relajo promoted the consumption of alcohol, student antagonism, and violence.[84] The tradition being violated was measured specifically in terms of the order and modernity that the governing elite wanted to promote inside the schools.

Authorities made several promises to ban hazing rituals and the burning of effigies. During the rectorship of Brito Foucher (1942–1944), for example, novatadas were officially made illegal after three young students accidentally lost their lives when some pranks apparently got out of hand.[85] Two years later, a group described as "thugs impersonating students" had allegedly taken advantage of these celebrations to extort money from newcomers.[86] Teachers and parents demanded that authorities ban novatadas "once and for all."[87] What complicated any possible response to this demand, however, was the fact that this group of so-called thugs, led, among others, by *El Fakir, El Aracuan, El Turco, El Pelón Valencia,* and *Upa el Cavernario,* were widely known within the schools to enjoy the political and financial support of the university's rector.[88]

A new brand of "excessive relajo" had come to characterize novatadas and the various rituals that revolved around American football celebrated in the streets beginning in the 1940s. The public in general was confused by the celebratory vandalism and abandonment of traditional values, especially by the cream of the crop, the universitarios, in which they had placed such high hopes.[89] Mexican criminologists, intellectuals, and independent social critics, like their counterparts in the United States, became increasingly preoccupied with what they saw as the rampant problem of youth delinquency in the slums of the emerging metropolis.[90] Juvenile delinquency was seen as an outgrowth of the destabilizing effects of rapid industrialization and urban growth upon the social order.

Films deemed by the state as "unpatriotic" served an important role in illustrating and modeling the details of a rebellious youth subculture to a new and anxiety-ridden middle-class generation. In particular, Luis Buñuel's controversial film Los Olvidados ("The Forgotten") questioned the premature celebrations of Mexico's economic boom by exposing the life of street gangs in poor Mexico City neighborhoods. Jaibo, the unscrupulous leader of a gang of youths resorting to petty thievery—reminiscent of the Chicos Malos from Peralvillo, the Gatunos from the south of Mexico City, the Nazis from Portales, and the Azotes from Narvarte—represented the worst fears for middle-class parents and nationalist (and even leftist) intellectuals about the development of their own sons.[91] Parmenides García Saldaña, a key figure of Mexico's countercultural movement, writes, "Their small victories in street brawls made these gangs famous beyond their neighborhoods. People feared and loathed them. They were the most Wretched Kids of Mexico."[92] In Buñuel's film, the youth delinquency of the time is attributed, not solely, or even primarily, to the individuals themselves, but to the never-ending cycle of poverty and despair in which they found themselves.[93] These marginalized kids appropriated the streets of their neighborhoods to protest against their exclusion from the "economic miracle" of Mexico.[94] In particular, they resisted the plastic models of better-off youth espoused in the press and glorified in the creation of new spaces like the Ciudad Universitaria and American football stadiums.

Cold War anxieties over rebellious youth in the United States made their way south through the important influence of American cinema in Mexico. The most influential of these films was Marlon Brando's The Wild One (1953), translated into Spanish as El Salvaje, or The Savage.[95] García Saldaña explains that this film gained a wide audience among the children of the lumpen pro-letariat. Frustrated with their regressive class status, these young *brandos* (as García Saldaña calls these early fans of the film) embraced Marlon Brando's body language, attitude, and dress to undermine state-sponsored notions of productivity as well as traditional good values. Speaking on behalf of the brandos, García Saldaña referred to Marlon as "our idol to propagate." He was the "multiple man in search of his importance." By imitating the "attire" of "our hero," he explained, "we became the heroes. We all assumed his spe-cial way [of being . . .]."[96] Because the Mexican brandos could not adopt the original language of their hero, they instead opted to revalue their street lan-guage, which, in turn, became a "shield and a dagger." On the one hand, Gar-cía Saldaña noted, student used street language to insult, challenge, and reject "the moral values" assumed by society. On the other hand, this new genera-tional attitude, in general, "became a defense" and a "shelter of prohibited customs."[97] Brando's performance in *El Salvaje*, in short, was one model with which disaffected youth created an entire subculture that included a defiant attitude, seditious clothing, and foul language.

The new and much more "damaging" version of relajo bubbling up from below was identified among young people as desmadre. Along with the related phenomenon of relajo, this style of rogue defiance shared a sense of disaffec-tion with time, place, and society. As the Mexican philosopher Jorge Portilla once fittingly noted, the youth's sense of "self-destruction, dissidence, [and] irresponsibility," went hand in hand with a feeling of little or no concern for the past or the future.[98] Anthropologist Roger Bartra wonderfully captures this sense of discontinuity in these uncommitted youths as follows:

> They [the *desmadrosos*] are unenthusiastic about an efficient modern age, and they have no desire to restore the promise of a proletarian industrial future. Nor do they believe in a return to the golden age, to a larval primitivism. They have been hurled from the original paradise and expelled from the future. They have lost their identity, but do not regret it: their new world is an apple of discord and contradictions. Without ever having been modern, they have become *desmodern*.[99]

In historian Eric Zolov's influential study of the rise of the Mexican counter-culture, he describes the difficult-to-translate "desmadre" as "an offensive, lower-class slang word" that "expresses a notion of social chaos introduced by the literal 'unmothering' of a person or situation"[100] A form of violent uprooting or counterculture, it can also be understood as the "antithesis to that Mexican phrase, *buenas costumbres* (good traditional manners) which encapsulates all that is proper and correct."[101] The adoption of desmadre was manifest in extreme self-promotion and resorting to violence as needed to make a statement. García Saldaña further expands on what being in the groove of desmadre might have meant for others: "[H]itting your enemy with a solid blow . . . being the sharpest [of the group] . . . , having the best girl . . . , being the toughest guy when it came to fighting, being able to consume the most alcohol."[102] Beyond the disorder, insubordination, and discontinuity inherent in the practice of relajo, the more aggressive and offensive expression of the "desmadre" subculture stressed extreme short-term hedonism, masculine aggression, disdain of work, spontaneity, and excitement performed as an end in itself.[103] Living outside the ethos of productivity and modernity presumed responsible for Mexico's economic miracle, young, defiant desmadrosos of the lower classes detested that order, particularly as promoted by the postrevolutionary state.[104] More important, they distinctively began to destroy it every chance they had and in every way they could, with physical and/or symbolic power.

Left to their own devices, the poor youth subculture might have remained isolated and forgotten, but the picture was complicated when middle-class students began gradually to adopt the language, dress, defiant attitude—in short, the "desmadre"—that was originally attributed to the lower classes. According to various sources, this took place sometime around the mid-to-late 1950s in the form of a generational response among a small yet increasing number of *niños bien* (well-to-do kids).[105] Initially this took the form of an effort on the part of these niños bien to differentiate themselves from their well-to-do parents. For these middle-class kids, their parents, to use the words of Jorge Portilla, appeared as *apretados*, or "uptight squares."[106] The niños bien embraced desmadre as their own private revolution and liberation. For them, the parent (read: apretado) culture symbolized, quite the contrary, a spirit of seriousness bounded by restrictions and values that to a large extent paralleled those of the authoritarian patriarchal state (*papá gobierno*).[107] In this conflicting dichotomy, the apretado dressed impeccably in search of the approval of the middle class, while the desmadroso rearranged his appearance to shock it. The apretado was defined by his beloved possessions, while the desmadroso destroyed or showed very little respect for them. The apretado excluded from his world all those who appeared different from him, while the desmadroso included them as part of their desmadre. The apretado loved liberty, but was constrained by his greater admiration for order and productive time. The desmadroso, in contrast, liberated himself from order, traditional values, and productivity by destroying them at every opportunity.[108] In this conflicting situation, the possibility of dialogue vanished; but more important, the integrity of the national spirit that the governing elite so desperately tried to promote during these incipient moments of the Cold War was threatened and thus dreams of greatness were destroyed. Or, in the language of desmadre, dreams of greatness "went to fucking hell" (se [fueron] a la chingada).[109]

The association of desmadre with youth/student culture, given expression in imported American films like *The Wild One* (1953) and *Rebel without a Cause* (1955), created a rift between youth and the general public. Zolov explains: "[In] the public mind-set[,] the relationship between films and juvenile delinquency was so close that the press appropriated the phrase *rebeldismo sin causa* (rebellion without a cause) as its standard description for youth disorder."[110] Life, art, and the media mingled as the young originators of desmadre began to be labeled via the lens of a frenzied media. In this process, those identified as *rebeldes* (rebels), *delincuentes* (delinquents), *profanes* (vulgar), or desmadrosos (defiant rogues) were increasingly seen as "outsiders" and challengers to national unity.[111] The print media saw the issue in black and white terms and insisted that the dangers of defiant youth be recognized. It therefore had no sympathy for what they saw as lenient intellectual microanalysis. For example, in Illustration 2.3 the famous cartoonist Rafael Freyre ridiculed the naivete of traditional parents who failed to recognize the problems of insubordinate students. The caption mockingly reads: "According to the doctor, our son is originally endogenous, naturally exogenous, and from a socio-economic point of view, [he is] conceptually etiological."[112]

Part of a reinforcing cycle well recognized by British, U.S., and Latin American scholars of postwar youth, conflict and hostility between youth culture and parent culture (or authority figures in general) gradually and systematically began to increase. American sociologist Howard Becker describes the cycle as follows: "methods of defense" by rebellious youth against "outside interference" from the parent culture became a preoccupation of the members, and a subculture grew around this set of problems.[113] This subcultural or defiant attitude, covered with greater frequency in the mass media, created a growing public concern that alluded to a possible crisis of political author-

ILLUS. 2.3. Freyre, "Paternal Innocence," *Excélsior*, August 25, 1958. (Reproduced with permission from *Excélsior*.)

ity.[114] Thus, as Paul Rock and Stanley Cohen illustrate for the subculture of English "Teddy Boys" of the 1950s and, as Valeria Manzano has more recently examined for the case of youthful rebellion in the case of Argentina, public concern did not suddenly develop out of thin air.[115] Rather, such concern grew out of a step-by-step process composed of a series of occurrences. This scholarship painstakingly demonstrates how an association between appearance and a delinquent self "requires reinforcement by a number of notorious incidents and, in many cases, a dramatic event."[116]

In the case of Mexico, the culture of student hazing (novatadas, hazings, effigy rallies, and the like) supplied the needed series of notorious incidents to prompt a concern with desmadre and the eventual mushrooming of a youth crisis. The 1956 student movement (Chapter 3) would serve as the nation's "dramatic event" that confirmed the crises of both the nation's youth and the state's political authority, as well as the opening salvo of the long sixties. Thus, in terms of youthful defiance, it is important to note that it is not an isolated phenomenon, but rather better described as part of an interaction between the person who commits the rebellious act (that is, the desmadroso, the rebelde, the radical student) and those who respond to it (that is, the press, the parent culture, school authorities, government officials, and so forth).[117] To authorities it became clear that the ascent of youthful defiance into the ranks of middle-class youth represented a threat that necessitated a response, an attempt to return to order. A tradition, not of revolutionary democracy, but of paternalism and patron-client relationships, could once again be drawn upon to fill this need. It would, however, need to adapt to the novel and unpredictable subject of a creative, though uninitiated, student culture.

Conclusion: Youthful Contestation of "Revolutionary Nationalism"

The cultural practices associated with youthful fun were multivalent performances emblematic of the ambivalent attitude students expressed toward the new cosmopolitan and consumerist vision of postwar modernity proposed by authority figures in the guise of revolutionary nationalism.[118] This nationalistic vision embodied in the students' preference of American entertainment contrasted with the older notion of modernity sponsored by the postrevolutionary state. As Jorge Portilla reminds us, relajo can be defined as the suspension of, or disengagement from, seriousness in the face of a value proposed to a group of people in a certain situation. Relajo in this sense has a "moral motivation" and "seeks liberation" from specific forms of responsibility. In the face of enveloping rules it finds untenable, its adherents find meaning in sustained expressions of not choosing responsible courses of action.[119] Thus, while the rituals of relajo—including novatadas, the burning of effigies, and cheerleading—opened a space for rival students to engage symbolically in a political and social duel while at the same time celebrate their emergence as young adults, consumers, and national subjects, these same rituals also allowed students to suspend the seriousness of and, thus, undermine the received models of economic progress, revolutionary nationalism, and traditional values.[120] Postwar Mexico's youth, in sum, exposed the fissures, limitations, and cracks of national unity and economic prosperity. This was particularly evident in the adoption of rogue desmadre on the part of the well-off niños bien from UNAM. As remarkably captured in Juan Ibañez's 1966 film, *Los Caifanes*, the blurring of these class tensions would only further intensify in the next decade.[121] As "classless" desmadrosos, the middle-class youth came to be regarded by the public, in general, and in the print media in particular, not only as "outsiders" of the nation but also, like the working-class politécnicos, as a potential problem for the state. Paradoxically, in managing this perceived youth crisis, the Mexican state relied on charismatic intermediaries and sponsors of fun (what I call padrinos del relajo). Rather than dismissing American football and cheerleading as by-products of Yankee imperialism, it embraced them—even commercialized them in films—as genuinely Mexican. But as the student "problem" would further intensify in the long sixties, the mechanisms of co-optation and control associated with entertainment would acquire a more violent character.

PART II

The Rise of Mexico's "Student Problem"
and the Consolidation of
"Charrismo Estudiantil" in the Early Sixties

3 "¿Manos Extrañas?": The 1956 Student Protest and the "Crisis" of Authority

O N APRIL 14, 1956, three days after more than twenty-five thousand *politécnicos* launched a massive student strike that would nearly paralyze the educational system for more than three months, famous conservative caricaturist Antonio Arias Bernal published a cartoon in *Excélsior* emphasizing a change in attitude toward Mexican youth by portraying the students of the National Polytechnic Institute (IPN) as no longer mere "ungrateful children of the Revolution" but rather, as a "genuine threat" to be feared (see Illustration 3.1).

Specifically, Arias Bernal warned his readers that the "white donkeys" of the Politécnico had not only become a nuisance in American football games, as many others had lamented, but had also recently behaved as "dangerous puppets" of the "International Communist Party."[1] Echoing the voices of dozens of journalists working in various newspapers, Arias Bernal grew increasingly concerned with the alleged "infiltration" of communists inside the Politécnico and warned his readers that without national support young Mexican students could be "manipulated" by *manos extrañas*, or "dangerous agents of unpatriotic forces."[2]

Indeed, the 1956 student protest at the Instituto IPN marked a defining moment in the history of student politics and resistance that redefined the conception of Mexico's youth. More than any other national student protest, this dramatic event signaled the end of one era in student activism and the beginning of a new one. The 1956 protest was the last in a series of student

ILLUS. 3.1. Arias Bernal, "No Comments,"
Excélsior, April 14, 1956. (Reproduced with
permission from *Excélsior*.)

demonstrations demanding a return to cardenista popular politics. Yet, as
one of the most massive student protests in Mexican history, this important
episode also represents the first direct challenge to the state of the Cold War
era, and thus, the opening salvo of the long sixties. This is the period when
a new culture of student politics emerged, where students are first identified
as a "subversive threat" to the nation by the governing elite and the Right-
leaning print media, and where a new culture exploiting student-centered
violence has its origins. While the official history states that student democratic activism began during the 1968 movement, in actuality a discourse on
democracy—specifically calling, in this case, for greater participation in the
management of their schools and student organizations—had begun to form,
however vaguely articulated, more than a decade earlier. Distinctively, the
democratic, but also increasingly violent, challenges to corporatist notions
of power and corruption emerging at the time were argued in public. Politéc-

nicos made it a point to take their demands directly to the streets using innovative strategies that would be wheeled out by their predecessors in future student uprisings.

Student Demands and Central Tensions in the Protest

On April 11, 1956, what began as a strike supported nearly unanimously by IPN's 25,000 students soon exploded into the first massive student protest in Mexico's history. The event mushroomed into a show of force that was over 100,000 students strong. The protest spread successfully by drawing in to the cause students from the National Teachers' School, the Normal School, the School of Physical Education, and some thirty-three Rural Normal and Practical Agricultural schools.[3] The diverse student bodies represented in this virtual city of protesters made it apparent that what was brewing was a movement national in scope, one that was bound to get the attention of the presidential palace and the nation as a whole.

The two most important demands made by the politécnicos were the immediate dismissal of seven of the school's administrators (including the director of the IPN, Rodolfo Hernández Corso) and the implementation of a New Organic Law that would grant students autonomy and participation in the governance of the IPN. In terms of educational resources, the students demanded increases in scholarships and allowances, an increase in class hours, and more efficient teaching. Several demands called for immediately funding improvements in school facilities. These included building new hospitals for the Homeopathic and Rural schools, the construction of new dormitories, and a better transportation system within the school district altogether.[4]

From the demands made by the students one can distill many of the central tensions that underlay the conflict. First, there was the political tension between students and their leadership. Students simply were at odds with much of the current school administration. They had become convinced that nothing less than the wholesale removal of key administration officials would bring about the changes they needed. Second was tension over the issue of student autonomy. Politécnicos differed markedly from their leadership regarding the issue of how much independence students should be granted to perform functions such as representative membership in school administration, defining the mission of the IPN, and shaping its pedagogical goals. This naturally led to related conflicts over measuring and evaluating the influence the Mexican government should have on the operation of the schools. Students struggled to decide whether reform or revolution would answer their needs, while the existing corporatist power structure scrambled to maintain the status quo. Tension over the bread and butter issues of school resources, of course, were apparent as students saw themselves sorely neglected in terms of school facilities, particularly as compared with the resources granted and planned for the preferred class at the National Autonomous University of Mexico (UNAM). The struggle over resources became linked to the tension over deciding what place Marxist-socialist ideas should have in the mission and life of the schools. Some, even persons with genuine Left leanings, would argue that such an ideology was overwhelming intellectual freedom, while others saw it as one of the best ways to safeguard such freedom and distribute resources fairly and equitably. This tension over Marxist ideology must be understood within the larger geopolitical context of the Cold War, a topic that led to debates over the policies of the colossus of the north, the United States, and its dominance in Mexican affairs. These stresses both echoed older battles between the populace and the government at the same time that they reflected an adjustment to novel conditions fundamental to the formation of a New Left (see Chapters 5 and 6).

From the standpoint of the politécnicos, IPN director Hernández Corso epitomized the insidious influence of the United States and its Cold War–influenced international development policies, which, many believed, had infiltrated every sector of society beginning in the 1940s.[5] The fact that the IPN director was educated in the United States (earning his M.A. at Northwestern University and his Ph.D. at Stanford) raised suspicion among students of favoritism toward the U.S. at the expense of his native Mexico.[6] But it was Hernández Corso's support for a "Plan Columbia [Teacher's College]" initiative that established his iconic status among students as a symbol of "Yankee imperialism."

As illustrated in a student poster, the endorsement of the Plan Columbia by the Ministry of Public Education (SEP) and the "overbearing" presence of the "tyrannical image of Uncle Sam" in postwar Mexico not only threatened the system of popular education but also "killed" the aspirations of all politécnicos in their ability to make important contributions to the nation.

The Plan Columbia initiative, as one document from the Department of State notes, was a "Point Four project carried out under contract by Columbia Teachers College of New York to make a survey of the needs in Mexican

ILLUS. 3.2. Politécnicos Protesting against the Plan Columbia. Reproduced with permission from the Archivo General de la Nación, Fondo Hermanos Mayo, No. 10.096 [n.d.].)

industry for technically trained workers and personnel and the facilities available in Mexico for such training."[7] The Teacher's College initiative was linked to the fourth of five main goals of the Truman Doctrine. Known as the "Plan Truman" in Mexico, the Truman Doctrine was a Cold War–era policy that allocated military and economic measures ostensibly in defense of the Western Hemisphere. But it has been viewed by the Left, including by many at the IPN at the time, as part of an effort to secure American imperial control (see cartoon of Uncle Sam figure executing a student of the IPN with the support of the SEP in Illustration 3.2). As directed toward nations seen as "threatened by communism," the five goals of the Truman Doctrine included intervention in (1) military cooperation, (2) the organization and education of the armed forces, (3) armament unification, (4) the utilization of human capital, and (5) the creation of a continental census. Plan Columbia arose from point four, but students saw it as part of a U.S. strategy to maintain Mexico in a semicolonial state of economic dependence.[8] More specifically, for politécnicos, the Plan Columbia represented the latest and most egregious attempt by North American investors to remove all individuals who favored Mexican nationalized industries and institutions.[9]

IPN student efforts to reject Plan Columbia gained inspiration from the events at the Antonio Narro School of Agriculture in Saltillo in September of 1955. There, students had successfully expelled a number of American teachers from their schools. The expulsions in effect foiled an agreement between the governments of Coahuila and Texas that had worked together to implement Plan Columbia at the Narro School.[10] IPN students took the victory at Saltillo as potentially the start of a larger anti-plan effort. Their efforts seemed to pay off, at least in the short run. U.S. teachers were not invited to the Politécnico and, thus, this aspect of Plan Columbia was never implemented. In the longer term, the story is more complicated. In the 1960s the Rockefeller and Ford foundations, as well as the Agency for International Development (AID), would occupy a strong presence in the Geology (mining and so forth), Agricultural, and Engineering departments of the IPN, UNAM, and other schools. Although the IPN was never fully privatized as many in the movement dreaded, the IPN would lose much of its populist cardenista legacy after the strike: for example, many scholarships for low-income students, funding the school dormitory, and so forth.

In addition to representing North American imperialism, Hernández Corso also came to epitomize for students the corrupt and abusive management typical of many government authorities. In a student newspaper, politécnicos accused him and his close associates of funding their own political campaigns by deliberate manipulation of the school budget. Students rejected in particular Hernández Corso's "politics of *charrismo*" as a mechanism for blatant abuse of power inside the schools.[11] Students labeled Hernández Corso and his cronies "academic *charros*" who, for example, threatened to take away scholarships if students dared to vote for the "wrong" student representative.[12] Yet it was also clear to students that Corso was merely the tip of an iceberg whose main mass lay deeply hidden within the depths of state politics. All the blame for corruption in the Politécnico could not be laid solely at the feet of Hernández Corso and his group. The authoritarian character of the Politécnico was embedded in its very structure. It was found, for instance, in the way the president had handpicked directors with close ties to the government, and he had done so with absolutely no consultation with the student population.[13] In order to both democratize the schools of the IPN and challenge the older generation of cardenistas, the umbrella IPN student federation FNET (National Front of Technical Students) looked to a legal tool that would officially institute a different balance of power. They proposed a "New Organic Law" that demanded the creation of a "Mixed Commission" composed of school authorities and students with equal power.[14]

Students recognized that their cause could not hope to succeed without taking their democratic messages out into the streets in a more public and confrontational fashion. To this end they devised a number of innovative strategies and opened the streets as legitimate spaces of contestation. Yet, as it would happen throughout the long sixties, the students' recourse to violence that frequently accompanied this new defiant attitude would also expose the vulnerability of their incipient notions of democracy primarily understood by the young students, at this time, as a struggle to gain greater access to the management of their schools and eventually put an end to academic charrismo.

Innovative Strategies of Contestation and Female Participation

The emphasis the politécnicos placed on direct action during the 1956 student protest superseded the more passive tactics previously employed by students during the demonstrations of 1942 and 1950. Their activism includes the democratic transformation of a variety of public spaces. Convinced that the common practice of negotiating with the government had led only to insignificant achievements in the past, these young students believed that the most effective way to pressure government authorities was to stir up support in other sectors of society by embracing a more confrontational stance against the government in public. In this effort, "informational brigades" would play a vital role. Information brigades were efforts on the part of students to educate the public about their cause through organized sessions off campus. With names that specifically stressed a nationalistic and ideological stance, such as Brigada Francisco Villa, Brigada Emiliano Zapata, and Brigada Lázaro Cárdenas, these brigades traveled to other schools, to factories, and to nearby pueblos. The information conveyed in the informational brigades was not confined to the demands of the strike. Many of the young students who participated in them also took advantage of this opportunity to inform the pueblo about the importance of their strike. In some cases the more radical students read passages from student newspapers calling for solidarity networks with other sectors of society to defeat a "common enemy."[15] At one brigade event, for example, a student read the following message out loud: "The authorities of the Ministry Education try to destroy our just strike by applying the disastrous politics of RUÍZ CORTINES. Their goal is to crush our dream and struggle for a better Politécnico."[16]

Information brigades took a variety of forms. Some students, for example, organized informal conferences on street corners. Others, with the help of cyclists, jammed traffic by blocking entire avenues, thereby transforming them into physically and conceptually "open" spaces for discussion.[17] Brigades not only crossed the gulf from the Politécnico to points outside, they sometimes also came with invitations for reciprocation. In cars borrowed from their parents, students distributed leaflets in "as many corners of the city as possible," inviting people to come visit the schools of the IPN "so they could witness for themselves how abandoned they were."[18] The more radical activists hijacked school buses, equipped them with loudspeakers on the roof, and drove them as far as Tlaxcala, Puebla, Guadalajara, Monterrey, Michoacán, and Chihuahua to deliver their messages.[19] The tactics of the informational brigades were especially effective in the state of Michoacán, where a very similar student protest in defense of popular education blossomed quickly at the main Universidad Michoacana de San Nicolás de Hidalgo.[20]

Women students also played a crucial role in the student movement, most visibly with respect to the informational brigades.[21] Restricted by the cultural mores of the time, the majority of young politécnicas who participated in these brigades were often in charge of cooking meals for the male comrades and organizing paperwork. In addition, as FNET president Nicandro Mendoza points out, they often provided important moral support for the young male combatants who clashed with authorities: "The enthusiasm and self-sacrifice of these *jovencitas* encouraged all of our *compañeros* of the Politécnico to stay strong during our daily battles."[22] However, not all of the female participants in the informational brigades were content to wait patiently inside the schools while their male comrades went out to the streets to confront authority.[23] Perhaps influenced by the thousands of young women who had taken part in the teachers' and railroad strikes organized earlier that year, a number of the most radical politécnicas took advantage of the opportunity to defy notions of power in a uniquely public manner. They took to the streets alongside their compañeros to distribute leaflets, organize walkouts, collect money for the movement, and march with banners that read "Politicians only try to repress the students."[24]

This "radical attitude" and public activism embraced by a few female students was shocking for many witnessing the protests. By taking an equal stand against authority along with their compañeros, these women acquired the mark of the *revoltoso*. Not only this, traditional gender standards that framed women as passive and apolitical made such actions all the more offensive to many onlookers. Questions were raised about female participation even from some unlikely quarters. For instance, in a "cordial and vigorous call" made by the feminist organization Ideario Político de la Mujer, director Julieta Domínguez asked young politécnicas to "reflect" on their roles and responsibilities as young women because joining the student protest was "unpatriotic." Young women had no business getting involved in "dirty politics." As Domínguez put it, they should

> intervene in the ill-intentioned actions of their compañeros, so that the restlessness of the male students takes a more progressive turn because it is important that the Nation benefits from the vigorous energy of the young . . . on behalf of the great Mexican family.[25]

What Julieta Domínguez failed to realize, however, was the fact that many of the young students of the Politécnico no longer identified with the authoritative model of the traditional "great Mexican family." On the contrary, the 1956 protest, unlike previous student demonstrations, represented a conscious attempt by students to defy what they perceived to be an increasingly authoritarian system.[26] Although relatively small in numbers, a fraction of the most "radical" politécnicas also embraced this rebellious attitude and overtly confronted a system of authority that openly celebrated the marriage of patriarchy and patria (the nation).[27]

In addition to the informational brigades, politécnicos also adopted a more spontaneous and confrontational tactic that came to be known as *mítines relámpago*. Roughly translated as "hit-and-run political rallies," these mítines relámpago were composed of three or four students who quickly organized political meetings, without prior express permission, at factory gates, street corners, markets stalls, and schools. These rallies had to be organized "in small numbers" and "performed rather quickly" because, as a politécnico noted later during an interview, "[the thugs for hire] were always on our backs."[28] Mítines relámpago represented an innovative way for students to express viewpoints that they found repressed in official statements inside the Politécnico and in media representations outside. They were organized to denounce the "false accusations made daily against the students in the mercenary newspapers," which, according to the students, "had sold out to imperialismo yanqui."[29] Organizing mítines relámpagos "was necessary because we had no other channels of communication available," later remarked a leader of the strike.[30] In close collaboration with the Ministry of Education and radio stations, the principal newspapers had joined forces with the government to create a campaign of lies against the students. Mendoza further recalled during an interview that "we had to find a way to contradict such public lynchings."[31] These impromptu, small-scale, and effective rallies delivered a jolt of truth, as the students saw it, to a public citizenry that would otherwise be subject to "authoritarian propaganda."[32] Further, as would become the case throughout the long sixties, the mítines relámpago were also particularly effective in distributing propaganda and raising money for the movement. Politécnicos would also try to take advantage of these rallies to create coalitions with other sectors of society. However, as would happen again in 1968, this strategy failed primarily because of the recourse to violence often embraced by the most militant students.[33]

For some of the more radical students, direct action also meant the taking physical possession of property and spaces at the risk of controversy and confrontational violence. At first, this took the form of hijacking school buses. But, as the uprising continued and the stance of the authorities hardened, a group of students began to apply more pressure by taking physical possession of buildings.[34] Once in physical possession of the buildings, the politécnicos organized "self-defense guards" to defend what they identified as "their liberated territories."[35] The first buildings taken by the students were inside the schools, and consisted of classrooms, cafeterias, dormitories, and administrative offices. To communicate that the strike would continue, they displayed signs of liberation (primarily black and red banners), which represented their genuine demands and an effort to internationalize their protest. But as the movement further intensified and as new and more militant brigades began to surface in the strike, students also occupied some buildings outside their schools, including two nearby hotels on August 14. Once in control of these symbolic buildings (perhaps meant specifically to protest the closing of the dormitories), the disgruntled students declared that they would not leave the hotels until IPN authorities guaranteed housing and social services to all students from the provincia.[36] The students set up self-defense guards and, as they would do throughout the long sixties, they placed red and black flags outside the windows. The police responded by sending several battalions to remove the students from the hotels. Initially the students fought back, but eventually they lost control of the hotels as more members of the police were sent on August 20–21 and students were arrested.[37] As would become the norm thereafter, the print media would welcome the government's determination to discipline the young revoltosos.

A Call for Action against the "Dangerous Students"

Efforts to liberate spaces temporarily gave politécnicos a number of small victories. But, partly through the lens of a mostly unsympathetic and one-sided press, the confrontational violence embraced by a small but growing number of student activists affected public perception quite negatively. Unable to accept the violence as a symptom of genuine social protest and, likewise, unable to see the students themselves as deliberate, reasoning, and adult dissenters, the "older generation" attributed the student violence to their immaturity and their vulnerability to dangerous "outside influences." In one version, the public interpreted student confrontations with authorities as the result of the revoltosos' unbridled primal being instincts allowed to run wild. As the government supporter, Freyre, sarcastically dramatized it, the problem of the "psychostudent" was in his head, such that an ordinary medical doctor found himself unable to "diagnose" the young politécnico (see Illustration 3.3).

Freyre's depiction of the students as having apelike features and being pigeon-toed appears intended to underline the uncivilized nature of the stance they had adopted in public.[38]

In another version, more radical students were characterized as spoiled brats who were unappreciative of the hard-won benefits granted to them by authority figures. These authority figures began with their parents but could extend on up to the leaders in the national government, who were framed as transmitters of the benefits of the revolution. Just a few days after the student strike first erupted, one reporter, referring to the social subsidies politécnicos received from the government, angrily condemned the young students as

ILLUS. 3.3. Freyre, "Psycho-students," *Excélsior*, June 15, 1956.
The caption reads: "I am sorry, but I cannot diagnose [your
son]." (Reproduced with permission from *Excélsior*.)

"egotistical brats . . . who had neglected to appreciate what the pueblo had
given to them."[39] Similarly, another journalist lamented:

> So long as there are children who go to schools without breakfast; so long as
> there are insufficient schools for the student population . . . ; so long as there
> are hundreds of thousands of rural families lacking the most basic essentials,
> the Government cannot adopt as its children a few rebellious students who
> have pretensions to eat, be clothed, and be paid as though they were the
> children of "pequeños burgueses" and not adolescents and young people
> who through effort and sacrifice are to construct a "patria nueva."[40]

"What can we expect from this generation," an editorial page likewise
lamented, which "prefers subversion and anarchy?"[41] The outcries against

the "increasingly violent" and "ungrateful" politécnicos would continue to appear on almost a daily basis not only in *Excélsior* and *El Universal* but to a much lesser extent also in the more radical *Siempre!* and *El Popular*.[42]

What the public seemed to find most troubling of all, however, was student vulnerability to the influence of "foreign agents" (manos extrañas)—that is, to the influence of communists. And no one incarnated this Cold War menace more than Nicandro Mendoza, the president of FNET and principal spokesperson of the student protest of 1956. Mendoza was a well-known student leader whose affiliation with the Partido Popular (Popular Party or PP, an opposition party of the Left founded by Vicente Lombardo Toledano in 1948) became a central theme of discussion in the newspapers. For the politécnicos, however, the fact that Mendoza was a member of the PP allegedly demonstrated that the student protest was genuinely inclusive and democratic.[43] They pointed out that, in addition to members of the Partido Popular, the protesters welcomed into their ranks student representatives of the Institutional Revolutionary Party (PRI), the Mexican Communist Party (PCM), the Mexican Worker-Peasant Party (POCM), and the National Action Party (PAN).[44] From the standpoint of the newspapers and government authorities, however, Mendoza represented the most convincing evidence that the student protest had been organized by external forces. Some journalists in Mexico and abroad went so far as to suggest that in collaboration with Guatemalan students who had participated in the Arbenz Revolution and were now "hiding" in the dormitories of the IPN, politécnicos hoped to destabilize the nation in order to spark the next "Marxist Revolution."[45]

Indeed, with the Cold War as a backdrop, the media consistently sought to portray the students of the Politécnico as "pawns of the International Communist Party."[46] Political cartoons were especially effective in depicting threats of this nature to the nation. The most dangerous politécnicos featured in the newspapers were the infamous *fósiles* (students who spent several years enrolled in the schools as aging "fossils" without ever completing a degree), who were depicted as sympathetic to the internationalist communist movement.[47] Reporters asked parents to dissuade their children from getting involved with foreign demagogues like "Nicandovich Mendoza," as one reporter sarcastically dubbed him, who had taken over the schools and converted them into a "dangerous environment" for young, impressionable minds. In one particular depiction, Freyre, who along other cartoonists and journalists had been hired in 1954 by the National Editorial Association

ILLUS. 3.4. Freyre, "Back to School," *Excélsior*, May 28, 1956.
(Reproduced with permission from *Excélsior*.)

to create an atmosphere that made it easy for the Latin American public to
accept the U.S. overthrow of the Arbenz government, portrayed Mendoza as
a "deceptive communist" who took advantage of the innocence of the young
(see Illustration 3.4).[48]

The perception that the schools were experiencing something that could
spread like a contagion to affect the nation and entire society led to a call for
action. Since the root cause of student unrest supposedly could be found in a
lack of respect for presumably justified paternal and patriotic authority, the
public and Right-leaning press saw discipline as the only proper response.
Journalists and influential conservative cartoonists, such as Bernal and Freyre,

in particular, began to demand a more authoritarian stance on the part of the government in order to control the "increasingly dangerous" students.

In the opinion of some, sanctions needed to come from the top. To meet this national "crisis of authority," as one editorial commentator put it, the legal apparatus of government could be applied in the form of a strict constitutional law that spoke directly about "obligations," just as laws existed that spelled out "constitutional rights."[49] One individual expressed outrage with the red and black strike banners that hung over the entrances of all schools of the IPN, as well as with collective acts of vandalism. Echoing the sentiments that would be published in numerous letters to the editor sent in by private citizens, this person implored the president "to discipline" the "little Red demagogues"—with "force if necessary"—if they continued to "refuse to obey orders from their older authorities."[50] In a letter sent to President Adolfo Ruíz Cortines and José Ángel Ceniceros, the secretary of the Ministry of Education, a person who had grown tired of the "delinquent" students, wrote, "[It] is time that you reined in the students of the Politécnico . . . those lazy, cunning little scamps (bribones) who think that the poor pueblo is working hard so that these scoundrels can get an education." Negating that "money grows on trees," he then went on to say:

> Sr. Presidente and Sr. Minister of Education, do what leaders in other coun-
> tries would do: close the schools and take care of these lazy bums by sending
> them to do hard work on the land so that they can see with their own sweat
> on their foreheads what their parents have to do so that they can get an edu-
> cation . . . . All they do is to create difficulties for the government . . . . They
> ought to be punished with rigorous energy.[51]

For an increasing number of "concerned citizens," however, public calls to the president were no longer enough to address the growing student problem. Many people who wrote to the newspapers argued that the "indecent" and "politically foreign" behavior of the students in public had become so "out of control" that a call for vigilantism must go out to various sectors of society.[52] On June 15, El Universal "called for serious consideration of the formation of vigilante citizen groups to protect the city from student outrages."[53] The implication, of course, was that the government, like an overindulgent parent, had been too soft with the revoltosos, and thus ordinary citizens needed to confront the students more directly in order to "reestablish order."[54] Vigilantism directed against the students did not take long to appear. That same month, a group of students were chased away from local markets and factory gates as they attempted to organize their mítines relámpago. In one of these instances, a surveillance report noted that "proprietors of stalls in La Merced Market pelted the students with a variety of decayed vegetable matter, putting them to rout."[55] Some factory owners went so far as to say that they would not hire any more graduates of the IPN, who had proven "to be nothing more than political agitators."[56]

Influential representatives from other political parties also voiced their concern about the future of Mexico. They expressed their disapproval of the dangerous politécnicos publicly. They went further than other critics of the students, however, in advocating that the politécnicos be punished for their "unpatriotic actions." Members of the PAN, for example, demanded that "the government should act more vigorously and should not ostrich-like hid[e] its head in the sand." Similarly, representatives of the more conservative Partido Nacionalista Mexicano (PNM) urged the government to take more "drastic measures, including expulsion of the strike leaders and the 'fossils,' or students who apparently found the limited rewards of continued attendance over many years at the Politécnico more enticing than honest work."[57] For their part, the governing elite would eventually respond to the "student problem" more harshly through both legal and extralegal mechanisms of control. But first, they would attempt to create a truce with the recalcitrant students by proposing a set of concessions.

On June 21, 1956, politécnicos returned to their studies after the seventy-two-day strike was officially called off. Like previous student demonstrations, the 1956 student protest ended after representatives of FNET met with government authorities to negotiate a number of agreements that appeared to begin to address several student demands. The following accords were made public by President Ruíz Cortines:

— A New Organic Law of the IPN would be sent to Congress to be discussed during the next session.

— Investments in the infrastructure [of the IPN] by the Federal Government would increase from 10 million pesos in 1956 to 20 million in 1957.

— A mixed commission, composed of equal numbers of students and professors and led by the Director of the IPN, would study the main technical and academic problems of the Politécnico.

— Another commission of a composition similar to that mentioned above would study the social problems related to the lack of students' benefits.[58]

Absent in these agreements was any discussion of the fate of Hernández Corso, whose "immediate removal from the Politécnico" was a major point of the 1956 list of demands (*pliego petitorio*). Fearing for his safety, Hernández Corso never set foot inside the Politécnico again.[59] At first he tried to manage the IPN "in exile" from an office outside the school. But as small student demonstrations began to crop up and the mítines relámpago began to agitate among the people once again throughout the city, Hernández Corso was finally asked by SEP authorities to resign on August 20, 1956. He was replaced by Alejo Peralta, who, the politécnicos would quickly discover, would prove to be a much more authoritarian figure than Hernández Corso.

Conclusion: The Emergence and Reactions to the Rise of Mexico's "Student Problem"

Because of its magnitude and strategies of direct action, the 1956 protest should be seen as the dramatic event that inaugurated the turbulent political activism of the long sixties. Traditional governmental mechanisms of controlling student activism prior to this episode, such as using corporatist structures and *relajo* to negotiate with student leaders in public, began to lose their effectiveness as students, demanding an embryonic notion of "democratic reform" in the form of greater management of their schools (free of charro control), became more adamant and confrontational. Students expressed their dissatisfaction with the system through a series of innovative practices designed to close the gap that divided their working-class educational struggles from kindred struggles in the society and nation that surrounded them. These included, in increasing order of assertiveness, information brigades, hit-and-run rallies, and building takeovers. These were seen as creating new physical and conceptual spaces for democratic reform to evolve. A small but dedicated number of female activists stood right alongside their male compañeros, forging a path of their own for women and a model for the decade to come.

An older generation of paternalistic cartoonists and a nativist press coverage toward student protesters, mounting public hostility, and pressure from opposition parties (seeking to gain an advantage from the unrest) together led the Mexican government to agree to a set of concessions enacted on June 21, 1956. But this would prove to be only a temporary truce. Continued student protest in the late summer and early fall of 1956 could not be suppressed by even more physically aggressive forms of maturing student charrismo.

4 The Re-establishment of Authority

O N SEPTEMBER 27, 1956, a student brawl erupted outside the Comedor Universitario (Student Cafeteria) after school and government authorities jointly announced that subsidized meals to low-income students of the National Polytechnic Institute (IPN), the National Autonomous University of Mexico (UNAM), and the Normal School would end.[1] The event made front-page news in several influential newspapers. Journalists differed in their details but generally agreed that a large number of *granaderos*, secret agents, and other police officers were present, yet allowed the brawl to continue.[2] Further, they were in accord that the melee had started when Augusto Velasco, president of the Comedor, and student Luis Muñoz, "violently attacked" another group of students opposing the demonstration against the closing of the cafeteria. The latter was accompanied by a group of students who were quoted as saying prior to the attack: "We don't want any more agitation. [What] we want is to study."[3] As proof of this "student attack," *Excélsior* printed a large front-page photograph with the following description:

> THE BATTLE BETWEEN students unfolded with great fury. Licenciado Castillo Mota (center) is shown giving the medical student Luis Muñoz a phenomenal beating. The picture speaks for itself: Mota demonstrates his fighting abilities while Luis Muñoz falls to the ground. It all occurred as a result of a division between students from the Universidad, those from the Politécnico, and those from the Normal School.

Students were outraged at this and other coverage of the event by the mainstream newspapers, and they began to circulate a variety of accounts that differed greatly from the media's portrayal. To begin with, *politécnicos* and *universitarios* rejected the "division between students" rationale for the altercation. Students in the Comedor were more likely divided by regional differences than any rigid divisions based on their schools of origin.[4] More important, they contended that the student brawl did not in fact take place. What actually happened was that a group of *golpeadores* (hit men), led by Castillo Mota, made a well-planned attack on the defenders of the cafeteria. The *Excélsior* photograph documents this, but the accompanying narrative of its front-page photo completely distorts the event taking place. A student newspaper angrily asked, "Exactly, which students was *Excélsior* referring to?" It couldn't be the individuals depicted in the photograph, it added,

> because we all know that they are hired provocateurs. [In fact] the "universitario" who appears to be hitting the authentic student in a very cowardly way . . . is none other than an agent of the Public Ministry . . . and his "bodyguard" [shown in the photograph holding a stick] is a professional wrestler whom we all know is paid at UNAM to be an "Instructor of Physical Education."[5]

According to the students, Castillo Mota, shown in the photograph wrestling down a young man, was part of a gang of provocateurs; moreover, he had had a lucrative career as a secret agent for the Public Ministry.[6] Along the same lines, another student manifesto argued that the golpeadores had received a large amount of money to pay for their attack and the destruction of the Comedor that occurred as a result.[7] Similarly outraged by the twisting of the facts on the part of the media, a student leader at UNAM wrote, "It is inconceivable to think" that provocateurs "such as those who attacked the students of the Comedor are still employed" by the schools today. But the fact that these thugs are "portrayed in the media as the defenders of the real students is [even] more inconceivable."[8]

Indeed, as it became clear that politécnicos were developing into a formidable force of protest, a concerted campaign of provocation and violence to discredit student protesters by various powerful individuals began to take shape at the IPN but also at UNAM. Whether the violence involved the destruction of school or private property, and whether the broken noses and bones belonged to students or their opponents, did not matter, as long as the blame could be placed squarely on the student activists of these two institutions and their cause. In addition to relying on the use of force permissible under existing laws, this campaign relied importantly on various extralegal tactics to intimidate or implicate students. Such tactics included hiring professional nonstudent thugs to rough up students, the implantation of disruptive pseudo-students into student social activities and political elections, the co-opting of legitimate students, the recruitment of opportunistic students more interested in their own political advancement than any loyalty to a real cause, and the muddling of legitimate student concerns during elections with what students identified as *grilla,* or empty, opportunistic, apocryphal, and/or confusing rhetoric and propaganda.

All together, students identified these various mechanisms of manipulation and exploitation of student-centered violence as *charrismo* and its front men as *charros.* In addition to using violence outright to threaten and intimidate activists, students at UNAM and the Politécnico argued that charros covertly encouraged violence in genuine student activism. Charros also created violent masquerades to serve the same purpose. Part of the formula of this mechanism consisted of a "divide and conquer" strategy that pitted conservative, pseudo, unwitting, co-opted, and opportunistic students against other students. Accompanied and buttressed by officially sanctioned aggression and force that relied on the interpretation and abuse of the law, the strategy of charrismo time and again proved itself effective for disrupting and discrediting student activism of the 1950s as a whole. However, with emergent signs that charrismo was failing to maintain unrest at an agreeable simmering point at the IPN, the Mexican state resorted to applying the lid of brute force to its relatively unique demographic of internal dissenters in an effort to maintain its house in order. As would happen again in 1968, it would enact more forceful measures to quell the student activism, including, in the 1956 Politécnico case, the closing of the main student dormitory, the occupation of the schools by the Federal Army, and the incarceration of key student activists and other "troublemakers." At UNAM, influential figures representing competing political powerbrokers would rely on charros to take control of the different schools. By the time of the inauguration of Ciudad Universitaria in the mid-1950s it would become evident that conservatives, who had maintained a significantly strong political base in the 1920s, 1930s, and 1940s, had lost control of UNAM to government and leftist forces.

The Development of Student Charrismo at the Politécnico

The temporary truce reached between student protesters and authorities in late June of 1956 did not last. By August 1956, many in authority lamented that "delinquent activism" had spread to other schools in Mexico, including a number of *preparatorias* in Mexico City as well as other universities in the *provincia*.[9] People writing in the newspapers demanded that the activists "needed to be stopped."[10] Like politécnicos, these students had also begun to challenge their respective school authorities through violent confrontations. This was the situation faced by Alejo Peralta, the new director of the IPN. With a background as a wealthy businessman, Peralta believed that all problems of the IPN could be solved if the institute were managed "like a private enterprise."[11] To this end, he argued that what was needed was a series of "pragmatic objectives," including a detailed and completely apolitical plan for the future of the IPN. But Peralta would soon find that his new job entailed messy business indeed.

Alejo Peralta soon joined the chorus in the conservative newspapers favoring a more authoritarian approach in order to "discipline" all *revoltosos*, whom he argued, had been implicated in fomenting "disorder and lack of discipline" at the Politécnico since the 1940s. He looked first to building a closer relationship with police authorities, though he accused them of being too lenient with *fósiles* and "reds" in the past.[12] Indeed, coincident with the arrival of Peralta, the head of the Police Department, Miguel Molinar, initiated a much harsher campaign against the rebellious students. However, not everyone concerned about the increasing "chaos" in the Politécnico was content to wait patiently for police authorities to discipline the "subversive" students. Documents now available from the Office of Federal Security (DFS) reveal that many influential figures in various positions of power financed a series of systematic acts of violence and provocation against politécnicos. As noted earlier, the purpose of this strategy was to discredit all student activists and encourage a more aggressive effort on the part of the government to put down the revoltosos.[13] For these strategies to be successful, the violent acts had to be clearly associated with bona fide students. As one student activist explains:

> [Authorities] went so far as to organize porras composed of pseudo-students who committed outrages, attacks, and all kinds of disturbances in public places, such as movie houses and small shops, with the intention of

provoking the anger of the pueblo at the [politécnicos] . . . who were accused of being responsible for these crimes.[14]

One of the many flavors of charro profiles was the so-called gorilla gang, whose covert modus operandi would be applied to Nicandro Mendoza, a key figure in the movement and principal leader of the National Front of Technical Students (FNET). On August 23, 1956, newspapers reported that a group of students wearing sweaters of the Politécnico had vandalized the movie house Variedades.[15] A closer look at student accounts reveals, however, that these so-called revoltosos had nothing to do with the activists. Following the vandalizing of the movie house, a group of protesters wrote the following declaration on a blackboard outside the main school of the Politécnico for all to read:

> Pueblo of Mexico: [The politécnicos] would never dare assault the pueblo simply because we are part of it. It is the enemies of popular education who defame our glorious IPN through malicious and evil tricks. [It is them, moreover,] who finance gangs of criminals . . . who create chaos in various parts of the city wearing sweaters with the colors of our school [white and maroon].[16]

The incident provided evidence for a phenomenon where authorities hired professional thugs to intimidate student activists and to discourage potential sympathizers. These *gorilas* ("gorillas"), as they came to be called, were a brand of "thugs" infamous for their violence.[17] The name derives from a gang actually called by that name, and it was this gang that was linked to the Variadades vandalism. Members of this gang included the Gama brothers (from the American football team the Pumas), their leaders Leopoldo and Mario Basurto, and Castillo Mota, who had also been involved in the student brawl outside the Comedor Universitario. These, among others, had apparently offered their services to university authorities in connection with student disturbances that had exploded at other schools.[18] Authorities sought out gorilla candidates from students who had acquired a reputation with their fists as well as a number of co-opted political agitators who could be bought if enough money was offered. This group included low-income interns who took advantage of these opportunities to improve their social and economic situation at the Politécnico. Others included what many students identified as "sellouts" from leftist student organizations, those who allegedly engaged in violence, ostensibly in the name of activism, in order to advance their political careers.[19] The student status of gorillas was sometimes in order, but more often it was questionable or nonexistent.[20]

As leader of the FNET, one could imagine that Nicandro Mendoza might become the target of surreptitious violence. On July 20, 1956, a group of ten individuals associated with the gorilla gang violently attacked Mendoza.[21] A DFS report provides interesting details that disclose who might have been behind this attack. The document states that the attackers were sympathizers of Baudelio Alegría, an important member of the Confederación de Jóvenes Mexicanos (CJM) who had ties to, and received support from, the Juventudes Socialistas (Socialist Youth).[22] In turn, the Juventudes supposedly had financial backing from Jorge Prieto Laurens, the president of the Frente Anticomunista Mexicano, or Mexican Anticommunist Front (FUA).[23] One could surmise that the attack was part of an attempt by Prieto to take control of FNET and perhaps remove all students sympathetic to communism from important positions of power within the IPN. There were additional groups unaffiliated with the Institutional Revolutionary Party (PRI) allegedly implicated in charrismo to gain control of FNET, as documented by the DFS. Reports reveal, for example, that the Antonia/o Pastrana Flores Group also retaliated against Mendoza, and that this was supported by Mendoza nemesis Hernández Corso. In addition, there is a record on the Mario Molina group. This group derived its name from the general secretary of FNET, who had his eyes on taking Mendoza's place as FNET's leader.[24] But the documents of the DFS also provide evidence of who in particular within the PRI might have been involved in seeking control of the IPN's organizations, provoking violence, and promoting tensions between students. For example, according to one report, Rodolfo González Guevara was implicated several times in the sponsoring of professional thugs, and, on one particular occasion, he hired a group of *pistoleros* to attack Mendoza and his friends outside the schools.[25] During this time, González was president of the Regional Committee of the PRI in the Federal District, a position he held until 1964. The extent of his political influence was felt in the Chamber of Deputies, which he ran in 1954. By 1958, Rodolfo González had become a close ally of Alfonso Corona del Rosal, governor of the Federal District (1966–1970), and their relationship would continue in subsequent years.[26] Additional and equally influential figures within the PRI would also get involved in the consolidation of *charrismo estudiantil* following "Operation P," the military occupation of the IPN in late September that would receive significant approval from different sectors of society as portrayed in the press.

"Operation P" and Government Approval

Tensions associated with the distinction between "real" and "pseudo" students were felt keenly inside the dormitory of the IPN (*internado*) as young men continued to arrive at the Politécnico from provincia without a substantial safety net. In the absence of official support, these students physically took over the dormitory and made it their home. As the internado became more and more crowded, however, these students began to occupy other available spaces where they could spend the night, further exacerbating tensions between them and the established *internos* (interns). Earning the nickname *gaviotas* ("gulls"), these young students became known for "landing" in empty classrooms, sleeping underneath stadium bleachers, and waiting in the cafeteria to "share" the remains of food left over by the internos. Obviously, not all students of the IPN were pleased with the influx of the gulls, nor were they necessarily "happy about the poor manners these students had brought from the provincia."[27] This tension often boiled over into very violent brawls between internos and gaviotas.[28]

The media exploited these negative images of the gulls, making the argument on numerous occasions that the closing of the internado would be the best solution to the increasing social and political problems of the Politécnico. For the media, the gulls had come to represent the students at their worst. It was these *holgazanes* ("lazy bums") and revoltosos, many newspapers angrily protested, who had "corrupted young students" with their bad manners from the provincia. "Gaviotas," one reporter for Martin Luis Guzmán's weekly magazine *El Tiempo* wrote, were entirely responsible for all the "chaos" and "social vices" plaguing the IPN. Betting on games, consumption of alcoholic beverages, carrying of illegal weapons, frequent visits of loose women, and acts of homosexuality, he continued, were frequent in the internado and threatened the innocence of the true politécnicos.[29] However, by putting all the blame on the gaviotas—as well as fósiles and pistoleros—the media failed to address the role corrupt school authorities may have played in the social deterioration of the internado.

On August 10, 1956, Ministry of Public Education (SEP) authorities announced the immediate suspension of all assistance to the students of the internado. According to the authorities of the SEP and the IPN (especially Director Peralta, who earlier had called for the closing of the Comedor Universitario), suspending these services was a "necessary" step at this point in order to protect the "real students" from the "political agitators" and fósiles who had taken over the internado since 1950.[30] For Police Chief Molinar and Director Peralta, there was no doubt that the gaviotas had been involved in the illegal appropriation of the two hotels (described below) that had generated a backlash against all students involved in the strike of the Politécnico.[31] Yet they used this particular case that involved a minority group of radical students to rationalize a belief that all politécnicos who sympathized with their cause, or with the "absurd" student protest for that matter, must be punished.[32] Like the media, they contended that student activists should be prosecuted as enemies of the nation, according to the most rigorous statutes of the law.[33] To this end, Molinar issued specific instructions to the "motorized battalion, the new body of granaderos, and members of the Secret Service" to "put a definite stop to all disorderly behavior" promoted by the politécnicos by arresting all "subversive students" who refused "to cooperate" with the authorities. These orders were given after consulting with Peralta in the week after Peralta took office on August 22. After giving these orders, Molinar directed that "guards" be deployed in the areas surrounding all schools of the IPN until "order was restored."[34]

The clampdown would soon reach new heights. On September 23, 1956, President Ruíz Cortines called in the Federal Army to occupy the schools of the IPN. Labeled "Operation P," this action was led by Secretary of Defense Matías Ramos Santos and involved eighteen hundred soldiers from the Eighth and Twenty-fourth Infantry battalions of the Mexican Army, more than three hundred riot police, and more than one hundred officers from the Department of the Judicial Police. In addition, an indeterminate number of agents of the DFS also participated in this battle of the Cold War waged upon the young students. In collaboration with Peralta and Ramos Santos, a group of DFS agents were sent onto the grounds of the major schools to disable the telephone and electric networks. Other DFS agents were assigned to patrol the area surrounding the various schools of the IPN in unmarked cars in order to keep the troublemakers under surveillance "twenty-four hours a day" until order was restored in Mexico.[35] These were supported by prominent officials within the Federal Army and the police department who arrived at the Politécnico in jeeps and armored vehicles ready for combat.[36] Once the schools of the IPN were occupied by the soldiers, the battalion was then ordered to arrest all "troublemakers" who refused to cooperate with the school authorities and government officials. If violence was required in order to bring the agitators into custody, soldiers were told "not to hesitate" to use their weapons, including "gas bombs and clubs," if necessary.[37]

Students of the internado were the first to be affected by Operation P. The commander in charge ordered his forces to go into every room of the internado at five in the morning to wake up the internos with reveille (toque de Diana) for interrogation. Surprised, and undoubtedly terrified, all the internos were told to pack up their belongings and exit the buildings in a single line. Once the students of the internado were lined up, the secretary of defense (with the backing of IPN director Peralta and the director of the internado, Manuel Burriel Ruíz) ordered the immediate imprisonment of all individuals who could not prove that they were full-time, bona fide students at the IPN. Of the 1,500 internos, it is difficult to determine how many individuals living in the internado were not officially enrolled at the IPN. Some U.S. Department of State documents put the number of gaviotas at 300, Excélsior estimated the number at "more than 400," and Alejo Peralta pegged the number at 204—"10 of which," he claimed, "had been found completely drunk" during the operation. However, other sources claimed much smaller numbers. The editors of Problemas de Latinoamérica asserted that only "53 young men had taken advantage of the social services illegally." The more mainstream El Universal surprisingly agreed with this estimate. They reported that, of the 200 students arrested, as many as 150 were able to produce their credentials later.[38]

Thus, mirroring the often-murky student status of many of the gorillas, the exact status, affiliation, and loyalties of the so-called gaviotas were tough to determine—a fact that could be used advantageously to serve political purposes. What does seem to be clear is that more than 300 students of the IPN were turned over to the judicial authorities for investigation. While students were detained for questioning, 204 were put in cells. It is also known that, of this group, 52 were subjected to heavy fines and short jail sentences. Finally, we know that, following the initial operation, the remaining students were put in buses and then dispersed throughout the city to avoid immediate reprisals.[39] Following the massive arrests of the internos, Alejo Peralta ordered Burriel Ruíz, the director of the internado, to give all the internos with legitimate credentials "200 pesos each" so that they could find a place to stay, "learn to live on their own," and stay quiet. In addition, they were warned that the dormitories would "never open their doors again." Instead, "the internado would be transformed into permanent barracks for the military," until order was restored. And "if FNET was found to be involved in a single act of protest that endangered the lives of the students," Peralta added, "we will ask the Federal Troops to use all the force that is necessary."[40] Peralta told a reporter present at the time: "It is a shame that we are forced to take such drastic measures," but the students, he alleged, had given them "no other choice." And regarding the occupation of the IPN, Peralta said to the politécnicos, "[It] is for the well-being of the good students." He concluded with the following patronizing threat: "I don't like to use force, but much less having to use it."[41] In a similar vein, Secretary of Defense Ramos Santos told the students: "You are to be blamed for all this. It is a shame that you were not able to appreciate all that the state has given to you."[42] To another group of internos accused of being responsible for the rampant corruption at the Politécnico, he said, "You have given us no other choice but to use violence."[43]

Although the politécnicos did not dispute the problems of corruption and professional agitators and fósiles that needed to be removed, they held the school authorities completely responsible for them. To clarify their position, they composed a collective testimonial, *El Poli Habla* ("The Politécnico speaks"), in which they made the following accusations:

> Those people who claim that politécnicos only spend their time stirring the student body up concerning unworthy causes ARE LYING! The only people wasting their time are the authorities who have refused to attend to the main problems of the [Politécnico] . . . . Indeed, it is true that one should not take advantage of the social services that the school offers; [yet] it is also true that as long as [Mexico] remains an underdeveloped country, the state should continue to provide financial assistance to poor students. What is intolerable is the way the authorities have handled the allotment of social services. And if anarchy prevails [in the Politécnico] as the authorities have always claimed, it does not mean that they have the right to assault or close [the internado].

They contended that it was the authorities who were to blame for the corruption at the IPN. They further noted:

> [It] is the authorities who have brought about corruption [inside the internado] . . . they are the ones who have illegally embezzled funds; they are the ones who have refused to allot the social services to the [real] students due to the lack of will or fear for their well-being; they are the ones who have traditionally managed the dispensation of scholarships and [political] plazas

through the threat of withdrawing such benefits to students who refuse to support the "right" political candidate; they are the ones who have co-opted student leaders and have provided social services to [pseudo] students.[44]

With the forces of the Federal Army occupying the major schools of the IPN, however, these and other accusations made by the politécnicos almost went unnoticed. As Nicandro Mendoza would later note in an interview, the accusations failed to gain attention in part through direct suppression: "[S]ecret agents and agent provocateurs had become infamous for threatening all students who dared to distribute propaganda." In contrast, "provocateurs were allowed to distribute as many apocryphal manifestos and student newspapers in the schools as they wished."[45] To make matters worse for the politécnicos, the print media refused to publish any student manifesto, and virtually no reports expressing a sympathetic view of the student protest were allowed to appear in the press. Instead, nearly all of the major newspapers (with the exception of the leftists' *El Popular* and *La Voz de México*) celebrated the severe measures taken by the government.[46] As one U.S. source enthusiastically reported, once the internado was closed and the politécnicos had returned to classes on October 1 (following their September vacations), "the watchwords 'order and discipline' had replaced 'anarchy and agitation.'"[47]

According to contemporary media reports, the pueblo could not be any happier. "At last," a number of individuals who wrote to the newspapers earnestly proclaimed, "the strike had ended," "youth rebellion" had been "tamed," and "the nest of revoltosos [the internado] had been shut down."[48] A number of politicians hastened to join the chorus of approval. In the opinion of the National Action Party (PAN), for example, the closing of the internado was said to be "necessary."[49] Government officials voiced their support for the action in the newspapers and made sure to single out Alejo Peralta for praise. In *Novedades*, for example, the deputy of the Federal District offered his congratulations on the closing of the internado to both the president and Peralta. That same day in *Excélsior*, the senator of Oaxaca expressed his gratitude by referring to the military occupation as a "magnificent step." Like others, he expressed his "trust that the authorities" that decided to take these drastic measures only after having studied the problem of the Politécnico in depth. Luis I. Rodríguez, the senator of Guanajuato and president of the Foreign Relations Committee, similarly referred to the military operation as a "necessary measure ordered by the Sr. Presidente." After all, he and others insisted that the behavior of the students of the Politécnico had gone too far.

They "had trampled the most vital rights of the people." The government, he concluded, "only did what should have been done a long time ago."[50] Similarly, an official at the Department of State stressed that following the military operation at the Politécnico, government officials had received the support of the responsible press, labor organizations, and other social sectors. "Order, discipline, and a sense of responsibility among students and teachers," it specifically noted, had finally reappeared.[51] Overall, it was estimated that Peralta had supposedly received, in "just two days" more than five hundred telegrams of "support, sympathy, gratitude, and admiration" from local neighbors, politicians, state officials, businessmen, teachers, and private individuals.[52] Peralta declared the occupation of the IPN a "glorious victory" for the nation and a lesson for its rebellious youth.[53]

Besides endorsing an iron fist inside the Politécnico, Alejo Peralta and his supporters also used other authoritarian tactics to intimidate and repress the students. Back in 1957, Peralta had announced that only "students with 'good character' would be accepted to the Politécnico."[54] It is no great stretch to conclude that Peralta had intended to filter out from enrollment students who expressed views sympathetic to the Left. Those who had already been admitted could be kicked out of the IPN if they participated in acts of rebellion. As it happened, the total number of students enrolled in the Politécnico in fact dropped from 25,277 in 1956 to 22,187 in 1958.[55] But Peralta would eventually pay the price for his authoritarianism. By the end of 1958, the highly unpopular director was met by a group of angry students who threw rocks and Molotov cocktails at him.[56] On February 28, 1959, Peralta was forced to offer his resignation, at the recommendation of the president, as additional student demonstrations broke out in various schools of the IPN. Ten days later, President López Mateos appointed Eugenio Méndez Docurro as the new director of the Politécnico.[57]

The Reinstallation of Corporatism and the Invocation of "Social Dissolution"

Once the internado was closed and the federal troops were in full control of the IPN, the state continued to blend the lines between youth rebelliousness and "unpatriotic" political activism and moved to imprison all the principal leaders in charge of the student protest. In this effort, authorities relied repeatedly on the revived catchall Law of Social Dissolution. As noted earlier, the law was first promulgated during World War II in response to the international threat of fascism posed by the Axis powers and then amended during the administration of Miguel Alemán to allow the government to imprison anyone convicted of endorsing "foreign ideas" that led to "rebellion, sedition, riot, or insurrection."[58] As the 1956 student protest took shape, such "dangers" came to mean the communist threat represented by the politécnicos, who—in the context of the Cold War—were portrayed in the media and elsewhere as dangerous demagogues who had imported foreign ideologies into Mexico.

For Nicandro Mendoza and Mariano Molina, the general secretary of FNET, the sting of the Law of Social Dissolution would be felt following the September 27 incident that took place outside the Comedor Universitario. Dozens of "young agitators"—representing the Comedor Universitario, the Confederación de Jóvenes Mexicanos, and the youth wings of the Communist Party and the Partido Popular—would soon join them.[59] On October 5 and 6, Nicandro Mendoza and his "gunmen," as several newspapers described other FNET representatives, were sentenced to prison after being convicted on a charge of social dissolution without the possibility of posting bail. According to the official document provided to *Excélsior* by the district attorney's office, the alleged perpetrators had been arrested because they had orchestrated "a series of acts to disturb social and public order." In addition, it was alleged that they had instigated students to take up arms and attack the soldiers stationed at the Politécnico.[60] Other specific charges included unlawful bearing of arms, inciting to riot, disturbance of public order, assault, resistance to authority, and even indecent behavior.[61]

Once the students had been sentenced to prison, the authorities made public all the evidence that connected these "subversives" with communism. In the case of Nicandro Mendoza, for example, it was widely reported in the Mexican press and stipulated in a U.S. government report that he had "recently returned from a trip behind the Iron Curtain financed by some mysterious source,"[62] an accusation he fervently denied in the press.[63] For some of his detractors, however, the certainty behind Mendoza's alleged visit to the Soviet Union seemed irrelevant. What mattered to many harsh critics of the strike, such as Audiffred, the well-known anticommunist cartoonist for *El Universal*, was the dangerously cozy relationship that Mendoza had established with the "King" of the "communist forces," Vicente Lombardo Toledando, whose recent visit to the leader of FNET in prison, Audiffred further suggested, should concern his readership.[64]

ILLUS. 4.1. Audiffred, "Lombardo, the Red, Knights Nicandro, the Little Red,"
El Universal, October 13, 1956. (Reproduced with permission from *El Universal*.)

Audiffred depicts the "aging demagogue" of the suggestively "anachronistic" Popular Party, carrying a Soviet hammer and sickle–tipped saber, knight-
ing the imprisoned young leader of FNET in recognition of Mendoza's selfless
dedication to the Left. For the commentator of *El Universal*, and dozens of
journalists who expressed similar anxieties in the press, there was no doubt
that unless the "little red troublemaker" of the IPN stayed in prison, he would
mature soon enough and become the next important leader of Mexico's communist forces.[65] This did not occur. Rather, Mendoza would remain imprisoned on charges of social dissolution until December 1958, when President
López Mateos would offer him general amnesty. In 1961 he would move to
Morelia, as the condition of his amnesty and, again, he would be accused
of inciting a student riot that supposedly led to the burning of the Instituto
Cultural México-Norteamericano.[66] Decades later, however, Mendoza would
continue to deny that he was a communist.[67]

In the late 1950s, with key protest leaders arrested and effectively removed
from power, a project to shift the direction and leadership of FNET to align it
with state policy began to develop. For an eight-year period, beginning in 1956,
a corporatist relationship between the IPN and the government sedimented
into place. During this period the student federation FNET was transformed
at the same time that, not coincidentally, tens of millions of government pesos

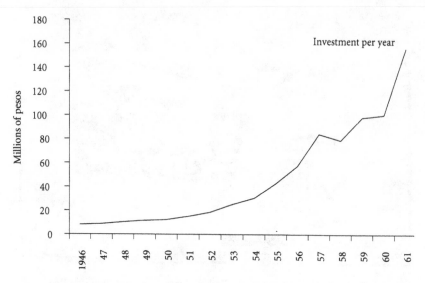

FIG. 4.1. Investment Growth: IPN, 1956–1961. (Data from IPN, *50 años*, 161.)

liberally flowed into the institute. After a series of only gradual increases since the mid-1940s, the Politécnico's budget began to grow remarkably a decade later (see Figure 4.1).

As investment rose, many participants spearheading the strikes of 1942, 1950, and 1956 witnessed with suspicion and dismay the rising fortunes of those who remained loyal to the school directors and the government of Adolfo López Mateos. In the years following the 1956 student protest, those loyal to authority benefited both financially and politically, as they became members of a transformed FNET. It did not take long after the official end of the 1956 strike for factionalism to set in as groups with various political affiliations vied to see who would hold power in FNET's new order.

The leaders of FNET that would replace Nicandro Mendoza and Mariano Molina were to be elected during the Ninth Congress of Technical Students that took place between October 22 and 26, 1956. Several factions put forth candidates for the presidency of FNET at the Congress, including the Francisco J. Velázquez Group and the Manuel Ochoa Velázquez Group. These groups stood on opposite sides with respect to their support of Director Peralta.[68] However, as the political climate intensified in the Congress, it became clear that two new networks, the Agapito Rios Group and the Benjamín Nieto Group, would emerge as the two most important factions contesting the FNET presidency. This in effect set up an opposition between "ramiris-tas," a group financed by Enrique Ramírez y Ramírez, distancing itself from the Partido Popular; and "lombardistas," a group remaining loyal to the policies of the aging leader of the Old Left, Vicente Lombardo Toledano.[69] Prior to the outcome of the election the two groups engaged in violent clash-es and accused each other of corruption and gangster politics. Yet they both demanded the immediate withdrawal of the Federal Army from the IPN.[70] As early as October 24, it had become evident that the ramirista group had triumphed, and with the victory came a consolidation of support from stu-dent leaders.[71] In November a new crop of students took on important local and national positions in FNET, but Enrique Ramírez y Ramírez continued to wield power behind the scenes, as he would continue to do until 1964. The ramiristas were also backed by López Mateos until the last day of his *sexenio* (1958–1964). The closer the ramiristas moved to the PRI, the further away they got from their Partido Popular origins. In exchange for loyalty to the government during this time, the ramiristas, amid unprecedented levels of corruption, acquired substantial political power and imperviousness to attack from FNET leaders.[72] In short, in the aftermath of the military occu-pation of the IPN, FNET became another charro organization at the service of the government, and its association with the Left remained nominal, a hollow artifact of history.

In 1964, the ramirista era would come to a close, only to be followed by a time dominated by an even more authoritarian and corrupt group of leaders who were financed by a number of influential *alemanistas* and *diazordistas*. Among these leaders were Alfonso Corona del Rosal and Jesús Robles Mar-tínez, who developed close ties with President Díaz Ordaz. They used all their power with the National Union of Educational Workers (SNTE) and the Fed-eration of Government Employees' Unions (FSTSE) to manipulate FNET.[73] Dominant *porro* leaders, such as "El Johnny," would work in opposition to the leaders of the 1968 student protest. By then, it would also soon become clear that FNET could not hold its own in this conflict, as it completely vanished from the IPN that same year (see Chapter 8). A similar situation would take place at UNAM. New and competing student organizations would emerge in the 1950s, only to see their power challenged, first by government-sponsored charros, and subsequently by new and more independent student organiza-tions demanding a more democratic nation.

The Consolidation of Charrismo during the "Golden Years" of UNAM

Many scholars have unreservedly referred to the decade and a half following the end of World War II in Mexico (the period from 1944 to 1960) as the "Golden Years of the University."[74] After all, this period saw the founding of Ciudad Universitaria (CU), an increase in federal funding, and relatively few massive student protests.[75] Yet, for an emerging generation of students who struggled to transform UNAM into a genuinely autonomous and democratic space, this so-called golden era of the university actually marked a tainted chapter in the history of this institution. In the words of two young scholars of student groups during the period: "[T]he student organizations of the University fell into one of their worst crises" during the 1950s. They explain that, in fact, this period was characterized by "gangster politics" and manipulation, or rather what students often broadly called *maniobrismo*, in which confusion and opportunism became the norm.[76]

Indeed, during the 1950s a new political environment with striking similarities to charrismo in the labor sector came into being at UNAM. The depoliticizing objective of "gangsterism" was one means by which the Mexican government could help stem a tide of genuine activism that might spread from the more radical IPN to UNAM. Mimicking the modus operandi applied in the labor sector, this student charrismo (charrismo estudiantil) was characterized by a host of competitive and corrupt practices. These included co-opting genuine leadership by granting various sorts of financial and political favors, installing false leaders who endlessly broadcast their empty rhetoric, and, in some cases, intimidating students with aggressive and violent tactics to undermine student elections.

Testimony by former students is particularly telling with regard to the atmosphere in the university and features of charrismo during this period. When asked to describe student politics during the 1950s, for example, Oscar González provided the following depiction during an interview:

> Borrowing from [Othón] Salazar, [Demetrio] Vallejo], and other important labor leaders we began to use the term "charrismo estudiantil" to identify all the corrupt leaders within the student organizations that we knew received complete support from government and school authorities. [With time,] many of these people became key leaders within the government. Other, more successful, charros became state governors or wealthy entrepreneurs.

Others became extremely popular among the student body. Like Palillo, they helped students who never attended classes to get their diplomas or when necessary helped them collect money for parties, graduations, or small political campaigns.

But above all, he added with greater emphasis in a louder voice,

[T]hese young leaders became famous for opening new opportunities to students interested in politics. They accomplished this by splitting the FEU into different student organizations; and therefore, multiplying the opportunities to create additional political networks with more and more influential padrinos.[77]

While student charrismo could rely substantially on extralegal means once it was put into place, a specific piece of legislation passed earlier in the mid-forties set the groundwork for making its grip on student organizing and behavior possible: the Caso Law of 1945. As noted earlier, the law represented a significant step backward in the negotiating capabilities of students and professors, including shelving their ability to choose the university's rector and school directors. Once the law took effect, the number of student intermediaries instantly multiplied and the political rivalry intensified. The new governmentally sanctioned authorities regained a strong political grip on the FEU and the student societies under its structure by removing conservative students from important political positions and replacing them with leaders who were more closely aligned with the government. Thus, despite Alfonso Caso's alleged intentions to depoliticize the university, the 1945 law laid the foundation for these and other avenues through which student charrismo could flourish. This was particularly evident in the case of the FEU. By the 1950s it had come to resemble once again, as originally intended, a "client-patron organization (*una organización clientelar*)," as Ilán Semo so aptly described it. As he put it, the FEU's main function was to serve as a "transmission belt between the bureaucracy of the university, the machinery of the government, and the students," many of whom certainly made use of it to move up the social and political ladder.[78]

An important clause in the Caso Law illustrates in part how the machinery of this "transmission belt" functioned. The clause specified that any student with a respectable grade point average had the right to organize a *planilla*, or representative group, which could compete for the presidency of the multiple student organizations in each of the schools associated with the university, including its preparatorias. In turn, the elected leaders won the right to be represented within the University Council. The only other requirement was that these planillas had to be nonpartisan.[79] Adhering to the new law, the existing porras and student societies registered with the administrative offices of their schools with the understanding that they would not get involved in political matters. Rather, they would continue to foster school spirit and respect for university autonomy.[80] In exchange, members of the porras and the new student societies received identification cards, offices, sweaters with the school logo, and other items and privileges that legitimized their organizations.

However, as numerous manifestoes distributed by independent organizations during this time testify, a growing number of student societies virtually ignored the new law by adopting a very clear political stance in pursuit of supporting the prevailing *padrinos*. This was particularly true during the rectorship of Nabor Carrillo (1953–1961), in which one student newspaper article observed that it had become "common for a small group of two or three students to organize a legitimate new FEU or Student Society." Once registered as an official organization, these small groups then received financial resources and an office from the administrative department of the school. As the university rector had done with popular *porristas*, the bulletin further noted that "Sr. Nabor Carrillo" gave student leaders a number of specific and long-lasting privileges, such as school diplomas, "without ever having attended classes." As explained in the bulletin, "Every year, the Señor rector spends between one hundred thousand and a quarter of a million pesos on 'private' receptions." Here, charro leaders were rewarded with "special benefits," including trips to Acapulco where charro leaders allegedly organized pseudo student conferences.[81] These so-called conferences supposedly explored a variety of themes related to the social, economic, and political problems of the schools; but in reality, the charro leaders used these conferences "to go out on a binge."[82] A student bulletin from the ENP # 3 signed "Common Front against Alemanismo!" specifically remarked on the role corrupt padrinos played during student elections, as follows:

> We are aware that buying off pseudo students has been the preferred "method" employed to guarantee votes. We can testify to this because they too have tried to bribe us! Trips to Cuernavaca and Acapulco with "all expenses paid"; open accounts in the Hotels Papagayo and The Majestic; money in cash to presidents and delegates willing to sign with them . . . . [Money] to pay for manifestoes and "clarifications" to be published in the

newspapers . . . Etc. etc. These are the methods that have been employed to contain the corruption [that has characterized this era of] Alemanismo.[83]

Indeed, the private receptions, trips to various tourist resorts with all expenses paid, and manifestoes published in the newspapers proved to be good investments for the circle over which the university rector presided. For one, with the support of charro leaders, Nabor Carrillo took control of the student body that in previous administrations had remained in the hands of conservative forces, such as panistas and later the alemanistas, particularly during the rectorship of Luis Garrido (1948–1953).[84] Nonetheless, as one student bulletin concluded, this strategy worked, but "at a very high price." The new way of doing politics, for example, satisfied personal ambitions and corrupted many student leaders and teachers.[85] Scattered espionage reports similarly conclude that it was precisely during the rectorship of Nabor Carrillo (1953–1961) that the government effectively assumed control of student political activity as well as the board of trustees by eliminating what little remained of the conservative hegemony of the 1930s and 1940s. As noted by the students, these documents unequivocally explain that such control was made possible by the intermediaries' abilities to co-opt student leaders of the FEUs and student societies.[86]

Many charro and porra leaders would also exert their influence efficiently and without resorting to violence during this period through the effective and widespread use of empty propaganda. As a self-described fósil said during an interview, the term "grilla," or "cricket politics," in fact, emerged during this period as a colorful descriptor for this aspect. Once "co-opted" or "installed in government-sponsored student organizations," the school intermediaries that served as the workforce of charrismo relied on a seemingly interminable amount of leftist rhetoric to confuse and pacify students.[87] Oscar Gonzalez similarly explained that in such a climate of greater political opportunities but also fierce competition to win the support of the students and padrinos that characterized the administration of Nabor Carrillo, "the term 'grilla,' emerged." He explained during an interview:

We began to use the term "grilla" to describe the noise that all competing leaders made during their campaigns, as they presented to the students their ideas, agendas, and political platforms. At first, we thought that this was what democracy was all about. After all, these student leaders were competing for our political support and often addressed a number of important issues that concerned most of the student body. But soon we realized that the majority of these campaigns represented nothing but rhetoric; you know, with little results or concrete solutions to our problems. This is the moment when we began to say that these charro leaders who received great support from above made nothing but noise; you know, just like the crickets (*grillos*): noise, noise, noise, without any real political substance.[88]

Another student of this period paints a very similar picture. According to his testimony, his generation conceived of the term "grilla" as a reflection of the political mechanisms at play that students saw were taking place at the national level. He explains the elections of representative leaders of the various student organizations at UNAM and the important role *relajo* played in student politics, as follows,

> The student candidates running for office engaged in exhausting campaigns to convince intellectuals, sport fans . . . and especially those powerful leaders with devious reputations . . . of which the [aspiring leaders] had to negotiate with, by granting a variety of concessions in exchange for votes, [including] school parties, tickets for sport events . . . [etc.].[89]

He then gives his explanation of the origin of the term "grilla": "I will begin by saying that the term was first used [around the mid-1950s] by Rafael Millán Martínez. He was a student . . . who adopted the word "grilla" to mirror the [political] circumstances of the moment." According to this account,

> The grillo [or cricket] is an animal that is constantly chirping to the extent that it gets so annoying that it wrecks your ears and your nervous system; this is precisely what student leaders running for office did: they got on your nerves (*estar chingando sin parar*) until they obtained their "conceived votes."[90]

Whether Rafael Millán Martínez was the first student to use the term "grilla" is not certain or even relevant. What is important, however, is that grilla politics filled the student publications, halls, open spaces, and airwaves of the university as a particularly effective tool of student charrismo.

What many student testimonies often failed to acknowledge, however, was the diverse range of people who were behind the proliferation of charrismo estudiantil. Without a doubt, the PRI was largely responsible for splitting the FEU into different factions, as the majority of student manifestoes (as well as

TABLE 4.1. Political Networks in 1953 Student Elections. School of Medicine

Political affiliation:	Henríquistas Miguel Henríque (Planilla Verde)	Panistas (Planilla Blanca)	Priístas Efrén del Pozo (Planilla Azul y Oro)
Intermediaries:	Jesús Guzman R	Jorge Siegrist	Lic. Antonio Mena Brito
Charro leaders:	Luis Aurelio Sánchez	Eduardo Pol J. Rangel, Horacio Oliva Abarca	Ernesto Cordero Galindo, Luis Alcaraz García, Carlos Camarena O'Farril
Provocateurs:	El Margot , El Gamas	El Pato Tuma, El Horacio, El Diente, El Clímaco, El Rapaz, El Tepochón, Los Rectores, La Paloma Wells, El Luque, El Pelón, El Negro, Hmos. Palma, El Famoso, El Cavernario, El Socio, El Rapaz, Hmos Palma, El Famoso, El Negro	El Campiñera, Los Pistoleros, El Pistolo, El Pager, El Malacara, El Boxer, El Pinky, El Pelón, El Huevo, El Plumas, El Macomich

Sources: Data from scattered notes by DFS agents; separate interviews with Carlos Ortiz Tejeda, El Angel, El Chaparro, El Negro, and Oscar González.

the few scholars who have written on the subject) have stressed.[91] The party did help corrupt leaders, distribute apocryphal propaganda, and finance provocation and violence. Yet the PRI was not the monolithic power that is generally depicted in this historiography. The PRI met with some competition from the PAN and actors outside the government. What is more, it also would find its own ranks splintered by different competing leftist and conservative groups within the party, each vying for power inside the university vis-à-vis the financing of charro leaders. A closer look at student elections during this period, for example, gives a more complicated picture often revealing a factionalized state struggling to maintain its hegemony inside UNAM. For instance, in the 1953 election for the presidency of the student society in the School of Medicine, illustrated in Tables 4.1 and 4.2, one can identify several competing networks within as well as outside the government structure, including "henriquistas," "panistas," "pozistas," "romeristas," "alemanistas," and "cardenistas."[92]

Henriquistas (Planilla Verde) sought to gain a foothold on power as a third-party alternative to the PRI and PAN. General Miguel Henríquez Guzmán, who had failed in his second and final attempt to create a strong opposition party with the support of disenfranchised cardenistas a year earlier, led this group.[93] Demonstrating the often-blurred distinctions between official and kin relations occurring with client-patron organizations, Guzmán's nephew (Jesús) functioned as his principal intermediary. Like other rising leaders, he did so by funneling the financing of those charro leaders he was able to gather to his cause. Henriquistas, a relatively weak faction, had fewer subordinates and resources. For example, according to a government document, it could only come up with a measly ten pesos to give members to set up explosives on Election Day in 1953.[94]

A second and more important network involved in the spread of charrismo estudiantil during this period was the conservative panistas, represented as Planilla Blanca in the 1953 elections. This Planilla was organized and financed by Jorge Siegrist Clamont, the most influential conservative student leader of the 1940s and 50s; the elections of 1953 were a high point in his career in student politics. A brief sketch of Siegrist's background points to the efforts conservative students made to re-establish the hold they had on the university prior to the reorganization brought about by the Caso Law. Jorge Siegrist was a charismatic leader who came from a wealthy family.[95] Like many students of similar conservative backgrounds, he attended private Catholic schools as a youth. At UNAM he enrolled in the School of Law, where he became an active recruiter of younger students, who were impressed by Siegrist's conspicuous intelligence and impressive physique.[96] Government documents describe Jorge Siegrist as a natural born leader who was particularly popular in the ENP # 2, as well as in the Arts, Architecture, Medicine, Dentistry, and Philosophy schools where the burgeoning Left had little or no influence on the student body. With the support of students from these schools Siegrist became the vice president of the FEU before this organization began to splinter into different political factions in the late 1940s.

In 1951 Siegrist reached the zenith of his career as an intermediary in UNAM. During the nineteenth congress of the National Student Federation held in Monterrey that year, he was elected president of CNE (Confederación Nacional de Estudiantes) with the support of the PAN for a period of two years. Conservative students such as Siegrist argued that "fraudulent student elections" following the Caso Law had put the university "in the hands of outside agents."[97] In particular, Siegrist's group believed that "radical" students with "leftist tendencies," supported in the administration by priístas (see below), had compromised the autonomy of the university. They had turned UNAM into a "close-knit political apparatus of the government" in which the centrist position embraced by the state "in the name of the Revolution" determined the discourse, nature, and tone of student politics.[98] In addition, Siegrist's group argued that these "outside agents" had transformed UNAM into a training institution of technicians and government bureaucrats as opposed to one that emphasized philosophy and humanism, putting Mexico's traditional (Catholic) values at risk. The new CNE under Siegrist condemned what it saw as the social capitalism promoted by the revolutionary state because it led to exploitation and extremes of wealth.[99] In short, as historian Donald Mabry notes, what the CNE hoped to accomplish under the leadership of Siegrist was what the conservative opposition to the government led by the PAN was proposing at the national level—that is, to place socially conservative leaders with close ties to the Catholic Church in influential positions of power and eventually open up Mexico to business interests that promoted free markets.[100]

In 1953, at the twentieth congress of the National Student Federation in Durango, Siegrist was elected president of the CNE for two more years. José Vasconcelos, who had become an important mentor for conservative students during this period, served as an honorary guest. Upon re-election, Siegrist set forth two additional objectives for the CNE: to attack the Caso Law more directly and to eliminate the board of trustees indefinitely. The goal proposed by Siegrist this time was to return to students the power to elect the university rector and the directors of the schools, which they had lost under the Caso Law in the mid-1940s.[101] However, according to a government report, the PAN had grown increasingly impatient with Siegrist during the first two years of his administration of the CNE and believed that he had mismanaged funds that the party had given to him. Consequently in July of 1953 the PAN withdrew its support for him and moved to sponsor new leaders.[102] Siegrist retaliated with two techniques typical of charrismo—shock brigades and bribery. Recruiting from his primarily younger student following to form shock brigades, Siegrist launched a series of attacks against the new representatives of the PAN, whom he claimed had formed their own brigades financed by the American embassy.[103] He then went on to describe his shock brigades as "falanges" composed of young militant students associated with the athletic teams of UNAM, including several members of the wrestling and American football teams. In collaboration with younger students from the Preparatorias, who had achieved "a certain degree of respect with their fists," he argued that many people joined his group primarily because they were motivated by school spirit and dedication to their conservative movement. He observed, in fact, that what compelled young students to join his group "was not an economic interest." No one received money from him, he added. Rather, they joined his movement "for the thrill" of the adventure, for the political security that he made sure to offer to them, or for "respect to their true identity" as conservative universitarios.[104]

Perhaps there is a certain degree of truth in Siegrist's comments. It is possible that many students did join his shock brigades for political and/or ideological reasons. Nonetheless, as remembered by former activists and detailed in various government documents and student newspapers, there is no doubt that Siegrist (as well as his rivals) used large sums of money that they received from their padrinos to re-establish political control of the schools. Besides influencing student elections, key intermediaries such as Siegrist used financial resources made available to them to pay for the printing and the distribution of apocryphal propaganda, hire thugs to pressure school directors to resign, and to maintain a reliable base of supporters during relatively peaceful times.[105] As perfected by Palillo, several of these charro leaders solidified their base by sponsoring parties, hosting graduation ceremonies, guaranteeing free attendance to football games, and giving blank checks in bars, cafeterias, and movie houses.[106]

The Planilla Azul y Oro, associated with the PRI, represented the third and final group involved in the 1953 student elections. Efrén del Pozo, the general secretary of UNAM, led this network. Priístas won nearly all of the student elections of 1953, and they would continue to do so during the supportive rectorship of Nabor Carrillo, with whom they had close ties. However, in building up their political power in the rest of the schools affiliated to UNAM, influential intermediaries could not rely on a single padrino. The most illustrious intermediary, Palillo, for example, depended not only on the Carrillo/Pozo patronage but also on the alemanista network and other sponsors. Several competing and partially overlapping networks within the PRI would emerge amid the system of charrismo that characterized the period. The figures who became involved in student politics through the financing of charro leaders within the PRI during the rectorship of Nabor Carrillo were various, as were their motivations. Numerous government reports, for example, point to a diverse group of influential priístas as key individuals who allegedly kept a reliable group of universitarios from the FEU on their payrolls.[107] In particular, they point to the general secretary under-rector Nabor Carrillo, Efrén del Pozo, and especially Humberto Romero Pérez, who achieved his first political success in the 1940s when, as an aspiring student leader, he was able to create a balanced supporting network of powerful padrinos and influential porristas.[108] This network, which many tried to put together but only a few

TABLE 4.2. Two Factions of the FEU Sponsored by the PRI, 1959–1961

Padrino:	H. Romero, Efrén del Pozo	Miguel Alemán
Intermediaries:	José Manuel Rodríguez	Miguel Alemán Velasco (son), Agustín García López
Charro leaders:	J. López V., H. Romero Candado, Jorge M., Servio Tulio A.	Carlos Díaz de León
Subleaders:	José L. Preciado, Ángel González Caamaño, Arturo Rodríguez, Hugo Castro	Luis Nogueda del Pozo (nephew)
Provocateurs:	El Chiquitón, El Vitaminas, Los Gama, El Posada, El Leonardo	Los Colmenares, El Charro, El Cubano, El Tigre, El Gandaya

Sources: Data from scattered notes by DFS agents; separate interviews with Carlos Ortiz Tejeda, El Angel, El Chaparro, El Negro, and Oscar González.

talented leaders such as Romero were actually able to establish, proved to be the springboard for an extremely successful political career.

Like many other políticos in the governing elite, Humberto Romero Pérez got his start in student politics in the School of Law. As a student leader, Romero was rewarded with the presidency of the student association in the early 1940s. In 1946, Miguel Alemán named him general attorney, a position Romero held until 1952. With the new sexenio (1952–1958), Romero was named director of Public Relations for President Adolfo Ruiz Cortinez. During the administration of Ruiz Cortinez, Romero became one of the principal supporters of the charismatic leader, Palillo, whose main function was to keep students "entertained" and, not coincidentally, distracted from politics (see Chapter 2). Romero was named the private secretary under the presidential administration of López Mateos (1958–1964).[109] In this capacity he became particularly concerned by the radicalization of universitarios who had begun to challenge the corporatist structure of the FEU with the creation of alternative student organizations. During this period Romero extended his political network well beyond the students in Palillo's circle (see a sketch of his network on Table 4.2). He forged a solid relationship with a group of charro leaders who had demonstrated little ideological interests, but who had demonstrated their leadership skills in creating diverse networks with porristas, football players, and pseudo-students recruited from nearby street gangs.[110] Their goal was to put together shock brigades capable of countering groups organized by henriquistas and panistas. Although these had seen their power diminish, they still enjoyed substantial support inside specific schools of the university.[111]

Followers of former Mexican president Miguel Alemán also competed for student allegiance within the PRI. Headed by Miguel Alemán, Luis Garrido (the former rector of the university), and Alfonso Noriega, alemanistas deployed shock brigades in order to get their candidate (Agustín García López) elected as rector.[112] Other influential alemanistas identified in multiple government reports include Ernesto Uruchurtu, the chief of the Federal District, who allegedly created a strong base of close to 250 students in Preparatoria # 5 with the help of a student leader by the name of Nestor Zavala.[113] Another base of support for Alemán came from the leaders of the National Institute of Mexican Youth (INJM), who allegedly hired a group of universitarios from the FEU on numerous occasions "to avoid possible reprisals" against them.[114] Such efforts on the part of the INJM continued until the late 1960s when, under the direction of Píndaro Urióstegui, the institute began to move away from the alemanistas.[115]

Despite these efforts, however, by the end of the administration of Nabor Carrillo all of these political factions within the PRI—that is, romeristas, pozistas, and alemanistas—would lose out to the cardenistas and the independent Left that emerged at UNAM in the wake of the Cuban Revolution (see Chapter 6). Dr. Ignacio Chávez, who in February of 1961 would assume the position of rector, would represent this latter group. But the control of this group would come to an end in 1966 when a new group of intermediaries financed by close affiliates to President Gustavo Díaz Ordaz (1964–1970) would violently force the rector to resign. Hence, for student leaders in the FEU, the student societies, and the porras willing to embrace the centrist position of the government, the new cozy relationship that developed between UNAM and the state offered exceptional economic and political opportunities, particularly during the administration of Nabor Carrillo. For conservative students, on the other hand, this period saw the gradual loss of the political control they had enjoyed in previous decades. The same was true for the alemanistas as a result of the successful *charrista* efforts of romeristas and pozistas.

Conclusion: The Consolidation and Limitations of Charrismo Estudiantil

After the IPN strike of 1956 was officially called off by President Ruíz Cortines in mid-June, a number of people in different positions of power began to fund more aggressive mechanisms of control to repress the most politicized students. These efforts involved the manipulation of student-centered violence and provocation that were consolidated as "student charrismo." But it was becoming increasingly evident that sporadic violence and provocation facilitated by charro leaders was failing to contain the forces of student protest that were escalating despite the official end of the protest. Student charrismo strained to resolve its own "crisis of authority." Revealing that its distinction from more overtly repressive regimes in Latin America was less pronounced than it would like to admit, the Mexican state responded with direct force. In answer to mounting pressure, school and government authorities called for the closing of the internado, which was flagged as the place where major political and social problems of the Politécnico originated. President Adolfo Ruíz Cortines ordered the military occupation of the IPN and the imprisonment of the principal political activists. They would be charged variously with "treason," "terrorism," and a variety of other crimes as stated in the catchall Law of Social Dissolution. The principal leaders of the student protest were imprisoned, the internado was closed, and the IPN was occupied by the Federal Army. As financing began to flow into the institute in greater amounts, the state proceeded to dismantle the progressive and popular student organization, FNET, and convert it into a charro student federation. The organization retained the name and leftist rhetoric of its predecessor but was controlled by loyal supporters of the government. The now charro student federation of FNET would remain the governing body of the politécnicos until 1968, when a newly installed student protest would demand its expulsion from the Politécnico. Throughout the long sixties, students would also continue to resist the increasingly ineffective systematic student violence of charrismo first established in 1958.

Given the success of the IPN in gaining massive on-campus support from students, forming alliances with local labor, and upsetting the powers-that-be in the Federal District, why, one might ask, didn't the protest spread to include the potentially ample resources available from the UNAM student body, located only a few kilometers away from campus? When asked by a reporter about the possibility that *normalistas* (students at the Teachers' School) and universitarios would join forces with the politécnicos to challenge the occupation, IPN director Peralta answered without hesitation: "The Army has the capacity to stop them all."[116] Whether or not this threat had an effect on the students is unclear. Nevertheless, it should be noted that the universitarios never joined forces with the politécnicos to protest the occupation. In fact, except in some very minor isolated instances, UNAM students never supported the 1956 student protesters of the IPN at all. According to the newspapers, support at UNAM of the IPN never materialized, because of innate differences between the two student bodies. They pointed to "obvious class differences" and cultural antagonisms stemming from American football sports rivalries since the 1940s.[117] Accounts by former student activists of UNAM, however, paint a more complicated picture, one that widens the responsibility to include the broader context of student charrismo. They attribute the lack of support to threat, bribery, and deliberate diversion on the part of government, school authorities, and competing political powerbrokers, and in so doing fittingly suggest that for many students the "Golden Years of UNAM" were not as "Golden" as received history would dictate.[118] They can perhaps be more appropriately described as "Tainted Years" whose potentially shining moments were distinctly darkened by the coalescing oppositional politics of charrismo estudiantil. The 1958 student protest in defense of bus drivers that followed would emerge to a large extent as a direct response to the consolidation of this mechanism of control across the domain of labor and education.

5   The 1958 Student Movement
and the Origins of Mexico's New Left

O N AUGUST 22, 1958, dozens of bus drivers tried desperately to protect a bus terminal in the southern part of Mexico City from the onslaught of hundreds of enraged *universitarios*. Heavily outnumbered by the students, the bus workers quickly abandoned their defensive positions. Dumbfounded by the attack, the drivers could only watch as rebellious students proceeded first to commandeer more than sixty city buses, and then almost playfully to crash the buses against each other. Meanwhile, another group of more radical students, armed with sticks, stones, and other objects, moved into different parts of the city to commandeer additional city buses and burn them.[1] Once in front of the National Palace, the students painted slogans on the walls such as "Death to the Bad Government," "Down with the Monopoly [of Power]," and "Death to Charrismo." Making no secret of their affiliation to the university, the students then drove the buses to Ciudad Universitaria (CU) to the accompaniment of Goyas (university chants), like so many sports revelers. In the course of the unrest, the bus terminal was set ablaze, and forty people overall were injured during the incident. Within a week, the universitarios, now joined by dozens of students from the preparatory schools, had taken possession of more than three hundred city buses; completely taken over CU (which they proudly proclaimed was "student territory"); prohibited anyone from entering the occupied territory who failed to show proper student identification; stationed "guards" in the occupied schools "to prevent provocateurs from sabotaging the movement"; and man-

ILLUS. 5.1. Audiffred, "Vandalism," *El Universal*, August 25, 1958. (Reproduced with permission from *El Universal*.)

aged temporarily to paralyze the transportation system in a large part of the city.[2]

Like the bus drivers who had tried desperately to defend the bus terminal, newspaper reporters were also baffled by the students' actions, which combined an air of festivity with violence. The majority of reporters simply did not know how to react to this "celebratory vandalism."[3] Referring to the international youth subculture that had begun to create a great level of anxiety around the world, one group of reporters argued that these "spontaneous" acts of violence could only be understood as the proof that "rebels without a cause" (*a los que había que meter en cintura a como diera lugar*) had taken over the National Autonomous University of Mexico (UNAM).[4] Echoing the voices of many people who wrote to the newspaper, one reporter wrote: "What we are witnessing and suffering from today is not a simple 'student commotion' or something to that effect." Rather, the reporter explained that the hijacking of city buses should be understood as a "noisy demonstration" of the "alarming" problem of youth delinquency and, unfortunately, "another episode more, in its most extreme nature, of what lately has been called 'rebelliousness without a cause.'"[5] A second and more conservative group of reporters refused to accept this idea of *rebeldismo sin causa*. Instead, still distressed by the massive strikes organized by *politécnicos* two years earlier and sectors of the working class that same year, they depicted the universitarios who engaged in the hijacking of buses as "young thugs." If the students were not punished, the conservative pen of Audiffred predicted that they would "drag the nation into chaos" with "prehistoric ideas" promoted by communists (see Illustration 5.1).

Audiffred, *El Universal's* most famous cartoonist and one of the principal critics of the 1956 student protest, further echoed the concerns of many reporters in insisting that such acts of "vandalism" (far exceeding the jubilant rituals of the *novatadas*) could only be explained by the manipulation of *manos extrañas* ("foreign manipulation"). He suggested that red agitation (depicted in this case as a gigantic boy playing with toy buses) had let the genie of social dissolution out of the lamp (see Illustration 5.2).[6] Like Audiffred, many commentators were convinced that the Law of Social Dissolution would "magically" put an end once and for all to this latest "red agitation" organized against the nation.[7]

Both of these interpretations of the 1958 student revolt proved to be premature, reductive, and, therefore, misleading. To begin with, a closer look at this student protest reveals that the so-called *revoltosos* involved in the burning of the bus terminal and the commandeering of city buses had a real "cause." Universitarios engaged in these festive and violent acts for collective political reasons that went beyond individual psychology or coercion. Expressing grievances similar to those voiced by workers during the labor strikes organized earlier in the year, disgruntled students took this opportunity to protest

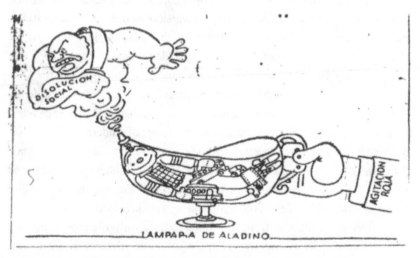

ILLUS. 5.2. Audiffred, "The Genie's Lamp," *El Universal*, August 27, 1958. (Reproduced with permission from *El Universal*.)

against the political corruption that they believed had come to characterize the postrevolutionary government. Employing the same language as the labor leaders, moreover, these students argued that the rampant problem of corruption in student politics was symbolized by the reviled image of the so-called *charro*, or what students identified as corrupt union leaders who allegedly received the financial and political support from the government.

Furthermore, the student protest of 1958 did not erupt spontaneously, as the reporters cited above claimed. Rather, this student protest must be understood as a symptom of the social and political crises that first came to a head in 1958 and reappeared throughout the long sixties. These crises were brought on by a number of factors, including: (a) an increasingly factionalized government that saw the presidential elections of November–December 1958 further diminish the authority of the president as well as that of the corporatist structure of the state;[8] (b) the corporatist structure of the University Student Federation (FEU), whose policies seemed anachronistic to a new generation of students; (c) the fading of the economic miracle, which had benefited the universitarios during the 1940s and early 1950s;[9] and (d) an inadequate transportation system that failed to meet the needs of a larger and more concentrated student population after the founding of Ciudad Universitaria in 1954.[10]

Unlike the protest organized by the politécnicos two years earlier, which received the support of key representatives of the Old Left (such as Vicente Lombardo Toledano and the Partido Popular), this latest action was the first massive student protest organized by universitarios during the long sixties that began to make a conscious attempt to challenge the leadership of the FEU. Students created alternative and more democratic organizations and forums of participation, such as *asambleas* (student assemblies) and the *Gran Comisión Estudiantil* (Grand Student Commission, GCE). Thus, despite the protest's short duration (August 22 to September 4), this event should be interpreted as one of the most important student actions of modern Mexico.[11] This defining moment—taken together with the 1956 student strike in the National Polytechnic Institute, and later the influences of Cuban Revolution—opened a new era of student activism, festive disorder, and violence that would give rise to Mexico's New Left. Following the 1958 strike, students began to see themselves as a collective front, *el estudiantado*, a unifying movement that would challenge (albeit momentarily) the institutionalized barriers of class differences that had traditionally kept students from different institutions apart. In particular, the uprisings of 1958 emerged to a large extent as a direct response to the consolidation of *charrismo* as a mechanism of control across the domains of labor and education in Mexico City.

The 1958 Student Movement

[Our] movement is a clear expression of the awakening of [our] new consciousness as young people. [We] have been asleep for a long time, which lately has been characterized by an atmosphere of prevailing deceit and corruption. [But today] we indicate that [our generation] has recognized that it is an endearing part of the pueblo, which inexhaustible vitality has recently found a vigorous energy in the struggles of the working class.[12]

Such were the sentiments voiced during August of 1958 by the universitarios responsible for the commandeering of city buses and the taking over of Ciudad Universitaria. Their goal was to announce the birth of what they saw as a "new movement" in student politics. They argued that, unlike previous revolts, this one "emerged to denounce the injustices that affected the ordinary lives of the pueblo, not just those of a small privileged minority."[13] They further explained how their "movement" was uniquely tied to working-class concerns:

We want to invite the public to see the social projection of our movement; a fraternal projection [that is] based on the struggles of the working class, whose vitality lies in the cleansing of the labor unions."

What they demanded was "a regime capable of guaranteeing the independence of the labor sector."[14] To safeguard this independence, they argued, it was "necessary to overcome an old formula" that had historically kept students detached from the needs of the common people. The dichotomous interactions of "The University to the Pueblo; the Pueblo to the University!" needed to be transformed in favor of "The University identified with the Pueblo."[15] As part of this effort the students presented a list of five specific demands. These included (1) an end to the private monopoly of city buses; (2) the expropriation of the bus system by the city; (3) better working conditions for bus drivers (as well as the right to form independent labor unions); (4) improvement in the transportation system without the raising of bus fares; and (5) the release of all students imprisoned during the strike and the withdrawal of federal troops and the city police surrounding Ciudad Universitaria and other schools, effective immediately.[16] Indeed the elaboration of these demands represented an unprecedented political act on the part of the universitarios, given the constituencies they attempted to bring into a single voice. Never before had students expressed an interest in siding with independent labor unions.[17] Previous strikes organized by these students had usually revolved around academic issues or school electoral politics. Universitarios had in the past acknowledged the need to create a unified front with the working class, but the elitism of university culture frequently prevented such a union from coming into being. An alliance between the different student bodies was also unprecedented. Not far from UNAM, the politécnicos had tried to join forces with sectors of the working class in the early 1950s. But because of the biased coverage in the media, as well as the distortion of the strike's aims by agents provocateurs, these students eventually lost the support of the popular classes.

The beginning of the student protest dates back to 1957, when the Alianza de Camioneros de México (ACM) first proposed to the authorities of the Federal District that bus fares be raised from to 45 cents to 65 cents per ride. The ACM was a privately owned bus company with ninety-six routes throughout the city, including one that ran from the old *barrio estudiantil* in downtown to the new Ciudad Universitaria. To investigate the proposal presented by the ACM, Ernesto Uruchurtu, the chief of the Federal District, assigned a Transportation Committee. A final decision by the committee was postponed for several months because the Federation of Workers of the Federal District (FTDF) threatened to go on strike in September of 1957 and later in January of 1958.[18] The FTDF accused the leaders of the ACM of having sold out to corrupt union leaders working for the Confederation of Mexican Workers (CTM), which, under the leadership of Fidel Velazquez, the nation's most powerful charro leader, had consolidated its leading position in the progovernment labor movement. The FTDF claimed that the ACM leadership had served as a key instrument of repression of all sectors of the working class since the 1940s.[19] In particular, the members of the FTDF argued that the ACM had violated a number of basic labor laws, including allowing unpaid vacations and providing an insufficient number of days off. The FTDF demanded a raise for all bus drivers, whose wages they claimed were well below the minimum wage. José Valdovinos, the general secretary of the ACM, responded that such demands could not even be considered unless the authorities of the Federal District granted the increase in bus fares of 20 cents.[20]

Meanwhile, as word of these developments reached the UNAM campus, a faction within the FEU, seeing this as a potential opportunity to strengthen their organization, made the daring decision to support the members of the FTDF. It issued the statement that an increase in bus fares, "as small as 5 cents per ride," would add to the economic burden faced by most universitarios, whose cost of living had increased recently. Claiming to speak on behalf of ordinary citizens, the FEU demanded that all city buses be overhauled and that new buses be put into service. Calling for more fundamental change, the FEU demanded, moreover, that the bus lines be operated by the city government, as opposed to a private monopoly.[21] Despite the combined efforts of the FEU and the FTDF, however, it had become clear by mid-August that the Federal District authorities had sided with the ACM. An increase in salaries and the overhauling of old buses would be contingent on a fare increase. Effective August 12, the Transportation Committee granted an increase in bus fares of 5 cents, with an additional increase of 5 cents to come when new buses went into service. The decision was approved by the CTM, which claimed to represent drivers on fifty-nine of the ninety-six bus lines that ran across the city.[22] Yet anger at the increase in bus fares was no longer limited to a small group of students within the FEU. Hundreds of universitarios now felt that, unless they took drastic measures, their voices would be ignored, just as had happened with the politécnicos two years earlier. On August 22 universitarios expressed their outrage as well as frustration at the seriousness and authoritarianism of the older generation of student activists by burning the bus terminal and engaging in a "defiant act of desmadre."[23]

The beginnings of a worker-student coalition presumably free of the tentacles of state meddling began to take shape. Once Ciudad Universitaria was occupied, a "Popular Committee" of self-described "independent students" organized an assembly that same night and invited bus drivers interested in organizing a massive strike to attend. To avoid the co-opting of their movement by government authorities inside UNAM, the Popular Committee collectively agreed that the FEU would not serve as the representative organization for the strike.[24] In addition, the Popular Committee stated that students would not return the hijacked buses until the ACM guaranteed in writing that the fare increase would be rolled back, the workers' salaries would be raised, and the transportation system would be improved. Convinced of their bargaining power, and now in possession of more than 150 city buses, the students adopted an increasingly violent position and announced that they would burn in public a bus for every driver fired by the leaders of the ACM for simply having sided with the students.[25] But elements within the FEU tried unsuccessfully to undermine the Popular Committee by claiming to have organized a meeting with Ernesto Uruchurtu that same night. As detailed in the press, the students had agreed to abandon their street positions at this meeting, and had promised that they would return the city buses to the ACM. After having successfully negotiated with the chief of the Federal District, they were reported to have agreed to an exemption for students to a raise in bus fares.[26] However, this attempt by the older representatives of the FEU to divide the students backfired. The Popular Committee exposed the different FEUs trying to take over their movement as "charro organizations." The initial negotiations with Uruchurtu actually magnified the strike's importance and intensified the coalition's grievances.[27]

The president's failure to negotiate also added impetus to the movement. On August 24, the committee hijacked additional buses, drove them to the Zócalo, and respectfully called on President Ruiz Cortinez to come out of the National Palace to address the students' demands. This was a practice that would be repeated in all of the major student uprisings of the long sixties.[28] It would be an error to see the students as unilaterally opposed to the president at this time. Numerous banners and Goyas professing support of the president were evident during the march. The president, however, declined to negotiate with the Popular Committee. Nonetheless, the students used this opportunity to try to dispel the myths they saw portrayed in the press regarding their own motivations and to set the record straight with regard to the underlying causes of unrest and violence. Before the National Palace in the historic Zócalo plaza, failing to address their own recourse to embrace a violent attitude, they spoke out to publicly accuse the ACM leaders of being responsible for the violence that had taken place during the burning of the bus terminal by having sent a group of provocateurs to instigate the students.[29] Moreover, they denied that their strike had been led by communists, as was so persistently stressed in the press.[30]

What had started as a small-scale demonstration had quickly evolved into a massive student protest and a movement beginning to spread beyond the university. Disappointed that the president refused to engage them in a dialogue, the students drove the buses back to Ciudad Universitaria. There, a smaller group of students from the Popular Committee had taken over the university's radio station and publishing house. These provided the platform for announcing and publishing their manifestoes and for keeping students informed about the latest developments of the movement.[31] The students' efforts caught the attention of two important figures symbolizing for the politicized student body resistance against the brutal forces of the *granaderos*: Demetrio Vallejo (associated with railroad strikers) and Othón Salazar (prominent leader in the teacher's movement). Both of these sent letters of support to the Popular Committee that leaders read out loud to the students.[32] Soon other key figures outside of the university joined the students, including a group of teachers, as well as outspoken *panistas* who saw this as an opportunity to expose the authoritarian and arbitrary role of the government in power.[33]

Significantly, the students managed to receive the critical support of Nabor Carrillo, the university's rector, who placed the events within a larger context of resistance. Carrillo stated publicly that, despite claims made by the ACM's José Valdovinos and the press, the protest was not a spontaneous reaction led by a small number of provocateurs financed by communist forces. Rather, it was part of a massive movement that had been sparked by a variety of social and economic problems. In exchange for his public support, Nabor Carrillo asked the students to "act with prudence." In particular, the rector pleaded with the universitarios in charge of the strike to learn from past mistakes and to reject acts of provocation and violence.[34] The involvement of rector Carrillo proved vital to the development of the strike. As historian Russell Morris notes in his study of political violence in Mexico during this period, "[By] defining the student protest as 'a grave social conflict' rather than a 'clear-cut conflict between the students and the government,'" both students and authorities "were absolved of blame, and the existing situation became 'a good opportunity to resolve the problem.'"[35] Carrillo's actions must be understood to be closely linked to a defense of the autonomy of the university as he saw it. He declared that his administration under no circumstances would tolerate the entry of the Federal Army or granaderos into the schools, as had happened two years earlier in the Politécnico.

The next day, August 25, the student protest led by the Popular Committee reached its climax when it created the GCE and took steps to implement important democratic innovations. The Popular Committee chose the name Gran Comisión Estudiantil apparently in homage to the independent union affiliated with Demetrio Vallejo called Gran Comisión Pro-Aumento del Salario.[36] According to an interview with one of its most vocal participants, it was formed "as a direct protest against the charro control of the FEU," which students began to see as "obsolete and at odds" with their "democratic" movement.[37] Another participant similarly remembered that faced with the threat imposed by charro leaders, "we came together and tenaciously planned the conditions that from then on leaders would have to abide by in order to represent the movement." He then went on to say, "After heated debates in a general assembly we collectively decided that we would not allow representatives from the Student Societies or from the University Student Federation to [co-opt] our movement for their own benefit." He concluded, "This is why we created an executive committee of struggle. [We] called [it] the 'Grand Student Commission.'" This decision, he insisted, was done "collectively to avoid both speculation and corruption within our movement."[38]

With the aim of breaking from the traditional vertical decision-making of the FEUs into something more democratic, the leaders of the GCE tried to implement a student apparatus in which all student representatives from the various schools had equal voting power concerning the direction of the strike.[39] Another innovation was the creation of asambleas, or student assemblies, in which "the most important decisions of the strike were made collectively." Oscar González later commented that these asambleas "defined student politics throughout the sixties," as did the "headaches that came along with them." He explained that, "from then on, all decisions inside the university were made collectively, often lasting long hours of the night primarily because of the various ideological positions endorsed by the students." And then he sarcastically lamented, "But despite our factionalism and the verbal attacks we were all convinced that we wanted to implement a more democratic system!"[40] Thus, practicing a new sense of democracy at the schools not only proved to be a difficult process but, as would happen throughout the 1960s, it was also frequently threatened by the students themselves in the forms of student violence and factionalism.

To further demonstrate student solidarity with the pueblo and their commitment to respecting the rector's plea for nonviolence, the GCE organized a peaceful torchlight parade on the following day (August 26) from the Monument of the Revolution to the Zócalo. The famous Palillo played a key role by getting thousands of students from the preparatorias involved.[41] The image of thousands of lit candles held aloft during the parade conveyed a civil demeanor of resistance on the part of the universitarios that earned the attention of more sympathizers.[42] Among the marchers were a group of intellectuals led by Carlos Fuentes, Jaime García Terres, and Fernando Benitez, whose public denunciations of the betrayal of the Mexican Revolution would soon pave the way for the emergence of a New Left within the university (see Chapter 6).[43] In a show of solidarity, the universitarios were accompanied in this parade by more than thirty thousand outspoken unionists, including teachers as well as railroad, petroleum, telegraph, and bus workers. These individuals displayed banners demanding the rescinding of the fare increases, the municipalization of the urban transportation system, an "end to charrismo," and, once again, respect for the president.[44] The universitarios were also joined by politécnicos and *normalistas* who saw in the momentum of the UNAM strike a chance to air their own grievances anew. Once the march reached the Zócalo, the protestors met with Benito Coquet, the secretary to the president, to whom the students presented their demands. They made it clear that they would continue their protest until all the students arrested during the strike were released from prison.[45] As noted earlier, such an act of solidarity between politécnicos, normalistas, and universitarios was unprecedented. The three groups of students understood the importance of this "exceptional moment."[46]

On the night of August 27, after three months of preparations, politécnicos, normalistas, and universitarios came together to form a "Tripartite Alliance," and a self-conscious understanding of the movement as reaching even beyond the boundaries of el estudiantado was born. Following a series of asambleas, they collectively celebrated the alliance with Goyas and Huélums (UNAM and IPN chants, respectively) previously used during American football games and other cultural events as expressions of school rivalries (see Chapter 2).[47] Swept up in the enthusiasm brought on by the Tripartite Alliance, students from then on began to speak of a "movement," as opposed to a student protest, uprising, or rebellion. The impact of this change in thinking as well as the *desmadre* that accompanied these protests would be felt throughout the 1960s in marches and assemblies in support of the Cuban Revolution, against the war in Vietnam and the 1965 U.S. occupation of the Dominican Republic, in solidarity with the medical student strike the same year, and especially against authoritarianism in Mexico as represented by the granaderos, corrupt police authorities, political prisoners, the Law of Social Dissolution, and the older generation of activists.[48]

Once united, the students used the Tripartite Alliance to expose what they saw as the authoritarianism of the postrevolutionary state and to pave the way for greater democracy in the labor sector and in their schools. The alliance demanded the eradication of the Law of Social Dissolution from the penal system, which was used freely by government authorities to punish students, and also the resignation of all school authorities who had allowed the Federal Army to occupy the schools.[49] In particular, the student alliance of 1958 called for the resignations of Alejo Peralta, the director of the National Polytechnic Institute (IPN), and José Valdovinos, the director of the ACM.[50] In the eyes of the students, both men represented the prototypical figures of charrismo. As noted earlier, Alejo Peralta was believed to have been personally responsible for the closing of the *internado*, the repression of politécnicos, and the transformation of the FNET into a charro student organization. As for Valdovinos, students were convinced that, in his attempt to recover the buses, Valdovinos had personally sent provocateurs dressed as students to harass the public, loot the streets, and incite students to take more drastic measures in the name of the movement.[51] The intent was to give the student movement a bad name. This was perhaps a return to a strategy that seemed to work in 1956 by creating a public outrage in the print media. According to the leading newspapers, the public had gone so far as to call for the creation of "vigilante citizen groups" capable of protecting the city from the young revoltosos (see Chapter 3).

The Tripartite Alliance dissolved when the student movement was officially called off on August 30 after a group of students from the GCE, together with Nabor Carrillo and Dr. Ricardo García Villalobos, the director of the School of Law, met with President Ruiz Cortinez to negotiate a peaceful solution. The end results appeared favorable to some students. The fare increase was canceled, and students who had been arrested during the disturbances were set free.[52] The students were notified of the president's decision in a letter that was first read to them by Carlos Tejeda, one of the principal leaders of the strike, on August 31. The letter was later published in the newspapers.[53] With the news, however, the students were immediately split into two conflicting camps. One group declared the student movement a great success and encouraged all students to return the buses to the ACM. The other and increasingly more militant group was determined to continue the strike until the question of municipalization was resolved and bus workers were allowed to form independent unions, free from CTM control. They accused the students who had met with Ruiz Cortinez, such as Oscar María Baruch and Alejandro Peraza, of having "sold out to authorities" and encouraged all students to keep the hijacked buses. Claiming that Baruch and Peraza had never fully severed their ties with the FEUs and had "betrayed" the movement, the two were expelled from the GCE.[54] With the Popular Committee split into two, the strike could not be sustained for much longer. By the first week of September the strike had ended. Students belonging to the more combative camp, who insisted on keeping the movement active, were instantly reduced to a small minority. Frustrated by the successful hijacking of the movement by charro leaders, this minority adopted a more militant strategy.[55] First, they engaged in a number of riots against the granaderos in support of labor strikes (such as those organized by the petroleum workers on September 6, 1958). Later they demanded more radical changes, including a call for a socialist system. Such divisions (that came hand in hand with calls for a more democratic Mexico) would remain the norm in student politics throughout the following decade.

Concessions and State Retrenchment

Under pressure from private interests in the last years of his six-year term, the tone of the Cortinez administration shifted to a much harder stance against the developing movement. Initially, the response of the Adolfo Ruiz Cortinez administration to some of the basic economic demands put forth by the workers seemed favorable. But the final months of the Ruiz Cortinez administration saw it become increasingly less tolerant. In part pressure came from divergent circles within the governing elite, the Right, the private sector, and the conservative press, who, echoing voices of disapproval from 1956, called for him to retaliate against the "traitors" to the nation with violence, if necessary. On the other hand, the president was also faced with an increasing number of workers who began to challenge the corporatist structure of the state by threatening to register with independent labor unions during elections, occupying larger public spaces (such as the Zócalo) during massive marches, establishing networks with other workers and students, and adopting more violent strategies.

Ruiz Cortinez issued his first official warning to the restive workers and students in his last presidential address on September 1, 1958. He stated in no uncertain terms that his government would use all the available power (*máxima energía*) to safeguard national unity, liberty, and economic progress. This was a radical change of tone from his previous presidential speeches in which Cortinez had repeatedly asked workers and campesinos "to have faith in the government" and to "be patient," as with time the fruits of the economic miracle would trickle down to all Mexicans.[56] Some excerpts from the president's speech illustrate his drastic change of tone: "We do not advocate violence," he said, "on the contrary, we condemn it. But when force becomes necessary to guarantee the law, the Government is obliged to employ it." Such was the case of the 1958 labor uprisings, when it had been clear that "certain agitators had launched systematic acts of provocation" against the nation. He explained, for example, that "confrontational and united," a handful of agitators in charge of these provocations had "compelled authorities to play a role which they cannot longer relinquish in order to guarantee" what he saw as the two principles that are necessary for economic progress: "order and liberty."[57]

The first organized groups to experience firsthand the meaning of such cautionary words were the teachers' union (the Revolutionary Teacher's Movement, MRM) and the Petroleum Workers' Union.[58] Yet actions against these unions came at the cost of losing the sympathies of the press. Marches organized by these striking workers, which enjoyed the support of the most radical group of universitarios, were violently put down by the still inexperienced and apparently poorly trained and largely uneducated granaderos, whose wholesale arrests of older female teachers and excessive use of teargas in the process outraged even the most loyal supporters of the government. Numerous editorial commentators wrote that, while the Mexican government should remain committed to ending the communist threat and disciplining the "rebels without a cause," it should not be at the price of transforming Mexico into another military state of Latin America.[59] Others, such as Abel Quezada, the famous and increasingly more defiant cartoonist, who distanced himself from the more conservative Freyre and Audiffred, were more direct in their criticism of the excessive use of force on the part of the riot police. They pleaded with city authorities to restore order but to do so institutionally through the application of the law.[60] Following the brutal campaign of repression by the granaderos, police authorities moved to imprison the labor leaders under the Law of Social Dissolution and replace them with new local bosses. Workers who had engaged in clandestine meetings were fired and their local headquarters were ransacked by Office of Federal Security (DFS) agents.[61]

A hard-line Cold War and nationalist rhetoric buttressed by the press against the labor movement initially ensued. As had been the case with the politécnicos two years earlier, a campaign of defamation was carried out via the conservative press. Accused of having connections with international communist forces, strikers were said to be storing firearms, Molotov cocktails, and Marxist propaganda in their homes and headquarters. They were also accused of taking advantage of the real workers in an irresponsible manner that threatened the stability of the nation and the safety and job security of all workers. As would happen again in 1968, the strike was labeled "illegal" and the strikers as "terrorists" and "saboteurs." The accusations against the workers served as a prelude to direct action against their movement's key organizers. Demetrio Vallejo, Hugo Ponce de León, and Alejandro Pérez Enriquez were imprisoned by applying, once again, the catchall crime of "social dissolution." Other lesser-known leaders were held incommunicado until matters cooled off. A total of nine thousand workers were fired from their jobs. Police and secret agents of the DFS broke into strikers' homes and, at gunpoint, forced them to go back to work. The headquarters of the independent unions as well as those of the Mexican Communist Party (PCM) were ransacked. In the end, the insurgent leaders were replaced by progovernment labor leaders or charros.[62] These solutions on the part of the government would continue to radicalize the more militant student groups of UNAM that, in the wake of the Cuban Revolution, would distance themselves from the moderate New Left by creating new organizations, opening new spaces of contestation, and adopting an increasingly violent position.

Conclusion: The Origins of Mexico's New Left

Unlike previous student demonstrations at UNAM, the movement that emerged in 1958 brought together for the very first time a broad coalition that included universitarios (including *preparatorianos*), politécnicos, and normalistas. These groups of students had traditionally kept apart because of their class differences, but also because of cultural and social rivalries. The tactics of charrismo had helped universitarios turn a blind eye to the massive strike of the politécnicos two years earlier. But the protests of 1958 challenged the control of charro leaders in both UNAM's FEU and the IPN's FNET. Unlike previous demonstrations, the demands collectively presented by the asambleas of the GCE directly challenged the vertical relations of power of the FEUs and student societies. These demands focused not on university academic policies but also on the same structural problems that had contributed to the consolidation of charrismo in the labor sector, including authoritarianism, corruption, and government-sponsored violence and provocation.

Importantly, the 1958 student strike, combined with other political movements, offered a "vital alternative" and a "unique perspective," as rising intellectual Carlos Monsiváis noted in his autobiography, that would give rise to Mexico's New Left.[63] In the context of UNAM, this innovative leftist movement was distinguished by a new wave of activism characterized not only by its democratic demands but also by its festive desmadre and violent approach. Indirectly drawing on the experiences of the politécnicos two years earlier, and especially the examples of the labor leaders, this new wave of student activism and festive desmadre fostered a public, more aggressive, and even violent form of resistance that would dominate student politics thereafter. In general, acts of protest by these rising representatives of Mexico's New Left were directed at repressive authorities (not necessarily at the government) and would eventually be framed in revolutionary terms. This rising wave of activism was distinguished by a more conscious effort to address larger structural problems of the nation. These problems included the rise of authoritarianism, political impunity, and the lack of democracy as represented by the granaderos, political prisoners, the FEU, and the Law of Social Dissolution. Student efforts notwithstanding, the 1958 student and labor strikes were not able to break away entirely from the corporatist structure of the state. This only began to take place on a larger scale with the creation of Comités de Lucha (fighting committees) by the new student organizations that would explode in numbers and thus further factionalize the student movement in the wake of the Cuban Revolution.

PART III

Student Unrest and Response
in the Aftermath of the Cuban Revolution

6 Contested Notions of Revolution

O N AUGUST 14, 1960, a group of young *universitarios* gathered together around the statue of Miguel Alemán in the middle of the night. The purpose of this meeting was to dynamite this monument to the former president and founder of Ciudad Universitaria (CU) in the name of "revolution."[1] Because of the students' lack of experience with this type of explosive, however, things did not go as planned. Nonetheless, the loud explosion did manage to destroy a significant portion of the presidential statue (see Illustration 6.1).

The press was outraged and demanded that a thorough investigation be undertaken and made available to the public.[2] Five days later, Manuel Rangel Escamilla, the director of the Office of Federal Security (DFS), delivered a report to the Ministry of Interior based on information collected by one of the countless informants working for his department on "student problems" during this period. In the report, Escamilla wrote, albeit with a degree of uncertainty, that the people responsible for the explosion of Alemán's statue were linked to a group of students who had tried unsuccessfully to blow up the statue two days earlier. In particular, the report pointed to the student group "Against the Statue" and to a young female actress enrolled in the university. The latter had recently appeared in Giovanni Karporaal's *El Brazo Fuerte* ("The Authoritarian Hand," 1958), an experimental film that, despite its censorship by the government, had been shown in one of the numerous *cineclubs* that had emerged at the National Autonomous University of Mexico (UNAM) during this period.[3]

ILLUS. 6.1. Rius, "Cartoon of the Week," *Siempre!*, August 31, 1960. The caption roughly reads: "They wanted to take a closer look at his savings account..." (Reproduced with permission from *Siempre!*)

Six years later, on June 4, 1966, on a more militant campus, a second and more successful attempt to destroy the statue with explosives was made. The bombers this time managed to decapitate this important symbol of ale-manismo. According to an article published in *Excélsior*, the "provocateurs" responsible for this latest act of vandalism were most likely associated with the schools of Economics or Political Science. By the mid-1960s the Trotsky-ites and the Maoists associated with these schools had become infamous for their use of violence.[4] As with the first explosion, the government's main institution of surveillance was asked to make a thorough investigation. In his report, the director of the DFS, Fernando Gutiérrez Barrios, determined that this violent act could not be attributed merely to a small group of disgruntled students. Instead, he concluded that at least two hundred young people, including several members of the infamous *porra* gangs, had been involved.[5] To prevent future attacks on the statue, two of the alleged leaders believed to have connections with the Mexican Communist Party (PCM) were arrested, and a group of pseudo students with close ties to former president Miguel Alemán were sent to protect what remained of the statue.[6] But rejection of the statue on the part of the disgruntled university community would continue. In 1968, a group composed of young students, intellectuals, and famous artists (including Adolfo Mexiac and José Luis Cuevas) launched a dual critique of alemanismo and the revolutionary nationalism of the muralist movement by painting an "ephemeral mural" over the metal sheets that school authorities had previously placed over the statue, as a despairing effort to avoid further attacks on Miguel Alemán.[7]

Clearly, the political climate inside UNAM had changed significantly during the 1960s. Condemnation of the government on the part of the students was no longer expressed solely within the confines of the National Polytechnic Institute (IPN). The student strike in defense of bus drivers in 1958 had made it clear that students at UNAM had also grown frustrated with the corruption and repression that had come to characterize Mexico during this period. Yet the emphasis on "revolution" during the 1961 statue bombing and the repeated defamations of the image of a former president, thereafter, suggests that universitarios had adopted a new language and attitude of dissent. For some, the notion of revolution would include the open sanctioning of violence. For others, as would happen in other parts of the world during the 1960s, it would rather be understood in countercultural terms.

Over the last forty years scholars from different disciplines have engaged in numerous debates concerning the legacy (or lack thereof) of the "turbulent" decade of the sixties. Yet, by now, they nearly all agree that the explosion of student protest that characterized this period was a global phenomenon. It was one that not only rejoiced in the possibility of progressive changes, but also ignited an unprecedented wave of reactionary violence.[8] Students residing in different corners of the world envisioned themselves as part of the same global fight against capitalist exploitation, communist repression, colonial rule, and imperialist domination.[9] For historians Arthur Marwick and Martin Klimke, the rise of this shared consciousness can be attributed to a number of structural changes that developed in most modern societies

in the aftermath of World War II. In particular, they point to a technological revolution in television and satellite communications, massive improvements in material life, a dramatic increase in university enrollment, and an
unprecedented international cultural exchange in music, film, and study-
abroad programs. Taken together, they allowed for greater student awareness
of the massive racial upheavals that had swept the United States since the 1950s
and introduced students to new concerns for civil and personal rights. They
also enabled students to forge alternative lifestyles that questioned traditional
Judeo-Christian sexual mores and Western notions of progress and modernity.[10]

Scholars of the sixties have stressed that the region of Latin America has
not been immune to the same structural changes that developed in Europe
and the United States. Literary critic Diana Sorensen has defined this period
not simply as a chronological decade stretching from 1960 to 1970 but as a
"heuristic" category spanning 1959 to 1973. Sorensen argues that the period
saw the emergence of a distinct "spirit of utopia" and "revolution," accompanied by a novel rhythm of "despair," reactionary politics, and political violence.[11] As others have argued, from this tension emerged an innovative sense
of "liberation," primarily epitomized by the Cuban Revolution and its mythical *barbudos* (bearded) leaders, Fidel Castro and Che Guevara. For university
and secondary students throughout the continent, the terms "liberation" and
"revolution" became the key words of the day. Without question, their field
of meanings was political. For example, the terms were centrally linked to
an unprecedented awareness of international solidarity and a revaluation of
the importance of ideology in nearly all Latin American campuses. Moreover,
they served as part of an innovative "language of dissent" used to articulate
with urgency the opposition to capitalism and imperialism. The terms would
also be put into service to oppose the reformism, authoritarian structure, and
corporatist apparatus of communist parties, labor movements, and an older
generation of leftist intellectuals.[12] But as other scholars have recently pointed
out, the terms "liberation" and "revolution" meant something broadly cultural as well. A globalized media in which they participated introduced Latin
American student activists to an almost instantaneous spread of news and
images of similar protests taking place in other parts of the world. It also
allowed them to construct a collective identity that opened the possibility for
alternative lifestyles and new countercultural spaces of expression.[13]

Student manifestoes, bulletins, and newspapers, as well as films, comics, and academic journals produced and consumed at UNAM during this period speak to the multiple meanings of the terms "liberation" and "revolution." However, an extensive look at these sources over the long sixties reveals that the overwhelming majority of leftist students did not want to overthrow the government or implement a socialist regime in Mexico. Rather, the demands for "revolutionary changes" were overwhelmingly "moderate" and "cultural" in nature. This continued to be the case following the Cuban Revolution, whose impact on Mexican student politics was evident in four significant ways: the explosion of new student organizations, the creation of innovative spaces of contestation, the revaluation of the importance of ideology, and the rise of reactionary violence. In particular, this chapter argues that, influenced by the spirit of the Cuban Revolution and supported by a new generation of Mexican intellectuals, UNAM students played a crucial role in the growth of Mexico's New Left. With the 1956 and 1958 student uprisings in the background, universitarios created new spaces of countercultural and political contestation by adopting an international language of dissent and by contrasting the massive improvements in material life in the nation's capital with everyday social problems, including their own highly overcrowded campus.[14] Here, students demanded the improvement of school facilities, but more significantly, they redefined the importance of Marxism, reconceptualized the meaning of the Mexican Revolution, and challenged traditional notions of *mexicanidad* (national identity promoted by the state). At the same time, the new student culture that emerged in the 1960s also factionalized the university. It introduced new forms of student violence that students welcomed to compete with the *porro* gangs and *granaderos*. In 1968, this decision would jeopardize the universitarios' democratic demands. As it had happened in the past, conservative critics of the student Left would reference this and other forms of student militancy as "proof" that the schools had been hijacked by "radical provocateurs" (see Chapters 7 and 8). Before examining the role these actors played in the radicalization of universitarios during the 1960s, it is crucial to explore how the "New Left" was conceptualized in Mexico as initially championed by a group of intellectuals and founders of the weekly magazine *El Espectador*. These magazine producers and contributors, along with Rius, the author of the cartoon depicted in the introduction, became extraordinarily influential in the cultural and political lives of universitarios. Their critiques portrayed a callous government that, they argued, had ostensibly betrayed its own revolution.

El Espectador and the Rise of Mexico's New Left

The Mexican left must reinvent itself by creating a new unity that takes into consideration the demands proposed by Mexico's democracy today. This [New Left] can no longer be imposed from above. [To avoid representing another] "progressive" ornament by the State, it must transform itself into a left from below.— *El Espectador*[15]

In 1959 Manuel Marcué Padiñas, Enrique González Pedrero, Víctor Flores Olea, Luis Villoro, and, most notably, rising intellectual Carlos Fuentes came together to form the monthly magazine *El Espectador*, the voice of the New Left in Mexico. Similar to the concurrent New Left in Britain and in the United States, the Mexican New Left consciously sought to distinguish itself from the communist institutions and figures endorsed by the Soviet Union, distant itself from dogmatic Marxism, make an explicit criticism of the apathetic tendencies in society, demand specific solutions to abolish the different structures of oppression, and open new democratic spaces in which people could exercise their constitutional rights from the bottom up.[16] In particular, Mexico's New Left argued that its supporters could move forward and assume the role of the "social activist," concerned with "global justice," "equality," "Third World solidarity," and "participatory democracy," without necessarily embracing the label of "socialist" or becoming an official member of the Communist Party. Rather than relying on guidance from the Old Left, the Mexican New Left emphasized a view "from below" that focused directly on the undemocratic qualities of local and national institutions.[17]

The influential young writers who founded the monthly magazine took on the role of expressing this emerging school of thought.[18] *El Espectador* first appeared in July of 1959 with the support of Manuel Marcué Pardiñas's *Talleres Gráficos de México*.[19] In its initial mission statement, *El Espectador* identified a "moment of crisis" in Mexico's political history resulting from the Old Left's abandonment of the core principles of the Mexican Revolution. Rather than enhance democratic principles, the close relationship of the Old Left with the postrevolutionary Mexican state had caused the former to succumb under the latter's authoritarian leadership structure.[20] In particular, *El Espectador* accused Communist Party leaders in Mexico and Vicente Lombardo Toledano's Partido Popular of failing to support the aligned labor and student movements of 1958 in their fight for the creation of "independent" unions. To the New Left, independent and uncorrupted unions were sacrosanct in national democratic history, given their role in the emergence of the Left in Mexico during the formative period of the revolution.[21]

The expressed goals for resolving the crisis resonate with the wishes and language circulating among the student bodies of the time. The collaborators of *El Espectador* argued that privileged intellectuals (like themselves) could no longer afford to play the role of passive observers, but instead should become "social activists" capable of "expressing with clarity and passion the needs of the people."[22] As writers they felt obligated to inhabit the role of "organic" social actor responsible for "informing [the people] in a more inclusive [voice], criticizing all reprehensible acts, praising and supporting the good ones, and including in their pages the opinions of those men whose democratic ideas were omitted in the [official] publications."[23] Only a commitment to defending freedom of speech and the creation of open spaces, they concluded, could undermine the multiple expressions of "paternal authoritarianism" that had historically characterized the different institutions sponsored by the state, including political violence and the different forms of neo-*caciquismo* that had developed in postrevolutionary Mexico, such as *charrismo*. To overcome these "superimposed" maladies, they claimed that the New Left must see the state for what it should be—that is, a "representative institution," and not a "mediator or supreme authority that paternally resolves the struggles of our social classes." Put differently, "[D]emocracy could never be imposed from above" but rather must be achieved from the bottom up, "when people decide to exercise it."

In more specific terms, the magazine's pages spoke of the "urgent need" to defend Mexico's natural resources from the two historical enemies of democracy and economic justice, "imperialism and colonialism." They insisted that the New Left must support the "neo-revolutionary movement" recently organized by the labor sector for the purpose of establishing independent unions. Once this victory was won, they advocated engaging the masses to pressure the state to invest in the most elementary principles of the revolution, namely:

> [To] complete the agrarian reform until communal lands were equally
> distributed among the neediest of rural Mexico, to progressively nationalize
> all natural resources, to restructure the economy so that it would benefit all
> Mexicans and not just a small minority within the "Revolutionary Family,"
> to create opportune and reliable institutions of credit, and to invest in the
> most basic industries of infrastructure.[24]

Stirred by that other hemispheric neighboring revolution, that in Cuba, this self-described "organic generation" of intellectuals declared, "[Our] Revolution of 1910 had acquired a new meaning. It had [the potential of] becoming alive," meaning that the New Left should be responsible for resuscitating the Constitution of 1917, "not because we believe that it represents a perfect law . . . but rather because in it we can find 'the will of the nation.'"[25]

Officially the fervor was short-lived, but the die had been cast. After a total of six issues, *El Espectador* ceased publication in 1960. But its principal protagonists continued to work together, first in the creation of the more radical weekly *Política* in 1960, and later in various other forums.[26] These included the National Liberation Movement (MLN) congresses supported by former president Lázaro Cárdenas, which would adopt many of the same ideas and programs originally proposed in the pages of *El Espectador*, including the demand for the coming together of existing progressive institutions, personalities, and political factions under a unified leftist front.[27] Once unified in 1961, members of the MLN further echoed the voices recorded in *El Espectador* by calling for greater national respect to the "sister Republic of Cuba" and demanding that the government embrace a more progressive internal policy that would guarantee better distribution of the nation's wealth, full control of Mexico's natural resources, and the achievement of greater political independence from the United States.[28] The contributors to the magazine also played an instrumental role in expanding other political spaces inside UNAM, including the Dirección de Difusión Cultural (DDC) and the Casa del Lago.[29] As historian Deborah Cohn has documented, these cultural centers "became key pole[s] in Mexico City's field of cultural production and outreach . . . where intellectual and popular culture converged." These intellectual activists, from *El Espectador*, "extended the university to the streets" by offering "courses, lectures, roundtable discussions, exhibitions, theater, ballet, recitals, films," and so on.[30]

At UNAM, the DDC and the Casa del Lago would also play a significant role in the politicization of students. As professors of political science, sociology, history, journalism, and the arts, key contributors to *El Espectador* would create new spaces of contestation that would influence the direction of student activism throughout the 1960s, most notably a revamped university magazine (*Revista de la Universidad de Mexico*), a renovated university radio station (Radio UNAM), and the creation of new cineclubs that would introduce students to experimental, countercultural, and international films.

Nonetheless, while the rise of this New Left would result in renewed energy, ideas, and organizations on campus, its growth would also become part of a process of bifurcation that would create a wedge between the Old Left and a set of energized radical groups on the far Left that, largely inspired by the Cuban Revolution, would call for more violent strategies in their activism.

The Polarization of Leftist Student Politics

An explosion of new student organizations characterized UNAM during the early 1960s.[31] The first of these initially demonstrated a low level of political and structural sophistication. But with the increasing support of national and international actors in the wake of the Cuban Revolution, a large number of them gradually evolved into sophisticated political entities broadly self-identified as "leftist." These organizations effectively radicalized the university. But despite various attempts at unification, these Left-leaning organizations never constituted a homogeneous front. Instead, there were at least three factions of the Left that radicalized student politics in Mexico during the 1960s, including the traditional Old Left, the moderate New Left, and the Orthodox Left. Ultimately, only one of these would have the greatest impact.

The traditional Old Left managed to create a temporary but nonetheless crucial base inside the university. By and large, this group was distinguished by the close relationship it established with the Mexican Communist Party (PCM), which, following the Cuban Revolution, began to increase its presence inside the university. According to a young member of the PCM, it did so by "paying greater attention to rising talented young members of the Juventud Comunista Mexicana (JCM) that since the 1930s had been ignored by the PCM."[32] Initially, the demands made by these student organizations were broadly characterized by a general (and often vague) support of the Cuban Revolution in which "national sovereignty," "economic development," and "anti-imperialism in solidarity with the Latin American people" became the most common slogans. With time, as these organizations grew in number and in importance, the demands became more specific. Echoing requests by politécnicos and other sectors of popular education during the 1950s, for example, they demanded the reincorporation of the internado and subsidized cafeterias, scholarships for students with low incomes, and "better schools."[33]

The support of the PCM bore fruit in 1963 with the emergence of the Central Nacional de Estudiantes Democráticos (CNED). It was originally conceived as a broad student front and, similar to Cárdenas's National Liberation Movement, CNED aimed to unite all the different national student organizations that broadly identified with the Left. To that end, CNED organized three national congresses at which representative delegates from all secondary schools and universities were invited to present their grievances. The first and most important of these congresses took place in Morelia, Michoacán, in March of 1963, as more than 100,000 students were said to have been represented by 250 delegates.[34] A group of students presented a political manifesto entitled "The Declaration of Morelia" that came to define the political tone of CNED as well as that of many other student organizations of the 1960s. In this declaration students presented an analytical critique of the principal problems in higher education, called for "greater national unity," and argued that "only the creation of a truly democratic student movement" would put an end to police brutality and political imprisonment at the hands of corrupt authority figures. In addition, the Declaration of Morelia stated that in order to bring such a movement into being, students would have to make a stronger effort to "incorporate the voice of the pueblo" by reappropriating the older banners of "popular education," "agrarian reform," "democracy," and "workers' independence."[35]

CNED would have a relatively short life. In 1966, just three years after the Declaration of Morelia, it would begin to lose many of its most vocal members to other student organizations that found the leadership of CNED too close to the government in power. In 1968 student activists would go so far as to accuse members of this organization of having sold their organization to *charro* leaders (see Chapters 7 and 8). However, the importance of CNED should not be underestimated. Its congresses supported by the PCM offered an important forum that representative leaders used to denounce what students at the base identified as violations of an authoritarian state that they alleged were otherwise ignored by the media, including the abuse of the Law of Social Dissolution on the part of the governing elite.[36] In addition, the delegates' insistence on reinforcing national student unity transformed CNED into a political mass movement that forged new political circles and a new leadership that would play a central role later in the 1968 student movement.[37]

Besides the front endorsed by the Mexican Communist Party, the leftist presence inside UNAM during the early 1960s also included a broad range of new groups that began to challenge the older generation of intellectuals. This heterogeneous group included representatives of the progressive wing of the Institutional Revolutionary Party, cardenistas, and militants of the JCM who briefly put aside their differences for a variety of reasons. Some factions joined together to support the rectorship of Ignacio Chávez (1961–1966) with the common goal of leaving alemanistas with limited control of the board of trustees and a diminished presence inside the student organizations. Others united to support the policies of the MLN and to promote a better understanding of the Cuban Revolution. With time, this broad coalition included a growing number of young male and female *político/as* and intellectuals who became involved in student politics but did not necessarily identified themselves as "chavistas," "cardenistas," "communists," "feminists," or official members of the MLN, but rather as "independent leftist thinkers"; together, they would be identified with Mexico's New Left. With names such as "The New Left," "The Patricio Lumumba Group," and "The Second Declaration of Havana Movement" (among others), these New Left student organizations challenged the hierarchical, authoritarian, and orthodox structure of both the state-sponsored University Student Federation (FEU) and the student organizations associated with the Old Left.[38] Furthermore, this new generation of leftists looked at recent historical events to underscore and define their movement in a more specific way than had previous student activists. They spoke of issues concerning students worldwide, including the Cuban Revolution, and to a lesser extent the liberation movements in Africa, the Black Power and Free Speech movements in the United States, and the North American invasions of the Dominican Republic and Vietnam.[39] But above all, the student organizations of the New Left were primarily concerned with local issues that universitarios felt impacted their lives much more concretely, including police brutality and the lack of democratic spaces inside their schools. Although the most outspoken women activists of these new organizations, such as Paquita Calvo Zapata, Margarita Suzán, and María Eugenia Espinoza Calzada (among many others), must have experienced discrimination from their male *compañeros* and certainly shared a new sense of freedom as they too protested in the public sphere, they in no way made a feminist statement (just yet).[40] The priority of these early student activists rather seemed to be on Marxism and social consciousness.[41] As in other parts of Latin America, questions related to the conflicting relationship between feminist movements and male leftists and eventually between feminists and nonfeminist women activists would not take place until the mid-1970s.[42]

Mexico's moderate New Left, inspired by the pages of *El Espectador*, would demand new leadership that better reflected their views and policies. They wished for an alternative to what they saw as the "anachronistic" image of Vicente Lombardo Toledano, the Partido Popular, and the Mexican Communist Party. Lázaro Cárdenas did not necessarily come to be seen as representative of the Old Left, but with the exception of his leadership of the MLN, students generally found him irrelevant to their struggle. Instead, the New Left that emerged around 1958 referred with greater frequency to the political efforts of popular leaders who refused to be subjugated to the revolutionary family, leaders like Othón Salazar in the teachers' movement, Demetrio Vallejo in the railroad workers' movement, and UNAM professor and writer José Revueltas. A year later, these politicized students of the New Left would find a more coherent voice through the example of Cuba and other liberation movements, and would adopt new "heroes" (see below).

To present their demands, these student organizations made use of both new and old strategies of struggle. As politécnicos had done in the past, universitarios of the early 1960s also distributed informational bulletins throughout the city, led numerous torchlight parades in front of their schools, organized marches to the Zócalo from the Monument of the Revolution, and created self-defense brigades to prevent attacks by agents provocateurs. New Left organizations notably held innovative asambleas in school auditoriums where students democratically discussed important decisions regarding a variety of issues. At the same time, reflecting an increasingly aggressive stance that simultaneously characterized the New Left, students also hijacked transportation buses and made the strategic blocking of streets fairly common tactics of political struggle. Some became known for erecting barricades inside the schools, as small groups of universitarios would momentarily take over the radio station to inform the public about their movement. Other students made a habit of breaking into publishing houses to print their copious manifestoes (which proliferated following the Cuban Revolution), while some became famous for organizing festive acts of protest in which symbolic elements of cultural celebrations (including novatadas) were reappropriated, destroyed, or disrupted. The most common of these defiant acts included the burial of the Mexican Constitution of 1917 (which students felt "had been violated by the government in power"), the burning of effigies, and the denigration of Uncle Sam figures representing American imperialism.[43]

Finally, leftist activity inside the university during the 1960s also included more militant groups that, armed with orthodox Marxism and greatly influenced by the writings of UNAM professor José Revueltas, sought revolutionary changes with a capital "R," as the prelude to the implementation of a socialist system. In particular, these self-proclaimed "Revolutionary" students of the New Left were influenced by Revueltas's piercing critiques of the Mexican Communist Party for having failed to take a leading position during the railroad workers' strike of the late 1950s; these students, in agreement with their mentor, saw these labor strikes as the most important confrontation led by the working class against the bourgeoisie up until that time. But especially resonant for these students was Revueltas's critique of the moderate New Left, concerning what he interpreted as the misguided assumption that the solution to the proletariat problem could be found in the Mexican Revolution. His intriguing metaphor referring to a "headless proletariat" is worth noting:

> It is difficult to find a parallel [in other countries] to the phenomenon
> that has taken place in Mexico: the consciousness of the working class has
> remained enchanted by ideologies that are foreign to its class. For the last
> fifty years, [members of the working class] have been particularly mad
> over the bourgeois ideology of democracy without having to first conquer
> [political] independence . . . .This historical madness . . . has transformed
> the members of the Mexican working class into proletarians without heads,
> [worse yet] into people whose heads over their shoulders are foreign to them
> [*un proletariado sin cabeza . . . que tiene sobre sus hombros una cabeza que no
> es la suya*].[44]

Here, and in other similar writings, Orthodox Left students noticed that Revueltas not only echoed what many intellectuals during this period were contending (such as those who participated in the Centro de Estudios Mexicanos)—namely, that the "Mexican Revolution was dead," but, more resonant to them, that neither the revolution's nationalist tendencies nor ideological tones were relevant to the interests of the working class.[45]

Broadly self-identified as "Maoists," "Trotskyites," and "Guevarists," these student organizations were characterized by self-criticism and ideological experimentation. In contrast to the moderate groups of the New Left, these more radical groups only represented a small minority of students.[46] Like comparable organizations elsewhere, these Orthodox Left groups believed that revolutionary consciousness was a struggle in which only a few students were capable of engaging, primarily as a result of the students' "bourgeois upbringing." To acquire the proper state of consciousness, they welcomed not only self-criticism but also heated debates regarding a variety of issues that ranged from the Cuban Revolution, to the writings and ideas of José Revueltas, Mao Tse-tung, Che Guevara, and Régis Debray, to the merits and errors of international and national models of resistance, such as those championed by the Black Panthers in the United States, the Tupamaros in Uruguay, and the peasant-student coalition that came together to attack the Madera Barracks in Chihuahua in 1965.[47]

One of the most polarizing issues was, in fact, the use of violence as a political strategy. For instance, one group of students, the Alianza de Izquierda Revolucionaria de Economía (AIRE), welcomed the second blast at Miguel Alemán's statue with enthusiasm and praised the Trotskyites behind it as "a sign of repulsion" on the part of the students against the "intolerable levels of corruption" that had come to characterize each of the different levels of the government "under the tutelage of the 'revolutionary family.'" Extending this argument, AIRE contended that by the mid-1960s there was very little difference between Miguel Alemán, Lázaro Cárdenas, López Mateos, or Díaz Ordaz. "State capitalism," they argued, "is no more than a socializing screen" employed by all the people in positions of power for "the accumulation of greater capital." They added:

> The "Revolution made Government"—is the administrative council of the same capitalists that exploit and repress our pueblo . . . . The beheading of Alemán's statue must be understood as an act of rebellion . . . . It symbolizes our culmination of a greater consciousness as militants and as [real] Revolutionaries who must join forces with the workers and the pueblo in the name of socialism.[48]

Thus, for these students, the explosion sent a clear message that alemanismo was finished at UNAM and that many universitarios disapproved of the "corruption," "lack of democracy," and "violent authoritarianism" that they believed characterized the administrations of Adolfo López Mateos and Gustavo Díaz Ordaz. To support their contention, AIRE noted that dozens of students present at the explosion had chanted "Death to Díaz Ordaz. Death to the bad government."[49] In contrast, other Orthodox Left students dismissed acts like these as "mindless adventurism" and argued that they only encouraged "provocateurs" to engage in similar behavior, which the government then exploited as an excuse to use force.[50]

Despite similar tactical and minor ideological differences, the majority of these Orthodox Left organizations shared a common dislike of students affiliated with the Mexican Communist Party, and what they identified as the "anachronistic" authoritarian leaders. In particular, largely influenced by the positions taken by Revueltas against the PCM, these students rejected the hierarchical structure that characterized the student organizations affiliated with the JCM and accused their members of elitism, calling them "defenders of the excesses of Stalinism," "puppets of the bourgeois government," and "opportunists who only cared about their personal political ambitions."[51] To demonstrate their alternative, these student organizations promoted the use of "rotating cells" in which all members of their organizations (regardless of seniority or intellectual skills) were required to share all of the different jobs that their struggle entailed, after undergoing an extensive program of Marxism. The Orthodox Left organizations also shared a deep distrust of all student activists of the moderate New Left, whom they accused of promoting bourgeois demands, and frequently disrupted their student assemblies with "verbal violence" by calling them "agents of the same system that repressed all students." Typically, the Orthodox Left students dismissed the idea put forth by the moderate New Left that all young people were capable of bringing about revolutionary change and argued instead that "only the radicalized students who had achieved a true understanding of Marxism-Leninism" could lead a proletarian revolution. For them, "Revolutionary change" could be achieved only by "becoming proletarians." To achieve this goal, they spent a great amount of time and energy organizing university workers, trying to create worker-student alliances, and attending work factories, where they built cells to "educate" workers about class struggle.[52]

Some attempts were made within the Orthodox Left to achieve some unity with other Left factions.[53] However, these fell short, and the Orthodox Left never really achieved the popularity that student organizations affiliated with the PCM did, let alone if we were to compare them to the reformist student organization of the moderate New Left. Many universitarios dismissed these Orthodox Left groups as "provocateurs," while the majority of activists grew increasingly impatient with their "verbal attacks."[54] By the end of the long sixties, disillusioned by their failure to forge strong political alliances with the working class and further convinced of the violent nature of the state—as would be demonstrated by the 1968 and 1971 student massacres—many of these radical students, including many young women, moved to marginal neighborhoods in Guadalajara, Cuernavaca, and Morelos or to isolated mountains in Chihuahua, Sinaloa, and Southern Mexico, to join guerrilla armies.[55] The leftist activism that came to dominate student politics inside UNAM during the early 1960s, in sum, experienced the same factionalism that had divided the Left at the national level for several decades. Yet each of these factions offered an innovative language of political contestation and all radicalized the student body of the university and their demands substantially.

Student Demands and the Creation of New Spaces of Contestation

> We do not want to be a rebellious generation but a revolutionary one.
> —*Nueva Izquierda*[56] [Student magazine]

While finding it important to articulate their more general goals associated with transforming the university into a genuinely democratic space, the students of the early 1960s presented a series of specific demands that would reappear on political banners throughout the decade and would eventually be represented at the national level during the 1968 student movement.[57] A wide assortment of activities aligned mostly with the moderate New Left blossomed on campus to help bring these demands to fruition. The most common student demands included the following:

— The firing of Federal District police chief General Luis Cueto Ramírez, whom students believed was largely responsible for incorporating violent mechanisms of mob control into police department tactics, including the use of tear gas and police vans known as julias.
— The immediate disbanding of the despised granaderos.
— The obliteration of the "social dissolution" provision from the criminal statutes, which students argued was "unconstitutional."
— Respect for the autonomy of the university with numerous references to "no more intervention in cultural institutions on the part of DFS agents, provocateurs, reactionary politicians, or the Federal Army," which had occupied the IPN in 1956 as well as the Teachers' School soon after.
— Immediate freedom for all political prisoners and "Liberty to all students, workers, and campesinos who were temporarily imprisoned or held incommunicado."

Other demands mentioned in their manifestoes and informational bulletins specifically referred to "Respect for the Constitution," "Respect for individual and social rights," "The disappearance of the American football team, por-ras, and the ultra conservative MURO," "The abolition of prison penalties for disturbance of public order," "Abolition of Article 82 from the University Statutes," which—like the Law of Social Dissolution—university authorities liberally employed to expel all students who engaged in "reckless behavior," "Democratization of the university's Board of Trustees," "Free education to all students regardless of social background or biased admission exams," and "Solidarity with all workers who were fighting to defeat charrismo."[58]

The "villains" most frequently cited by New Left students in their ideolog-ical war were primarily the authority figures whom students felt had abused their political and economic power. Particularly despised were those indi-viduals who were directly involved in the repression of students and work-ers, including "corrupt" school authorities, *porristas* who employed violence, "co-opted *grillos*" from the FEU, "charro leaders" in labor unions, the chief of police of the Federal District (Luis Cueto), and especially the granadero force, which was created in the 1950s to deal ruthlessly with civil disturbances and massive protests. To combat the different forms of political repression, stu-dent representatives of the New Left expressed (again, in a tone of voice simi-lar to that of the writers of *El Espectador* a couple of years earlier) the need to take a more active role in social politics inside the university. However, unlike the contributors of *El Espectador*, New Left universitarios refused to see the Constitution of 1917 as a panacea to Mexico's social problems. Instead, looking at UNAM as a microcosm of the modern world, they argued that democracy could be achieved inside their schools only when students were exposed to as many different ideologies, alternative ways of life, and aesthetic forms as pos-sible.

To this end universitarios of the New Left proceeded with a program that in effect widely radicalized the university. This transformation included the organization of an unprecedented number of conferences, roundtable discus-sions, workshops, film festivals, music concerts, art galleries, and literary con-tests.[59] Moreover, it would extend to the core business of the university cur-riculum itself. With the support of Left-leaning professors like José Revueltas, Enrique González Pedrero, Guillermo García Contreras, and Pablo González Casanova (many appointed by rector Ignacio Chávez), students from the schools of Law, Economics, and Political Science pressured the rector to add new courses on Marxism to the university curriculum and organize ad hoc seminars on the writings of Marx, Lenin, Stalin, Mao Tse-Tung, Che Guevara, and Gramsci.[60] In addition, with the active participation of various national and international editorial houses, such as *Progreso* in the Soviet Union, *Pueblos Unidos* in Uruguay, and *Fondo de Cultura Popular* in their own country, students were introduced to a significant number of classic texts on Marxism and decolonization in Spanish at affordable prices.[61]

Prominent international authors such as André Gorz, Erich Fromm, Irving Louis Horowitz, Pablo Neruda, Serge Mallet, Nicolás Guillén, and C. Wright Mills, among many others, were invited to courses organized during the winter and summer breaks by the School of Political and Social Sciences. There, the university community was invited to discuss the cultural advances of the Cuban Revolution, the crises of industrialized societies, the poor distribution of work and wealth, the structure of power, and the role of the media in authoritarian capitalist societies. A young professor at the time, Gerardo Estrada, remembers the importance of these courses as follows:

> The Winter and Summer courses . . . attracted hundreds of students who packed the Auditorium of [Political] Sciences. These courses allowed us to become acquainted with the latest political theories of the world and gave us the privilege of engaging in open, direct, and personal debates.[62]

Especially memorable was the visit to UNAM by Herbert Marcuse in February of 1966. Invited to talk about his landmark book *One-dimensional Man*, Marcuse addressed the university community with a dual critique of capitalism and the Soviet model of communism. What was most enduring, essayist Gabriel Careaga remembers, were the words highlighted by "Marcuse regarding the need for students and intellectuals to become agents of social change."[63]

In addition to being exposed to the writings of internationally known Marxist authors, a new generation of talented local and national Left authorship was also given an opportunity to express itself by publishing work with the editorial houses affiliated with the university.[64] This was largely made possible by the important backing of the Dirección de Difusión Cultural, and with scholarships from the Centro Mexicano de Escritores (CME). A rising generation of writers represented by José Agustín, Gustavo Saínz, Salvador Elizondo, and Sergio Pitol chronicled, in its own terms, what authorities were presenting as the "youth crisis." These young writers described a sharp division between what they (and most young students) saw as two very distinct worlds: the authoritarian, moralistic, traditional, and conformist world of the adults, on the one hand, and the exciting and adventurous world of young people seeking new ideologies, alternative ways of looking at life, and *desmadre* on the other. As Cohn recently noted, these writers of *la onda* (the wave) and the thousands of young people who identified with their innovative prose, fashion, and style, "revised stereotypes of national underdevelopment by fashioning themselves as cosmopolitan sophisticates . . . by refusing to engage with master narratives of national identity and history, by espousing popular cultural modes and models, and by rejecting prevailing conventions and mores (social as well as literary)."[65] Mexico's countercultural movement broadly known as *la onda*, Zolov similarly concludes, "permeated the student revolt. This was reflected as much in the long hair of many participants as in their language and expressed contempt for hegemonic values."[66]

Other young writers enrolled at UNAM who benefited tremendously from the new opportunities offered by the editorial houses of the university included Carlos Monsiváis, Roberto Escudero Castellanos, Paquita Calvo Zapata, and Miguel Álvarez, among others. They came together to create their own student magazines, including *Linterna*, *Combate*, and *Nueva Izquierda*, and would eventually be given an opportunity to present their concerns to a wider public in *Política, Siempre!*, *El Día*, and similar publications.[67] Inspired by their mentors in *La Casa del Lago* and *El Espectador*, these students also used their magazines to put together a series of events of their own inside the university with the intention of promoting their general and specific goals.[68]

Also particularly influential in the radicalization of student politics were the university's radio station (Radio Universidad) and journal (*Revista de la Universidad de México*). With the support from the rector, Ignacio Chávez, and his son-in-law, Jaime García Terrés, these "means of communist propaganda," as labeled in numerous pages of *Excélsior* and *El Universal*, were transformed in the 1960s into critical spaces of contestation. Here, students were introduced to Marxist teachings, countercultural ideologies, and a burgeoning sexual revolution.[69] Under the direction of Max Aub (1960–1967), Radio Universidad reached an unprecedented number of listeners, both inside the National University and in surrounding parts of the city. During this period universitarios were given an opportunity to listen to a variety of renowned guests, including many of the regular contributors to *El Espectador*, such as Carlos Fuentes, Francisco López Camara, and Victor Flores Olea. Guests also included Fernando Solana, Armando Ayala Anguiano, and the rising feminist writer and UNAM graduate Rosario Castellanos, who were invited to discuss the nation's most pressing social and economic problems on a nightly show called "Themes of Our Times." In its "Open University" program, students were offered the opportunity to enroll in English courses and take introductory seminars on psychoanalysis and Marxism. With the participation of its collaborators reporting from different parts of the world, the renovated Radio Universidad offered weekly updates on the cultural and political events in Paris, recorded the poems written by Pablo Neruda from exile, translated the work of Bertolt Brecht, and offered news from Latin America. The latter included a detailed report from a radio station in Habana where Cubans protested against the U.S.-sponsored Bay of Pigs invasion. The station also offered rising young writers and artists from Mexico and Latin America an opportunity to present their work in new shows. Figures such as Juan José Arreola, Ignacio López Tarso, Ofelia Guilman, and Gabriel García Marquez would appear in the shows "Poetry in a Loud Voice," "New Music," and "Live Voices of Latin America." On the Nancy Cárdenas and Carlos Monsiváis show, *El Cine y la Crítica*, universitarios heard satirical skits that used humor and irony to expose the contradictions and authoritarianism of both the Mexican state and the "stagnant" film industry. On "Live Voices from Mexico," students were introduced to political theories and literary texts of Spanish and Latin American intellectuals and politicians exiled in Mexico as recorded in their own voices. They listened to American jazz bands and Latin American political folk music (*música de protesta*), and they learned from "Bulletins of Information" about upcoming musical concerts, political meetings, conferences, art exhibitions, films, and provisionary courses.[70]

Similarly, under the directions of Jaime García Terrés (1953–1965), Luis Villoro (1965–1966), and Gastón García Cantú (1966–1968), a revised *Revista de la Universidad* also served as an important space in which the writings of political and countercultural figures became regular features. Here, students were introduced, for example, to Luis Villoro's interpretations of Hinduism, Maria Sabina's knowledge of alternative medicine, Miguel León Portilla's translations of Nahuatl poetry, Jean Paul Sartre's influence on existentialist philosophy, C. Wright Mills's notes on the Cold War, Herbert Marcuse's critiques of the aggressiveness of advanced industrialized societies, and Victor Flores Olea's expositions on democracy and Marxism.[71] In these pages universitarios also became acquainted with the modernist paintings and writings by José Luis Cuevas, where he frequently criticized the "nationalist" art of Diego Rivera. They also were exposed to Latin America's boom literature represented by Julio Cortazar, the feminist/*indigenista* poems by Rosario Castellanos, and the reviews of world cinema by Emilio García Riera. They were informed about the pro-Vietnam movement in Paris, the repression of Argentinean students, and the cultural accomplishments of the Cuban Revolution. Over the decade universitarios also read important manifestoes launched by intellectuals touching on a broad range of themes that concerned students all over the world. These included "The Fellowship Reconciliation," a document written by North American intellectuals to condemn all North American invasions. Also included was Erick Fromm's "Socialist Manifesto," Frank Waldo's "Call to Latin American Writers," Ricardo Pozas's denunciation of J. F. Kennedy's Alliance for Progress, and Carlos Monsiváis's critical assessment of Mexico's embryonic sexual revolution.[72]

Together, the university's radio station, its academic journal, and new seminars reached thousands of students who in turn participated in the "cultural revolution" that came to characterize the 1960s. As explained by British historian Arthur Marwick, this revolution in the arts, social attitudes, and politics took place worldwide, "*simultaneously* by unprecedented *interaction* and *acceleration*." It exposed the contradictions in the everyday life of the 1950s, including what Marwick identified as

> rigid social hierarchy; subordination of women to men and children to parents; repressed attitudes to sex; racism; unquestioning respect for authority in the family, education, government, the law, and religion, and for the nation-state, the national flag, the national anthem; Cold War hysteria; a strict formalism in language, etiquette, and dress codes; a dull and cliche-ridden popular culture.[73]

In the nation's capital, these and additional contradictions of an earlier era would also be exposed not only in the rise of a new rock music movement but also in the appearance of new political cartoonists, in the countercultural attitudes of new magazines, and in the internationalist language of the new cineclubs at UNAM.

"Una Revolución sin Fusil"

"Should we embrace violent tactics to bring about revolutionary changes? If so, what consequences would that bring to our movement?" According to Oscar González, these and similar questions (discussed with the author during an interview) took central stage during an informal meeting organized in 1960 by a group of leftist *universitarios* to discuss "the possible motives" behind the explosion of Miguel Aleman's statue. For this influential activist and leading founder of the militant magazine *Linterna*, the position championed by a group of students seemed clear: "This generation had been given no other option but to fight fire with fire." But the overwhelming majority of students strongly disagreed, and moving away from Che Guevara's more violent definition of revolution, "they called for *una revolución, pero sin fusil*." That is, a call to "an armless revolution" echoed in most Latin American campuses in the wake of the Cuban Revolution that implored students, artists, and intellectuals to assume a more active role in leftist politics by transforming their magazines, music lyrics, and cameras into more powerful weapons of contestation.[74] Yet, despite these persistently polarizing tactical and ideological differences, Oscar González remembered commonalities: "a new sense of urgency in promoting social and political consciousness; a new appreciation of rock music and provocative film; and a list of obligatory readings that would shape the political philosophy of our entire generation." He explained:

> We were all influenced by the same revolutionary figures, independent thinkers, and artists whose voices became louder by the end of the decade, but who—we believed—were otherwise censored, ridiculed, or ignored by the mainstream media. These voices ranged from those of the iconic Herbert Marcuse, The Beatles, and the controversial [Alejandro] Jodorowsky to the much more influential Rius, whose [comic] book, *Cuba para principiantes*, along with [C. Wright] Mills's *Escucha Yankee*, [Pablo González Casanova's] *La Democracia en México*, [Régis] Debray's *Revolución en la Revolución*, and the papers *Política, Siempre!*, and *El Día*, became required readings for all student activists.[75]

For the governing elite of the 1960s, it was no exaggeration for Oscar to reference the caricaturist Rius (Eduardo del Río) as a particularly influential figure of the Left, alongside the Beatles, the countercultural filmmaker Jodorowsky, and the German-American sociologist and key voice of the global New Left Herbert Marcuse. In 1968, faced with Mexico's largest student movement, President Díaz Ordaz described Marcuse as a "philosopher of destruction in favor . . . of nothing and against everything."[76] The Ordaz administration was equally critical of those who blurred the lines between rock music as fashion and rock music as social protest. As Zolov has demonstrated, the paternalistic administration of Díaz Ordaz grew increasingly concerned with the subversive nature of the psychedelic rock revolution that had emerged in most modern societies. Mimicking American hippies and British rock bands not only allowed the nation's youth "to belong to a global movement" but also to discover "new ways of *being* Mexican, ways that ran counter to the dominant ideology of state-sponsored nationalism."[77] The nation's defiant youth first felt the disciplinary hand of the president in 1965 when Mexico City authorities ordered the closing down of as many as twenty-five night clubs after being charged with disrupting order with "noise."[78] Films addressing "sensitive" political themes also faced harsh criticism and even censorship by the government throughout the 1960s. Thus works deemed to contribute to the "moral corruption" of the nation's youth, or those that referenced electoral fraud or the government's involvement in the financial support of corrupt caciques, would come under intense scrutiny. Representing the former was Luis Buñuel's *Viridiana* (1961), a film that told the story of a young nun raped by her religious uncle, and Alejandro Jodorowsky's *Fando y Lis* (1967), a psychedelic film that told the story of a young couple in search of ecstasy and freedom in the enchanted city of Tar. The latter included Giovanni Karporaal's *El Brazo Fuerte* (1958), Julio Bracho's *La Sombra del Caudillo* (1960), and Roberto Gabaldón's *La Rosa Blanca* (1961).[79]

But Rius, who presumably reached a much larger audience with his weekly comic, *Los Supermachos* (1965–1968), proved to be a more menacing figure than Marcuse, the Beatles, and Jodorowsky, combined. Throughout the sixties he was pressured to present his resignation as an editorial caricaturist from several newspapers. However, censorship only pushed Rius to become a louder and more dissident voice of the New Left. In 1968, the state forced him to end *Los Supermachos*. But in the midst of his participation in the student movement, Rius created new comics that were added to the obligatory list of required readings at UNAM. These included *La Garrapata* (The Tick, 1968), *Los Agachados* (The Downtrodden, 1968–1977), *Marx for Beginners* (1972), and his weekly cartoons in *Polítca, Sucesos,* and *Por que?* In 1969, after refusing to give in to the government's demands to "tone down" his razor-sharp critiques of the government, Rius was taken hostage to the mountains, where the police simulated his execution.[80] For the presidential administration of Díaz Ordaz, attempting to censor Rius did not constitute an isolated example. In 1969, the countercultural magazine *El Corno Emplumado/The Plumed Horn* also ran into trouble for supporting the student movement. It too, would be forced to publish its last issue (see below). The following year, the two most important films documenting the 1968 student movement, Leobardo López Arretche's *El Grito* (1968) and Oscar Menéndez's *Historia de un documento/ Histoire d'un document* (1970), were forced to go underground.[81] For the conservative administration of Díaz Ordaz, in short, there was very little difference between the Marxist revolution promoted by a small segment of Mexico's New Left, and the "armless" revolution with which universitarios came to identify throughout the decade, as expressed in the internationalist, countercultural, and satirical language of the cineclubs, *El Corno Emplumado*, and Rius's comics. A closer look at the critical discourse of these cultural aspects of the New Left's "armless revolution" explains why the presidential administration of Díaz Ordaz found these new spaces of contestation so threatening to the nation's youth.

Rius's Revolution

Rius was indeed an ideological force to be reckoned with. In his weekly comics, he praised the accomplishments of the Cuban Revolution and echoed the dissatisfaction of leftist student activists. He would dare to identify corrupt politicians by name (a taboo in political cartooning before the 1960s) and make the demand for freedom of the press a central priority.[82]

Like the students, Rius became a poignant critic of electoral fraud, imperialism, and the abuse of power. The targets of his criticism included local caciques, American entrepreneurs living in Mexico, "biased" journalists working for the government, and leading figures of the Catholic Church. He focused especially on the leading representative figures of the Institutional Revolutionary Party (PRI). For example, in *Siempre!* he accused *priístas*, wealthy figures of the private sector, and demagogues of the institutionalized Left of transforming American football at UNAM into a contested space of the Cold War primarily to benefit the economic interests of the governing elite (see Illustration 6.2). But perhaps more important, in the numerous cartoons published by the more radical weekly *Política* he made repeated references to the once sacrosanct image of the president. In one of these cartoons, for example, he drew López Mateos giving the baton of the iniquitous "Law of Social Dissolution" to the newly elected president, Díaz Ordaz, whose conceived "ugliness" and "animalistic" authoritarianism (as portrayed by the students) would become a symbol of ridicule and protest during the 1968 movement (see Chapter 8).[83]

Moreover, in similar language reproduced in dozens of student manifestoes, Rius also called attention to "the hypocrisy" of "Western democracy" by

ILLUS. 6.2. Rius, "No title," *Siempre!*, November 9, 1960. (Reproduced with permission from *Siempre!*)

making specific references to apartheid in South Africa, to biological warfare in Vietnam, and to U.S. military involvements in Guatemala (1954) and the Dominican Republic (1965). In recording the rise of the global counterculture, he also made numerous references to psychedelic drugs, the Beatles, vegetarianism, herbal medicine, hippie communes, sex, marijuana, Buddhism, and Zen.[84]

Yet Rius proved to be equally critical of the more moderate Left preferred by the univeritarios. For him, only socialism would bring real revolutionary change to Mexico. In making this point, Rius poked fun at "pseudo" leftist intellectuals who concealed their "bourgeois" ideas behind the institutionalized veil of the Mexican Revolution. Yet he also grew increasingly critical of young Mexicans who blindly embraced the hippy slogans of "freedom and equality" without reflecting upon the multiple contradictions of the countercultural movement. For example, in his 1969 issue "Help! The Hippies!" Rius noted that hippies were very critical of the Vietnam war, yet their passive response was simply to withdraw from society. They detested commercialism and conformity, yet their rejection of mainstream culture depended on a consumption of the same slogans that remained in the possession of media entrepreneurs. Hence, like the more radical elements at UNAM, he became critical of those activists who refused to embrace a more militant position. "Sitting down while smoking marijuana and eating flowers," Rius bluntly told his readers in one of his cartoons, would not challenge "the evils of this world." True revolutionaries, he insisted, wore an olive green uniform, stood up with dignity on their feet, and picked up arms.[85]

In short, the nonconformist Rius made a name for himself in the 1960s by attempting to increase the political awareness of his readership. And although he initially had hoped that his explanatory texts and dialogue balloons would appeal primarily to (and thus ultimately benefit) the working class, he eventually admitted that the overwhelming majority of his readership was composed by the more educated sectors of the middle class. This was particularly true of universitarios, who, despite their general objections to socialism, seemed to have welcomed Rius's version of desmadre, as well as his committed efforts in raising social consciousness as an inclusive characteristics of the critical discourse of the New Left.

El Corno Emplumado/The Plumed Horn

Also well received by a significant sector of the university community as yet another example of the "armless revolution" of the 1960s was the progressive literary journal *El Corno Emplumado/The Plumed Horn*. Created in 1962 as an international joint effort by American Beat poet Margaret Randall and her husband, Mexican poet Sergio Mondragón, *El Corno* was the first magazine to publish poetry, articles, essays, news, and letters in both Spanish and English. By making available as many as three thousand copies throughout Latin America, the United States, Canada, England, and India, their goal was not simply to attract a broader international readership but also to create a greater sense of global solidarity. In this way they could directly challenge the national and ideological borders that kept intellectuals and artists of the global New Left divided. This uniting effort, with specific attention to the American hemisphere, was evident in the origin of the journal's name itself. According to its founders, *El Corno Emplumado/The Plumed Horn* was meant to represent the "jazz horn of the north and the bright feathers of Mesoamerica's Quetzalcoatl."[86] In this effort, Randall and Mondragón used the journal to introduce European and North American readers to various countercultural protests and literary movements from Latin America. Many readers became familiarized for the first time with the violent anti-Catholic and "anti everything" manifestoes recorded by the *nadaistas* (nothingists) in Colombia, and the surrealist poetry in "search of a New World" from Venezuela. The journal also offered the contributions of the anticonformist happenings organized by the *tzánticos* (head shrinkers) in Ecuador, and the manifestoes against the "emptiness" in contemporary art by *Los Hartos* (the Fed-ups) in Mexico. In addition to the "cruelty theater" of Alejandro Jodorowsky, readers were exposed to the revolutionary pop art of Cuban artists and were given the opportunity to read English translations of the writings by Octavio Paz,

Rosario Castellanos, José Emilio Pacheco, Jaime Sabines, Raquel Jodorowsky, Nicolas Guillen, and Ernesto Cardenal, among many others. The editors of *El Corno* opened the possibility for Latin Americans to read in Spanish for the first time the works by Allen Ginsberg, Laurence Ferlinguetti, and George Bowering, as well as the "Concrete Poetry" from Brazil and the Eastern philosophy of D. T. Suzuki. Thus, like the editors of *Revista de la Universidad*, Randall and Mondragón presented their readers with a broad range of international artists, independent thinkers, intellectuals, and philosophers. Such figures challenged rigid notions of Christianity, nationalism, and progress. They also began questioning the sanctuary of the nuclear family, rejecting traditional sexual mores, and exploring alternative spiritualties.[87] But, unlike the academic journal published at UNAM, *El Corno* appeared to be more democratic. It gave equal space to Mexican and foreign contributors and opened new opportunities to rising artists and intellectuals who otherwise had difficulties publishing their work in other university journals precisely because of their blunt rejection of the status quo, in general, and academia, in particular.[88]

By the mid-1960s, *El Corno Emplumado* appeared to have been deeply affected by the intensification of the war in Vietnam and, following Margaret Randall's first visit to Cuba in 1967, it began to incorporate more direct references to specific political events.[89] The editors continued to privilege articles related to Beat poetry, literary essays, visual arts, Eastern philosophies, and the rising sexual revolution, but the gap between the counterculture and politics became significantly narrower. The political turn of the journal was evident in both its content and its appearance. Beginning in 1965, for example, the editors abandoned the traditional typographic covers and replaced them with provocative images. Among the most dramatic of these images were three separate photographs by Rodrigo Moya, Larry Siegel, and an anonymous journalist. In these photographs, viewers were invited to discuss the repercussions associated with the military presence of U.S. Marines in the streets of Santo Domingo, the antiwar movement that had flourished in different parts of the world, and the violent racial discrimination against African-Americans in the United States. The editors of the journal argued that these had given rise to the worldwide protest of the 1960s.[90]

In 1968, Sergio Mondragón abandoned the magazine after his divorce from Randall, and the American poet Robert Cohen became the new coeditor of the journal. By then, there was no doubt that *El Corno Emplumado* had evolved into a fervent supporter of the Cuban Revolution and a representative voice for Mexico's New Left. In its October 1968 issue, the editors demonstrated their solidarity with the student movement and made President Díaz Ordaz and Minister of Interior Luis Echeverría personally responsible for the violent repression of students. As a direct consequence, remembers Margaret Randall, "we lost most of our financial support[,] print shops were scared away from printing the journal[, and] we ourselves [faced] political reprisals and persecution." Fearing for their lives, they went underground.[91] At the end of that year they left Mexico. Randall went to Cuba, where she continued writing for the next decade and became one of Latin America's most influential feminist thinkers; Sergio Mondragón moved to the United States, and eventually to Japan, where he worked as a correspondent for *Excélsior* and expanded his interests in Zen Buddhism.[92]

For the founding editors and young readers of *El Corno*, the journal had represented a genuine tool of the "armless revolution" of the 1960s that came to be identified with the New Left. "Poetry," wrote the editors to the participants of the student movement in their 1968 issue, "will give you the courage to continue fighting against the corrupt system." And with the optimistic language that characterized many of their editorials, they added, "[T]he present and future is in your hands." For then twenty-one-year-old student José Vicente Anaya, these words could not come closer to represent his generation. He remembered reading those words as "if they were my own." The journal's protest of the government repression, he added, "symbolized the culmination of the strong spirit of *El Corno Emplumado*, its editors, and [his] generation."[93] Similarly, the new cineclubs, the university radio station, and UNAM's main academic journals would also come to epitomize the spirit of liberation and innovation of the 1960s.

The University's Cineclubs and the Nuevo Cine Movement

The history of the first cineclubs can be traced to Paris shortly after the end of World War I. In less than ten years, these social clubs could be found in most European cities. Initially, the founding members sought to create an alternative space outside the realm of the mainstream film industry, which itself was experiencing technological adjustments to sound. In these clubs, the participants were expected to discuss the technological, psychological, and aesthetic aspects of cinema, and exhibit films that were otherwise excluded from the commercial industry. These included many silent features, which many of the cineclub members nostalgically described as cinema in "its purest form." Further, they were expected to learn the latest techniques and appropriate language to "educate" the taste of their audiences and make libraries, cinématéques, and courses available to the larger public, especially to future filmmakers. These, in turn, were expected to improve the quality of cinema in their respective countries.[94] In Mexico, the roots of a cinematic movement first surfaced with the creation of the Cine Club Mexicano in 1931. Operating in the same European tradition, its founders intended to foster the appreciation of film as an artistic object of study in itself. To this end, they exhibited films from different parts of the world, trained other members to evaluate film as a medium, taught the history of cinema to a selected audience, and organized conferences on the aesthetic, technological, and social importance of film. Other, very selective, clubs were soon formed in different parts of the nation, including the famous Cine Club de México, which opened its doors in 1948.[95]

Nonetheless, a cineclub movement aiming to reach a wider public would not surface until the mid-to-late 1950s, following the direct involvement of a selected group of UNAM authorities, particularly Manuel González Casanova. In 1952, at the age of eighteen, González Casanova had been a founding member of the influential Cine Club Progreso.[96] Unlike the more elitist cineclubs of an earlier decade, the main goal of Progreso was to create a cultural movement capable of revitalizing the national film industry. Its members argued that the "nationalistic language" and "monopolistic power" in the hands of a few producers, directors, and stars had grown increasingly intolerant to aesthetic change and experimentation. Further, with a particular insistence on the part of González Casanova, Progreso published the first articles on the particularities of Mexican film, established contact with other cineclubs in Europe, and called universitarios to create cineclubs inside the new campus of UNAM, where he envisioned the movement would flourish.

The students responded favorably, and with the involvement of the DDC and the new Federation of Mexican Cine Clubs (FMCC), they founded the first cineclub inside UNAM in 1955, the Cine Club Universidad. Referring to themselves as "the intellectual vanguard" of Mexico's new cinematic movement, they announced the inauguration of their club as follows: "As students, we could no longer remain on the margins of this [new] cinematic struggle. We could no longer sit still witnessing the disappearance of our national cinema. .... As students, we have discovered the potential power of cinema in promoting the social and cultural development of our pueblos."[97] Additional cineclubs, expressing similar sentiments in the different schools and *prepa-ratorias*, soon appeared inside the campus.[98] Like the pioneer Cine Club Universidad, they too grew increasingly concerned with the overproduction of *churros* (low budget/quality movies), on the one hand, and the indiscriminate importation of commercial (and negative) Hollywood films, on the other.

Efforts to revive Mexico's film industry at UNAM were further strengthened in the late 1950s with the creation of the Asociación Universitaria de Cine Experimental (AUCE) and the Sección de Actividades Cinematográficas. Both of these institutions also received direct financial assistance from the DDC. From their respective offices, and with the enthusiastic support of González Casanova, they organized the first International Film Festivals, where students featured dozens of films that had otherwise never been introduced to Mexican audiences. These included films by Chaplin, Eisenstein, Clair, Pudovkin, Griffith, Vidor, Rosellini, Houston, Bergman, Passolini, Visconti, Kubrick, Castelloni, Aldrich, Carné, Cocteu, de Sica, and Kazan. Moreover, they called for the creation of cineclubs in all of the different schools and invited Nancy Cárdenas and Carlos Monsiváis to host "El Cine y la Crítica" (a weekly program at Radio Universidad, as we recall, that sarcastically poked fun of the stagnation of the national film industry). In 1959, UNAM also opened the Taller de Cine Experimental, a cinematic workshop that specifically emphasized the pioneer work of young Mexican directors. The following year Manuel González Casanova invited José Revueltas, Walter Reuter, and other renowned professors and film experts to lead "50 Lecciones de Cine," a seminar with a low cost to students of one peso per lesson that would give rise to Mexico's first School of Cinema, the Centro Universitario de Estudios Cinematográficos (CUEC).[99] Officially created in 1963, the CUEC would help foster a generation of young filmmakers whose experimental films and controversial documentaries of the late sixties would further expose the authoritarianism of the state and the stagnation of its film industry. Moreover, the CUEC would open the doors to the nation's first explicitly feminist and homosexual filmmaking of the 1970s, as represented in the works of Marcela Fernández Violante and Jaime H. Hermosillo, respectively.[100]

By the mid-1960s the CUEC had become one of the most important film schools in Latin America. Its archive, containing more than three hundred rare, independent, national classic and international films in 1967, also made the university's film library one of the richest in the continent.[101] By then it had also become evident that the cineclub movement had successfully fostered a generation of students who had a more critical view of cinema. The most active of these clubs included Proceso in the Law School, José Guadalupe Posada in the School of Anthropology, Flores Magón in the School of Economics, Eisenstein in the School of Political Science, and Cine-Club Coapa in the Preparatoria No. 5. In their respective schools, universitarios established cultural relations with many international embassies stationed in Mexico. With the collaboration and financial support of the DDC, they led festivals in which students emphasized the work of specific directors, as well as focused on particular themes, genres, and movements. In these new social clubs the university community was also exposed to cinematic representations of "Youth," "Satire," and "Horror." The innovative clubs demonstrated enthusiasm for black, Japanese, and Polish cinema, as well as animated shorts from Eastern Europe. Other clubs organized conferences that specifically featured representative films from the classical Hollywood era, the French *Nouvelle Vague*, the *Cinema Novo* movement in Brazil, the English "Free Cinema," and Italian Neorealism.[102] In the wake of the Cuban Revolution, universitarios also expressed special interest in the relationship between cinema, politics, and social change, as articulated in the work of Tomás Gutiérrez Alea and Glauber Rocha (among others).[103] In these academic festivals, UNAM created a space for the rise of Mexico's independent cinema, where Sergio Vejar, Archibaldo Burns, Alberto Isaac, Ruben Gamez, Benito Alazraki, Jomí García Ascot, Luis Alcoriza, and Arturo Ripstein featured some of their pioneering films. Moreover, students demonstrated a particularly keen interest in national classics that had either received scant attention or had yet to be introduced to the university community.[104] Finally, the cineclubs seized the opportunity to screen highly controversial films, including many films that had been banned by the state, the Vatican, or other countries for political and/or religious reasons.[105] But as the Cine Club Progreso had emphasized in the past, these films were not simply exhibited to a passive audience. Rather, beginning in 1960, students complemented many of their clubs with debate-style seminars (*Cines Debate Popular*) in which featured films were accompanied by open audience discussions and public lectures led by a new generation of cinephiles who eventually developed into Mexico's most important directors, film critics, and chroniclers.[106] The main goal of these participants was "to foster a more demanding public."[107] In this effort, both the organizers and lecturers also published articles, books, journals, and manifestoes in which they further discussed the important role of cineclubs in revitalizing the national film industry.[108] In his 1961 influential essay, "What Is a Cine Club?" Manuel Gonzalez Casanova argued that Mexican cinema was on the verge of collapsing, and he encouraged others to create their own movements capable of fomenting a generation of "new men" with "greater artistic sensibility."[109]

Outside UNAM, the loudest movement advocating a reawakening of Mexican cinema came from a group of intellectuals who called themselves the "Nuevo Cine." In their 1961 manifesto and monthly journal *Nuevo Cine*, its members, which included Manuel Gonzalez Casanova and Carlos Monsiváis, emphasized the educational importance of cineclubs. They also called for a number of reforms, including the formation of a filmothéque, the founding of a film school, the support of experimental film groups, and the publication of film journals.[110] Further, they demanded the renovation of the national film industry by opening it to new talent, promoting a better understanding of the history of Mexican film, criticizing the unions to protect only their economic interests, and blaming the state for its misplaced protectionism. They highlighted the importance of respecting the filmmakers' rights to freedom of expression; called for the production and exhibition of independent films, shorts, and documentaries; and asked others to join in the revitalization of the Reseña de Festivales, an annual event that brought films from major international festivals to Mexico.[111]

The journal *Nuevo Cine* published only a few issues, from April 1961 to August 1962. During this short period its contributors did not openly employ a leftist position, nor did they explicitly call for students to embrace the camera as a "revolutionary weapon" of the 1960s liberation movement, as many other Latin American intellectuals did.[112] Rather, the Nuevo Cine group was more concerned with renovation and artistic freedom and less with social and political justice and gender equality. Nonetheless, during this brief period, the journal created an important space in which its contributors successfully exposed the stagnation, monopolistic power, and anachronistic language of a mainstream film industry that refused to open its doors to new talent. They also played an instrumental role in the creation of the CUEC in 1963. Further, in collaboration with the cineclub movement, this group of intellectuals, who were to become Mexico's most important CUEC professors, independent filmmakers, and critics, helped foster the internationalist language that characterized the New Left at UNAM. Like José Luis Cuevas and Alejandro Jodorowsky in the arts, like Rius in political cartooning, like the contributors of *El Corno Emplumado*, and like the leftist universitarios who opened new independent spaces of contestation in their schools, the Nuevo Cine group also rejected the state-sponsored forms and language of cultural nationalism. Student life at UNAM during the long sixties, in short, radically challenged the conformity and nationalism of an earlier decade and further questioned the state-sponsored concept of "national unity." By the end of this period, the first generations of filmmakers at CUEC would be less concerned with film culture and increasingly more involved in the use of the medium as a component of broader social and political struggles. This can be seen as a direct consequence of the youthful disillusionment that emerged inside the schools in the aftermath of the student massacre of 1968.

Conclusion: the Radicalization of UNAM during the 1960s

The statue of Miguel Alemán legitimized state power and authority during the 1950s.[113] It represented the very institutionalization of the revolution. Its destruction in the wake of Cuban events, however, came to monumentalize the postrevolutionary state's incomplete modernity. Moreover, as humorously captured by Rius, it exposed a youthful sentiment of dissatisfaction and rebellion no longer confined to the schools of the Politécnico, but also throughout UNAM. Finally, and perhaps more importantly in challenging the conceived wisdom in the historiography, its destruction and the divergent definitions of revolution that followed illustrate how incredibly faction ridden the student population of UNAM was during this period.

The Cuban example provided a key ingredient for the birth of a new culture of protest characterized by a public and more aggressive form of resistance to parental, institutional, and revolutionary authority that dominated student politics thereafter. This new culture of defiance framed in "revolutionary" and primarily "masculine" terms was directed toward repressive authorities and imperialism. To reform the political system and educational institutions that represented them, male and female universitarios fought to put an end to political corruption, demanded the ability to speak freely and critically, and participated in the creation of new spaces of contestation where they insisted that their constitution be respected so as to allow them to express ideas in a more democratic environment.

Thus, like students in other modern societies during the long sixties, Mexican universitarios underwent a significant process of radicalization. As equal participants in this culture of student protest, they too began to conceive of themselves as new subjects of history and also to fight for the right to speak with a collective voice. This collective voice, however, never fully adopted Rius's radical version of revolution. A feminist movement would not materialize until the 1970s. The writing of Franz Fanon, Raúl Sendic, Mario Firmenich, Abraham Guillén, and Carlos Mariguella (who became so influential in the endorsement of urban guerrilla tactics in South American universities) was not widely read among students at UNAM during the 1960s.[114] Rather, like the participants of *El Espectador*, the overwhelmingly moderate New Left at UNAM primarily demanded respect of their constitutional rights. Moreover, like their North American and European counterparts, universitarios of the long sixties also understood "revolutionary" defiance in "countercultural" terms. An international language of dissent, but also satire, humor, violence, and desmadre, became representative characteristics of Mexico's New Left. This "armless revolution" was evident in the new interest in Eastern and Native American philosophies published in new academic journals, the satirical sketches and protest music aired in Radio Universidad, the disruptive style and irreverent attitude that came to characterize the literature of la onda, and the internationalist language celebrated in the cineclubs. In this new culture, young male and female students became not only a "spectacle," as in other parts of the world, but also a social and political problem that, authorities argued, needed to be controlled institutionally if possible or by force if necessary.[115] In many Latin American countries, the response to the student problem would come with an iron fist in the form of overt military campaigns of repression against their leftist youth.[116] By contrast, in Mexico, the government would prefer the use of extralegal mechanisms of control that, following the Cuban Revolution, would become increasingly more violent.

7 "No More Fun and Games": From Porristas to Porros

ON DECEMBER 1, 1958, Adolfo López Mateos replaced Ruiz Cortinez as the new president of Mexico. Universally revered by the Mexican and U.S. press, López Mateos was described as a younger, more articulate, and attractive leader than his predecessor. Some in the *New York Times* spoke of him as a "symbol of Mexico's rising middle class."[1] Others in the U.S. press simply described him as "an eminently practical man" and anticipated that the new president would govern Mexico in a much more progressive fashion. They were convinced that, unlike the older and more conservative General Ruiz Cortinez, the new civilian president would never bring shame to Mexico's democracy with the brutal use of the *granaderos* or the federal troops against ordinary citizens. Some reporters even suggested that, "at last, the new Cárdenas had arrived."[2] In Mexico, journalists tempered their enthusiasm but nonetheless expressed the hope that López Mateos represented what the nation needed during the difficult times of the Cold War: a leader who was "both humane and tough at the same time."[3] The optimism reported in the U.S. and the national press reflected the feeling of many people that López Mateos had performed well as secretary of Labor and Social Welfare during the administration of Ruiz Cortinez. In this capacity he had established a good relationship with the labor unions. With "conciliation and arbitration," an American journalist reported, "[the secretary of labor had] settled nearly 30,000 labor managerial disputes" prior to the massive uprisings of 1958. Similar results were thus to be expected regarding the ideological polarization that came to characterize Mexico in the wake of the Cuban Revolution.[4]

As reported to the U.S. Department of State by U.S. ambassador Thomas Mann, the new presidential administration initially found favor with the anticommunism of Miguel Alemán's Mexican Civic Front of Revolutionary Affirmation (FCMAR) and the nationalist tones of Lázaro Cárdenas's Movement of National Liberation (MLN).[5] However, when rumors began to surface that members of the two fronts wanted to transform their organizations into opposing parties, the presidential office took a number of steps to thwart their plans. As a general measure, Institutional Revolutionary Party (PRI) officials stated publicly that the only acceptable solutions to Mexico's problems were those embodied by the Mexican Revolution as institutionalized in the party. Under pressure from all sides, the administration of López Mateos tried to demonstrate its leftist intentions, on the one hand, and, on the other, it hoped to convince anticommunist forces in and out of government that Mexico would not become a hotbed of communism. In the first instance, in response to growing pressure from the Left to address the significance of Mexico's own revolution, the president made a statement that the "course and ideology" of his revolutionary government were of the "extreme left within the Constitution."[6] These remarks did not go unnoticed by various people and institutions concerned with the spread of communism in Mexico following the outbreak of the Cuban Revolution. When asked to explain what he meant, López Mateos cannily responded by stressing that "progress in agrarian reform, expansion of agricultural improvement and productivity, expansion of foreign markets, better education, social justice . . . and solidarity with the sister republic [of Cuba] and sympathy for their legitimate aspirations" would be the priority of his administration.[7]

With similar remarks the president reproached the "extreme" elements of the leftist and conservative constituencies of the MLN and the FCMAR. In particular, he reprimanded the cardenista front for embracing a "borrowed ideology" to attack the Mexican Revolution and simultaneously "upbraided the forces of reaction" within the FCMAR "for seeking to impede Revolutionary progress."[8] Moreover, hoping to weaken the polarizing opposition to the government, the López Mateos administration set its sights on wooing the MLN with the ultimate aim of turning them against the FCMAR. Kennedy's visit to Mexico at the end of June of 1962 provided one such opportunity. The trip was prefaced with a warning to leftist protesters that they "could expect some freedom of action as long as they maintain a circumspective attitude and not do anything to threaten national unity." The PRI then asked the leadership of the FCMAR to supply "thousands of its members and sympathizers to be deputized as special security agents along Kennedy's march route."[9] More important, in an attempt to co-opt leaders who might be strengthening ties to the FCMAR and MLN, the president invited all seven living former presidents "into the official family" by giving them each "a Government office." As noted in a U.S. Department of State document, this clever move "accomplished two things. First, it countered rumors about weaknesses in the PRI and lack of stability in the present administration, as the massive social movements of the late 1950s had shown. Second, it placed the more influential former presidents—Lázaro Cárdenas, Miguel Alemán, Adolfo Ruiz Cortines, and Abelardo Rodriguez—in a position "where they will work for, and answer to, López Mateos, busying themselves in constructive work rather than engaging in political maneuvering."[10]

At the local level, such as schools and factories, where struggles for power and ideological superiority took place, the López Mateos administration further countered rumors of any possible weakness of his administration by combining additional efforts of co-optation with a series of populist concessions. For instance, to undermine the rising popularity and power of its opposition and demonstrate the president's determination to create a productive dialogue with workers and students, the López Mateos administration gave the orders to free a number of key figures who had been imprisoned during the previous sexenio. The most noted of these was Othón Salazar, the principal leader of the Revolutionary Teacher's Movement (MRM). More important, in an effort to strengthen the corporatist structure of the state, the president granted a considerable wage increase to workers and met a number of specific demands presented during the 1958 labor strikes.[11] And as part of establishing a good relationship with students, the president in 1958 called for the withdrawal of federal troops from the National Polytechnic Institute (IPN) and personally ordered the release of Nicandro Mendoza, the "troublemaker" of the Politécnico, who, as we recall, would move to Morelia where he became involved in a new student uprising, and again be accused of corrupting Mexico's youth with communist ideas.[12]

However, when co-optation, popular concessions, and divide and conquer strategies failed to tame the opposition in the labor and school sectors, the López Mateos administration relied on the same repressive mechanism of control that had characterized previous sexenios. And when government agents and granaderos proved inefficient, it too relied on what other historians have alluded to as the "surgical power" of the military forces.[13] Such was the case on March of 1959 when military troops received executive orders to shut down the Normal School, close its dormitories, and crush a railroad strike that threatened to revive the possibility of bringing the different sectors of the working class together. Subsequently, the communist leaders Valentin Campa and Demetrio Vallejo were sent to prison for the violation of the law of social dissolution. In August the painter David Alfaro Siqueiros would suffer the same fate. Three years later, a group of soldiers were sent to Morelos to arrest the agrarian leader Ruben Jaramillo. On May 23, 1962, he was dragged out of his house and killed.[14]

This chapter examines both the surgical and the preemptive violence that developed inside the National Autonomous University of Mexico (UNAM) campus during the presidential administrations of Adolfo López Mateos (1958–1964) and Gustavo Díaz Ordaz (1964–1970) to strike the leftist student militancy and further accentuate the so-called burgeoning student "problem" of the 1960s. It pays particular attention to the more conservative and authoritarian leadership of Díaz Ordaz and argues that the "carrot and stick" approach that had characterized the previous administration in defense of Mexico's "preferred" revolution remained the favored government response to student dissent during the new sexenio. Nonetheless, in distinguishing between the multiple political actors involved in the consolidation of *porrismo*, it contends that the mechanisms of student control and mediation underwent a significant transformation during this period and in the process further intensified the political student culture at UNAM. Moreover, it argues that as the radicalization of the student Left became more apparent in the aftermath of the Cuban Revolution during the "authoritarian" rectorship of Ignacio Chávez (1961–1966), so did the political power and autonomy of *porros*, as the government-sponsored "lumpen" agents provocateurs who replaced the more charismatic and middle-class *porristas* of an earlier era became known during the administration of Díaz Ordaz. Shock brigades led by violent porros and more powerful intermediaries achieved their greatest victory in 1966 by violently breaking into the rector's office and forcing Ignacio Chávez to resign.

Thus, as historian Soledad Loaeza has argued, the authoritarianism that distinguished Mexico during the second half of the 1960s should not be reduced to a series of "paranoid" acts of a single president (as Enrique Krauze and others have insisted).[15] Instead, the political elite that governed Mexico during the administration of Díaz Ordaz—including its divergent responses to student unrest—must be understood within the broader political and countercultural context of the Cold War (described in previous chapters). As other countries in Latin America responded to their respective student problems overtly, this chapter argues, Mexico—concerned with maintaining the image of an "exceptionally peaceful" nation—preferred the more covert use of agents provocateurs and pseudo-student organizations.[16] Recruited from local street gangs by multiple and at times competing political power brokers, porros not only served as agents of school violence and *desmadre* but also successfully created powerful networks with wealthy *alemanistas* from the FCMAR, leftist politicians sympathetic to López Mateos, and more conservative *priístas* loyal to Díaz Ordaz. Moreover, in successfully infiltrating most of the schools during this period, they played a crucial role in further accentuating the so-called student "problem" stressed throughout the long sixties in the conservative press. School authorities and a right-wing media sympathetic to the administration of Díaz Ordaz efficiently blurred the lines between legitimate student activists, "thugs," "porros," and *desmadrosos*.

Porrismo in Defense of Mexico's "Preferred" Revolution

The official response on the part of the government to the radicalization of students during the 1960s was to invest in the promotion of Mexico's own revolution. To this end, it attempted to bring back to life the National Institute of Mexican Youth (INJM) and, with the encouragement of Carlos Madrazo, the party's new president, created a new youth wing of the government, the PRI Juvenil. When both of these strategies failed to contain the student problem, however, government authorities looked for alternative solutions. These included concealed attempts to create pseudo-student political and cultural organizations disguised as genuine representatives of the university Left and overt efforts to replace middle-class porristas with lumpen and working-class porros in the late 1960s.

The INJM was founded in 1950 in response to the political and social crises brought on by World War II. In the context of the incipient Cold War, President Miguel Alemán thought that if Mexico's youth were without institutional support and direction, they could be led astray by foreign ideologies, such as ultraconservative politics, or worse yet, communism. Following the Cuban

Revolution, when more than half of Mexico's population was said to be under twenty-five years of age, the administration of López Mateos tried to revive the INJM by encouraging Mexico's youth to embrace the centrist position endorsed by the government. The leading directors of the institute argued that once reintegrated into Mexico's own progressive system, young people, including *universitarios* and *politecnicos*, would participate in other programs designed by the state to solve the nation's basic problems.[17] Along these lines, and with a careful (and rather limited) collaboration with John F. Kennedy's Alliance for Progress, the institute tried to place greater emphasis on the multiple accomplishments of Mexico's own revolution by sending "Brigades of Social Action" to rural areas and poor neighborhoods in urban centers and creating "Youth Homes" throughout the nation.[18] By the mid-1960s the INJM had achieved a relatively large degree of success primarily in the poorest sectors of society located outside the nation's capital, allegedly claiming as many as 120,000 members nationwide. Despite these numbers, however, it had become evident that in Mexico City—where the so-called youth problem was particularly acute—the INJM had failed to attract the number of members that they had hoped for, particularly inside UNAM, where the Institute had been categorized by students as yet another *charro* organization.[19]

To deal with the radicalization of students and further secure its base among young voters, the Mexican government also created the PRI Juvenil (PRI Youth).[20] Dedicated to the tasks and goals of the government, this organization was founded in March of 1960 by Carlos Madrazo, the president of the National Executive Committee of the PRI (1954–1965), who tried to democratize the political structure of the party.[21] The goals of Madrazo were to attract young people throughout the republic, orient them toward the principles and programs of the Institutionalized Revolution, and draw universitarios away from "radical" organizations associated with the militant wings of the New Left.[22] To these ends, the PRI Juvenil offered young people internships in "parent" sectors of the corporatist structure of the party and sent representative leaders to national and international conferences. Moreover, under the close supervision of Madrazo, the youth wing of the party opened "centers of indoctrination" and organized council meetings, round-table discussions, patriotic observances, seminars, oratory contests, and workshops in which young politicos learned about leadership recruitment, finance, public information, and civic, social, and cultural action.[23] By the mid-1960s the PRI Juvenil had matured into an important youth wing of the state that generated myriad defenders of their representative government as well as a reliable group of local, state, and national politicians.[24] And despite constitutional regulations that prevented political parties from forming student organizations inside the schools, the success of the PRI Juvenil was also evident in UNAM, as it managed to penetrate student politics there.[25] The presence of the PRI represented by the Partido Social Progresista (PSP) and the Partido Estudiantil de Fuerzas Integradas (PEFI) was particularly noticeable inside the schools of Engineering, Law, and Social and Political Science.[26] Like other student organizations that emerged in Mexico following the Cuban Revolution, these groups also adopted a leftist platform, organized roundtable discussions, became involved in the *cineclubs*, put up candidates for student elections, and published their own periodicals, including *Integración* and *El Político*, in which they warned students of the "dangers of falling prey" to *grillos* who, they believed, threatened the spirit of the Mexican Revolution by exploiting empty and "foreign" Marxist phrases in order to get elected in student organizations.[27]

Yet, despite the PRI Juvenil's success, by the mid-1960s it had become evident that in order to contain the "student problem" the government of Díaz Ordaz also had to create pseudo-student organizations, or rather what many bona fide students frequently labeled *organizaciones fantasmas*.[28] These "ghost" organizations were usually quite short-lived, and they tended to appear as student protests gathered steam or in conjunction with political rallies. To give them legitimacy, provocateurs registered them as "cultural groups," hoping that they would offset the more independent and progressive representative bodies that had emerged inside the schools throughout the early 1960s. The specific goal, as one cofounder of a cultural group recalled, "was to create an environment of confusion among the student body and have fun in the process."[29] They did so by using the same language and symbols of "revolutionary" and "countercultural" change embraced by leftist student organizations. For instance, the overwhelming majority of these groups used easily recognizable icons representing national or revolutionary heroes in their names, such as "Che Guevara," "Emiliano Zapata," "Sandino," "Salvador Allende," and "Martin Luther King."[30] Most of these organizations sprang up within the schools of Law, Economics, and Political Science. That, of course, was no coincidence. The majority of leftist student organizations originated in these very same schools. For example, scattered government documents in the intelligence archives note that as many as forty-eight cultural organizations came into being inside the School of Law alone between 1966 and 1968.[31] As in the past, a broad range of competing power brokers within as well as outside the government structure were involved in the financial support of these organizations. These sources of surveillance reveal that the overwhelming support of these organizations came directly from the presidential office.

Particularly important in exposing the role that the administration of Díaz Ordaz played in promoting porrismo is a 1966 *Investigaciones Políticas y Sociales* (IPS) report. The document describes a step-by-step plan put together by government agents to be carried out by provocateurs in order to divide "the red agitation" inside the schools.[32] The specificity of the instructions buttresses a central argument of this book. Unlike other states in Latin America that launched overt military campaigns of repression against their youth during this period, the Mexican government preferred extralegal mechanisms of control, mediation, and diversion. In particular, the report calls for the sponsorship of pseudo-cultural and -political organizations capable of radicalizing the student body for the multiple purposes of fomenting factionalism, providing entertainment (or *relajo*), and presenting all activists as "dangerous pawns" manipulated by foreign agents. These organizations, the report specifically states, should appear naive, even romantic in their political views, yet competent in creating networks with "international communist forces" with the use of violence, if necessary. To this end, porra members should be divided into small yet highly organized shock brigades and distributed in different parts of the UNAM and IPN campuses to loot stores, paint Trotskyite, Guevarist, or Maoist propaganda on walls, disrupt student assemblies with the use of tear gas, and engage in violent confrontations with legitimate organizations. To confuse the student body (and perhaps the media), these strategic attacks should be done, for example, "in defense of the people in Vietnam." In addition, the report calls for the specific use of spurious propaganda as a key means by which to further factionalize the students. According to its anonymous authors, provocateurs were to distribute thirty thousand pamphlets throughout the schools under the name of Grupo Juvenil de Vanguardia "Van Troit."[33] The pamphlet that accompanies this report identifies this vanguard as the true representatives of students working inside the schools to end colonialism in the Third World. In contrast, the youth wings of the Mexican Communist Party (PCM) and the Partido Popular Socialista (PPS) are portrayed as "opportunistic forces" manipulated by "Yankee Imperialism." Only "violence," the pamphlet concludes, will bring about the "socialist revolution" needed in Mexico to defeat the "Yankee monopoly" that had Mexico in its grip.[34]

Additional government reports, testimonies of former porra leaders, and student manifestos of the time further point to the administration of Díaz Ordaz as a drastic turn, not only in the overt manipulation of student politics and in the distribution of apocryphal propaganda emphasized in the IPS report, but also in the life of charismatic porristas. Many porristas, such as the influential Palillo (who, as we recall, was sent to France in 1964 with a full scholarship), disappeared from the university for good. Other upcoming, yet less influential, intermediaries were forced to compete with a new generation of gang-like pseudo-leaders who infiltrated the formal and informal networks of mediation and diversion built by older style porristas to elevate their status, serve the needs of their *padrinos*, and ultimately counter the legitimate student organizations that had exploded in numbers in the wake of the Cuban Revolution.[35]

The broad range of sources also reveals that the most successful leaders profited financially and politically by transforming the "cultural" organizations that they helped to establish inside the schools into money-making enterprises. For instance, using the offices granted to them as springboards after registering their organizations with the university, they took control of the revenues generated by the schools' cafeterias and the cineclubs, offered security to new students during *novatadas*, and sponsored beauty pageants, football games, field trips to Oaxtepec and Acapulco, film festivals, and rock concerts. "El Gato," a porra leader of the Preparatoria #5 and at the time loyal supporter of the administration of Díaz Ordaz, remembered his involvement in the organization of these cultural events during an interview as follows:

> With the expulsion of Palillo from the university [in the mid-1960s], the preparatorias were suddenly up for grabs. But this was not the 1950s. Our environment was a more complicated one. Following the Cuban Revolution we realized that the control of the student body no longer simply relied on the management of American football and novatadas. Instead, organizing film festivals and rock concerts that alluded to some sort of liberation movement had become necessary. Some got into the business of the cine clubs. But I stayed away from that. Rather I achieved a certain degree of popularity by spending a great deal of my energy organizing rock concerts. The lefties preferred the boring música de protesta from South America, but the overwhelming majority of students wanted rock. So I gave it to them. I

invited local bands from various neighborhoods to the schools, frequently claimed that my intentions were noble (such as pretending that my concerts were organized in support of the people of Vietnam), charged students a modest fee to attend these concerts, and sold them mota at a very low price. Other things remained the same. You see, like Palillo, all of us also received the financial support from key school authorities and influential politicians who continued to rely on the same formula—you know: trying to keep students away from politics by keeping them entertained.[36]

In addition, the new leaders achieved a certain degree of notoriety by offering protection from competing gang leaders to small businesses surrounding the schools and guaranteeing diplomas to struggling students by threatening teachers.[37]

The criminal nature of the new "student" networks is reflected in their membership, which base of support differed greatly from the cheerleading squads of earlier decades. As explained by Larissa Lomnitz, in the vertical structure of these gangs "one finds several levels of command, according to personal closeness." She continues,

> The gang leader usually has two or three lieutenants who are very close to him, almost like brothers. Then there are two or three golpeadores ("hitmen"), who stick close to the leader and remain at his personal command. Then there is a group of boys called borregos ("sheep"), who may number ten or more. A fully grown porra may have twenty to thirty full-time members . . . . The leader acts like a charismatic father of all, and at the same time he is the negotiator on their behalf.[38]

When asked to comment on Lomnitz's descriptions of the internal structure of these gangs, El Angel not only agrees with her but also explains why the "new student leaders" became so feared inside the university during this period. According to this influential intermediary from the Preparatory School #2, "[O]ur job was to defeat all the radical student organizations that at that time we believed had been promoted by the leftist and authoritarian rector Ignacio Chávez" since he had taken power in 1961. For this, and instead of relying on football players and cheerleaders, they drew recruits from local street gangs, including "the infamous Nazis" but also Los Mopis, La Banda del Jeep, Los Gatos, and La Banda del Ataúd Gris.[39] At the Politécnico the most successful intermediary in achieving networks with powerful politicians, on the one hand, and a base of local street gangs, on the other, was Alfonso Torres Saavedra, also known as "El Johnny," whose long career spanning the long sixties and beyond illustrates the political ambiguities common at times of shifting patron-client relationships. Unlike the *tapatio* (native of Jalisco) Palillo, this historic porrista of the Politécnico was born in Mexico City in 1948. Like his predecessors, El Johnny was also born into a poor family. At a very young age he became fascinated with the rebellious attitude portrayed by Marlon Brando in the highly popular film *The Wild One*. Mimicking other Mexican "brandos" of his generation (see Chapter 2), he proudly sported his blue jeans and black leather jacket as badges of honor and generational protest. In the rough streets of the Colonia Buenos Aires neighborhood, the young Santiago achieved the reputation as a fierce fighter, a desmadroso, and a charismatic leader. As a young teenager, El Johnny joined the infamous gang *Los Ciud-adelos*,[40] and he hoped that one day he would overcome his poverty and own his own motorcycle. While enrolled in a secondary school (Secundaria #65) in the early 1960s, he became the president of one of the multiple Sociedades de Alumnos that emerged during this period to compete for the control of the *vocacionales* under the tutelage of FNET. The young leader held this and similar positions for several years (see below).[41]

Adding fuel to the public mania depicted in the press over the psycho-social waywardness of undisciplined youth in Mexican society, porra gangs led by El Johnny and other influential intermediaries brought new problems into the schools, including drug trafficking, armed robberies, violent territorial disputes (in which arms were commonly used), and even murders and rapes.[42] By the late 1960s, these problems were framed in the press as a social menace, a political threat to the autonomy of the university, and an affront to democracy itself. In short, the patriotic school spirit of the middle-class porristas increasingly came to be referred to in the print media by the more negative label of porro, or lumpen thugs-for hire.[43]

The overwhelming majority of the new porro leaders emerged in the preparatorias and vocacionales, a fact that helped reinforce parallels with urban gang activity. In effect, there was some connection between the two. El Angel notes:

> For many of us who grew up with limited options in poor neighborhoods where street gangs offered a sense of social and economic reassurance, porrismo offered us unprecedented opportunities to get an education and to move up the social and political ladder by simply exercising our street knowledge inside the preparatorias.[44]

At UNAM's secondary schools, the most influential of the new porro leaders included Armando Lara Montier (El Larita) and the Corona Brothers, in the ENP #2; El Superman in the ENP #5; León de la Selva in the ENP #6; El Nazi and El Goldfinger in the ENP #7; and El Mame in the ENP #8.[45] Like the porristas of earlier years, these new intermediaries were rewarded with legitimate student status that provided them with a number of privileges inside and outside the schools.[46] Similarly inheriting from the porrista profile, some of the new porro leaders became so valuable to their padrinos that they achieved a certain degree of immunity from interference by school authorities as well as a great deal of political independence inside the schools. For example, the new cartoonist of *Excélsior*, Marino, tried to distance himself from the more conservative Audiffred and Freyre by offering sharp criticisms of school and government authorities involved in promoting porrismo by drawing the figure of a menacing porro holding in his hand a school identification card with the logo of UNAM. In particular, Marino argued that porros not only had achieved the role of important actors inside the schools, but because of the political influence of their padrinos, they had also become "untouchable" in the eyes of the law.[47] Indeed, either fearing the porros or seeing them as useful, many school authorities, including Vicente Méndez Rostro, the general director of the preparatorias, tolerated the crimes committed by them inside the schools.[48] The UNAM logo in the hand of the porro drawn by Marino is telling concerning the porro's independence and immunity during this period. It reads: "The carrier of this ID is a porro. Authorities are implored to assist him in the best possible way so that he can carry out his mission."[49]

Mariano's comments were far from an exaggeration. Porros, in fact, were also often hired to function as an "informal police force."[50] Some were used as coercive instruments of social control to intimidate students during school elections. Others were hired to recover school buildings taken over by student activists and disrupt assemblies and political meetings by throwing stink bombs inside auditoriums and classrooms. On special occasions, as captured in a photograph by the communist newspaper *La Voz de México*, porros frequently cleaned up their image and, wearing suits and ties, served as bodyguards of their padrinos, as was the case during a visit by a smiling Díaz Ordaz to UNAM on February of 1967.[51] A broad range of authorities also hired porros to perform a number of duties on and off campus. These individuals were available to "clean up" the schools, metro stations, and other public spaces by destroying leftist propaganda, disrupting cineclubs, looting the offices of

Radio UNAM, and physically removing those deemed to be "bums," petty criminals, and unauthorized street vendors. Beyond this, padrinos frequently employed porros to actively carry out campaigns to misinform students, school authorities, the police, and newspaper reporters. As recommended by the IPS report noted earlier, they spread rumors and distributed apocryphal propaganda to infiltrate fighting committees and to provoke student activists by advocating more militant strategies, including the hijacking of school buses (which apparently had become such a rampant problem that the DFS had designated its own specific file of investigation titled *secuestro de camiones* or "the commandeering of school buses").[52] In short, what in the past had been legitimate tactics of student political activism and resistance were thus turned into "acts of desmadre." Their intention, as former porro El Angel claims, was "simply to discredit student activists."[53] For the multiple and, at times, competing padrinos, the acts of desmadre on behalf of the provocateurs usefully blurred the difference between bona fide students and porros in the eyes of the public.[54]

The 1966 Strike and the Rise of "El Fish"

On April 26, 1966, a group of leftist *fósiles*, allegedly financed by Leopoldo Sánchez Celis, the governor of Sinaloa and close friend of Díaz Ordaz, charged into Ignacio Chávez's office and held the rector hostage for more than six hours demanding his resignation, which he presented that same night.[55] With this violent act, this group of provocateurs claimed to be the legitimate representative body of the university Left, which had initiated a strike during the month of March demanding that the rector initiate a series of educational and political reforms. In particular, the leftist wings of the 1966 strike, representing multiple moderate, priísta, and Trotskyite organizations, contended that the administration of Chávez had violated freedom of expression as guaranteed in the autonomous status of the university. Specifically, they pointed to the rector's overuse of Article 82 of the University Statute, which enabled school authorities to expel students for political motives. But the Left was not the only front that attacked the rector. Ultraconservative students with links to influential actors from the Catholic Church, Miguel Alemán's FCMAR, the private sector, and the PAN led by the new University Movement of Renovational Orientation (MURO), whose founding members had been expelled from the university (after having burned an effigy of Fidel Castro in front of the School of Economics), also joined the multifaceted movement against the rector.[56] From their respective ideological positions the competing fronts called for the elimination of Article 82 from the University Statute and demanded the abolition of the university security force, the Cuerpo de Vigilancia, whose "brutality," both fronts alleged, paralleled that of the infamous granaderos.[57] A radical group of leftist students who had taken over the university radio station in mid-April to protest against U.S. president Lyndon B. Johnson's visit to Mexico made further used of this medium to call other sectors of the university community to join the strike.[58] Preparatoria students responded by going out into the streets to demand easier and guaranteed access to higher education. UNAM workers, leading representatives of Central Nacional de Estudiantes Democráticos (CNED), and a group of independent students from the Politécnico added more fuel to the fire by demonstrating their public support of the strike. Additional messages of solidarity also arrived from the universities of Guerrero, Durango, and Morelia (all of which had launched their own specific student protests and further proved to the authorities that the student problem had become a national concern). On April 28 the various leftist strike committees came together under the University Student Council (CEU). This was an independent organization represented by three delegates from each of the different schools and preparatorias who, in turn, had been democratically elected in public student assemblies. This innovative practice, meant to prevent charro leaders from co-opting the strike, would be repeated on a larger scale during the 1968 movement (see Chapter 8). Once united, the students presented additional demands including an end to the admission exams, a revision of the rector's three-year plan for the preparatorias, and the creation of subsidized cafeterias. Further, and more important, they demanded greater student participation in the election of school directors and called for respect for the students' right to organize freely. Students contended that despite the opening of the intellectual life of the university community in the form of greater access to new academic forums, journals, and cineclubs, the "authoritarian" Chávez, who had replaced "the more lenient" Nabor Carrillo, had grown increasingly intolerant of public student criticism, and thus his replacement in favor of a more democratic rector was necessary.[59]

Such fragmentation established a fertile ground for ambitious porro leaders to gain attention by latching on to a particular ideological stance. These included El Superman and El Mame in the preparatorias, El Nazi from the shocking brigades sponsored by MURO, and the members of the so-called Sinaloa Group from the Law School who had led the violent hostage-taking of Ignacio Chávez. But the most significant of these new porro leaders was Sergio Romero Ramírez, nicknamed El Fish. Like Palillo, Romero was also born in Guadalajara and raised in a poor neighborhood in Mexico City, to which his family had migrated when he was a young boy. In 1961, at the age of seventeen, Sergio enrolled in the relatively politically moderate School of Chemistry.[60] Ramírez initially was not known for his conservative leanings. Yet the antagonism that many of his new supporters felt toward the new rector presented him with an opportunity. In 1962 he decided to run for president of the Generation of Students on a platform against the "communist threat" allegedly posed by rector Chávez, as evident in the new emphasis on Marxist philosophy in the classrooms, the attention to psychoanalysis in the university seminars, and in the creation of new "radical" and "immoral" cineclubs.[61] In addition, successfully pandering to a significant sector of the conservative community at UNAM, he spoke of the need to restore the university to what it had been in "the glorious era of alemanismo."[62] On the basis of these two broad political messages (that resonated back to the Siegrist years described earlier), Sergio won the presidency of his school and instantly became a central player in student politics.[63] El Fish, as he would be recognized hereafter, held the position for two years (1962–1964).

The relationship that El Fish established with key individuals gave him access to economic and political resources made available through several networks of conservative power. Through Alfredo Medina Vidiela, a right-wing journalist with *Excélsior*, El Fish established connections with key alemanistas. Vidiela was also an active member of the FCMAR and a key supporter of MURO. The older leaders Carlos Cruz Morales and Pablo Monzalvo, in particular, sat at the center of a range of conservative student organizations, university administrators, and government officials.[64] With this broad support, El Fish claimed to have won the presidency of the FEU in 1964. However, the university rector Ignacio Chávez refused to acknowledge the legitimacy of this and similar organizations.[65] In an unsuccessful effort to put an end to *charrismo estudiantil*, Chávez pronounced all of the different factions of the FEUs null and void, and reiterated his promise (with little success) that he would do everything in his power to eliminate the factionalism and political violence instigated by the Left and the Right, including, if necessary, the use of the university police as well as the implementation of Article 82 from the University Statute.[66] In place of the FEUs, Chávez created the University Federation of Student Societies (FUSA), which sought to promote the official "revolutionary" ideology of the Mexican state in the wake of the Cuban Revolution but further factionalized the politicized student body. Humberto Roque Villanueva, whose conservative views could be seen via his close ties with the PAN and the CEM, led the FUSA.[67] In theory, through Morales's ties to Villanueva, El Fish had inside access to FUSA.[68] But the ambitious Romero did not settle for such secondary influence. In retaliation for the "authoritarianism" of Chávez, El Fish declared war on Roque Villanueva by occupying the FUSA headquarters on January 11, 1965, with the help of fifteen members of his porra gang. Villanueva, accompanied by his own shock brigade and by the university police, fought back by setting fire to the building occupied by El Fish. An internal investigation was ordered by the University Council to determine responsibility for the violence. Both leaders were suspended from their respective schools.[69]

The suspension from the university proved to be a defining moment in the political career of El Fish, who would shift loyalties toward a group of important politicians close to Díaz Ordaz. He would establish ties to this political wing by associating with two important organizations off campus and several administrative sympathizers at UNAM. Momentarily out of school, Sergio first found a job in the Press Office of the Department of the Federal District (DDF), where he started to sell information about student political activities to Alfredo Ríos Camarena, the secretary to Joaquín Cisneros, who, in turn, was the personal secretary of Díaz Ordaz himself. El Fish also established dealings with the DDF through Rodolfo González Guevara (general secretary of the DDF under Corona del Rosal and president of the PRI, 1955–1964) and Martin Díaz Montero (personal secretary of Corona del Rosal).[70]

The forced resignation of Ignacio Chávez in 1966 cleared the way for El Fish's return to the university and led to further opportunities to link with diazordistas. Surprisingly, El Fish enrolled in the radical School of Economics, where he distanced himself from his conservative base, adopted a new rhetoric that spoke to the leftist base of this school, ran for president of a new FUSA, and won.[71] During his one-year term as president, El Fish moved to cut ties with Cruz Morales and his political contacts expanded. El Fish continued to sell pertinent information regarding student political activity to the DDF through a key contact, Alberto Lanz, Press Department manager of the DDF. But he also established new relations of patronage with Díaz Ordaz supporters such as Vicente Méndez Rostro, the general director of the Preparatorias; Fernando Solana, the general secretary of UNAM; and Jorge Ampudia, the personal assistant of Solana. El Fish also developed a relationship with Coronel Manuel Díaz Escobar, the Subdirector de Servicios Generales, who in the late 1960s would become one of the main figures in the creation of the infamous Halcones, or Falcons, a paramilitary group responsible for orchestrating the Corpus Christi student massacre of June 10, 1971.[72] With this impressive network of political support, El Fish was able to transform himself from simply one of several student leaders of the FEUs and the new FUSAs into the most influential intermediary between the different porro leaders of the preparatorias and the state. He was able to offer financial and political support to his porros in the preparatorias from a number of different sources. Similarly, at the Politécnico, El Johnny would establish important connections with Alfonso Corona del Rosal, but also with Jesús Robles Martínez and Alfonso Martínez Dominguez.[73] Together, these two prevailing porros would try to undermine, with limited "success," the 1968 student movement (see Chapter 8).

The Struggle against Porrismo at the Close of the Decade

During the 1968 student movement members of the Comités de Lucha from the IPN presented a list of demands to the public that included the reduction of porrismo by calling for the abolition of FNET and the immediate dismissal of all students associated with it and similar groups financed by the PRI and the ultraconservative Right, such as MURO. The call was soon echoed throughout most of the schools (see Chapter 8). By 1969 the demands for the elimination of porrismo had become louder, more organized, and specific. The brutal killing of a student, Miguel Parra Simpson, on October 20, 1969, and at least ten additional homicides of porros that were the result of clashes inside the schools between porro gangs from 1969 to 1972 intensified public anti-porrismo sentiment. El Fish was thought by many to be the mastermind behind Simpson's killing.[74] An outcry against porrismo went up as news of the murder spread. Assemblies inside the schools, public demonstrations in the streets, and press conferences were organized to denounce the crimes committed by porros and the padrinos who sponsored them.

The new and more populist administration of Luis Echeverría (1970–1976), seeking to distance itself from Díaz Ordaz and the student massacre of 1968, responded to the student demands by arresting dozens of porro leaders.[75] El

Superman in the ENP #5, El Mame in the ENP #8, and a number of other pseudo-student leaders were picked up by police authorities and jailed in 1970. El Angel, who suffered the same fate, gave his own explanation during an interview of why police authorities arrested dozens of porros during this time:

> Yes, we enjoyed a great deal of political independence; yes, we had a lot of fun doing it; and yes, many of us made substantial economic profits from criminal activities associated with porrismo. But at the end we all had to come to grips with one single reality: We were all disposable figures. It was just a matter of time until someone from the top pointed the finger at one of us and for their own political purposes, and we ended up in prison. This is exactly what happened to many porros when Echeverrístas came into office. They cleaned the house.[76]

Disappointed that their padrinos refused to get them released from prison (as had been the case previously), these two porros publicly denounced Vicente Méndez Rostro, the general director of the Preparatorias, whom they named as their principal supporter.[77]

The accusations by El Superman and El Mame fanned the flames of public outrage concerning porrismo and the campus was in an uproar. Teachers organized strikes, threatening to shut down all of the schools unless the authorities "expelled all porros from the preparatorias for good" and forced Méndez Rostro to resign. Joint committees of parents and students supported the teachers by organizing "anti-porra campaigns" in most of the schools. The teachers, students, and parents collected hundreds of statements of denunciation against the porros and presented them to the judicial police. Many students erected barricades in front of their schools, set up alarm systems to warn students of potential attacks, and armed themselves with sticks and Molotov cocktails to prevent porros from entering the schools.

The campus administration responded with typical efforts at damage control. Pablo González Casanova, the new university rector (1970–1972), agreed that porrismo was a "national problem" and argued that unless the government invested in social programs in the marginal neighborhoods that surrounded the preparatorias, porros would remain a threat to democracy inside the schools. Octavio Sentíes, the minister of education, appeared on television and appealed to the students to avoid confrontation with the porros, asked their parents to join the government in its efforts to eliminate porrismo, and pleaded with school authorities to report to the appropriate authorities anyone who engaged in acts of vandalism inside the schools. The federal district attorney vowed that his office would take a more forceful approach in dealing with the porros and ordered the police department to "assist any citizen and genuine student who seek protection from 'porras' or other youth vandals." Similarly, the federal district government "called for any victim of the 'porras' to come forward to testify."[78]

Students were correct in believing that governmental anti-porro efforts were part of a "Machiavellian plan" orchestrated by the presidential administration of Luis Echeverría. The goal of the echeverrístas was to gain a foothold inside UNAM by using the so-called problem of the porras as an excuse to violate the autonomy of the university.[79] The new administration sent the police into the schools, not necessarily to "arrest" the porros, as mistakenly suggested by various journalists, but rather to harass the few students who remained committed to the moribund student movement. For this reason, the Comités de Lucha rejected the demands of the anti-porra campaigns that the police enter the schools and arrest the porros. For them, this was "a task that should strictly be carried out by the students" with the building of additional barricades in front of the schools and the organization of more self-defense brigades.[80] Furthermore, they correctly pointed out that porrismo was "a political problem" and "not a social problem," as was widely held in the press.[81] For the Comités de Lucha there was no difference between the "charro leader in the labor unions," the "white guards and the caciques" in rural Mexico, and the "porra leaders" in the schools.[82] Indeed, they were all agents of repression and mediation deployed by the government and competing political power brokers.

Conclusion: "Student" Violence during the Administration of Díaz Ordaz

A more authoritarian era took hold of the schools of UNAM during the polarizing decade of the 1960s. Authorities close to government officials and competing political power brokers provided financial support to charismatic intermediaries who paradoxically served as a form of quasi guardians of order to counterweight the multiple leftist and cultural organizations that emerged inside the university in the wake of the Cuban Revolution. "In exchange," as Palillo aptly noted during an interview, these new student leaders were given "a green light inside the schools to engage in desmadre," student politics, and cultural activities as long as they "remained within the accepted political parameters" established by their padrinos.[83] At the same time, desmadre and student radicalism offered authorities a useful label to repress, imprison, and undermine anyone who engaged in such defiant behaviors that threatened Mexico's "preferred revolution," including legitimate student activists. Some intermediaries, such as the influential Palillo, found it difficult or impossible to adjust to the changing tactics of manipulation that came with the shifting presidential administration of Díaz Ordaz and changing approaches to growing student dissatisfaction. New charismatic leaders arose to take advantage of the opportunities available, until they too found themselves disposable. This would be the case of El Angel, El Fish, El Johnny, and many other leaders who, despite their loyalty to their padrinos, would be taken prisoners or forced to go underground in the midst of the 1968 student movement, only to be replaced by a new generation of even more callous porros loyal to the secretary of interior and future president of Mexico, Luis Echeverría, 1970–1976.

The 1966 strike, which indirectly influenced the proliferation of porrismo at UNAM, also marked an important chapter in the history of student activism in Mexico. It brought together, albeit momentarily, the various leftist fronts that under the umbrella of the CEU collectively pointed to a series of social and political problems that would come to the fore during the 1968 student movement. On May 11, 1966, Javier Barros Sierra became the new rector of the university—a post that he held until 1970. Still in possession of various school buildings, the students warned Barros Sierra that red and black flags would continue to be waved inside the campus unless the rector publicly announced that he would meet the students' demands. The strike finally ended after the new administration called for the abolition of Article 82 as well as the elimination of all the different FUSAs and the university police. Moreover, Barros Sierra ordered an investigation of those students who had been expelled during the strike, assured that preparatoria students would be automatically accepted to the university, and pledged that freedom of speech would be respected during his administration.[84] His pledges as well as the political stability of UNAM—and the Politécnico—would be tested in 1968.

8   Conservative Mexican Exceptionalism: Body Politics and the "Wound" of '68

ON OCTOBER 23, 1968, twenty-one days after the Tlatelolco massacre, the following letter by the young Helena Paz Garro appeared in the conservative newspaper *El Universal* directed to her father, Octavio Paz, who had publicly resigned his post as Mexican ambassador to India on October 3, 1968, in protest against the ruling party:

> The old men who pose as guides or inspiration for the youth [Marx, Althusser, Marcuse, Lévy-Strauss], in reality are their enemies . . . . The Rudy Dutsckes, Cohn Bendits, Beatles, hippies, yuppies, etc. are the ones who listened to the intellectuals' dead phrase: "the failure of western culture" .
> . . . I'll give you an example: while student riots broke out in Mexico, they were breaking out in Cuba. Here [in Mexico], there were 50 dead and 100 detained. In Cuba there were hundreds shot and thousands imprisoned. At the same time, the Soviets also murdered an entire nation: Czechoslovakia. Why do the intellectuals of Mexican liberty accept the crimes of the Cuban youth [and] of the Czech people . . . ? Because cadaverous rigidity has seized their minds and the countries in which these mass gravediggers reign . . . . I know your perceptiveness, which will let you see the moral and intellectual destitution of those inciting the tragedy that is developing in Mexico.
>
> . . .
>
> You weren't there for the resounding insults [of the teachers and students in the] Che Guevara auditorium, nor their calls to crime, sabotage, and insurrection. Nor did you speak, as I did, with their victims, the

terrorist youths, to whom your "correspondents" outfitted with high-powered weapons, dynamite, and hatred. Your sentence should have fallen upon the complacent authorities, who threw out the youth dispossessed of fortune to death and destruction, and who also snatched away [their] future.

. . .

I should tell you that there has not been one single voice, except that of the government itself, that is concerned about the fate of these youth, destroyed by their materialistic (and therefore opportunistic) guides. We return to you . . . . Now I don't see what [evidence] you put forward for your renouncing the "use of force exercised over peaceful people." The youth . . . were not peaceful . . . . I am with the youth-victims and against their teachers. If you consider yourself part of the group of these teachers, I'll congratulate you and feel pride at your renouncing. But I fear that you have been the "scapegoat" . . . . You see, we find ourselves by different paths in the same arena once again.[1]

Many "ordinary citizens," workers, parents, and teachers sent hundreds of letters with a similar condemnatory tone to the presidential office welcoming a stern response to the "escalating" student problem.[2] Yet sentiments regarding the Tlatelolco crisis and the broader social movements with which it was associated represent a response that to date has been under-represented, even ignored, by the dominant historiography of this period. The same is true regarding the role conservative journalists and right-wing writers played in "protecting" the nation from the new "international threats" and "propagandistic lies" aimed at damaging Mexico's image abroad that, many of them argued, had "peaked" during the 1968 student movement. By incorporating these voices, I argue in this chapter, the administration of Díaz Ordaz perfectly understood that, in order to gain popular support for the open repression of the student movement, it was vital to continue portraying the students as "misguided," "bitter," "utopian," "insecure," and/or "dangerous" pawns manipulated by external enemies of Mexico. As in the past, the role of loyal *porros* and journalists, as well as the distribution of apocryphal propaganda, became indispensable tools in such an enterprise. However, the increasing frustration toward the student movement, its militancy, and its *desmadre* (emphasized here) far exceeded the authoritarian, yet strikingly weak, structure of the Institutional Revolutionary Party (PRI). Put differently, the lack of popular approval of the student movement, overlooked in most analyses of 1968, must in part be attributed to the broad support that the government received from a wide range of influential conservatives, who not only created their own '68 literature in defense of the president but also renovated the language and mission of the Right.[3]

To the surprise of many readers, the young Helena—cited above—did not write to *El Universal* to offer support for her father's bold resignation in India. Instead, expressing similar arguments voiced by her mother (Elena Garro) elsewhere, she offered a poignant and personal critique of "irresponsible teachers" whom she accused of manipulating the minds of young students, and of the way her father had been blinded by his Marxist ideas, betrayed by the Left, and designated as the latest "scapegoat" who would further damage the image of Mexico.[4] But Helena and her mother were not alone in explicitly contending that President Díaz Ordaz had saved the nation from anarchy, ideological subversion, and further violence. Several books written by influential journalists and intellectuals, close to a dozen published between 1968 and 1972 alone, chronicle negative responses to currents seeking change during the long sixties in Mexico. Many of these were more clearly ideologically conservative. Such work supplemented a substantial body of writing in the popular press along similar lines. But what deserves note is the diverse makeup of constituent allegiances of these authors, juxtaposed with their generally agreed unity in opposition to the movements emanating in and out of Mexico City. The participation of renowned intellectual Martin Luis Guzmán, and others, in such discourse provides a prime exemplar of the depth of complexity of such loyalties. Together, their response complicates any simplistic picture of a unified and monolithic conservative opposition. They speak instead to the strength of an established undercurrent of traditional allegiance and, in so doing, raise important questions challenging the notion of the narrow singularity of the events of 1968.

From this perspective, the major events of '68 can be thought of not so much as "watershed"—a term often raised as a dominant metaphor in the historiography—but more as a "wound."[5] This wound, undoubtedly opened up to reveal the internal contradictions of Mexico's authoritarian political culture, was nevertheless clumsily stitched in the national response, mended enough such that the status quo would continue. As with the infrastructural cleanup before and after the Olympics, the purposes of the state continued to be served. It seems that this could only be possible if an established undercurrent of consent of the populace, formed across the body politic before and during the long sixties, was stronger than that of the forces of "genuine" change.

Two intertwined events of 1968, the Tlatelolco massacre and the Olympics—the latter anxiously anticipated, and the former, a fear that came to
pass—demanded some form of referendum by the Mexican people on the
import of the student-led uprisings that had begun forming since the 1950s.
And so, young protesters found themselves inhabiting the canvas of two
divergent would-be portraits, ephemerally painted on an international backdrop. One, adopted by the Left, was a self-portrait that portrayed them as
both victims of an authoritarian Mexican state and vanguards of a new Mexico, connected to similar revolutionary movements worldwide. This image,
as described in previous chapters, had come to capture the imagination of
much of the scholarship of the period ever since. To conservatives and far-
Right influential figures, however, the students were at times still victims,
but now victims of the coercive forces of what they saw as socially, politically,
and economically misguided intellectuals and political subversives, part of
an international malaise of the Left. When students moved beyond peaceful protest to active (and violent) resistance, they were more often than not
portrayed by traditionalists as "criminals," "porros," and, even as "purveyors
of terror." The general dividing lines and distinguishing categories for the
two interpretations, chosen depending which side one stood on, became well
rehearsed by the late '60s—in categories like the typical "targets of threat" on
each side (parents, intellectuals, administrators, the students themselves),
strategies for change (peaceful resistance, militant action, negotiation, desmadre, Zen, counterculture, *porrismo*, brigades), and institutions under
scrutiny (governmental, educational, religious, cultural). The same was true
regarding nations deemed influential benefactors or threats referenced in
this chapter (Cuba, France, Vietnam, the Soviet Union, the United States), as
well as demons and saints (Mao, Díaz Ordaz, Che Guevara, Trotsky, Villa),
press allegiances (*La Nación, El Tiempo, Política, El Universal, El Sol de México*), leading intellectuals (Marcuse, Paz, Freire, Gúzman, Garro, Novo), and
literary and artistic voices calling for action or restraint (Rodríguez Lozano,
Moheno, Illich, Solana, Fuentes, Flores Zavala, Borrego, Siqueiros, Rius,
Monsiváis).

Given the tension implied by this dividing line, my concern in this concluding chapter is to shed light on how conservative opposition to the movements of the long sixties, although by no means monolithic, effectively
sutured the wound created by 1968, leaving a scar, but not a devastating and
debilitating injury. The Games of state continued on. This chapter addresses

this question by dissecting the components of the central myth considered under threat, Mexican exceptionality, into the institutions that constitute it, especially those considered most threatened.[6] Because of its uniquely liminal relationship to Mexico, the conservative response to the "Colossus of the North" is given its own brief treatment, as is the response of Martín Luis Guzmán, whose periodical *Tiempo* exemplified particularly well some of the more nuanced origins of the resilient conservative opposition in its preservation of business as usual. Although the conditions for conservative resilience were long in the making, the discussion begins in 1968 itself. A highly detailed description of the two Janus-faced events of 1968 made so iconic in the literature—the Tlatelolco assault and the Olympics—can be found elsewhere, and is not needed for the purposes of this concluding chapter.[7] However, a sweeping chronology of the movement, with an emphasis on the failure of the *granaderos* and porros in containing the student movement, is provided next as a brief reminder of the harsh realities that formed the backdrop for the domestic and international damage control that conservatives would so assiduously seek during this time.

The Student Movement of 1968: A Brief Chronology

The movement began as a direct response to a long history of police brutality.[8] It got its start on July 22 following a street brawl between two groups of students. Rival street fights were common, but with the involvement of two neighboring gangs and government-sponsored provocateurs, the brawl took a particularly violent turn.[9] Clashes continued the next day. The authorities sent the infamous granaderos to re-establish order, swinging their clubs at students, female teachers, and school employees alike. Four days later, students engaged in two parallel demonstrations: one organized by *politécnicos* to protest against the police invasion of their schools; and a second led by a group of leftist *universitarios* to commemorate the anniversary of the Cuban Revolution. Police reacted by beating both groups callously. The rival students fought back by, surprisingly, joining forces with porros and creating the first *comités de lucha* (fight committees). By July 28, countless students, porros, and granaderos had been injured, at least one young man had died, and hundreds more had been imprisoned.[10]

As more disgruntled youth joined the uprising, government authorities responded by sending military tanks and armored cars to all of the secondary schools that had been taken over by the students. On the night of July 29, the government ordered a group of paratroopers to use a bazooka to blow apart

the two-hundred-year-old wooden door of the historic San Ildefonso Preparatory School. Subsequently, the uprising began to acquire a more political
overtone. The direct involvement of Javier Barros Sierra, the rector of the
National Autonomous University of Mexico (UNAM), further legitimized
the incipient movement; lowering the national flag to half-mast and inviting students to participate in a "funeral march" on August 1, Barros Sierra
protested the violation of the autonomy of the university. Speaking to a crowd
of more than 100,000 people, he encouraged students to articulate their grievances peacefully. Four days later politécnicos and universitarios came together in the first massive demonstration of 1968. At that time, they called for the
unification of the different factions of the Left, demanded that President Díaz
Ordaz personally and publicly recognize their strike, and threatened government authorities that any attempts to co-opt their movement would only lead
to a broader national uprising. By August 8, the various comités de lucha had
come together to form the National Strike Council, or CNH. Collectively,
they made public the following six demands:

1. Liberty for all political prisoners;
2. Abolition of the granaderos;
3. Dismissal of the Mexico City chiefs of police;
4. Elimination of Article 145 (a law of sedition) from the Penal Code;
5. Indemnification for the victims of repression; and
6. Justice against those responsible for the acts of repression.

As in the past, government authorities claimed that "foreign elements" were
behind the students.[11] As early as July 26, the police, upon ransacking the
headquarters of the Mexican Communist Party, allegedly found half a ton
of communist propaganda that, they claimed, had arrived from "Socialist
Cuba." The offices of the communist newspaper La Voz de México and Central Nacional de Estudiantes Democráticos (CNED) suffered the same fate,
and several foreign students accused of promoting urban guerrilla warfare
were expelled from the country. Government authorities made vague accusations in the media claiming "to have evidence" that competing "international" forces were attempting to infiltrate the CNH to prevent Mexico from
becoming the first developing nation to host the Olympic Games, which were
scheduled to begin on October 12. Further, as porros organized by El Fish at
UNAM and El Johnny at the National Polytechnic Institute (IPN) led the first
violent attacks against the comités de lucha, the authorities called for "real"

students to come together in defense of the "democratic" institutions of the Mexican Revolution.

On August 12 the students organized a massive demonstration in front of the National Palace. Meanwhile a CNH chapter claimed that two more students had been killed, six had been gravely injured, and eleven more remained missing. During this demonstration it was estimated that as many as 200,000 people had participated in the march, including thousands of parents and professors. CNH representatives stated that the strike would continue until the government accepted the six demands. They oversaw informational, artistic, and film brigades in various parts of the city that independently documented and presented student grievances to the wider public, reiterated that their broader movement had no intentions of disrupting the Olympic Games, and demanded that all negotiations with the government aimed at resolving the conflict be made in public with press, radio, and television coverage. On August 27, students organized yet another massive demonstration (of more than 400,000 people) leading to the Zócalo, where they named UNAM and the IPN "free territories" of Mexico. They demanded that the "public dialogue" be held in front of the National Palace on September 1 (the same day as the presidential address) and accused the media of orchestrating a dirty campaign that blurred the lines between provocateurs and bona fide activists.[12]

The August marches in the Zócalo were jovial, multitudinous, and, at times, violent.[13] A festive attitude of desmadre—in the form of offensive *corridos* (revolutionary folk songs) insulting specific government authorities, fierce verbal attacks stressing the "animalistic" appearance of the president (performed in front of the National Palace), spontaneous street plays mimicking the granaderos, and the commandeering of transportation buses—offered students opportunities for the direct exercise of freedom and solidarity in the face of police repression, state authoritarianism, generational distrust, and gender discrimination.[14] This was particularly true for the thousands of young female students who publicly defied traditional notions of femininity and chauvinistic stereotypes by leading their own comités de lucha, enabling the movement to spread outside the schools, sleeping over at the occupied schools with their male compañeros, marching in the vanguard of massive demonstrations, and engaging in heated debates in front of male audiences.[15] The same was true of the "re-baptizing" of school bathrooms ("Díaz Ordaz," "Luis Echeverría"), classrooms ("Camilo Torres," "Patricio Lumumba"), and auditoriums ("Che Guevara"), the reappropriation of the state-sponsored

Olympic graphs, the burnings of effigies of politicians, and the symbolic bury-
ing of coffins representing the Constitution of 1917.[16] These and additional acts
of protest and desmadre exposed the inability and unwillingness on the part
of government authorities to mediate the movement. Simultaneously, they
reinforced the opinions of many who began to see the "anarchist" elements
of the movement with great dismay. This was particularly true following the
massive demonstration on August 27, when a significant number of students
welcomed the radicalization of the movement by breaking into the cathedral,
ringing the bells, placing an image of Che Guevara in one of the altars, and
setting off fireworks that had been prepared for Independence Day in mid-
September. Equally offensive to many "ordinary citizens," who protested in
the press and sent hundreds of letters of support to the presidential office, was
the raising of the anarchists' red and black flag in front of the National Palace
that same day.

The administration of Díaz Ordaz responded the best way it knew how. On
September 1, during his Fourth Annual Address to the Nation, the president
explicitly warned students that his administration would not tolerate anarchy,
offered his outstretched hand to those who would take it, and cautioned the
"enemies of Mexico" that government repression will only escalate unless all
students returned to their classrooms.[17] Students failed to appreciate the seriousness of the president's ultimatum.[18] They refused to end their strike and
further mocked the image of Díaz Ordaz by jocularly suggesting that their
movement would accept his outstretched hand only so that experts "can have
it tested for gun powder."[19] They insisted that their grievances were moderate
in nature, reiterated that they would continue to respect the Constitution of
1917, gave evidence that the government had hired provocateurs to undermine
their movement, and organized self-defense brigades to kick the porros out of
the schools.[20] Moreover, hoping to regain popular support, students organized
a Silent March on September 13. Although significantly smaller than previous demonstrations, its peaceful demeanor sent a powerful message of civil
disobedience that the CNH utilized to insist that their movement was both
national and democratic, and not foreign, as their critics insisted. In making
this point, students put tape over their mouths, temporarily toned down their
insults of the president, and replaced anti-U.S. placards and images of Che
Guevara with iconic posters of Emiliano Zapata.

By mid-September it had become evident that the systematic use of provocateurs and granaderos had met their match within the recalcitrant nature

of the movement. Further, there was no longer any doubt that Díaz Ordaz would participate in a public dialogue with the students or risk disruption of the Olympic Games.[21] The same was true of the radical wing of the CNH, which labeled "all forms of negotiation," including a public dialogue with the government, as a betrayal of the movement.[22] On September 18, as public support for the movement continued to wane, the president ordered the military occupation of the UNAM campus. A week later, additional troops were sent to occupy the schools of the IPN, which politécnicos defended fearlessly by forming self-defense brigades and engaging in a violent battle with the military that lasted for more than ten hours.[23]

On Wednesday, October 2, an estimated five thousand people gathered at the Plaza of the Three Cultures in Tlatelolco to discuss the appropriate measures students should take in the next stage of their movement, formulate a strategy to attract popular support (which had sunk to its lowest level), seek ways to receive more international attention, discuss the strategy for a ten-day hunger strike in support of the political prisoners, and demand the departure of troops, which had abandoned the UNAM campus but still occupied the schools of the Politécnico. But as more people continued to arrive at the plaza, government-sponsored snipers opened fire with automatic weapons. Their bullets not only made their way to students peacefully demonstrating but also hit bystanders fleeing to the adjoining Tlatelolco housing project. Soldiers and granaderos who had been sent by the government to oversee the demonstration and arrest the main leaders of the CNH also found themselves in the line of fire. Chaos rapidly unfolded, as the white-gloved members of the Olympic Battalion joined in the shooting.[24] The soldiers, mostly inexperienced in the function of this paramilitary battalion and with massive urban uprisings, fired indiscriminately, while a handful of armed students returned fire with pistols.[25] By the time the smoke had cleared, an undetermined number of people (in the hundreds) had been killed, thousands more injured and/or imprisoned. The government blamed radical elements of the student organization CNH for the massacre, claiming that it had been these students who had fired the first shots.[26]

International Exposure and Critique

The student massacre in the Plaza of Tlatelolco got immediate international attention, and shifted the Mexican showcase, at least temporarily, from eager anticipation of a romanticized and/or renewed Mexico City as the site for the upcoming Olympics, to alarm that this event, and Mexico itself, were not immune to the protest and unrest that were surfacing globally. Under international pressure, the leading representative figures of the government released multiple reports claiming that between thirty and forty people had lost their lives in Mexico on October 2.[27] From their respective countries, however, Mexican ambassadors wrote back to the secretary of state reporting that students and journalists in Canada, the United States, Europe, and Latin America not only questioned the assertion of these numbers but also had organized several demonstrations in which they made the Mexican president personally responsible for the student massacre in Tlatelolco.

These reports were not exaggerations. In Copenhagen, students tried to dissuade Danish tourists from attending the Olympic Games by marching into the streets with signs that read *Tag Med Coca-Cola til Mexico og Drk Blod* ("Go with Coca-Cola to Mexico to Drink Blood").[28] Similarly, in Helsinki, a group of students led a street demonstration chanting "Gold, Silver, Bronze, Blood. Guevara Yes, Díaz No!" In Toronto, Hamburg, and Grenoble, young activists demanded their respective governments withdraw from the Olympics altogether, while, in London, a group of students proclaimed, "Their fight is our fight. We demand the immediate withdrawal of all troops from Mexico City . . . . We are confident that with international solidarity, the students of Mexico will [persevere]."[29] In Caracas and Managua, students rallied in front of the Mexican embassies calling Díaz Ordaz an "Assassin."[30] More aggressively, in Guayaquil, a militant youth group set a car on fire in front of the Mexican consulate and threw stones at the building. Similar acts were reported in the capitals of Panama and Guatemala.[31] In Bogotá, students demonstrated their camaraderie by jamming traffic and singing corridos of the Mexican Revolution in front of the embassy while, in Montevideo, members of the weekly magazine *Marcha* honored those who had died by hosting two filmed testimonies of the student massacre, *Testimonio de una agresión* and *Comunicados Cinematográficos del CNH*.[32] In California, the faculty of the UC campuses represented by Herbert Marcuse (among many others) sent telegrams to the Mexican government protesting against "the brutal killings and imprisonments of university students and others who [have] peacefully and constitutionally participated in the movement."[33]

A slew of initial commentary largely critical of the Mexican government also took place in the international press. The Swedish newspapers *Afton-*

bladet and *Expressen*, for example, challenged the ads promoted in Europe by the Olympic Committee (led by Pedro Ramírez Vázquez) by specifically asking, "Is this the scene that we should expect from the host of the Olympics: military tanks chasing students?"[34] Similar questions were raised in televised reports aired on Belgian, Dutch, Austrian, and Swedish television programs—suggesting that, despite Mexico's "grandiose" attempts at portraying the nation as "modern," it still resembled the "negative" picture so vividly captured in Oscar Lewis's *The Children of Sánchez* (which a Mexican ambassador angrily lamented "was a well-read" book throughout Europe).[35]

Political cartoons published in various international newspapers were particularly effective in providing riveting condemnations of the government and suggested that, perhaps, the Olympic Games should be canceled altogether. For example, a cartoon published in *The Hindustan Times* depicts Mexico as an unworthy Olympic host that can only understand violence (see Illustration 8.1). The Olympic torch is borne in the right hand by a Mexican marathoner, who simultaneously is firing shots from a rifle from his left. A smiling Mexican official extends a greeting to a concerned Olympic Committee in the background on the torch side, while, opposite, an overturned bus sits in flames, a clear reference to recent student-led violence. This, and similar cartoons from countries such as France, Germany, Austria, and the Netherlands, suggested that the only games Mexico knew how to play were those that involved rebellion and government-sponsored repression. While the arguably chauvinistic overtones in these illustrations (the grimacing, mustached torch bearer, the sombrero-capped Mexican official dressed in traditional *charro* garb) provided Mexican officials some level of rejoinders to grasp at, the injury these romanticized and pejorative representations inflicted to the national image was undeniable. They seemed to reinforce the very Hollywood caricatures of Mexicans as bandits, ruthless revolutionaries, and *pistoleros* that the government had hoped the Games would help to dispel.[36]

Journalists in the North were not the only ones to launch critiques. Latin American cartoonists contributed as well.[37] One Central American cartoonist suggested Mexico seemed to be on its way to becoming yet another right-wing state in Latin America (see Illustration 8.2). The cartoon calls attention to a "sad resemblance" between the three foreground figures, representing Mexico, Peru, and Honduras. All have in common an exaggeratedly long right arm that extends fully to the ground, symbol of their mirrored right-wing politics. They also share a landscape filled with the projectiles of war cruising above

"Don't worry, Senors, they're only practising for the Games!"

ILLUS. 8.1. "Mexican Olympics," *Hindustan Times*, October 5, 1968. (Reproduced with permission from the Archivo Histórico Genaro Estrada, Dirección General de Asuntos Diplomáticos, III-5893-1. No. 315.)

a ground of scarcity and economic blight, as vultures lie ready to pick at the desiccated bones of dead cattle. The Brazilian daily *O'Globo* made explicit the critique implied by the same cartoon, arguing that the massacre in Tlatelolco marked "the end" of the "Mexican miracle" (described in previous chapters), which, in the past, had prevented Mexico from becoming another military dictatorship in the Americas.[38] In so doing, it simultaneously called into question the ruling PRI, the party that had presided and claimed credit for the miracle.

Back at home, some of the earliest and most poignant critiques of the administration of Díaz Ordaz came from the National Action Party (PAN) and its official newspaper, *La Nación*.[39] Throughout the movement, both *panistas* and the Left denounced the excessive use of state force against the students and, with provocative photographs published in their respective periodicals, they provided visual evidence of the unwarranted violence of the granaderos.[40] In *La Nación*, but also in congressional and Chamber of Deputies meetings, panistas were particularly strident in condemning the government's violation of the autonomy of the university. Besides the unconstitutional presence of the military inside the university campus, they argued that the PRI had historically violated the autonomy of UNAM through the illegal use of charro leaders and agents provocateurs. In this, they viewed the 1968 student movement as no exception. They specifically accused Alfonso Corona del Rosal and the charro unions of Fidel Velázquez of hiring shock brigades to provoke further violence, confusion, and fear in this latest strike.[41] Representative voices of the PAN refused to accept the president's allegations that "international communist forces" had taken over the movement and, instead, depicted the student strike as part of a long history of social uprisings that had historically questioned the monopolistic power and authoritarianism of the PRI.[42]

ILLUS. 8.2. "Sad Resemblance," Honduran Newspaper Unknown, October 9, 1968. Caption reads: "Wouldn't you agree that our right hands are exaggeratedly long?" (Reproduced with permission from the Archivo Histórico Genaro Estrada, Dirección General de Asuntos Diplomáticos, III-5893-1. No. 515.)

What made critiques from the North, from the kindred South, and from right at home so biting was that they challenged a core myth the government wished to assert—that of Mexican exceptionality. It would be this national myth that conservatives would rely upon most, though not exclusively, to muster enough of a counternarrative to the critiques to keep government legitimacy intact. The concept of Mexican exceptionalism became a central point of contention through which the dividing lines mentioned above intersected. As conservatives advanced it as their motto, it became the core value potentially threatened by enemies internal and domestic. To the opposition, such claims were a farce. But, it should be noted, the case on both sides hinged on the same focal point—the extent to which the Mexican revolution was a living presence in the life of the country, a resource of inspiration for moving forward. Conservatives were ready, willing, and able to garner a defensive strategy, even, and especially, in the face of the furor after the Tlatelolco embarrassment. Their response amounted to a defense of the idea that Mexico was still the country of institutions established and evolved from the vision of revolutionaries and symbolic founders like Pancho Villa, Carranza, Madero, and Zapata, with no greater bearers of the torch than the party that had ruled since those times, the party under scrutiny during the long sixties, the PRI. This myth of Mexican exceptionality, oriented toward national cohesion, but which by definition encompassed an international positioning, was perceived as under threat from without. It thus required a defensive strategy.

The International Character of the "Threat" to Mexico's Exceptionality

On September 3, 1968, the office of Mexico's secretary of interior sent an urgent telegram to all embassies requesting information about recent political uprisings in their respective countries. Concerned with the continuous growth of the decade's largest student movement in Mexico, the government asked ambassadors specifically to identify the various "administrative, legislative, and military" methods employed in their assigned countries to control student uprisings.[43] The initial reports arrived from Paris, where it was reported that French government authorities continued to "formulate plans" to isolate the student protestors.[44] By the end of the month, the administration of Díaz Ordaz had received as many as twenty-one detailed reports from various Latin American countries, as well as from Germany, Italy, Egypt,

Indonesia, and Japan. In these briefings, the ambassadors not only confirmed that youth uprisings had become a worldwide phenomenon in 1968, but also noted that government authorities had grown increasingly frustrated with the internationalist character of the student problem.

Telegrams noted that students in Lima, Beirut, and Rome, for example, hoping to achieve the level of success accomplished in France, had made deliberate efforts to strengthen ties of solidarity with the working class. In Jakarta and Munich students had supposedly established networks of cooperation with French and American students, respectively. In Panama, Quito, La Paz, Santo Domingo, and Tokyo, the student uprisings had become particularly violent.[45] To deal with this unprecedented wave of student uprisings, various government authorities relied on numerous mechanisms of control. In La Paz, for example, the Mexican ambassador reported that the Bolivian government was considering implementing a new law that would make it illegal for more than four students to assemble together in public. In Egypt and Italy, the respective authorities had ordered the closing of several universities. In the Dominican Republic the U.S.-trained marines did not hesitate to use "extreme violence" inside the schools. And in Japan, where the students had become particularly hostile, the authorities had made great efforts to modernize their antiriot police.[46]

But for the Mexican government, the most alarming report arrived from Venezuela, where a group of international students, allegedly "armed with handguns, long-barreled weapons, machine guns, and high-explosive grenades," was said to be training in guerrilla warfare with the sole purpose of "sabotaging the Olympics" and thus preventing Mexico from becoming the first underdeveloped country to host such an important international event. Addressed to the minister of interior (Luis Echeverría) by the secretary of foreign affairs (Antonio Carrillo Flores), the report set out its author's suspicions that members of the so-called General Commando of the Caribbean had infiltrated the Mexican student movement after entering the nation with Colombian and Panamanian passports.[47] Additional reports noted that Venezuelan authorities had undertaken several measures to suppress the "radicals," including the arrest of more than seven hundred students for having violated a new "University Law" that prohibited the distribution of any political propaganda inside the schools "that threatened the principle of the nation or offended proper [Venezuelan] values." Moreover, the office of Díaz Ordaz was informed that several foreign students had already been expelled from the nation, including the German "professional agitator" Daniel Cohn Bendit, who had allegedly traveled to South America to create an international student front.[48]

For Mexican authorities, the diplomatic reports confirmed that the worldwide student revolts of 1968 had established a collective identity of youthful dissent and direct action that transcended traditional notions of nationalism. In late September of 1968, following the military occupation of UNAM, Luis Echeverría, the minister of interior and future president, sent a telegram to Mexican embassies scattered across the globe with a directive to alert the international community about "criminal" and "antisocial elements" that had taken over the UNAM campus since late July. The "illegal" and "antipatriotic" occupation of the schools made a return to classes by bona fide students and teachers impossible, the telegram explained. Although the government "has been patient," hoping that students "will return to their senses," the telegram went on to say that authorities had been given no other choice but "to use public force." If necessary, it concluded ominously, more severe measures would have to be implemented.[49]

A plan to put a final end to the movement by force seemed to be in place. The use of more overt and brutal tactics by the Mexican government to this point has been well highlighted in the literature. But, consistent with the emphasis of this work as a whole on also highlighting more covert and symbolic mechanisms of control (for example, those of porrismo), the remaining sections of this chapter will describe a multidimensional conservative counternarrative that, in successfully shielding a "threatened" Mexican exceptionality, made continued overt brutality less necessary.

In Defense of National Sovereignty

Overall, the various voices of the Right emphasized that exposing the truth about the 1968 uprisings was their "patriotic duty," a defense of Mexico's exceptionality and its very sovereignty. Like Helena Paz Garro, they described the global threat of the sixties as a multifaceted assault ultimately destructive of the nation, but focused initially on the "soft underbelly" of the nation's vulnerable youth. These writers described the events that unfolded in Tlatelolco as tragic and unfortunate occurrences that would not have taken place had it not been for the unpatriotic forces that had infiltrated the schools in the wake of the Cuban Revolution. In particular, they blamed corruption of the student body, as influenced by a wide range of actors, including what they broadly categorized as "foreigners," "Marxist teachers," "progressive Catholics," and "disgruntled politicians." Each of these antagonistic categories can be viewed as representing an institution "under attack," whose discursive defense we will consider in turn, beginning with the so-called "foreign" threat.

One of the earliest attempts at counternarrative came in the form of the release of several apocryphal pamphlets and books that exaggerated student leaders and intellectuals as violent revolutionaries under the influence of "anti-Mexican" infiltration.[50] It would be revealed in time that the source of this apocryphal literature was none other than the DFS. For example, a fabricated "memoir" called ¡El Móndrigo! Bitácora del Consejo Nacional de Huelga (and distributed throughout the schools by porros) became available for free not long after the Tlatelolco killings.[51] This "intimate diary" is a daily account of the CNH during the most active period of the 1968 student movement, from July 26 to the day of the student massacre (October 2) in the Plaza of Tlatelolco. The apocryphal author is "El Móndrigo" (meaning "poor sod" or a "despicable person"), whose dead body, along with his "testimony," the reader is told in the prologue, were allegedly found in one of the buildings in the Plaza of Tlatelolco. According to the author of this "revealing testimony," the CNH advocated that students adopt a more violent strategy in the battle with the government by endorsing an urban guerrilla movement. Echoing the words of the government, El Móndrigo tells the reader that the "naive leaders" in charge of the student movement, "intoxicated with drugs," "armed with ammunition," "connected with international communist forces," and "ready to employ their 'snipers,'" were willing to take all the necessary steps "to stop the Olympics" from taking place in Mexico. The ultimate goal of the "radical students" in charge of the movement, El Móndrigo insists throughout the book, was "to bring about a socialist revolution." Díaz Ordaz, by contrast, is characterized as a misunderstood leader, even a victim, of a violent student movement that refused to have a public dialogue with the state.[52]

The book ends with a chilling description of the moments before the student massacre in which the author implies that people died because of the radicalism of a few self-centered leaders. One of these móndrigos, or poor sods, who hijacked the student movement, was "Raúl" who, according to the author, gave the "signal" for the snipers to open fire on the masses.[53] He writes in his memoir prior to his death: "October 2: Raúl told me that the signal would appear behind the church in the form of Bengal lights. . . . 6:03: The soldiers arrive. I wait for Raúl's signal. There are many [military] tanks. This is the moment. It's 6:15."[54] Moments later El Móndrigo was shot and killed, along with hundreds more students.

In a similar vein, after Tlatelolco, several testimonies were released in the media of militant students who claimed to have received financial support from disgruntled politicians such as Carlos A. Madrazo, who, in collaboration with none other than Elena Garro, was alleged to have been planning to orchestrate a coup d'etat. The suspected presence of pseudo-students among those cited, along with questions of testimony under the coercion of torture and food deprivation, raises serious doubts about such claims.[55] Supplementing such propaganda was a substantial, and perhaps more effective, argumentative discourse on international threats and exceptionality that found, and/or helped to shape, a resonance and receptiveness among the Mexican public.

The first book published in defense of Mexico's revolutionary institutions and its leaders in the wake of the Tlatelolco massacre was Rubén Rodríguez Lozano's *El Gran Chantaje,* or *The Great Extortion* (1968).[56] According to the author, what was key to realize was that students had refused to understand and value the evolutionary character of the Mexican Revolution. In agreement with the prominent economist Manuel Germán Parra, Rodríguez Lozano argues that the revolution had neither failed nor ended.[57] As such, he chastises the nation's youth for failing to appreciate the "unique" character of Mexico, a country, he stresses, that had already fought a violent civil war for the benefit of all its citizens. In contrast with Mexico, in Brazil, a military dictatorship had taken over the government to deal with the continental menace of communism. In France, schools had been turned into ideological trenches by a small group of radical Maoists whose main goal was to undermine Western notions of progress. By contrast, Rodríguez Lozano asserts that revolutionary Mexico had created the necessary institutions to guarantee economic stability, individual liberty, democracy, and political independence from the countries behind the Iron Curtain and the United States.[58] Though conceding that the political system that had emerged from Mexico's popular revolution was far from perfect, it was one that was determined to continue searching for idiosyncratic solutions to Mexico's most detrimental problems, including the upgrading of an educational system incapable of keeping up with the explosion of the student population in the nation's capital.[59]

Stressing the vulnerability of the "crisis of youth," Rodríguez Lozano (like Helena Paz Garro) argues that students had fallen victims to a "dangerous extortion" that had erroneously convinced students that Western civilization and capitalism threatened the future of democracy in the developing world. He condemns the numerous references to Mao Tse Tung embraced by young radicals at both UNAM and the IPN. In setting this perceived ideological "trap," Maoist teachers had taken advantage of the schools to create confusion and ultimately launch a cultural revolution that would bring socialism to Mexico.[60] Because of this perceived threat, the "fraternal" administration of Díaz Ordaz had been given no other choice but to defend the schools with force. In agreement with the president, Rodríguez Lozano insists that the autonomy of UNAM, which had been a key accomplishment of the Mexican Revolution, should be defended from the Maoist forces of CNED. What happened in Tlatelolco, therefore, could not be blamed on the government, as the Left insisted, but instead on the "unpatriotic" forces from abroad that had infiltrated UNAM, the Politécnico, and their respective secondary schools.

In *Historia de una Infamia* (1969), Roberto Blanco Moheno, the influential journalist of *Impacto* and *Siempre!* and self-described nonideological "independent thinker," portrays students as victims of an *infamia*, or "disgraceful act," bred by "unpatriotic teachers of hate" who cared more about communist Cuba and the "misconstrued" writings of Che Guevara than about Mexico, its rich revolutionary heritage, and its historically conservative people.[61] Like Rodríguez Lozano, he also refers to the student strike as a direct threat to the accomplishments of the revolutionary state. In these "particularly stressful times" he felt "compelled" to offer his unconditional support to the government and encourages his readers to do the same. Otherwise, he fears, the nation runs the risk of becoming another military state in Latin America.[62]

In aligning himself with the leadership of the PRI, the author of *Historia de una Infamia* points to the "de-mystification of Cuba" as the main goal of his book. In this effort, Blanco Moheno gives a detailed history of the island, stressing the "subversive nature" of its revolution and its "authoritarian" leaders who, despite their "rhetoric of freedom," he argues, had betrayed the libertarian and "genuine Latin American" spirit of José Martí. In particular, he offers a scathing critique of Che Guevara, whom he describes as an irresponsible husband and father who gives up on his national roots to despotically aid campesinos viewed as "inferior dupes" of a homogenous capitalist elite.[63] Like the author of *El Gran Chantaje*, Blanco Moheno also demands that his readers seek national solutions to Mexico's problems, not "vague" and "foreign" Trotskyite, Maoist, or Guevarist slogans, but rather, the progressive elements of the 1917 Constitution. He persists that unlike Cuba, revolutionary Mexico had truly championed freedom of the press and assembly. Similar sentiments regarding the so-called subversive nature of Cuba and the Mexican student strike are also evident in Gustavo de Anda's *Resumen del Pensamiento Libre de México* (subsequently published in *Maquina Infernal*, 1975), Manuel Urrutia Castro's *Trampa en Tlatelolco* (1969), Rafael Solana's *Juegos de Invierno* (1970), Luis Spota's *La Plaza* (1972), Carlos Martínez's *Tlatelolco* (1972), and Ernesto Flores Zavala's *El Estudiante Inquieto* (1972). All of these accounts reiterate the image of students as "puppets," as articulated earlier by Helena Paz Garro, who had been manipulated by "external hands"; they also all unreservedly excuse the "progressive" and "prudent" administration of Díaz Ordaz for the "necessary use" of force implemented in Tlatelolco.[64]

Adding to book-length treatments were a slew of articles written by journalists in periodicals such as *El Sol de México, El Universal, Novedades*, and *El Heraldo de México*, all echoing many of the same arguments in which they too questioned the legitimacy of the student movement and thanked the government for re-establishing order. Renowned intellectuals Salvador Novo and Agustín Yañez, as well as Vicente Lombardo Toledano (who had been a principal supporter of the 1956 movement), and the famed historian Daniel Cosío Villegas, if not openly siding with the government, also grew increasingly concerned with the *revoltosos*. Former presidents Lázaro Cárdenas and Miguel Alemán, agreeing with Cosío Villegas, asked their respective constituents to come together in the name of "national unity" and to reject "foreign elements" that they agreed had infiltrated the movement.[65] Other, more conservative writers, such as René Capistrán Garza, toned down their critics of the "anticlerical" government, but further collaborated in highlighting the "foreign elements" of the student uprising.[66]

In Defense of the Church and Religious Values

Endorsing a more reactionary tone, Manuel Magaña Contreras's *Troya Juvenil (Trojan Youth* 1971) and Salvador Borrego Escalante's *México/Futuro* (1972) argue that the international threat of the sixties manifested itself in different political shapes and cultural forms.[67] They agreed that Mexico was an exceptional country in Latin America, but instead of emphasizing its revolutionary past, they pointed to its Catholic heritage and its unique geographical relationship with the Colossus of the North. In their version of Mexican exceptionality, Mexico was, even after the extensive divestments and restrictions written into the 1917 Constitution, a Catholic country at its core. Thus conservatives opposed the evils of secularization coming from both extra-Church sources and from clerics sympathetic to the demands of the student-led uprising.

Writers Manuel Magaña Contreras and Borrego Escalante were among the ultra conservative Right who framed their defensive discourse in religious terms, fusing Catholicism with a Mexican national character that they saw being compromised. From their moral conservative perspective, teachings about subjects such as sexuality, countercultural reform, Left politics, and psychoanalysis amounted to an anti-Catholicism rampant in the school system. In his *Troja Juvenil*, Magaña Contreras shares with Helena Paz Garro and others a long list of figures responsible for the "demoralizing" attitude embraced by the Latin American youth throughout the sixties.[68] However, he dismisses the allegations made public by Alfonso Corona del Rosal, among other government officials, which claimed that groups linked to "the extreme right," such as the University Movement of Renovational Orientation (MURO), were ever involved in radical student politics. Instead, he points to *Marxistas en sotana* (Marxists in priest clothing) as the leading figures responsible for the corruption of Mexico's youth. At the top of his list of enemies is Sergio Méndez Arceo, the "red bishop," whom he accuses of transforming Cuernavaca into a "decadent nest" for "pseudo priests," "degenerate monks," "atheists," and "foreigners" interested in destroying the Catholic Church by "importing" liberation theology to Mexico.[69] Specifically, he links the bishop of Cuernavaca to the representative leaders of the International Documentation Center (CIDOC) and the directors of the Universidad Iberoamericana (UI). In part of his critique, he attempts to feminize both of them by accusing them of "hiding behind" their religious *faldas* or "skirts" to influence and thus radicalize the young minds of students.[70]

In reference to vague notions of Marxism and U.S. imperialism, Magaña Contreras and Borrego Escalante also pointed to Protestantism, North American liberal values, and Judaism as dangers to Mexico.[71] They claimed that such values came to the fore at UNAM during the cardenista rectorships of Elí de Gortari in Michoacán (1961–1963) and Ignacio Chávez in Mexico City (1961–1966). As such, they describe cardenismo, not as a unifying force that had successfully consolidated the modern nation state by the 1950s, as the historiography, the Left, and the state tend to suggest, but rather as an irrefutable threat to Mexico's Catholic identity and its Hispanic past.

While exaggerated and often groundless, such critiques did occur in response to a set of important interventions and in the face of activism. The workshops and publications organized and published by CIDOC in Cuernavaca and the Universidad Iberoamericana (UI) in Mexico City independently promoted the need for dramatic social and political changes on a grand scale. They advocated rigorous sociological analyses of poverty and openly called for a fruitful dialogue with Marxists, agnostics, and even atheists committed to radical change in the less-industrialized world. In this effort, for example, Iván Illich, the founder of CIDOC, invited many of the same intellectuals and activists to his seminars in Cuernavaca who had contributed, or would later contribute to, the political and/or countercultural debates in *Revista de la Universidad* and *El Corno Emplumado*, including Paulo Freire, the author of *The Pedagogy of the Oppressed* (1968); Erich Fromm, the professor of psychoanalysis at UNAM; Ernesto Cardenal, the Nicaraguan poet; and Grégoire Lemercier, the Belgian abbot who experimented at his monastery in Cuernavaca with the use of psychoanalysis in community life.[72] As the leading member of these seminars, Illich became particularly critical of what he called the "self conscious altruism" of "charitable" groups traveling to Latin America, including John F. Kennedy's Peace Corps as well as foreign religious missionaries. "Next to money and guns," Illich argued, "the third largest North American export is the U.S. idealist." In making this argument, Illich taught Spanish to Europeans and North Americans and called them to fully integrate their learning into the communities they visited so that they could help empower those in need, not patronizingly from above but, rather, collectively from below. Dozens of young Latin American priests who wanted to take the church to the people rather than the people to the church responded favorably to Illich and enrolled in his seminars.[73] Similarly, *Comunidad*, the new and equally "subversive" journal published at the Jesuit University (UI), also opened an important space for progressive priests and laymen to build a more democratic, humanistic, and pluralistic nation.[74] Here, the Catholic students of the UI (many of whom had participated in the movement) were introduced to and thus engaged in dialogue with the same individuals accused by Magaña Contreras of degenerating the minds of young Mexicans during the 1968 movement.[75]

In Defense of Education and the Minds of the Youth

All roads of conservative criticism seemed to lead to the nation's "rebellious" youth, and no formal institution connected with Mexican exceptionality was closer to students than the nation's schools and educational establishment. Its leadership was time and again described in menacing terms from a variety of sources, including the PAN and conservative journalists such as Blanco Moheno (and others). At heart, it was the minds of the youth themselves, subject to the corrupting influence of "teachers of hate," that were considered up for grabs.

After its initial favorable backing of the student movement post-Tlatelolco reviewed above, the PAN grew increasingly critical of the "militancy" and "lack of political clarity" of the student movement, which gave it a convenient platform to launch against its rival PRI.[76] While not excusing the repressive tactics of the PRI, violent street confrontations between students and the granaderos, they argued, only gave the government greater ammunition to repress the students, and anyone else who dared to challenge the "supreme" image of the president and the PRI's overall "dictatorial" power. *Panistas* saw themselves as exposing the unwillingness of both the government and school administrators to create pragmatic solutions that would allow the necessary "dialogue" to bring a peaceful resolution to the conflict.[77] Among administrators targeted for criticism was university rector Barros Sierra. Like the government, panistas argued, the university rector had "irresponsibly" claimed that both "internal" and "external" hands had infiltrated the movement; but in so doing, he had failed to make the direct connections that panistas believed existed between student violence and government authorities. A good number of self-defined communists might have played a role in the movement, they concluded, but the massive proportion of the strike was not under their direction. Failures of students, administrators, and the Mexican government to come together hurt the ideals that Mexico's unique combination of educational freedom and advancement had supposedly created.

Criticisms of leadership figures associated with the schools would also be leveled by influential journalists and writers. Blanco Moheno's accusations serve as a good example. His broad-stroked denunciations included key founders of *El Espectador* and contributing figures of Radio Universidad, the university *cineclubs*, the Dirección de Difusión Cultural (DDC), *Comunidad*, and the more radical magazine *Política*, for allegedly encouraging students to endorse new forms of urban guerrilla violence. Thus men like Carlos Fuentes, Carlos Monsiváis, Demetrio Vallejo, Alfaro Siqueiros, Barros Sierra, José Revueltas, Herberto Castillo, Eli de Gortari, and Víctor Rico Galán would all come under attack. Similarly, in his *México/Futuro*, Borrego Escalante accused universitarios and politécnicos of "mimicking" Parisian barricades, yippie attitudes, and "homosexual behavior."[78] He pointed to "teachers of hate" as mainly responsible for the urban violence and anarchy that he alleged had tinted Mexico's economic miracle during the 1960s. But to the already familiar list of leftist teachers and intellectuals, he also identified Max Aub, Erich Fromm, Abbie Hoffman, Jerry Rubin, Paul Krassner, Alejandro Jodorowsky, Mick Jagger, John Lennon, Daniel Cohn-Bendit, Rudi Dutschke, and Mark Rudd, as predators on a bewildered global youth. "Smoking marijuana" at Ciudad Universitaria, "watching pornography" at the cineclubs, reading "degenerate comics," playing a role in the "fashioning" of *la onda*, attending workshops on psychoanalysis, and participating in "pseudo-religious" seminars led by Marxist priests, he stressed (in a moralistic—even paranoid—tone), had contributed to the radicalization and alienation of Mexican youth. In dwelling on this point, he also made poignant accusations against the "mainstream communist media" and specifically laid blame on the new (Jewish) directorship of *Excélsior* for turning its back on the newspaper's patriotic origins.[79] In its cultural pages, but also in the university radio station and cineclubs, he argued, Mexico's youth had been exposed to the "erotic" and "homosexual" nature of European films, to the "widespread" consumption of drugs in the developed world, and to the seditious and hedonistic nature of the U.S counterculture, as promoted in the American magazines *Come Out*, *Mad*, and *The Realist*.[80] Like *Excélsior*, Borrego Escalante also argued, the equally subversive pages of *La Nación*, *Siempre!* and the more radical *Política*, and *Por qué?* lessened the significant role communists played in the 1968 student uprising, elevated the Cuban "experiment" into mythical proportions, caricatured the heroic granaderos, and dangerously portrayed the Mexican government, the president, and the army as both sadistic and dictatorial. In stressing the uncertainty of Mexico's "future," both Borrego Escalante and Magaña Contreras invited their readers to support the government's efforts in "re-nationalizing" UNAM, the IPN, and their respective student bodies. Like Rodríguez Lozano and Helena Paz Garro, they all claimed that "true" intellectuals, as well as the working class and the peasantry, were fully aware of the accomplishments representing Mexican exceptionality, including the potential of its educational system, and this is why they refused to be subjugated to the *gran chantaje* of student radicalism.[81]

The Dual Role of the U.S.-Meddling Threat and Envied Model

As it has been for many issues in the conjoined histories of Mexico and the United States, conservatives viewed U.S. influences and opinions related to strategic political affairs, economic relations, and cultural influences post-Tlatelolco in a bifurcated way. Often, and more publicly, the view was negative on two fronts. First, American countercultural forces were viewed as an external corrupting influence on Mexican youth and society. Second, even views from the United States that agreed with traditional Mexican "values" were received with a suspicion in order to reinforce the ethos of Mexican exceptionality, which cared little about the opinions of its neighbor to the North with which it shared such a contentious political history. Yet, naggingly, deep down the United States undeniably represented a "First World" model against which conservative elites, often educated in the most prestigious of U.S. colleges and universities, measured that very Mexican exceptionality.

For what it was worth, initially, as Eric Zolov has documented, "Americans were ready and eager to see Mexico succeed as the first developing nation to host the upcoming Olympics." Such success, of course, would do nothing to upset the cart of presumed American superiority, and the American government quickly reversed direction from an enthusiastic support of the administration of Díaz Ordaz to a more critical view of the president's handling of the student movement. The confidence in the Mexican state quickly deteriorated in mid-September of 1968 and, particularly, after the Tlatelolco massacre, as Americans "came to adopt a more critical assessment of the Mexican Miracle and of the PRI."[82] Joining the concerns of the European press over growing protests, the U.S. press also began to dismiss "the [Mexican] government's claims that behind the protests lay a communist-led conspiracy to disrupt the Olympics," and, instead, gradually admitted that the student movement was overwhelmingly moderate and democratic.[83] For example, by September the *New York Times* and *Time Magazine*, both of which had been supportive of the Mexican government, began raising doubts about this explanation, suggesting instead that the governing authorities in fact had made exaggerated claims of an "international conspiracy," if not fabricated the story altogether.[84]

Since the early 1960s, however, the U.S. State Department's Cold War anxieties that civil unrest could lead to a Mexican turn to "radical politics" and "communism" had led to greater surveillance targeting Mexican schools and student activists. Through various channels, U.S. agents had attempted to gauge the political winds on the UNAM campus. A U.S. agent reporting at the beginning of the decade about students whom "he has come to know fairly intimately" described them as having the failings of rebellious youth—"hot-blooded, idealistic, insecure, and resentful":

> Because of his unfavorable social and economic standing, [the Mexican student] is plagued by innumerable complexes and suffers from a feeling of insecurity. He is resentful of his own society and more so of those societies which enjoy a degree of well-being and prosperity.[85]

The psychosis plaguing Mexican youth led to an acute vulnerability. They argue that the universitarios were constantly "seeking some institution and some body of truth to which they can cling."[86] The "hot-blooded, insecure, and vulnerable psyche," they added, became particularly problematic in the eyes of government agents when, additionally, it was bound to an historical antipathy for the United States, one that was exploitable by the "countries behind the Iron Curtain."[87]

There is little left to the imagination to decipher the congratulatory self-reference to the United States itself in the quotation above, referencing "those societies which enjoy a degree of well-being and prosperity." And while the majority of Mexicans might take issue with the arrogance, this language mimicked references to an "inferiority complex" of Mexico's youth that was stressed in many conservative (and leftist) accounts arising in Mexico at the time. Díaz Ordaz himself in his September 1 "Address to the Nation" expressed something akin to it, and a variant of it could be read into Octavio Paz's influential *Labyrinth of Solitude* (1950) as well. Ultimately, whether a failing based on envy that the United States could boast about, or an envy that Mexican conservatives could say was unpatriotic, or one that Mexican intellectuals could claim got in the way of challenging injustice, the psychic orientation of students came out of the literary wash as a failing nevertheless, and the locus of such a failing was the students themselves.

As mentioned earlier, when activism was closest to direct action, sympathies regarding any inferiority complex met nothing but the strongest condemnation; about this, the counter-countercultural American and Mexican press, and their sympathizers, could chant in unison. For example, many ordinary American citizens went so far as to thank Díaz Ordaz personally for sending the military forces to the Plaza of Tlatelolco to put a final end to the revoltosos. Consider the way conservative Mexican sentiment, already described, appears paralleled in the language used by one individual in the United States writing directly to Díaz Ordaz:

> Dear Sir, . . . while I am sympathetic to the lives lost and the innocently hurt, when unruly mobs refuse to hear the call to order it is then that force must be met with force. I strongly regret that events here in my country were permitted to get out of hand before authorities here too realized that the only way a mob will respond to civilized rule of law is by force . . . . The current breed of hippies, yippies and the like seem to think apparently, that by going into the streets and demanding attention by any means is just and proper. It is not. The authorities in Mexico City and recently in Chicago proved that prompt action and decisive action is responsible action.[88]

Similarly, another "friend of Mexico" residing in the United States noted, "A mike rusher with his teeth bashed in and left laying in the streets is not so likely to have too much to say on the air that evening. I'm sure most Americans support the prompt action of the Mexican government . . . especially since we seem to lack the guts to do it in our own country. Good luck to your government and your armed forces. They have my respect."[89] These vignettes did not represent two isolated examples. Hundreds of similar letters in support of Díaz Ordaz arrived at the presidential office throughout the 1960s.[90]

The conservative discursive field in both countries could place its faith equally on the effectiveness of nonviolent and extralegal measures for managing tensions. From the beginning of the 1968 student movement, American agents stationed in Mexico and key representatives of the U.S. media confidently reported that the PRI's mechanisms of student control and mediation would have no difficulty in co-opting the movement.[91] At the same time, Mexican conservatives could use the tenets of the nation's exceptionality identified with racial tolerance and military restraint to distance Mexico from disturbances in the United States, seen as a uniquely American domestic failure. In his gran chantaje treatment, for example, Rodríguez Lozano states that the polarized society of the United States—caught between a "racial upheaval" and an "excessive" use of imperialist force in Vietnam—had contributed both to the disillusionment of their nation's youth and to the rise in popularity of the violence endorsed by the Black Panthers, the "anarchist" takeovers of Berkeley and Columbia, and the vile killings of John F. Kennedy and Martin Luther King. He also denounced the "excessive presence" of the United States in Latin America and Vietnam by encouraging his readers to realize—once and for all—that the revolutionary pueblo of Mexico "would never accept a red, yellow, or white imperialist dictatorship."[92] Despite such distancing, the general agreement in opposition to the perceived threat of communism and cultural revolution, patently obvious in a shared rhetoric on both sides of the border, suggested that some identification and cooperation was certainly possible, and made attempts at strict adherence to a distinct Mexican exceptionality a tricky dance indeed, as historian Sergio Aguayo has demonstrated.[93]

Guzmán and Tiempo, Exemplar of
the Complexity of the Conservative Response

The remarkably long and prolific career of Martín Luis Guzmán as a revolutionary, politician, historian, and journalist came to personify the changing trajectory of the state and its institutionalized revolutionary party.[94] At the age of eighty-one he became one of the most outspoken supporters of Díaz Ordaz's violent reaction to the student movement of 1968. He serves especially well as an illustration of how the flexibility in interpreting the Mexican Revolution and Mexican exceptionality could serve to broaden the reactionary response in '68, as during the entire period of the long sixties.

In 1900, at the age of thirteen, Guzmán had started his first periodical, *Juventud*, and subsequently formed part of the illustrious Youth Athenaeum Group.[95] During the outbreak of the revolution, Guzmán became a zealous critic, first of Victoriano Huerta and, later, of Plutarco E. Calles, whom he accused of "corrupting the ideals" of Francisco Villa and Emiliano Zapata. Following a brief sentence in the infamous Lecumberri prison, he left for exile in Spain, where he made a comfortable living as a successful writer until 1936. During this period he joined the Republican forces against Franco and published two of the most influential accounts of the Mexican Revolution, *El Águila y la Serpiente* (1928) and *La Sombra del Caudillo* (1929). Upon his return to Mexico, the more mature Guzmán became a cautious supporter of President Lázaro Cárdenas. Guzmán wrote the first volumes of his renowned *Memoirs of Pancho Villa* and contributed numerous articles for various leading newspapers, including *El Universal*, where he celebrated the accomplishments of the institutional phase of the revolution. In 1942 he founded the influential weekly magazine *Tiempo (Semanario de la Vida y la Verdad Hispano Americano)*. A decade and a half later, in 1959, President Adolfo López Mateos rewarded the iconic revolutionary *caudillo* for his long support of the revolutionary government by putting him in charge of the National Commission of

Free Textbooks, a new educational program of publication and nationwide distribution of free schoolbooks to all elementary and secondary students. In these textbooks, students learned the civics of the liberal constitution, as well as the official history of Mexico, including the dictatorial abuses of Porfirio Díaz, the ongoing accomplishments of the Mexican Revolution, the unifying symbols of the nation's mestizo culture, and the "fanaticisms" of both the clerical and leftist political oppositions.

During the administration of Díaz Ordaz, Martín Luis Guzmán relied on the widely read pages of *Tiempo* to construct a counternarrative to the anti-government critiques depicted in the oppositional weeklies *Siempre!* and the more radical *Política*.[96] In a striking contrast, the images of the president published in *Tiempo* capture, not a ruthless leader of an increasingly militaristic state (as Rius had humorously stressed in various magazines and comics), but rather a caring, yet stern, "father" of a nation "under attack." In these turbulent times, photographs depict a caring president being welcomed with opened arms by the business, the military, and the popular sectors. Others present Díaz Ordaz not as leading "gorilla" tanks with "Olympic wheels," as widely depicted by the students, but rather distributing the fruits of the revolution to the poorest sectors of society, inaugurating the new infrastructure built for the Olympic Games, leading workers in the construction of the METRO (Mexico's subway system), reaching out for the support of the private sector, signing the papers for the distribution of communal lands in rural Mexico, granting authority to the new graduates of the Military School, giving memorable speeches to gratified masses, and engaging "in dialogue" with indebted students who joyously walk side by side with the president in front of their schools.

As chief editor of *Tiempo*, Martín Luis Guzmán provided a detailed chronology of the movement in which he drew a striking contrast between the "violent" student strike and the "democratic nature" of the Mexican Revolution. He offers what he sees as detailed descriptions, statistics, and further photographic evidence of the "anti-revolutionary" elements of the movement.[97] Also highlighted are the familiar dividing lines between the main actors involved in the student movement. In Guzmán's meticulous coverage, he draws a sharp distinction between the "provocateurs" and "revoltosos" who participated in violent acts, on one hand, and the young athletes representing Mexico at the Olympics, the female students or pretty *edecanes* ("in psychedelic miniskirts") who served as models for the advertising of the Games, and the young granaderos who "risked their lives" to re-establish order, on the other.[98] He portrays granaderos as "victims" of a leaderless mob engaged in the burning of city buses, the building of barricades with public property, the ransacking of commercial stores, the robbing of innocent bystanders, and the dishonoring of national symbols (including the Mexican flag, the Zócalo, and the president).

In the editorial letters of *Tiempo* (written to and overseen by Guzmán), teachers, parents, workers, and "real" students express their support of the government and the army for what they highlight as the "prudent" handling of the social uprisings of the 1960s. All the categories of Mexican exceptionality and the institutions being defended in the discussion above (sovereignty, the Church and religious values, education, and so forth) appear in *Tiempo*'s estimation and funneling of popular sentiment. Mexicans living abroad write to the editor to "correct the lies" found in foreign newspapers, such as *Marcha* in Montevideo and *L'Express* in Paris, pointing to the Mexican government's alleged "inability" to host the Olympic Games. Letters from "ordinary citizens" in Mexico share their concerns regarding the "foreign elements" that they too believed had infiltrated the schools during this period. In general they offer their support to the editor of *Tiempo* for revealing "the true" and "seditious" nature of the strike. In nationalistic tones relating back to the Mexican revolution, they draw a strong contrast between the "failed attempts" by Che Guevara and the successful and truly popular revolutionary strategies and accomplishments of Pancho Villa.[99]

The editorials likewise embody the dual portrayal of students and youth as a whole as both victims of the "teachers of hate" and violent villains responsible for the current crisis. Accusing Marxists teachers and the "philosophers of destruction" of taking advantage of the vulnerability of the nation's youth, "indignant parents" reach out to their children, pleading with them not to fall prey to the lies of these "pseudo leaders" and the "dangers" associated with the consumption of drugs, which they argued, had reached an unprecedented level of approval by the late 1960. Schoolteachers and former supporters of the movement made accusations against Siqueiros (who had appeared in several televised reports in Europe condemning the Mexican government), and questioned the "real motives" behind the resignation of Octavio Paz. Workers wonder whether students also have the right to organize a strike. Echoing classist and paternalistic views published in newspapers during the 1956 and 1958 uprisings, the letter writers accused middle-class universitarios of adopting the same working-class attitudes of the politécnicos, chide irresponsible parents for having failed to provide a patriotic upbringing to their children, condemn young señoritas for getting involved in dirty politics, and scold "real students" for failing to accept the president's willingness to create a dialogue with the movement. An overall reactionary feeling mixing disappointment, alarm, and determined opposition emerges from these editorials that thank the editor for providing clarity during these "difficult times" of "anarchy," countercultural *libertinaje* ("licentiousness"), and "global chaos."[100]

Martín Luis Guzmán died of a heart attack while editing the pages of *Tiempo* in his office in 1979 at the age of ninety-two. For his critics, the long political life of this cultural caudillo resembled that of the main character in Carlos Fuentes's highly influential book on Mexico's New Left—*The Death of Artemio Cruz*. Like the main character in this book, Guzmán risked his life during the violent phase of the revolution. But during the post-Cárdenas period, he became a unifying and institutionalized voice of the nation and ultimately died profiting from both the symbols and the rhetoric of the Mexican Revolution (of which he played a key role in constructing). For his supporters, however, Martín Luis Guzmán came to resemble the conservative voice of a significant section of the nation, which grew increasingly frustrated with the student radicalism of the era and remained, if not supportive of the government, at least silent in the aftermath of the Tlatelolco massacre. They welcomed the peaceful celebration of the Olympic Games as a sign that Mexico (and by extension the PRI) would continue to embark on its revolutionary path to order, peace, and prosperity.

Conclusion: The Successful Containment of the Gran Chantaje

The leading representatives of Mexico's intelligence agencies clearly understood that neither the Soviets nor the Cubans had ever been involved in the 1968 student movement.[101] The Cuban Revolution and its *barbudo* leaders enjoyed a mythical status during the massive street demonstrations, but the overwhelming majority of students who participated in the CNH brigades, including those who engaged in multiple violent street battles against the granaderos, simply wanted respect for their constitutional rights. The disruption of the Olympic Games and the hope of implementing a socialist society in Mexico might have been echoed in numerous autonomous brigades, but such radical ideas never received the overwhelming support from the students.

Regardless of the strike's massive demeanor, the movement never achieved a truly popular or national dimension.

Despite concrete knowledge of this information by the intelligence services, however, the wounded administration of Díaz Ordaz realized that, in order to receive support for the repression of the student movement, it was crucial to continue portraying the students as foreign threats to the nation. Agents provocateurs and journalists also played important roles in promoting such picture of the student activists. But, as has been emphasized in this and previous chapters, the increasing frustration toward the young revoltosos far exceeded the authoritarian hand of the president and the priísta structure. The lack of popular approval of the student movement (minimized in the historiography) must in part be attributed to the broad support that the government received from a wide range of influential conservatives.

Meanwhile, the students of 1968 proved incapable of transforming their strike into a broader democratic movement. As Herbert Braun has documented, they saw the people of the pueblo and members of the working class as "dupes" of a dictatorial government and thus incapable of creating a strong alliance with their movement.[102] Moreover, like the government and the Right, the leading representatives of the movement also insisted that "foreign elements" (financed in this case by the CIA) had infiltrated their strike and, as an earlier generation of activists had done in the past, they too labeled anyone who endorsed a more militant attitude an "agent provocateur" and/or "sellout."[103] But perhaps more important, because of a long history of corporatist control (described in previous chapters), the students of 1968 tried but ultimately failed to create alternative channels of dissent that transcended the nation's capital and voice innovative demands. The six points articulated by the CNH brigades had been echoed throughout the long sixties, while the students' insistence on creating a "public dialogue" with the president only seemed to reinforce the same paternalistic structure that the movement had wished to destroy.

The 1968 Olympics offered Mexico an opportunity to showcase the accomplishments of its economic miracle, and it opened a global space for the movement, which the students proved incapable of fully comprehending. By contrast, for the multifaceted conservative Right, it was precisely the international character of 1968 that appeared particularly threatening to Mexico's "exceptionality" and it was this "threat" or chantaje that brought their different factions together. As planned, the Olympic Games were inaugurated with great joy and popular support on October 12, 1968. By then, the overwhelming majority of student leaders were either in prison, underground, or in exile. On December 5, the CNH published its last manifesto titled "October 2" declaring an official end to the strike and encouraging all students to return to their respective schools.[104]

My goal in this last chapter has been to present an aspect of the movement that has only received scant attention in the literature. Hundreds of memoirs, plays, novels, and essays have been written on the 1968 student movement over the last forty years.[105] These accounts have failed to examine the divergent conservative reactions to the student movement and instead have tended to reduce '68 to the student massacre in Tlatelolco; they have overwhelmingly described the strike as a unified movement, prioritized the perspectives of leftist male leaders enrolled at UNAM, and minimized the important role student violence played in combating the infamous granaderos.[106]

A closer look at some of the multiple events that unfolded in 1968 within the broader international context of the Olympic Games as differently perceived by competing actors reveals that the movement never constituted a monolithic protest. Further, it demonstrates that, in comparison to the more radical uprisings in Europe and the United States, the Mexican case did not achieve a "popular" dimension. Rather, its limited support came primarily from leading voices of the middle class, including parents, teachers, and intellectuals. By contrast, the deviating sectors of Mexico's conservative community, including influential journalists and leading intellectuals as well as "ordinary citizens" who "felt compelled" to write letters of support to the presidential office, grew increasingly critical of what many of them broadly interpreted as the "anarchist" and/or "communist" nature of the movement. As in the past, the public acts of youthful desmadre and the student militancy that came to characterize the 1968 strike served as a double-edged sword. As leftist intellectuals and supportive groups from the international community denounced the government's involvement in the student massacre, dozens of conservative voices simultaneously came together in defense of the administration of Díaz Ordaz and in so doing created their own "68 literature." Hoping to offer a counternarrative to the highly influential "leftist" interpretations of the movement published at the same time by Ramón Ramírez (*El Movimiento Estudiantil de México* [1969]), Elena Poniatowska (*La Noche de Tlatelolco* [1971]), Luis González de Alba *(Los Días y los Años* [1971])*, and Carlos Monsiváis (*Días de Guardar* [1971]),[107] this other literature blurred the lines between the global counterculture and the student radicalism that characterized 1968. It indiscriminately depicted the sexual revolution, the progressive move to the Left within the Catholic Church, the "subversive" nature of the student uprisings, the hippie counterculture, and even homosexuality as inclusive parts of an international conspiracy that threatened the "exceptional" character of Mexico. Some of these authors traced this exceptionality to the ideals of the Popular Revolution of 1910. Others emphasized Mexico's Catholic heritage and/or the conflicting proximity to the United States. All wrote in support of the government and indirectly dismissed the testimonial accounts by Poniatowska, Monsiváis, and González de Alba (among others) as "lies" aimed at destroying the legitimacy of Mexico and the pax-priísta.

In comparison to the French, German, Italian, and U.S. cases, historical studies illustrating the complexity, as well as the autonomous and even chaotic and violent nature of the Mexican student movement, remain surprisingly low in number. But the same is true of the diverse reactions to the movement, as differently expressed by competing sectors of the national and international communities.[108] In this sense, I agree with historian Ariel Rodríguez Kuri, who argues that at this point it is inconceivable to speak of any revisionist accounts of the student movement.[109] First, we have to establish a better understanding of the "messiness" and contradictions and of the multiple reactions to a long wave of student radicalism that I argue began in 1956 and reached its peak in 1968.[110] Thus, as has been stressed in previous chapters, I also agree with Barry Carr, who questions "1968" as the watershed moment (*parteaguas*) of Mexico's democracy. As he suggests, "'*partemadres*' [skull-breaker] would more accurately convey the iconoclastic character of the [1968] events."[111] The wound inflicted, like the images of bandaged heads of student survivors and political prisoners, were effectively submerged in the historical annals to come.

Conclusion: The End of an Era

O N JUNE 10, 1971, a gang of "thugs"—sporting military clipped haircuts and armed with long kendo sticks, baseball bats, chains, electric pods, and guns—brutally suppressed a peaceful student demonstration.[1] The demonstrators had gathered near the Politécnico's Casco de Santo Tomás in support of a student uprising in the northern city of Monterrey, which had voiced dissatisfaction with President Luis Echeverría's educational reforms, called for the creation of independent labor unions, and demanded freedom to all political prisoners.[2] Four days later, Echeverría spoke on Jacobo Zabludosky's televised *24 Hours* news program and promised that those responsible would be identified, brought to justice, and punished. As in the past, however, the president claimed that *manos extrañas*—manipulated, this time, by "right-wing" forces—had financed the attack. Their goal, he and his supporters would insist throughout Echeverría's administration, was to launch a war against the president's "democratic aperture" and, thus, attempt to undermine his goals of assuming the "progressive" leadership of the Third World.[3]

Four years later an anonymous publishing house released *Jueves de Corpus Sangriento* ("Bloody Corpus Christi Day").[4] The book claims to be the autobiography of Solis Mimendi—a *porro* leader from a preparatory school allegedly involved with the formation of the Halcones, or the "Falcons." As correctly pointed out by the author, this was the same gang of lumpen youth transformed into a paramilitary group that was responsible for violently suppressing the student demonstration noted above. In this apocryphal memoir, however, Solis Mimendi (or whoever the author is) mixes factual information with exaggerations and lies. The author, who claims to have met all the different *padrinos* in charge of creating this paramilitary group, argues that the main figure responsible for this latest student massacre was Díaz Ordaz. Yet there is no longer any doubt that President Luis Echeverría and Manuel Díaz Escobar, the Subdirector de Servicios Generales, were the key figures responsible for ordering the attack against the students on that feast day of Corpus Christi when twenty to forty students were killed and hundreds more were injured and imprisoned.[5] Díaz Ordaz at the same time (and until his death in 1979) stubbornly insisted on protecting the myth of a unified Mexico that not only was "Revolutionary" and "modernized" but also "democratic."[6]

Similarly mixed observations can be made regarding the rich descriptions of *porrismo* provided by Solis Mimendi and discussed at greater length, here, in this book. The author accurately notes, for example, that a broad range of school and government authorities used political violence, provocation, and *desmadre* throughout the 1960s in order to bring under control a politicized student body portrayed in the media as increasingly "more radical" and "violent." Yet many of the details concerning the padrinos who promoted extralegal mechanisms of control throughout the sixties are not entirely accurate. For instance, Solis Mimendi wrongfully asserts that one of the main figures responsible for the campaign against the "leftist" administration of Ignacio Chávez (1961–1966) described in Chapter 7 was the university rector who succeeded him, Javier Barros Sierra (1966–1970). Mimendi thus ignores the involvement of competing key figures. Among those whom he fails to mention are the numerous individuals from the National Action Party (PAN), the Catholic Church, and the private sector. These groups were involved in sponsoring the University Movement of Renovational Orientation (MURO) to crush the countercultural and leftist "crusade," which the ultraconservative group argued had proliferated inside the National Autonomous University of Mexico (UNAM) during the cardenista rectorship of Chávez.[7] Instead, Mimendi wrongfully links MURO with progressive sectors of the Catholic Church that—influenced by the Second Vatican Council—hoped to promote a pragmatic dialogue with the Left.[8] In addition, the author of *Jueves de Corpus* further echoes the arguments put forward by the different sectors of the Right (discussed in Chapter 8)—namely, that leftist intellectuals such as Herberto Castillo, Raúl Alvarez Garín, and Gilberto Guevara Niebla, among many others, were as "guilty" as the armed forces for the student massacre of 1968. For these "irresponsible leaders," Solis tells the readers, a massacre of innocent lives was "necessary" in order to win the sympathy of the masses, crucial for sparking a "socialist revolution."[9]

This, and similar apocryphal narratives of the era (such as *El Móndrigo*), did not fall on deaf ears. The conservative response that emerged with the rise of Mexico's so-called student problem in the mid-to-late 1950s and the divergent voices that later came in defense of Díaz Ordaz drew similar conclusions; in doing so, they effectively portrayed students as a "danger" to the nation's "revolutionary" projects. For the divergent voices of the Right, moreover, the "internationalist" revolution of the long sixties and the desmadre that became associated with it were responsible for the moral stagnation, anarchy, and social decline that many came to believed had reached a boiling point in 1968. Thus, as in other parts of the world, Mexico's Right also emphasized 1968 for its own specific ends.[10] At times in collaboration with, but also independently from, the government, the Right launched its own campaign of disinformation that portrayed the otherwise brutal response in Tlatelolco as an instance of national defense in the face of foreign provocation.

Another key figure accused by Solis Mimendi of having played an important role in the manipulation and profiting of student violence is the iconic intermediary El Fish. In a recent interview published in *Proceso*, El Fish confirms that he was indeed a crucial player in the consolidation of porrismo inside UNAM during this period.[11] In this confession, however, El Fish denies that he had anything to do with the student massacre orchestrated by the Halcones. According to him, the Ministry of Interior (Gobernación) put together *Jueves de Corpus* by using information provided by the director of the Dirección Federal de Seguridad (DFS), Luis de la Barreda Moreno (1970–1976). The intention of the government of Luis Echeverría, he convincingly argues, was to manipulate the history of recent events by putting all the blame for the 1968 and 1971 student massacres on diazordistas—including the numerous porros under the control of El Fish who were imprisoned with the shifting powers of the new *sexenio*.[12] The new *comités de lucha* that emerged in the aftermath of the Tlatelolco massacre agreed with this interpretation, suggesting that the only reason the new administration had launched a "fight" against porros was to divert attention away from the crimes committed by the government against the students in the late sixties.[13] A U.S. Department of State report entitled "Anti-'Porra' Campaign" came to the same conclusion. For the U.S.

embassy stationed in Mexico, the "crackdown" against the porras during this period was "a response to widespread public demands." It was "an attempt to take some of the heat off the government resulting from the general knowledge that elements of the GOM [Government of Mexico] bore responsibility for the bloody repression of the June 10 student demonstration by the 'Halcones.'" It explains:

> The denunciation of the "Halcones" following the June 10 repression of the student demonstration brought forth an outcry, not only from student groups but at the beginning from the press as well. Following President Echeverría's announcement that he had instructed Attorney General [sic] Sanchez Vargas to make a thorough investigation of the affair, there was speculation shortly afterward that the report would be ready in about two weeks. This has not happened, and it is quite possible that it will never be released, at least in a believable form that clearly fixes responsibility for the "Halcones" action on the Government. The Embassy believes it quite likely that the current concentrated effort to control the "porras" is an attempt on the part of the GOM to take some of the heat off itself because of lack of a forthcoming Attorney General report on the June 10 events. The report has not been forgotten by the students, who are certain to bring the matter up again, but at least the GOM will be able to point out that it has taken vigorous action against other, similar right-wing groups.[14]

The report on the student massacre of 1971 was never released to the public, and recently (in 2009), at the age of eighty-seven, Echeverría was acquitted by a federal court of charges of genocide stemming from the Tlatelolco massacre.[15] "The worse part about this," a porro angrily lamented during an interview, was the fact that this "lack of accountability" and "impunity" initially took place during Echeverría's "so-called democratic aperture."[16] Indeed, as others have pointed out, the president's populism (reminiscent of López Mateo's "carrot and stick" politics described in Chapter 7) came with a high price. On the one hand, the press, but also iconic figures of the New Left who voiced their support for Echeverría, such as Carlos Fuentes, congratulated the new president for releasing hundreds of political prisoners, giving leftists intellectuals key positions of power in the government, allowing greater freedom of the press, allocating greater resources to the creation of new schools, portraying Mexico as the champion of the Third World, and/or publicly supporting Allende's socialist revolution.[17] On the other hand, however, porrismo became much more violent during the "populist" administration of Luis Echeverría. Little, in fact, changed inside the schools following the 1968 student movement regarding political patronage and state sponsored violence.

As an effort to demonstrate Echeverría's "intentions" to eliminate porrismo, his administration introduced new "anti-porra campaigns." In reality, however, these were used to undermine the leadership of diazordistas inside the schools. Further, they provided government authorities with an opportunity to infiltrate the schools in order to further weaken the leftist student organizations. As a result of the anti-porra campaigns endorsed by Echeverría, Vicente Méndez Rostro was forced to resign from the director's office of the Preparatorias in April of 1970. Without this key backer, El Fish (and other influential intermediaries such as El Superman, El Mame) lost their hold on the *preparatorias* as new porro leaders associated with the new presidential administration, such as El Larita and Los Pancho Villa, came to power.[18] The end of the sixties, in short, saw the progressive student culture that had characterized the era and its strikingly moderate demands co-opted by the state. Porrismo, for its part, entered into a more violent phase. The violent intermediary tactics of, not charismatic and popular porristas like Palillo, but more clearly porros like El Larita at UNAM and El Johnny at the Instituto Politécnico Nacional (IPN), were recognized and challenged by new comités de lucha. But the tension created by the battles between these groups only left intermediaries like El Johnny vulnerable to betrayal as they themselves became the publicly acknowledged targets of government accusations and public scorn.[19]

Students would continue to engage in political dissent during the mid-to-late 1970s, but the "will to act" in the name of "revolution" that had been massively voiced in public during the long sixties seemed to have vanished in Mexico City with the Corpus Christi massacre.[20] As portrayed in the media and as captured in a new cinematic movement, "alienation" and the "consumption of drugs"—along with the more "lumpen" phase of porrismo described above—became the new "problems" associated with Mexico's youth.[21] At the end of this period, moreover, the "threat" of communism now seemed increasingly relegated to outside the nation's capital—where hundreds of militant students abandoned their "bourgeois" leftist organizations, broke ties with the PCM, joined the radical wings of the New Left, and fled to rural Mexico to join the guerrillas. In short, the sixties were over and the new period of the "dirty war" had begun.

A "Kaleidoscope" History of the Long Sixties

Scholars of modern Mexico have devoted significant attention to social movements to explain the ways in which ordinary citizens have shaped the processes of state formation and democracy. In this scholarship, "1968" (and more specifically October 2) has almost always been described as the transformative moment in Mexico's transition to democracy.[22] The longer history of student unrest and *relajo*, the plurality of the Left, and the divergent conservative responses from competing political powerbrokers described in this work complicate this picture. An emphasis on the different, and at times competing, political powerbrokers behind porrismo and desmadre, moreover, paints a fragmented picture of a highly divisive, and at times particularly fragile, Institutional Revolutionary Party (PRI).

The student massacre of 1968 did not take place because of the "dictatorial powers" of a "leviathan" government entirely led by a paranoid and all-powerful father of the nation, as the literature insists.[23] Rather, it occurred because of the weakness of the PRI's political apparatus. The internal caciquelike disputes within the government, the brutality of the ill-trained *granaderos*, the unsuccessful attempts to completely censor the New Left, and the student massacres of '68 exposed the limits of state power that only became further evident in subsequent decades with the crumbling of the income substitution economic model.

At the same time, the presidential administrations of this period seemed incapable of creating the necessary channels for a burgeoning middle class that had benefited tremendously from the economic miracle. The working-class students of the Politécnico were particularly adamant at questioning this and additional contradictions. It was they, moreover (and not exclusively the "generation of '68"), who had been at the vanguard of student activism and militancy in the struggle for democracy throughout the long sixties. But it has been their history—as well those of the campesinos in rural Mexico and those who fought against *charrismo* in the labor sector and the Normal and Chapingo schools—that has been neglected in the "memory of 1968."

In comparison with other countries, the memory of 1968 in Mexico has not been a highly contested terrain, but one that, despite its relatively thick scholarship, remains overwhelmingly "forgotten" today.[24] Hoping to generate more public interest in anticipation of the fortieth anniversary of 1968, the Cultural Center of UNAM, in collaboration with the Ministry of Public Education (SEP), recently opened the *Memorial of 1968* in the Plaza of Tlatelolco. But as literary critic José Ramón Rulsánchez Serra has lamented, the museum only "receives a few visitors, either by members of the 68 generation or by those of younger generations. So the question of silence remains."[25] According to Sergio Raúl Arroyo, the director of the museum, such silence is attributed primarily to the Mexican government, which over the last forty years has made sure that 1968 is forgotten. He explains:

> First, [it silenced] all testimonials and experiences that broke out of the ideological cages of the post-revolutionary period; then [it] created a sort of vacuum around historical facts and played down all troubling circumstances until they were merely banal. Finally, [it waited] until the remains of any particular testimonials or memories had grown so old and mute that they acquired the opacity that the distance of time spreads along its paths.[26]

To a large extent, these explanations are true. After all, as others have pointed out, the school textbooks that were distributed nationwide from 1968 to 1992 made absolutely no reference to the student uprisings of the 1960s, and little, in fact, has changed in the history books since then.[27] However, I would add that those who have reduced—even commercialized—the memory of 1968 to one hegemonic group of people also share a significant degree of responsibility.

A closer look at the selected voices chosen to represent the *Memorial* reveals, in fact, that little effort has been made by the *sesentaocheros* (68ers) to contest, complicate, or expand their own memories of 1968. From a total of more than four hundred memorial vignettes (representing over fifty participant witnesses of '68) included in the museum, for example, more than half originate from the same hegemonic voices that have dominated the scholarship—namely, Gilberto Guevara Niebla, Raúl Alvarez Garín, Carlos Monsiváis, Marcelino Parelló, Roberto Escudero, Salvador Martínez (El Pino), Gerardo Estrada, Paco Ignacio Taibo II, and Luis González de Alba. Only a fifth of the testimonies collected in the *Memorial* are given by women (primarily to talk about their "feminine experience of '68"), and nearly all represent the selected memories of leftist *universitarios* and intellectuals.[28] By comparison, the experiences at the IPN, the preparatorias, the *vocacionales*, and the Normal and Chapingo schools are limited to the voices of fewer than five people, most of whom have already published their testimonies elsewhere.[29] With the exception of two brief vignettes by Pedro Ramírez Vazquez, the architect of the Olympics, these memories do not try to capture the different ways in which government authorities might remember the movement today. Here, moreover, the paranoid personality of Díaz Ordaz is remembered at length, but those who came in support of the president are forgotten. Also excluded from the *Memorial*, in particular, and from the scholarship of the period, in general, are the testimonies of the undetermined number of students who refused to join the movement, of those (the majority, really) who still recalled the image of Che Guevara but who at the time had otherwise grown increasingly critical of the Cuban Revolution, and of those school authorities who became impatient with the movement for economic, social, and or ideological differences.

Future studies must also make an effort to remember the hundreds of granaderos who fought violent battles with the students in the streets. The student testimonies that we have available frequently allude to the darker complexion of the riot police. Yet we don't know how, if at all, a racialized discourse manifested itself during these street battles. We also know very little about the role regional differences might have played in the numerous students' disputes that emerged between *capitalinos* and *provincianos* during this period. The same is true of the relationship that students established with the different political parties and the working class. Many students who belonged to the progressive wings of the PRI and religious institutions also participated in the movement. Yet the voices of these and additional actors have yet to be remembered in the history of the sixties in Mexico.

As an American historian has argued, "The Sixties was a drama acted out on many stages." Yet scholars of modern Mexico have yet to provide what he calls a more "kaleidoscopic history" of this turbulent period.[30] A deserving historicization of this crucial period in Mexican history becomes possible only when we move beyond the same hegemonic voices zealously guarded by the sesentaocheros, and recently brought together by the *Memorial*, to approach a kaleidoscope history of the long sixties.

REFERENCE MATTER

Notes

Introduction

1. These letters can be found in the *Archivo General de la Nación* (hereafter AGN), Fondo Presidencial Gustavo Díaz Ordaz (hereafter FGDO), Vols. 501, 502. They are also referenced in Rodríguez Kuri, "El lado oscuro de la luna."

2. The PRI has its roots in the National Revolutionary Party (PNR). Founded by President Elías Calles in 1929 as a coalition of the military, social, and political forces, it changed its name, first in 1938 to the Mexican Revolutionary Party (PRM), and finally in 1946 to the Institutional Revolutionary Party (PRI). The PRI lost the presidential elections for the very first time in 2000 to the conservative opposition, the National Action Party (PAN).

3. Anonymous director of the IPN; conversation with the author, notes, Mexico City.

4. Ibid.

5. As noted in Chapter 1, Mexico's "economic miracle" refers to a period of sustained growth of 3 to 4 percent annually, with low inflation of 3 percent from the 1940s until the 1970s. See also Aguilar Camín and Meyer, *In the Shadow of the Mexican Revolution*, 159–198.

6. See, for example, Guevara Niebla, *La libertad nunca se olvida*; Vázquez Mantecón and Arroyo, *Memorial del 68*; Aquino Casas and Perezvega, *Imágenes y símbolos del 68*; Consejo Nacional para la Cultura y las Artes, *1968: Un archivo inédito*; Valle, *El año de la rebelión por la democracia*; Monsiváis, *El 68: la tradición de la resistencia*; and Gómez, *1968: la historia también está hecha de derrotas*.

7. See, for example, Carey, *Plaza of Sacrifices*; Estrada Rodríguez, *1968, estado y universidad*; and Rivas Ontiveros, *La izquierda estudiantil*.

8. On the "long sixties," see De Groot, *The Sixties Unplugged*; Marwick, *The Sixties*; Gould, "Solidarity under Siege"; Sorensen, *A Turbulent Decade Remembered*; Klimke, *The Other Alliance*; and Horn, *The Spirit of '68*.

9. Zolov, "Expanding Our Conceptual Horizons"; and Gosse, *Rethinking the New Left*.

10. Camp, *Mexico's Military on the Democratic Stage*.

11. Aguayo Quezada, *La Charola*; Jardón, *El espionaje contra el movimiento*; and Navarro, "Political Intelligence."

12. The best studies available on porrismo include Guitán Berniser, "Las porras"; Durón, *Yo Porro*; Lomnitz, "The Uses of Fear"; and Sánchez Gudiño, *Génesis, desarrollo, y consolidación*. On the role of agents provocateurs outside of Mexico, see Marx, "Thoughts on a Neglected Category."

13. In making this argument, I draw from two key texts: Portilla, *Fenomenología del relajo*; and Bartra, *The Cage of Melancholy*.

14. Zolov, *Refried Elvis*.

15. Especially relevant is Cohen's classic study on "moral panics," *Folk Devils*. See also Manzano, "The Making of Youth in Argentina."

16. Particularly telling are Servín, *Ruptura y oposición*; and Padilla, *Rural Resistance*.

17. See, for example, the collection of essays in Joseph et al., eds., *Fragments of a Golden Age*; and Moreno, *Yankee Don't Go Home!*

18. On the PRI recently described as a "perfect dictatorship," see many of the essays in Herrera Calderón and Cedillo, eds., *Challenging Authoritarianism*; Condés Lara, *Represión y Rebelión*; and Fiscalía Especial para Movimientos Sociales y Políticos del Pasado, "Informe Histórico a la Sociedad Mexicana, 2006." For more balanced studies of the PRI, see Padilla, *Rural Resistance*; Servín, *Ruptura y oposición*; and Rubin, *Decentering the Regime*.

19. Particularly important are the collection of essays in Joseph and Spenser, eds., *In from the Cold*; and Spenser, ed., *Espejos de la guerra fría*.

20. Joseph, "What We Now Know," 17.

21. Particularly relevant are Knight, "The Modern Mexican State"; Brachet-Márquez, *El pacto de dominación*; Knight, "The Weight of the State"; Pansters, "Theorizing Political Culture"; Pansters, "The Transition under Fire"; Camp, *Intellectuals and the State*; and esp. Lomnitz, "Horizontal and Vertical Relations."

22. See, among others, Agustín, *La tragicomedia mexicana*; Monsiváis, *Dias de Guardar*; Gilabert, *El hábito de la utopía*; Verkaaik, *Migrants and Militants*; and Moore, *Music and Revolution*.

23. See, for example, Niblo, *Mexico in the 1940s*; Aguilar Camín and Meyer, *In the Shadow;* and Rubenstein, *Bad Language, Naked Ladies*.

24. Alonso, *El movimiento ferrocarrilero*; Niblo, *Mexico in the 1940s*; and Carr, *La izquierda mexicana*.

25. One of the best theoretical works to tackle "modern" forms of caciquismo is the collection of essays in Knight and Pansters, eds., *Caciquismo in Twentieth Century*

Mexico. Here, Maldonado Aranda and Hernández Rodríguez examine, in their respective chapters, how urban *caciques* (strong—and often charismatic—local bosses) in key positions of power institutionalized charrismo in the labor unions throughout the Cold War to control, intimidate, repress, negotiate with, and co-opt disgruntled workers who threatened to break away from the corporatist structure established by the state in the 1920s and 1930s. Wil Pansters extends the debates by attesting that "institutions that accompanied modernization, centralization and bureaucratization of power and the state apparatus in postrevolutionary Mexico have always embodied personalistic and clientelistic practices" (297).

26. All interviews were conducted in Mexico City through the course of one to six visits to each interviewee during the summers of 2003, 2009, and 2010, and more extensively between April 2004 and July 2005. At the request of most of my subjects, all interviews were exclusively recorded in handwritten notes taken during these sessions and complemented with additional comments that were immediately appended at the end of each meeting.

27. Luis "Palillo" Rodríguez was the main leader of the Porra Universitaria (UNAM's cheerleading squad) and one of the most important intermediaries inside the university and its preparatorias during the 1940s and 1950s. His American football rival, Jorge "Oso" Oceguera, was the leader of the Porra Politécnica from 1950 until 1957. Oscar González was an influential student activist at UNAM during the 1950s and early 1960s. He was enrolled at the National School of Economics, where he became a key member of the Grupo Linterna and key representative leader of Lázaro Cárdenas's National Liberation Movement (MLN).

28. Nicandro Mendoza was the president of Frente Nacional de Estudiantes Técnicos (FNET), the main leader of the 1956 student strike, and one of the first political prisoners of the long sixties who was arrested for having allegedly violated the Law of Social Dissolution. Carlos Ortiz Tejeda was a student representative of the PRI in the Law School of UNAM and one of the most outspoken leaders of the 1958 student strike.

29. If a nickname was not given during the interview, one was assigned. Some preferred to be cited "anonymously" or referenced with a pseudonym. In total, I interviewed more than a dozen people labeled and or self-defined as a provocateur (or porro).

30. Two important exceptions include David Vega (from the IPN) and Salvador Ruíz Villegas (from UNAM's School of Engineering). Both were representative members of the 1968 National Strike Council (Comité Nacional de Huelga, or CNH).

31. Carey, *Plaza of Sacrifices*, 192; Cohen and Frazier, "No sólo cocinábamos"; Cohen and Frazier, "Mexico '68"; and Tirado Villegas, *La otra historia*.

32. Additional research is required to see how the media and other sectors of society responded differently to the hundreds of female students and workers who also participated in street protests during this period. For two relevant and comparative perspectives, see Alegre, "Las Rieleras"; and Rayas, "Subjugating the Nation."

33. Braun, "Protest of Engagement." See also Pensado, "The (Forgotten) Sixties."

The literature on the Mexican student movement of 1968 is too thick to list in one citation. For a review of the major trends and political debates that have dominated this historiography over the past three decades, see Markarian, "El movimiento estudiantil." For a bibliographical list of the major works published on 1968, see Sánchez Saénz, "Bibliografía sobre el movimiento."

34. Other key events that are important in the history of Mexico's democracy but are otherwise mentioned only in passing here include the medical student strike at UNAM in 1965 and the long history of student protests in Chihuahua, Puebla, Michoacán, Guadalajara, and Guerrero. On these, see Pozas Horcasitas, *La democracia en blanco*; Garza, de la, et al., *El otro movimiento estudiantil*; Gómez Nashiki, "El movimiento y la violencia"; Zolov, "¡Cuba sí, yanquis no!"; Rangel Hernández, *La Universidad de Michoacana*; Henson, "Madera 1965"; Aviña, "Seizing Hold of Memories"; Herrera Calderón, "From Books to Bullets"; Pansters, *Politics and Power in Puebla*; and Blacker-Hanson, "Cold War in the Countryside."

35. Servín, "Propaganda y guerra fría."

36. On the importance of photographic images during this period, see Mraz, *Looking for Mexico*; and Castillo del Troncoso, "El movimiento estudiantil de 1968." On Mexico's "discreet" anticommunism, see Meyer, "La guerra fría."

37. Other political cartoonists under the periodic payroll of the U.S Department of State and/or the Association Press, included Medina de la Vega, García Cabral, Guasp, and Facha. See Rius, *Un siglo de caricatura*, 92–93; and Freyre, *Mira lo que me encontré*, 9.

38. See, for example, Agnew, "¡Viva la Revolución!"; Hinds and Tatum, *Not Just for Children*, 69–110; and Zolov, "Jorge Carreño's Graphic Satire."

39. See Chapter 1; and Aguayo Quezada, *La Charola*.

40. In addition to the DFS and IPS documents, President Fox ordered the Interior Ministry "to collect and deposit in the National Archive documents from other government agencies," including the Secretary of Defense (Secretaría de Defensa Nacional, SEDENA), "that contained information related to Mexico's dirty war." See Human Rights Watch, *Lost in Transition*.

41. Many of the reports contain erroneous information, exaggerated descriptions, and even rumors presented as fact, as historian Raúl Jardón found in his analysis of these documents relating to the 1968 student movement. These shortcomings notwithstanding, the sheer number of documents produced by these two agencies yields a great deal of information if one adopts a cautious approach. Jardón, *El espionaje contra el movimiento*.

42. On the different DFS directors, see Aguayo Quezada, *La Charola*.

43. "El Angel," interview with the author, notes, Mexico City.

44. Ibid.; and "El Caballo," anonymous, and "El Negro," interviews with the author, notes, Mexico City.

Chapter 1

1. Skidmore and Smith, *Modern Latin America*, 53. On ISI promoted as "revolutionary nationalism," see Lomnitz, *Deep Mexico*.

2. Lomnitz, *Deep Mexico*.

3. See, for example, Hofstadter, *Mexico, 1946–73*, 23–24; Cline, *Mexico: Revolution to Evolution, 1940–1960*; and Loaeza, *Clases medias*, 119–175.

4. Schmidt, "Making It Real," 33.

5. Krauze, *La presidencia imperial*, 110–111; and Loaeza, *Clases medias*.

6. Schmidt, "Making It Real," 33. On the accelerating growth of U.S. investment from 1940 to 1957, see González Casanova, *Democracy in Mexico*, 212–213.

7. Hart, *Empire and Revolution*, 403.

8. Moreno, *Yankee Don't Go Home!*, 229.

9. Hansen, *The Politics of Mexican Development*, 72–73.

10. Historian Jeffrey Bortz also found a sharp decrease in workers' real wages from 100 percent in 1938 to 45.8 percent in 1945, 57.1 percent in 1955, 64.7 percent in 1961, and 79.9 percent in 1965. For a complete list of percentages from 1938 to 1982, see Table 2 in Bortz, "Wages and Economic Crisis in Mexico."

11. These numbers exclude the top 4.8 percent of families.

12. Or 14.2 percent, if one were to include those students whose head of the families were "housewives."

13. Jorge "Oso" Oceguera, interviews with the author, notes, Mexico City.

14. Nicandro Mendoza, interview with the author, notes, Mexico City.

15. Mendieta y Nuñez, "La clase media en México."

16. Based on a sample analysis of family income in 1963, Lorey noted that 4.6 percent of the universitarios who participated in the census were from the lower-class, and 9.6 percent from the lower middle-class sectors ("transitional middle"); the overwhelming majority of students were from the middle- and upper-class sectors (85.98 percent). Lorey, *The University System*, 148–149, 197.

17. I use the term "professional" in reference to those parents identified in Covo's study as *profesionales y técnicos, funcionarios y directivos públicos y privados, empresarios*, and *propietarios*. I use the term "white-collar worker" in reference to *trabajadores administrativos, comerciantes o vendedores*, and *trabajadores en servicios diversos*. Finally, I use "blue-collar workers and campesinos" in reference to *obreros y artesanos, campesinos*, and *otros*.

18. Levy, *University and Government*, 24–25. See also Appendini, *Historia de la Universidad*.

19. The university was closed first in 1823 by President Goméz Farias, again in 1857 by President Comonfort, in 1865 by the foreign emperor Maximilian of Habsburg, and finally in 1867 by President Benito Juárez.

20. Appendini, *Historia de la Universidad*; and Garciadiego Dantan, *Rudos contra científicos*.

21. Secundarias, or secondary schools, were created in 1923 under the administration of the National University. Two years later, these were incorporated into the Office of Secondary Education. See Levinson, "Una etapa siempre difícil,'" 145.

22. Mabry, *The Mexican University*, 30, 57–88; and Mendoza Rojas, *Los conflictos*, 67–68.

23. Mayo, *La Educación Socialista*, 75–100.

24. Burke, "University of Mexico," 268; and Mabry, *The Mexican University*, 112.

25. Burke, "University of Mexico," 268.

26. On the conservative control of students and UNAM during the 1930s and early 1940s, see Contreras Pérez, *Los grupos católicos*; and Espinosa, "Student Politics."

27. Ornelas Navarro, "La Educación Técnica," 36.

28. Britton, "Urban Education," 237. For a list of the key figures responsable for the creation of the IPN, see Robles, *Educación y sociedad*, 161; and Instituto Politécnico Nacional (hereafter IPN), *50 años*, 56.

29. Britton, "Urban Education," 235.

30. The proposal was originally published in *El Universal*, January 1, 1936.

31. FNET, "El Movimiento Estudiantil Politécnico," Colección Cuadernos Estudiantiles, November 20, 1960, 30, in Fondo Personal de José Enrique Pérez (hereafter FPJEP).

32. Brito Lemus, "Cambio generacional," 239.

33. Ornelas Navarro, "La Educación Técnica," 40.

34. For the inauguration speeches given at the First Congress of Technical Students, see "Estudiantes Técnicos," *Excélsior*, May 1, 1937.

35. See, for example, Niblo, *Mexico in the 1940s*; Middlebrook, *The Paradox of Revolution*; and Russell Morris, "Political Violence."

36. Schmitter, "Still the Century of Corporatism?," 93–94.

37. Anderson and Cockcroft, "Control and Co-optation," 232.

38. By "UNAM students," I refer to students from both Facultades and Escuelas Superiores, while "ENP students" refers to students of the preparatorias in Mexico City, which by 1966 were located in nine different buildings. "IPN students" refers to students from the various professional schools. "Voca students" includes all middle students from the seven vocacionales associated to the IPN. On population increases in the nation's capital, see Ward, *Mexico City*, 33.

39. The total numbers for each year include both UNAM and ENP students.

40. The majority of female students enrolled in UNAM between 1959 and 1965 were located in five schools: Nursing, Philosophy and Letters, Music, Science, and Social and Political Science. See Covo, "La composición social," table IV. Unfortunately, there is no reliable data with a similar analysis for the IPN.

41. See Chapter 3; and Carey, *Plaza of Sacrifices*.

42. These included the schools of Law and Economics that in the 1960s would become the most important centers of leftist political activism, as well as violent arenas of contestation between activists and provocateurs.

43. As detailed in Chapter 2, the old barrios estudiantil was the site of the most flamboyant novatadas. See also Martínez Assad and Ziccardi, eds., *1910*.

44. For a list of these schools, see Britton, "Urban Education"; and IPN, *50 años.*

45. IPN, *50 años,* 133.

46. Gómez Nashiki, "El Movimiento y la Violencia."

47. See, for example, Camp, "Education and Political Recruitment," 295–321; and Smith, *Labyrinths of Power.*

48. Camp, "Education and Political Recruitment," 298.

49. Krauze, *Mexico,* 587.

50. Lomnitz, *Deep Mexico,* 133, 121.

51. As noted earlier, the construction of Ciudad Universitaria began in the late 1940s, but it was not but until the mid-1950s when all professional schools were transferred to the new location. For a history of CU, see Díaz y de Ovando, ed., *La Ciudad Universitaria.*

52. President Miguel Alemán, as cited in ibid., 298.

53. For a photograph of the statute, see *Tiempo,* May 9, 1966, front cover.

54. See, for example, the student responses to the founding of CU cited in Díaz y de Ovando, ed., *La Ciudad Universitaria,* 294.

55. The old barrio estudiantil had been a space of political contestation and youth rebelliousness since at least the late nineteenth century (and particularly during the 1920s and 1930s); see, for example, Garciadiego Dantan, *Rudos contra científicos.*

56. On the ideological shift to the right, see Córdova, *La política de masas;* and Niblo, *Mexico in the 1940s.* On the emergence of Cold War politics, see selected chapters in Spenser, ed., *Espejos de la guerra fría,* 11–28, 95–117, 119–149. On the consolidation of a stronger central government, see Brachet-Márquez, *El pacto de dominación.*

57. Niblo, *Mexico in the 1940s,* 299.

58. On the rise of an "official" and "discreet" anticommunism, see Meyer, "La guerra fría"; and Loaeza, *Clases medias,* 119–175.

59. González Casanova, *Democracy in Mexico;* and Middlebrook, *The Paradox of Revolution.*

60. See, for example, Semo, "El ocaso de los mitos"; Alonso, *El movimiento ferrocarrilero;* Loyo Brambila, "El marco socio-económico"; Loyo Brambila, *El movimiento magisterial;* Loyo Brambila and Pozas Horcasitas, "La crisis política de 1958"; and Pellicer de Brody, *México y la Revolución Cubana.*

61. Stevens, *Protest and Response,* 105.

62. Monsiváis, "La sonrisa, disfraz de la perfidia," *Proceso,* no. 343 May 28, 1983, 19.

63. Teichman, *The Politics of Freeing Markets,* 38.

64. See, for example, Gil, *Los ferrocarrileros;* Maldonado Aranda, "Between Law and Arbitrariness"; and Hernández Rodríguez, "Challenging Caciquismo." On the DFS during the mid-to-late 1950s, see Aguayo Quezada, *La Charola.*

65. Semo, "El ocaso de los mitos," 38.

66. Foweraker, "Popular Organization," 45–46.

67. Navarro, "Political Intelligence," 238–239.

68. Ibid., 189–190, 210, 237–238, 240, 242–243.

69. Ibid.; Aguayo Quezada, *1968;* and Aguayo Quezada, *La Charola.*

70. An extended version of the law is available in Stevens, *Protest and Response*, 253.

71. Stevens, "Legality and Extra-legality," 64.

72. Ibid., 70. See also Cockcroft, *Mexico's Hope*, 144; and Loyo Brambila, *El movimiento magisterial*, 83–85.

73. *El Popular*, March 31, 1959, as quoted in Alonso, *El movimiento ferrocarrilero*, 153.

74. Cockcroft, *Mexico's Hope*, 121; Vaughan, *Cultural Politics*, 5; Britton, "Urban Education," 235; and Ornelas Navarro, "La Educación Técnica," 48.

75. Cline, *Mexico: Revolution to Evolution*, 194–196.

76. Medina, *Del cardenismo al avilacamachismo*; and Niblo, *Mexico in the 1940s*.

77. On CONCAMIN and its closer ties to the government in the 1940s, see Cockcroft, *Mexico's Hope*, 219.

78. Silva Herzog, *Una historia de la Universidad*; and Mabry, *The Mexican University*.

79. On the control of the university by conservatives during this period, see Contreras Pérez, *Los grupos católicos*.

80. Alfonso Caso, as cited in Navarro Palacios, "La Reforma Universitaria," 105.

81. Ibid., 53.

82. Ibid., 123.

83. Ibid., 103.

84. Alfonso Caso, as cited in ibid., 131–132.

85. Ibid., 53, 54, 107–108, 121, 126.

86. Alfonso Caso, as cited in ibid., 131–132.

87. Caso y Andrade, "Ley Orgánica de la Universidad," 233–249; and Lomnitz, "Conflict and Mediation," 320–321.

88. From then on it would be called the National Autonomous University of Mexico, or UNAM.

89. Lomnitz, "Conflict and Mediation," 320.

90. Mabry, *The Mexican University*, ch. 4.

91. Ibid., 189–190.

92. Contreras Pérez, *Los grupos católicos*.

93. See, for example, Silva Herzog, *Una historia de la Universidad*; and Mendoza Rojas, *Los conflictos*.

94. See Marcúe Padiñas, "La crisis de la educación," 12, 36–37; and IPN, *50 años*, 114.

95. For additional demands, see IPN, *50 años*, 114–115.

96. "Los causantes de la agitación," *El Universal*, March 6, 1942.

97. Clarot T. Canto, "Corrido Huelga de 1942," Archivo General de la Nación, Fondo Manuel Ávila Camacho, Vol. 703, Exp. 2/210.

98. On Véjar Vázquez's anticommunist attitudes, see Niblo, *Mexico in the 1940s*, 96.

99. Marcúe Padiñas, "La crisis de la educación," 37; and CJM, *25 años*, folleto, no. 4, in Cuadernos de la juventud, 1942, 64, FPJEP.

100. On the list of IPN directors who were forced to resign by the students during this period, see IPN, *50 años*, 176.

101. Wilebaldo Lara Campos, "El movimiento estudiantil en el IPN," FNET, "El Movimiento Estudiantil Politécnico," Colección Cuadernos Estudiantiles, 29–30.

102. Marcúe Padiñas, "La crisis de la educación," 39.

103. Jacinto Licea, as quoted in IPN, *50 años*, 137.

104. On the "darker side" of the miracle, see also Padilla, *Rural Resistance*; Servín, *Ruptura y Oposición*; and Ochoa, *Feeding Mexico*.

105. One of the earliest critiques of Mexico's revolutionary projects was Cosío Villegas, "La crisis de México" (1947). Others would soon follow, including Buñuel's classic 1950 film, *Los Olvidados*; and Fuentes, *La Región más transparente* (1958) and *La muerte de Artemio Cruz* (1962).

Chapter 2

1. Porte Petit, *El Instituto de la Juventud*, 18.

2. See, ibid.; and "Discurso pronunciado por el Señor Presidente de la República, Lic. Miguel Alemán," March 30, 1952, Princeton University Latin American Pamphlet Collection. Government in Mexico. Roll #1; in Regenstein Library, University of Chicago (hereafter RL).

3. See, for example, Manzano, "The Making of Youth in Argentina." On earlier conceptions of Mexico's youth, see Pensado, "Between Cultured Young Men"; and the collection of essays in Pérez Islas et al., *Historias de los Jóvenes en México*.

4. Nuwer, *Wrongs of Passage*, 99.

5. In France, a form of ragging known as *brimade* also became common among students. Brimade included "hazing, fagging, silly and dangerous jokes, and forced drinking." See Ghosh, *Ragging*, 10–11.

6. Alejo Montes, *La Universidad de Salamanca*, 313–314; and Torremocha, *La vida estudiantil*, 32–35.

7. José Joaquín Fernández de Lizardi, *The Mangy Parrot*, 21–22.

8. Villaseñor y Villaseñor, *Guillermo*, 56–62.

9. See, for example, Antic Novel, "El Popocho," *El Imparcial*, June 22, 1905; and Villaseñor y Villaseñor, *Guillermo*.

10. Villaseñor explains that *Chante* was an indigenous word, yet used as a derogatory term to define all indigenous people who worked in the mines. See Villaseñor y Villaseñor, *Guillermo*, 61.

11. Ibid.

12. Vogeley, *Lizardi*, 83–84.

13. Palillo, Jorge "El Oso" Oceguera, Jesús Flores Palafox, Nicandro Mendoza, Carlos Ortiz Tejeda, and Oscar González López, interviews with the author, notes, Mexico City; Elizondo Alceraz, *Universidad*; and Arenas, *La Flota*.

14. Nicandro Mendoza, interview with the author, notes, Mexico City.

15. Palillo, interview with the author, notes, Mexico City.

16. As cultural critic Phil Cohen points out, territoriality is not only a way in which students live the subculture of youth as a collective behavior but also the way in which the subcultural group becomes rooted in the situation of its community. See, for example, Cohen, *Rethinking the Youth Question*, x.

17. Arenas, *La Flota*, 61.

18. Elizondo Alceraz, *Universidad*, 105. Brooms "symbolically used by novatos to sweep away their pasts" were brought to the author by Palillo during an interview.

19. Nuwer, *Wrongs of Passage*, 94; and Ghosh, *Ragging*, 10.

20. Nuwer, *Wrongs of Passage*, 98.

21. Viqueira Albán, *Propriety and Permissiveness*, 104.

22. As Julio Moreno has argued, "The simultaneous display of different forms of Mexican nationalism and the spread of American values and ideals made it difficult to make a distinction between 'Mexican' and American." American football played at Mexico's universities during this period was certainly emblematic of this. Moreno, *Yankee Don't Go Home!*, 129. See also Arbena, "Sport, Development."

23. See, for example, Amador de Gama, *Historia gráfica del fútbol americano*; and Noguez Quintanar, *Primero y Diez*.

24. Amador de Gama, *Historia gráfica del fútbol americano*; and "Nuevos campos," *Excélsior*, December 4, 1938.

25. Confederación Deportiva Mexicana, *60 Aniversario*; and López Cabrera et al., "Ensayo histórico de la educación física."

26. Jorge "El Oso" Oceguera, interview with the author, notes, Mexico City.

27. Arbena, "Sport, Development"; and Moreno, *Yankee Don't Go Home!*

28. For earlier examples, see the words pronounced during the anniversary of the Mexican Revolution on November 20, 1933, by Carlos Riva Palacio, president of the National Revolutionary Party (PNR). See Confederación Deportiva Mexicana, *60 Aniversario*, 14.

29. Monsiváis, "Sociedad y Cultura," 272.

30. On the link between advertising, commercialization, identity, and youthful entertainment during this period, see Palacios, "Yo no soy un Rebelde," 321–348; García Saldaña, *En ruta de la onda*; Arana, *Guaraches de ante azul*; and Zolov, *Refried Elvis*.

31. On the production of revolutionary slogans during World War II, see Rankin, *¡México, la patria!*

32. See, for example, the speeches made by national authorities during the inauguration of the Revolutionary Games organized in 1941 to commemorate the anniversary of the Mexican Revolution in Secretaría de Educación Pública, *Memoria de los juegos*.

33. Department of State Documents, Washington, Mexico—Politics, Government, and National Defense Affairs (hereafter DSDW, M-PGNDA), 1963–1966, "A Summary of the Instituto Nacional de la Juventud Mexicana," Desp. A-1064, May 15, 1965.

34. "Discurso pronunciado por el Señor Presidente," March 30, 1952.

35. Hanson, *Go! Fight! Win!*, 41.

36. Ibid.

37. Ibid.

38. See, for example, Morlet de Varela, *Yo dirigí la porra*.

39. Many female students who participated in these parades did so to be "discovered" by the flourishing movie industry. Some students who made it to the big screen included Miraslova, Martha Roth, Teresa Sánchez Navarro, and María Luisa Leal. Jorge "El Oso" Oceguera, interview with the author, notes, Mexico City. See also Palillo, *Goya*, November 12, 1955; and E. R. R., "Palillo, el primero de los 'porros,'" *Contenido*, June 1977, 35–40.

40. Some famous actresses who agreed to endorse the football games included María Félix, María Elena Marqués, Chula Prieto, Ana Bertha Lepe, Cristiane Martell, Lilia Prado, Ana Luisa Peluffo, Kalantán, Su Muy Key, Sátira, and Kitty de Hoyos. See E. R. R. "Palillo, el primero de los porros," *Contenido*, June 1977, 37; *Cine Mundial*, November, 1954; and "La Doña entregó trofeo al campeón," *Cine Mundial*, April 7, 1957.

41. For an example demonstrating the mixture of wild abandon and school spirit, see Noguez Quintanar, *Primero y Diez*, 47.

42. The burning of effigies has a long history in Mexican popular culture. See, for example, Beezley, *Judas at the Jockey Club*.

43. Rivas Hernández, *Grillos y Gandallas*, 17–18.

44. The Goya cheer went like this: "Goya/ Goya/ Cachun Cachun Ra Ra/ Cachun Cachun Ra Ra/ Goya/ Universidad." The Huélum cheer went like this: "¡Huélum! ¡Huélum!/ Gloria/ A la Cachi Cachi Porra/ A la Cachi Cachi Porra/ Pin Pon Porra/ Pin Pon Porra/ Politécnico, Politécnico/ ¡Gloria!" Palillo, interview with the author, notes, Mexico City. For an image of this ritual, see Díaz y de Ovando, ed., *La Ciudad Universitaria*, Illustration no. 31.

45. Oscar González López, interview with the author, notes, Mexico City.

46. See, for example, Kemper, "The Compadrazgo"; and Vélez-Ibañez, *Rituals of Marginality*.

47. Carlos, "Fictive Kinship," 75.

48. See, for example, Camp, *Intellectuals and the State*, 17; Pansters, "Theorizing Political Culture," 14; and Smith, *Labyrinths of Power*.

49. Lomnitz, "Horizontal and Vertical Relations."

50. In all relations of power, as Michel Foucault explains, "there is a capillarity from below to above" and vice versa. Foucault, *Power/Knowledge*, 201.

51. Lomnitz, "Horizontal and Vertical Relations," 54.

52. Note that in this scheme, a person can serve as leader (patron) with a given following, and simultaneously as an intermediary/client, to a larger pyramid to which the person belongs, and so on up and across a pyramidal network.

53. In general, Wil Pansters explains, the "political culture of the pyramid is center-oriented, vertically structured, and the 'cement' that holds it together is the culture of personalismo." See Pansters, "Theorizing Political Culture," 9, 16.

54. Wolf, "Aspects of Group Relations," 1075–1076.

55. See Chapter 1 for a more detailed discussion of these changes in UNAM's formal organization.

56. Wolf, "Aspects of Group Relations."

57. President of the FEU, as cited in Domínguez, "El perfil político," 264.

58. Lomnitz, "Carreras de vida en la UNAM," and "Conflict and Mediation."

59. In the 1940s, Palillo was also the nickname of a famous comedian; thus, also alluding to Luis's presumed sense of humor.

60. Salvador Ruiz Villegas, interview with the author, notes, Mexico City.

61. The exact year of his birth is not something he liked to talk about, a fact that only added to his legendary status. When asked about his birth date the famous porrista responded enigmatically, "[S]ometime around those conflicting years of revolutionary chaos and European uncertainty." Like many people during this time, the Rodriguez family migrated to the capital to escape the violence of the revolution. Palillo, interview with the author, notes, Mexico City. To reconstruct his story I have also relied on additional interviews as well as the following published interviews and articles: Jaste, "'Palillo' dice que no esta loco," *El Mundo Universitario*, June 1946; Camapru, "Palillo, ¿rector?" in *El Mundo Universitario*, June 22, 1948; E. R. R., "Palillo"; Andrés Peralta Santamaría, "El Dr. Luis Rodriguez ('Palillo')," *Gaceta ENP*, Vol. III, no. 8, July 1988, 42–43; and Jorge Laso de la Vega, "¡Cachun, cachun ra, ra!," *Revista de Revistas*, no. 3989, June 11, 1986, 26–31.

62. By the 1950s, for example, Palillo made a number of cameo appearances playing himself in the movies: Urueta, *Serenata en Acapulco* (1951), Cortes, *Viva la Juventud* (1956), and Díaz Morales, *Al compass del rock and roll* (1957).

63. Carlos Ortiz Tejeda, interview with the author, notes, Mexico City.

64. See, for example, the photograph of Palillo in Arana, *Guaraches de ante azul*, 31.

65. Oscar González López, interview with the author, notes, Mexico City.. "Pintas" refers to informal gatherings organized by students to miss school. In English these are often called "ditching days."

66. El Negro, interview with the author, notes, Mexico City.

67. Palillo, interview with the author, notes, Mexico City.

68. Jorge "El Oso" Oceguera, interview with the author, notes, Mexico City; and E. R. R., "Palillo," 38.

69. Palillo, interview with the author, notes, Mexico City; and Laso de la Vega, "¡Cachun, cachun ra, ra!"

70. Palillo stayed in Paris until 1972. Palillo, interview with the author, notes, Mexico City.

71. Jorge "El Oso" Oceguera, interview with the author, notes, Mexico City. On the gaviotas, see Chapters 3 and 4.

72. Anonymous, interview with the author, notes, Mexico City.

73. Oscar González López, interview with the author, notes, Mexico City.

74. Carlos Ortiz Tejeda, El Oso Oceguera, and El Angel, interviews with the author, notes, Mexico City.

75. Palillo, interview with the author, notes, Mexico City. For the photograph, see De la Vega, "¡Cachun, cachun ra, ra!," 31.

76. For an excellent collection of essays that describe urban local bosses, or caciques, see Knight and Pansters, *Caciquismo*.

77. Besides head of the federal district between 1952 and 1966, Uruchurtu was also subsecretary of government (1946–1966) and secretary of government (1951–1952). See Camp, *Mexican Political Biographies*, 710.

78. Before being private secretary for López Mateos, Humberto Romero Pérez was the general attorney of Mexico (1946–1952), director of publicity for the Secretariat of Labor (1952), and director of public relations for President Adolfo Ruiz Cortinez (1953–1958). See ibid., 620.

79. Palillo, interview with the author, notes, Mexico City.

80. See, for example, Archivo de la Dirección Federal de Seguridad (hereafter ADFS), "UNAM," Exp. 63-1-954, L-1, H-349; "Facultad de Derecho," Exp. 63-1-955, L-4, H-4; and "UNAM," Exp. 63-1-1957, L-5, H-92.

81. Letter by Guadalupe H. B. Plascencia to President Don Adolfo Ruíz Cortines, April 17, 1956, in Archivo General de la Nación, Fondo Adolfo Ruíz Cortines (hereafter FARC), Vol. 11, Exp. 111/404. Capitalized emphasis is in the original. There were so many of these and similar letters sent to the government, historian Elena Azaola points out in her study of correctional institutions, that the president often felt compelled to respond. See Azaola, *La institución correccional*, 108–109.

82. Jorge "El Oso" Oceguera, interview with the author, notes, Mexico City.

83. Nicandro Mendoza, interview with the author, notes, Mexico City.

84. See, for example, "Novatadas," *Tiempo*, February 25, 1944, 38; and "¿Promesa no cumplida?," *Tiempo*, March 31, 1944.

85. "Novatadas," *Tiempo*, February 25, 1944, 38.

86. Sanchez Gudiño, *Génesis, desarrollo, y consolidación*, 185.

87. Palillo, interview with the author, notes, Mexico City.

88. Sanchez Gudiño, *Génesis, desarrollo, y consolidación*, 185.

89. See, for example, "La Universidad en Crisis," *Excélsior*, July 28, 1944; "La crisis de la Universidad," *Excélsior*, April 26, 1948; "Escandaloso zafarrancho," *La Prensa*, June 24, 1951; "Temen otro choque," *El Universal*, June 25, 1951; "Crisis de la autoridad," *La Nación*, no. 765, June 18, 1956; and "El Vandalismo estudiantil," *Excélsior*, August 26, 1958.

90. See, for example, Whyte, *Street Corner Society*; and Cohen, *Delinquent Boys*.

91. On Mexico's negative reaction to Buñuel's film, see Acevedo-Muñoz, *Buñuel and Mexico*; and Mraz, *Nacho López*, 91–102.

92. García Saldaña, *En ruta de la onda*, 37–38.

93. To stress the universality of this problem, the viewer is warned with the following opening statement: "The poverty you are about to be see is not Mexican ... [these events] could occur anywhere in the world." Buñuel, *Los Olvidados*.

94. Gomezjara, "Juventud ¿Y la banda que?," 93–134.

95. As several authors have demonstrated, other influential films included *Blackboard Jungle (Semilla de Maldad*, 1955), *Rebel without a cause (Rebelde sin causa*, 1955),

and *King Creole* (*Melodía Siniestra*, 1959). See, for example, García Saldaña, *El Rey criollo*; Arana, *Guaraches de ante azul*; and Zolov, *Refried Elvis*.

96. García Saldaña, *En ruta de la onda*, 54–55.

97. Ibid., 55–56.

98. Portilla, *Fenomenología del relajo*, 39.

99. Bartra, *The Cage of Melancholy*, 176; italicized emphasis is in the original. *Axolotl* is a type of salamander found in Mexico City, which Roger Bartra adopts to signify the Mexican identity. See a similar reference to Mexican identity in Portilla, *Fenomenología del relajo*, 93.

100. Zolov, *Refried Elvis*, 27.

101. Ibid., 27.

102. García Saldaña, *En ruta de la onda*, 57.

103. Thus desmadre can be interpreted as a "subterranean value" in direct opposition to work values (that is, differed gratification, conformity to bureaucratic rules, high control over detail, predictability, and so forth) See, for example, Young, "The Subterranean World," 73.

104. García Saldaña, *En ruta de la onda*, 57.

105. See also Agustín, *La tragicomedia*; Arana, *Guaraches de ante azul*; and Zolov, *Refried Elvis*.

106. As described by Portilla, apretado can be translated as a conceited person or a snob. In the context of youth culture, I would employ the term apretado here as "square." This latter term was originally introduced to scholars by sociologist Howard Becker in his study of jazz musicians as an antithesis to "hipness." See Becker, *Outsiders*.

107. Agustín, *La tragicomedia mexicana*, 150.

108. Portilla, *Fenomenología del relajo*, 87–93.

109. "To go to *la chingada*," as Christopher J. Hall notes in his translation to Roger Bartra's book, "originates from the verb *chingar*, meaning 'to fuck, to spoil, to annoy,' is roughly equivalent to the English 'fuck off, go to hell.'" See Bartra, *The Cage of Melancholy*, 142 n. 20.

110. Zolov, *Refried Elvis*, 39. Anthropologist Carles Feixa points out that, beginning in the early 1950s, young rebels were spawned around the world with names like the "gamberros, blousons noirs, teddy boys, vitelloni, raggare, rockers, beatnicks, macarras, hippies, halftarkers, provos, ye-yés, rockanroleros, pavitos, etc." See Feixa, *El reloj de arena*, 43, 51; Manzano, "The Making of Youth in Argentina"; Passerini, "Youth as a Metaphor for Social Change"; and Rock and Cohen, "The Teddy Boy."

111. Becker, *Outsiders*.

112. See similar descriptions in "El cine inmoral," *La Extra*, October 28, 1957; "La juventud ha olvidado la tradición moral," *La Extra*, September 12, 1957; "Patente de impunidad" and "Ante lo Intolerable," both in the editorial page of *Excélsior*, August 25, 1958; and "Jóvenes desorientados," *Últimas Noticias*, September 1, 1959.

113. Becker, *Outsiders*, 57.

114. Cohen, *Folk Devils*, 9.

115. Rock and Cohen, "The Teddy Boy"; and Manzano, "The Making of Youth in Argentina."

116. Rock and Cohen, "The Teddy Boy," 292.

117. Cohen, *Folk Devils*, 14.

118. For more on the contradictions inherent in hegemonic models of modernity and nationalism in Mexico, see Bartra, "La crisis del nacionalismo," 215.

119. In short, the ironic and mocking ways of relajo in this context illustrate that "[i]rony seeks truth, humor seeks liberty, and relajo [embodying both] seeks irresponsibility." See Zirión, "Phenomenology in Mexico," in which he discusses Portillas's *Fenomenología del relajo*.

120. Beezley, *Judas at the Jockey Club*; and Arbena, "Sport, Development."

121. Juan Ibañez, *Los Caifanes*, 1966.

Chapter 3

1. A similar cartoon depicting politécnicos as puppets can also be seen on the cover page of *Siempre!*, no. 150, May 9, 1956.

2. *Excélsior*, April 14, 1956.

3. See the *New York Times*, April 18, 1956; "Veinticinco mil estudiantes," *Excélsior*, April 12, 1956, 9; "Alumnos del Politécnico," *El Popular*, April 11, 1956. Department of State Documents, Washington: Mexico—Internal Affairs, 1955–1959 (hereafter DSDW, M-IA), Desp. 1348, June 8, 1956; and Cuevas Díaz, *El Partido Comunista*, 64.

4. See "Pliego Petitorio de la FNET," IPN, *50 años*, 146.

5. Nicandro Mendoza, interview with the author, notes, Mexico City.

6. *Hispanic American Report*, 1956, Vol. IX, no. 4, 163.

7. DSDW, M-IA, Desp. 1191, April 20, 1956.

8. Medina C., *EE. UU, y la independencia de América Latina*, 145.

9. Student attitudes toward the issue were noted in multiple DFS documents. See, for example, ADFS, "IPN," Exp. 63-3-1956, L-2, H-253–255. On Corso's interest in implementing the "Plan Columbia," see DSDW, M-IA, Desp. 1191, April 20, 1956. This fear was also shared by a number of leftist intellectuals. See, for example, *La Voz de México*, April 12, 1956.

10. Mendoza, "Relaciones Estado-IPN," 85.

11. Jesús Flores Palafox, interview with the author, notes, Mexico City.

12. See "¡No Ceder, Poli! La Agresión a los Internos, Primer Paso del Programa del Gobierno Contra el Instituto Politécnico," *Fuerza de la ESIME*, no. 3, October, 1956, in Fondo Reservado de la UNAM—Impresos Sueltos, Movimientos Socio-Políticos (hereafter FR-U-IS, MS-P), Vol. 26. Similar accusations will later be made in "Testimonio: El Poli Habla," IPN, *50 años*, 150.

13. See, for example, "¡No Ceder, Poli!," *Fuerza de la ESIME*, October, 1956; "Crisis de la autoridad," *La Nación*, no. 765, June 18, 1956.

14. "Pliego Petitorio," IPN, *50 años*, 144.

15. "No es un simple cambio de Autoridades," in the Student Newspaper, *La Chispa*, n.d., ADFS, Exp. 63-3-1956, L-3, H-32.

16. Ibid. Capitalized emphasis is in the original.

17. See, for example, ADFS, "IPN," Exp. 63-3-1956, L-3, H-1.

18. ADFS, "IPN," Exp. 63-3-1956, L-3, H-4.

19. Nicandro Mendoza, interview with the author, notes, Mexico City; "Mitin en Tlaxcala," *Excélsior*, April 15, 1956, 1, 3; and ADFS, "IPN," Exp. 63-3-1956, L-3, H-1; and Exp. 63-3-1956, L-2, H-253–255.

20. See, for example, Gómez Nashiki, "El Movimiento y la Violencia."

21. Nicandro Mendoza, interview with the author, notes, Mexico City.

22. See Mendoza, "Relaciones Estado-IPN," 85.

23. Nicandro Mendoza, interview with the author, notes, Mexico City.

24. For additional descriptions of student banners, see the same document, ADFS, "IPN," Exp. 63-3-1956, L-3, H-2–5. On the participation of young women in the teachers' and railroad strikes, see Loyo Brambila, *El movimiento magisterial*; and Alegre, "Las Rieleras."

25. "La mujer mexicana," *El Universal*, June 4, 1956, 8.

26. Nicandro Mendoza, interview with the author, notes, Mexico City.

27. It is difficult to determine how many female students participated in these brigades. In one DFS document, it was estimated that only 1 percent of the total number of people in a protest were women, but much more needs to be researched to establish a more accurate estimate.

28. Jorge "El Oso" Oceguera, interview with the author, notes, Mexico City.

29. Jesús Flores Palafox, interview with the author, notes, Mexico City. See also ADFS, "IPN," Exp. 63-3-1956, L-2, H-253–255; and ADFS, "IPN," Exp. 63-3-1956, L-3, H-1.

30. Nicandro Mendoza, interview with the author, notes, Mexico City. One just has to look at the major newspapers to confirm the validity of this statement. I, for one, did not find a single article in the newspapers (*Excélsior, Universal, La Nación,* or *Tiempo*) that sympathized with or even objectively reported about this student protest.

31. Nicandro Mendoza, interview with the author, notes, Mexico City.

32. Ibid.

33. Ibid.; and ADFS, "IPN," Exp. 63-3-1956, L-2, H-253–255.

34. Physical takeovers like these, as subcultural studies have noted, could be read as acts of liberation "in opposition to authority." See, for example, Marsh, Rosser, and Harré, "Life on the Terraces."

35. Nicandro Mendoza, interview with the author, notes, Mexico City.

36. ADFS, "FNET," Exp. 63-3-1956, L-6, H-50.

37. "Hoy arrestarán a los que cometan delitos," *Excélsior*, August 22, 1956; and ADFS, "FNET," Exp. 63-3-1956, L-3, H-129.

38. On the response of the mass media to student activism beyond the Mexican case, see Gitlin, *The Whole World Is Watching*; and McMillian, *Smoking Typewriters*.

39. "Cierre del Internado," *Tiempo*, October 1, 1956, 4.

40. This translation of the *Excélsior* report is available in DSDW, M-IA, Desp. 1248, May 11, 1956. See also "El dinero del pueblo," *Excélsior*, April 21, 1956.

41. "Crisis en la juventud," *Excélsior*, April 20, 1956.

42. See, for example, "El Poli en acción," *Siempre!*, May 2, 1956; "El Politécnico, una lección más," *Siempre!*, June 27, 1956; "Recuerda Usted, Señor Ministro?" *Siempre!*, June 27, 1956; "Lombardo exhorta a los jóvenes," *El Popular*, July 14, 1956; and "Opinión del PP," *El Popular*, October 5, 1956.

43. This argument was made, for example, by Mariano Molina, general secretary of FNET, when asked by a reporter whether he belonged to any political party. See *Tiempo*, May 14, 1956, 4.

44. Marcúe Padiñas, "La crisis de la educación," 45.

45. These arguments were also made outside México. See, for example, "Los comunistas agitan en México," *La Prensa* (Lima, Peru), April 21, 1956; "Lo del Politécnico," *El Espectador* (Guatemala), September 29, 1956; and "Libertinaje Estudiantil," *Nuestro Diario* (Guatemala), October 8, 1956; all in "Huelga del Instituto Politécnico," Archivo Histórico Genaro Estrada, Dirección General de Asuntos Diplomáticos (hereafter AHGE, DGAD), Exp. III 664 (72).

46. See, for example, "Apoya abiertamente la Huelga," *Excélsior*, April 14, 1956; "Comunistas y pepistas," *Excélsior*, April 30, 1956; and "Hay que erradicar el comunismo," *Excélsior*, May 3, 1956.

47. DSDW, M-IA, Desp. 1310, May 25, 1956; *Excélsior*, May 6, 1956; and "Politécnicos y normalistas," *La Nación*, May 10, 1956.

48. See also DSDW, M-IA, Desp. 1248, November 5, 1956; and "Lecciones de la Huelga," *Excélsior*, April 27, 1956.

49. "Cierre del Internado del IPN," *Tiempo*, October 1, 1956, 5.

50. "Crisis de la autoridad," *La Nación*, no. 765, June 18, 1956.

51. Letter to President Adolfo Ruíz Cortines and Secretario de Educación Pública José Ángel Ceniceros, by Joel Ibarra on May 10, 1954, in FARC, Vol. 11, Exp. 111/404.

52. "La verdad sobre la huelga," *Excélsior*, April 19, 1956; "Crisis en la juventud," *Excélsior*, April 20, 1956; "Hay que erradicar el comunismo," *Excélsior*, May 3, 1956; and "¿Una conspiración roja?," *Excélsior*, May 8, 1956.

53. DSDW, M-IA, "Political Developments in Mexico during June 1956," Desp. 28, July 10, 1956.

54. See, for example, "¿Hay huelga en el Poli?," *Excélsior*, May 17, 1956; "Nuestra más alta Escuela Técnica," *Excélsior*, May 21, 1956; "Ya es demasiada tolerancia," *Excélsior*, May 29, 1956; and "Nuestro deber," *Excélsior*, June 6, 1956.

55. DSDW, M-I, Desp. 1281, May 19, 1956.

56. DSDW, M-IA, "Political Developments in Mexico during June 1956," Desp. 28, July 10, 1956.

57. DSDW, M-IA, Desp. 1204, April 27, 1956; and "Crisis de la autoridad," *La Nación*, no. 765, June 18, 1956.

58. Extended versions of these agreements are available in "Resolvió anoche el

Presidente el conflicto," *Excélsior,* June 16, 1956; and "Presentan hoy sus demandas," *El Popular,* April 21, 1956.

59. Politécnicos, in fact, threatened that Hernández Corso never enter the IPN again. See, for example, "El Comité no acepta a Hernández Corso," *Excélsior,* June 17, 1956; and "Se reanudan clases," *Excélsior,* June 21, 1956.

Chapter 4

1. The Comedor was a publicly and privately financed cafeteria in downtown that served subsidized and/or free meals to hundreds of low-income universitarios, politécnicos, and normalistas. The people who wanted to see an end to the cafeteria included Alejo Peralta, IPN director; Nabor Carrillo, the UNAM rector; and Morones Prieto, the secretary of Health and Welfare. See "Trifulca estudiantil," *Excélsior,* September 28, 1956.

2. "La UNAM, nido de juniors y niños popof," Fondo Reservado del Instituto de Investigaciones Bibliográficas (hereafter FRIIB), Vol. 1, Exp. 73, n.d., in Archivo Histórico de la UNAM [AH-UNAM].

3. "Trifulca estudiantil"; and Russell Morris, "Political Violence," 370.

4. A student manifesto, for example, demonstrates that some conflicting differences existed between students from Veracruz, Michoacán, and Tlaxcala. See "¿Rectitud o vandalismo?," FRIIB, Vol. 1, Exp. 24, June 1956, in AH-UNAM.

5. "La verdad sobre el atentado gangsteril," *El Cometa Universitario,* no. 3, October–November 1956, in FRIIB, Vol. 1, Exp. 91, AH-UNAM.

6. Ibid. Some students went so far as to say that the attack had been paid for by Nabor Carrillo through his private secretary, Efreén del Pozo. See, for example, ADFS, "UNAM," Exp. 63-4-953, L-1, H-2.

7. "Los judas del comedor," *El Cometa Universitario,* no. 3, October–November 1956, in FRIIB, Vol. 1, Exp. 91, in AH-UNAM.

8. "Opinión de los estudiantes," *El Cometa Universitario,* no. 3, October–November 1956, in FRIIB, Vol. 1, Exp. 91, in AH-UNAM.

9. After the eruption of new student disturbances, both Preparatoria #5 and #2 were closed "to prevent further bloodshed." See DSDW, M-IA, Desp. 116, August 3, 1956; and "'Prep' Students," *Washington Post,* August 22, 1956. Before that, during the month of June, students from the University of Michocacán organized a violent demonstration in support of the Politécnicos. See, for example, Gómez Nashiki, "El Movimiento y la Violencia." The following month more than two hundred students from the Escuela Nacional de Medicina Homeopatica also went on strike to demand the immediate removal of that school's director—Luis Salinas Ramos. See Russell Morris, "Political Violence," 366.

10. "Peralta ve fácil lo del Politécnico," *Excélsior,* August 25, 1956.

11. Born into a successful entrepreneurial family (his brother was the owner of the Hotel Regis), Alejo Peralta began his industrial career at the age of eighteen when he founded a small mechanical shop that he named Peralta Hermanos. Three years

later he graduated from ESIME (Superior School of Mechanical Engineering—associated with the IPN), expanded his shop, and renamed it IUSA. In 1945 he founded one of Mexico's largest electrical industries, Compañia Electrocerámica, S.A. Nine years later, he became one of Mexico's most prosperous millionaires after investing in the baseball teams Azteca and Tigres Capitalinos. See Suárez, *Alejo Peralta*; and Marcúe Padiñas, "La crisis de la educación," 46.

12. See, for example, *Zócalo*, August 27, 1956.

13. Politécnicos were aware of such strategies on the part of school and government authorities. See, for example, "¡No Ceder, Poli!," *Fuerza de la ESIME*, no. 3, October, 1956, in Fondo Reservado de la UNAM—Impresos Sueltos, Movimientos Socio-Políticos (hereafter FR-U-IS, MS-P), Vol. 26, in AH-UNAM.

14. Anonymous student, as cited in Marcúe Padiñas, "La crisis de la educación," 43. The word "porras" is used here in reference to a "gang" or a group of people.

15. See, for example, "Los estudiantes retan a la policía," *Excélsior*, August 24, 1956.

16. Cited in Marcúe Padiñas, "La crisis de la educación," 43.

17. These groups often consisted of older students ("fossils") leading a band of pseudo-students. Eventually the term "gorila" was generalized to mean any "thug" preying on students, including the granaderos (riot police).

18. Jorge "El Oso" Oceguera and El Angel, interviews with the author, notes, Mexico City.

19. Oscar González, interview with the author, notes, Mexico City.

20. Earlier in the year, gorillalike tactics were used on April 12, 1956, when "a group of hoodlums" tried to take over the Strike Committee by force. The fact that they had "arrived in ten police cars" left no doubt in the minds of the politécnicos that these provocateurs were in cahoots with the police. See, for example, "Sangrientas refriegas," *Excélsior*, April 13, 1956.

21. ADFS, "IPN," Exp. 63-3-1956, L-5, H-265, July 23, 1956.

22. The Juventudes Socialistas was one of the many leftist student organizations that emerged in the 1930s during the administration of Lázaro Cárdenas. The CJM was created in the 1920s as part of a state corporativist effort to represent youth in government.

23. ADFS, "FNET," Exp. 63-3-1956, L-6, H-29, August 10, 1956. Jorge Prieto Laurens was a nationalist politician who fought against the "Communist invasion of the Soviet Union" in Latin America. Like many Latin American anticommunists during this time, he was also a fervent critic of American imperialism. For an example of his writings during this time, see Prieto Laurens, *Llamado a la América Latina*.

24. ADFS, "FNET," Exp. 63-3-1956, L-6, H-50, August 16, 1956.

25. Ibid.

26. Camp, *Mexican Political Biographies*, 304–305.

27. ADFS, "IPN," Exp. 63-3-54, L-1, H-17, April 8, 1954.

28. Jorge "El Oso" Oceguera, interview with the author, notes, Mexico City; and ADFS, "IPN," Exp. 63-3-956, L-2, H-170.

29. "Cierre del Internado del IPN," *Tiempo*, October 1, 1956, 4.

30. "Contra los falsos Estudiantes," *Excélsior*, August 27, 1956.

31. ADFS, "FNET," Exp. 63-3-1956, L-6, H-50.

32. See, for example, "Futurismos: historia de un fracaso," *El Universal*, June 7, 1956.

33. Sánchez Hidalgo, *Trazos y mitos*, 173–174.

34. "Se ordena a la policía detener a los estudiantes," *Excélsior*, August 22, 1956. See also "Peralta ve fácil lo del Politécnico," *Excélsior*, August 25, 1956.

35. *Últimas Noticias*, September 24, 1956.

36. For a list of the officials within the Federal Army and the police department charged with suppressing this "national threat," see "Cierre del Internado del IPN," *Tiempo*, no. 752, October 1, 1956; "El Toque de 'Diana,'" *Excélsior*, September 24, 1956; and "Se acabó el foco de agitación," *El Universal*, September 24, 1956.

37. "El Toque de 'Diana,'" *Excélsior*, September 24, 1956.

38. From the Department of State, see DSDW, M-IA, Desp. 275, September 14, 1956; and ARA to Mr. R. R. Rubottom, October 8, 1956. For the other estimates, see "El Toque de 'Diana,'" *Excélsior*, September 24, 1956; Marcúe Padiñas, "La crisis de la educación," 50; "Cierre del Instituto," *Tiempo*, October 1, 1956, 3, 6; and *El Universal*, September 24, 1956.

39. DSDW, M-IA, Desp. 275, September 14, 1956; "El Toque de 'Diana,'" *Excélsior*, September 24, 1956; and Marcúe Padiñas, "La crisis de la educación," 50.

40. Alejo Peralta as quoted in ADFS, "IPN," Exp. 63-3-56, L-6, H-216, September 24, 1956.

41. "Tropas Federales Clausuraron el Internado," *Excélsior*, September 24, 1956.

42. *Excélsior*, September 24, 1956.

43. As quoted in Loyo Brambila and Pozas Horcasitas, "La crisis política de 1958," 109.

44. FNET, "El Poli Habla," n.d., IPN, *50 años*, 150. See also "¡No Ceder, Poli!," *Fuerza de la ESIME*, October, 1956.

45. Nicandro Mendoza, interview with the author, notes, Mexico City.

46. "El Toque de 'Diana,'" and "Reacción favorable," *Excélsior*, September 25, 1956.

47. See, for example, in DSDW, M-IA, Desp. 340, October 5, 1956.

48. Many comments such as these were published in editorial pages in *Excélsior* and *El Universal*.

49. See, for example, "Fondo político en la huelga estudiantil," *La Nación*, no. 762, May 20, 1956, 7–8; and "Crisis de la autoridad," *La Nación*, no. 765, June 10, 1956, 3–4.

50. See *Novedades*, September 25, 1956; and *Excélsior*, September 20, 1956, respectively.

51. See, for example, in DSDW, M-IA, Desp. 358, October 10, 1956.

52. "Cierre del Internado del IPN," *Tiempo*, October 1, 1956.

53. *Excélsior*, October 1, 1956.

54. Russell Morris, "Political Violence," 372.

55. IPN, *50 años*, 154.

56. Russell Morris, "Political Violence," 372.

57. Méndez Docurro adhered to the authoritarian policies of his predecessor until 1963, when he himself was replaced as director.

58. See Chapter 1.

59. For a more comprehensive list of students arrested in 1956 under the Law of Social Dissolution, see "Gaviotas con el sweater de la UNAM," *El Universal*, September 27, 1956; "Politécnicos disfrazados de universitarios," *Excélsior*, September 27, 1956; "Nicandro Mendoza entre los detenidos," *El Universal*, September 28, 1956; "Molinar, líder de la FNET en la redada," *Excélsior*, September 29, 1956; and "Los líderes Nicandro Mendoza y Molina," *Excélsior*, September 30, 1956.

60. See "Nicandro Mendoza y sus socios," *Excélsior*, October 2, 1956.

61. See ibid.; and DSDW, M-IA, Desp. 340, October 5, 1956.

62. DSDW, M-IA, Desp. 340, October 5, 1956.

63. See, for example, "Nicandro Mendoza entre los detenidos," *El Universal*, September 28, 1956; and "Los líderes Nicandro Mendoza y Molina," *Excélsior*, September 30, 1956.

64. DSDW, M-IA, Desp. 380, October 19, 1956.

65. See, for example, "Molinar, líder de la FNET," *Excélsior*, September 29, 1956; and "Los líderes," *Excélsior*, September 30, 1956.

66. Zolov, "¡Cuba sí, yanquis no!"

67. Nicandro Mendoza, interview with the author, notes, Mexico City.

68. Alejo Peralta and Rodolfo González, the president of the Regional Committee of the PRI in the Federal District, were the principal supporters of the Francisco Velázquez Group. See Russell Morris, "Political Violence," 373; and ADFS, "IPN," Exp. 63-3-56, L-6, H-266.

69. The Rios Group united all the students from the Bloque de Estudiantes Técnicos (Bloc of Technical Students), and it was supported by Baudelio Alegría of the Confederación de Jóvenes Mexicanos (CJM). Baudelio Alegría for his part enjoyed the financial support of Enrique Ramírez y Ramírez, who had been the general secretary of the Partido Popular but in the early 1950s had broken ties with the Partido Popular and had moved closer to the corporatist structure of the PRI. Besides Vicente Lombardo Toledano, the Benjamín Nieto Group was also supported by Salvador Gamiz. Lombardistas made it a primary goal to get Nicandro Mendoza and Mariano Molina released from prison as part of a plan to re-establish the Partido Popular as an influential player inside the IPN. For a list of the different factions that participated in the Congress for the presidency of FNET, see ADFS, "IPN," Exp. 63-3-56, L-6, H-306–352. On the dispute that developed between Lombardo and Ramírez, see Schmitt, *Communism in Mexico*, 77–119.

70. "Repudio a los líderes de la FNET," *Excélsior*, October 23, 1956; and ADFS, "IPN," Exp. 63-3-56, L-6, H-319.

71. For a list of students who accepted the ramirista victory, see "No más violencia," *Excélsior*, October 24, 1956.

72. David Vega, interview with the author, notes, Mexico City.

73. Fernando Gutiérrez Barrios, "Instituto Politécnico Nacional," July 18, 1968, in IPS, Vol. 2912, Exp. 105; "Los porros," *Proceso*, no. 21 (March 1977); and Durón, *Yo Porro*, 233. On Jesús Robles Martínez, Alfonso Martínez Domínguez, and Rómulo Sánchez Mireles, see Camp, *Mexican Political Biographies*, 441–442, 600, 652.

74. See, for example, "Una paz cuasi octaviana, 1948–1966," in Silva Herzog, *Una historia de la Universidad*, 98–149; and Mendoza Rojas, *Los conflictos*, 95–120.

75. Silva Herzog, *Una historia de la Universidad*, 98–149.

76. Rojas Bernal, "Por la Federación Estudiantil," 31; and Ortiz Tovar, "Informe político," 42. See also Domínguez, "El perfil político."

77. Oscar González López, interview with the author, notes, Mexico City.

78. Semo, *¿Una oposición sin atributos?*, 30.

79. Navarro Palacios, "La Reforma Universitaria," 195–196.

80. Palillo, interview with the author, notes, Mexico City; and Ortiz Tovar, "Informe Político."

81. *El Nigromante*, no. 1, 1959, in FRIIB, Vol. 2, File 119, in AH-UNAM.

82. Rojas Bernal, "Por la Federación Estudiantil," 31; Walter Ortiz Tovar, "Informe político"; and Domínguez, "El perfil político."

83. "A los alumnos de la ENP No. 3," n.d., FPJEP. Alemanismo—although not always associated with Miguel Alemán—became a common phrase used by students in reference to corruption.

84. Oscar González López, interview with the author, notes, Mexico City.

85. *El Nigromante*, no. 1, 1959, in FRIIB, Vol. 2, File 119, in AH-UNAM. See also "¿La política en la UNAM?" *Palabras*, c. 1958, in FRIIB, Vol. 2, File 134, in AH-UNAM.

86. See, for example, AIPS, "Porras," Vol. 2944 (A), n.d.

87. El Negro, interview with the author, notes, Mexico City.

88. Oscar González López, interview with the author, notes, Mexico City. Similar definitions of the term "grilla" could also be found in Lira, ed., *Diccionario del Español usual*, 469; and Mejía Prieto, *Así se Habla el mexicano*, 83.

89. Rivas Hernández, *Grillos y Gandallas*, 9–12.

90. Ibid.

91. See, for example, "Manifiesto del Partido Estudiantil Socialista," n.d., in FRIIB, Vol. 3, File 162, in AH-UNAM; Rojas Bernal, "Por la Federación Estudiantil"; Ortiz Tovar, "Informe Político"; Domínguez, "El perfil político"; and esp. Rivas Ontiveros, *La izquierda estudiantil*; and Sánchez Gudiño, *Génesis, desarrollo, y consolidación*.

92. The information noted in this table was compiled from a collection of documents sent to President Adolfo Ruiz Cortínez from July 11, 1953, to February 3, 1954, in "Memorandum Universidad," FARC, Vol. 729, Exp. 534/60.

93. In 1951, Miguel Henríquez Guzmán was expelled from the PRI for having organized a premature campaign. In 1952 he ran as candidate for the Federation of People's Parties of Mexico. For a detailed analysis of henriquismo, see Rodríguez Araujo, "El henriquismo"; and Servín, *Ruptura y Oposición*.

94. ADSF, "UNAM," Exp. 63-1-53, L-11, H-130.

95. Jorge's father was a wealthy Swiss banker. His father-in-law was the former senator from the State of Chihuahua (1940–1946) and director of the Cooperative Sugar Mill of Zacatepec, Morelos, Eugenio Prado. See Guitián Berniser, "Las porras," 29–38; González Ruiz, *MURO*, 300–308; and Yañez Delgado, *La manipulación de la fe*, 203.

96. Guitián Berniser, "Las porras," 29.

97. Ibid.

98. Oscar González López, interview with the author, notes, Mexico City. See also ibid., 29, 33.

99. Guitián Berniser, "Las porras," 29, 33; and Mabry, *The Mexican University*, 205–206.

100. Mabry, *The Mexican University*, 205–206.

101. "Memorandum Universidad," July 21, 1953, in FARC, Vol. 729, Exp. 534/60; and ibid.

102. As a replacement for Siegrist, panistas moved to sponsor the vice president of CNE, Armando Ávila Sotomayor. Sotomayor was a more conservative young leader who, following the Durango congress, created a new organization, the National Confederation, with PAN funding. Its purpose was to challenge Siegrist's CNE, and although it never fulfilled the ambitions of its president, it did become a key player during student elections in the early 1950s.

103. Guitián Berniser, "Las porras," 36.

104. Jorge Siegrist, as cited in ibid., 35–37.

105. See, for example, ADSF, "UNAM," Exp. 63-1-53, L-11, H-130; and "Memorandum Universidad," FARC, Vol. 729, Exp. 534/60.

106. Oscar González López and Carlos Tejeda, interviews with the author, notes, Mexico City. See also "Memorandum Universidad," August 20, 1953, in FARC, Vol. 729, Exp. 534/60.

107. Other people included Antonio Mena Brito (Secretariat of Public Education, 1952–1958); Fernando Román Lugo (official mayor of the Secretariat of Government, 1952–1953, Subsecretary of Government, 1953–1958; and attorney general of the Federal District and Federal Territories, 1958–1964); and Manuel Moreno Sánchez (senator from the State of Aguascalientes). See, for example, FARC, Vol. 729, Exp. 534/60, August 18, 1953; ADFS, "UNAM," Exp. 63-1-62, L-16, H-202; and ADFS, "UNAM," Exp. 63-1-62, L-16, H-202. See also Camp, *Mexican Political Biographies*, 461–462, 487–488, 616–617.

108. "Nuevo rector," *Tiempo*, February 20, 1961; and Romo Medrano, *Un Relato Biográfico*, 220–221.

109. Camp, *Mexican Political Biographies*, 620.

110. On the network of charro leaders financed by Humberto Romero, as reported by the DFS, see ADFS, "UNAM," Exp. 63-1-62, L-16, H-202. See also Rivas Hernández, *Grillos y Gandalla*; and Romo Medrano, *Un Relato Biográfico*.

111. In addition, they retained the backing of prominent factions within the PRI

such as the cardenistas and the alemanistas, from whom Humberto Romero had distanced himself during the sexenio of López Mateos. The principal intermediary between this group of charro leaders and Humberto Romero was José Manuel Rodríguez, the president of one of the FEUs. Oscar González López and Carlos Ortiz Tejeda, interviews with the author, notes, Mexico City; "Pistoleros en la CU," *Política*, no. 9, September 1960, 20–21; and Rivas Ontiveros, *La izquierda estudiantil*.

112.   Luis Garrido Díaz served as rector of UNAM from 1948 to 1952. With Alemán's influence in the Board of Trustees, he was re-elected, but ultimately resigned in 1953. Alfonso Noriega had been professor of law since 1939 and director of that same school from 1944 to 1945. Agustín García López had been one of the most influential professors of Miguel Alemán. He was also the former director of the Law School (1938–1939), current director of the School of Comparative Law, the secretary of Statistics for the presidential campaign of Miguel Alemán, former secretary of Public Works (1946–1952), and personal friend of Luis Garrido. See Camp, *Mexican Political Biographies*, 265, 503.

113.   ADFS, "ENP #5," Exp. 63-1-957, L-4, H-253.

114.   ADFS, "INJM," Exp. 63-1-1957, L-5, H-99.

115.   DSDW, M-PGNDA, 1963–1966, Desp. A-1064, May 15, 1965; ADFS, "FEU," Exp. 9-27-950, L-4, H-54; ADFS, "UNAM," Exp. 63-1-62, L-16, H-202; and "¡Fuera el gorilismo de la Facultad!," n.d., FPJEP.

116.   See "Cierre del Internado del IPN," *Tiempo*, October 1, 1956, 7; "Por la Clausura," *Excélsior*, September 25, 1956; and "Toda agitación será reprimida," *Excélsior*, September 26, 1956.

117.   See, for example, "La Universidad no se hará eco de la agitación," *Excélsior*, September 26, 1956.

118.   For example, Carlos Ortiz Tejada (a leftist student of the PRI) would later remember the 1950s during an interview as followed: "[W]ith the help of the famous captain of the Porra, Palillo, [all the principal student leaders were] kindly advised by Nabor Carrillo, who offered some very attractive incentives, not to get involved in the problem of the Politécnico. That is, of course, if we still desired a career in politics in the near future." Oscar González López (a leftist student at the National School of Economics,) similarly noted: "[T]hose of us who did not care about a career in politics were simply threatened with being kicked out of school. In retrospect, I think we should all admit that we were young and very naïve for having accepted such 'invitations.' We should have supported the politécnicos when they needed us. After all, we seem to have faced the same enemies. Instead, we opted to continue to have fun with Palillo." Oscar González López and Carlos Ortiz Tejeda, interviews with the author, notes, Mexico City.

Chapter 5

1.   Carlos Ortiz Tejeda, interview with the author, notes, Mexico City; and "Con actos vandálicos," *Excélsior*, August 23, 1958.

2. "Con actos vandálicos," "Escándalos estudiantiles," *El Universal*, August 23, 1958; "Estudiantes contra el monopolio camionero," *La Nación*, no. 882, August 31, 1958, 16–21; "Protesta estudiantil," *Tiempo*, September 1, 1958, 3–7; and Paul Kennedy's articles in the *New York Times*, August 24–September 1, 1958.

3. See, for example, "El Vandalismo estudiantil," *Excélsior*, August 26, 1958.

4. "[T]hose of whom need to be disciplined at any cost necessary." See "Patente de impunidad," *Excélsior*, August 25, 1958; "Delincuencia juvenil," *Excélsior*, August 29, 1958; and "Estudiantes contra el monopolio," *La Nación*, no. 882, August 31, 1958, 17.

5. "Ante lo intolerable," *Excélsior*, August 25, 1958.

6. Audiffred was not alone. See, for example, "Los profesionales de la agitación," *Excélsior* September 1, 1958.

7. See, for example, "Con comunistas en acción," *Excélsior*, August 26, 1958; "Ahora sí ven rojos en todas partes," *El Universal*, August 28, 1958; and "Operación Moscú," *El Universal*, August 30, 1958.

8. Loyo Brambila, "El marco socio-económico"; and Pozas Horcasitas, *La democracia en blanco*.

9. The first symptoms of an "economic crisis," as will be shown later on, were manifested in the mid-1950s, following the devaluation of the peso in 1954.

10. Díaz y de Ovando, ed., *La Ciudad Universitaria*, 15; and Silva Herzog, *Una historia de la Universidad*, 133.

11. Unlike the 1956 student strike, this later revolt has enjoyed greater attention on the part of scholars. The best available studies on the 1958 protest include Estrada Rodríguez, *1968, estado y universidad*; Rivas Ontiveros, *La izquierda estudiantil*; and Russell Morris, "Political Violence," 334–341. An important study and a memoir also include Semo, *¿Una oposición sin atributos?*; and Rivas Hernández, *Grillos y Gandallas*, respectively. Other scholars who have briefly touched upon the importance of the 1958 student protest include Mendoza Rojas, *Los conflictos*; Domínguez, "El perfil político"; and Mabry, *The Mexican University*.

12. La Gran Comisión Estudiantil, "Ideario del movimiento universitario," FPJEP.

13. Carlos Ortiz Tejeda, interview with the author, notes, Mexico City.

14. La Gran Comisión Estudiantil, "Ideario del movimiento universitario," FPJEP.

15. Ibid.

16. For a longer list of the specific demands, see ibid.

17. See, for example, the various student protests examined in Garciadiego Dantan, *Rudos contra científicos*.

18. DSDW, M-IA, 1955–1959, Desp. 228, September 4, 1958.

19. On Fidel Velazquez, see Middlebrook, *The Paradox of Revolution*.

20. DSDW, M-IA, 1955–1959, Desp. 228, September 4, 1958.

21. Carlos Ortiz Tejeda, interview with the author, notes, Mexico City.

22. DSDW, M-IA, 1955–1959, Incoming telegram, Department of State, no. 14880, August 24, 1958.

23. Oscar González López, interview with the author, notes, Mexico City.

24. Rivas Hernández, *Grillos y Gandallas.*

25. For a complete list of demands and agreements, see "Protesta Estudiantil," *Tiempo*, September 1, 1958, 4. For a dramatic illustration of the burning of these buses, see the photograph in Casanova and Konzevik, *Luces sobre México*, no. 211374.

26. "Estudiantes y regente dan solución," *Excélsior*, August 23, 1958.

27. Carlos Ortiz Tejeda, interview with the author, notes, Mexico City.

28. See, for example, Braun, "Protest of Engagement."

29. Carlos Ortiz Tejeda, interview with the author, notes, Mexico City.

30. Ibid. See also "Bus Rise Sparks Mexico," *New York Times*, August 24, 1958; and "Tumultosa fue la Manifestación," *Excélsior*, August 24, 1958.

31. Rivas Ontiveros, *La izquierda estudiantil*, 98.

32. Monsiváis, *Carlos Monsiváis*, 40.

33. "Estudiantes contra el monopolio," *La Nación*, no. 882, August 31, 1958.

34. "Gestiones del Rector," *Excélsior*, August 24, 1958; "El rector condena la violencia," *El Universal*, August 25, 1958; and "Serenidad demanda el rector," *Excélsior*, August 25, 1958.

35. Russell Morris, "Political Violence," 337–338.

36. Demetrio Vallejo, "El Conflicto Ferrocarrilero," *El Espectador*, no. 2, June 1959, 18–20.

37. Carlos Ortiz Tejeda, interview with the author, notes, Mexico City. The new GCE was represented by forty-five leaders including all the presidents of the Sociedades Alumnos as well as the delegates of the FEUs from all twenty-three schools of UNAM. See "Concretan sus peticiones," *Excélsior*, August 25, 1958.

38. Rivas Hernández, *Grillos y Gandallas*, 73.

39. Rivas Ontiveros, *La izquierda estudiantil*, 486.

40. Oscar González López, interview with the author, notes, Mexico City. In his book, sociologist Ricardo Pozas Horcasitas argues that asambleas were first organized in 1965 during the medical student movement that emerged that year. However, as noted above, my findings suggest that student assemblies—as a democratic alternative to meeting organized by the FEUs and student assemblies—were first organized during the 1958 student strike and thereafter.

41. Palillo and Carlos Ortiz Tejeda, interviews with the author, notes, Mexico City; and Monsiváis, *Carlos Monsiváis*, 41.

42. This solemn demonstration of peaceful resistance would be repeated a decade later on a much larger scale during the September 13 "Silent March" in 1968.

43. "Al pueblo y al gobierno," *Excélsior*, August 30, 1958.

44. DSDW, M-IA, 1955–1959, Incoming telegram, Department of State, no. 17109, August 27, 1958; "Fue muy ordenada la manifestación," *Excélsior*, August 27, 1958; and "Mexico's Students Stage a Big Rally," *New York Times*, August 27, 1958.

45. "Se someterán al presidente," *El Universal*, August 27, 1958; and "Así lo informó el licenciado," *El Universal*, August 27, 1958.

46. Carlos Ortiz Tejeda, interview with the author, notes, Mexico City.

47. "Fue muy ordenada la manifestación," *Excélsior*, August 27, 1958; and Carlos Ortiz Tejeda, interview with the author, notes, Mexico City.

48. Oscar González López, interview with the author, notes, Mexico City. See also Pozas Horcasitas, *La democracia en blanco*.

49. "Estudiantes y agitadores," *Excélsior*, August 28, 1958; Loyo Brambilia, "El marco socio-económico," 355.

50. "Llevan la agitación al Politécnico," *El Universal*, August 28, 1958.

51. Carlos Ortiz Tejeda, interview with the author, notes, Mexico City.

52. "Acordaron los delegados estudiantiles," *Excélsior*, August 31, 1958; and "Protesta Estudiantil," *Tiempo*, September 1, 1958.

53. Carlos Ortiz Tejeda, interview with the author, notes, Mexico City.

54. DSDW, M-IA, 1955–1959, Desp. 228, September 4, 1958; and "En el mitín del Zócalo," *El Universal*, August 31, 1958.

55. Oscar González López, interview with the author, notes, Mexico City.

56. "El gobierno reprimirá las agitaciones con la máxima energía," *Excélsior*, September 2, 1958; and "Head of Mexico Warns on Strife," *New York Times*, September 2, 1958.

57. President Ruiz Cortinez, as cited in Loyo Brambila and Pozas Horcasitas, "La crisis política de 1958," 109. For a full description of the speech, see "Texto íntegro del informe presidencial," *Excélsior*, September 2, 1958.

58. On the MRM, see Loyo Brambila, *El movimiento magisterial de 1958*.

59. See, for example, "La Opinión Pública y el Gobierno," *Excélsior*, August 30, 1958.

60. Abel Quezada, "Piénselo dos veces," *Excélsior*, September 8, 1958.

61. Alonso, *El movimiento ferrocarrilero*; and Loyo Brambila, *El movimiento magisterial*.

62. Ibid.; Stevens, *Protest and Response*, 99–126; and Estrada Rodríguez, *1968, estado y universidad*.

63. See, for example, Monsiváis, *Carlos Monsiváis*, 41.

Chapter 6

1. ADFS, "UNAM," Exp. 63-1-60, L-11, H-88–90; and "La Guerra Fría," *Tiempo*, August 22, 1960, 3–9.

2. "¿De quién es la universidad?," *Siempre!*, August 31, 1960; and "Un hecho injustificable," *Siempre!*, August 31, 1960.

3. ADFS, "UNAM," Exp. 63-1-60, L-11, H-88–90. According to film critic Emilio García Riera, Giovanni Korporaal's political satire was banned by the government until 1974, primarily for having criticized the political corruption of this period, as epitomized by a ruthless cacique with close ties to the "revolutionary government." See García Riera, *Historia Documental*, 321–324. See also "Korporaal abrió camino," *El Universal*, February 16, 2004.

4. "Decapitaron la estatua," *Excélsior*, June 5, 1966.

5. ADFS, "UNAM," Exp. 63-1-966, L-39, H-172–173.

6. ADFS, "UNAM," Exp. 63-1-66, L-44, H-107–113; and ADFS, "UNAM," Exp. 63-1-63, L-23, H-262. See also the students' accounts in Cabecilla, "Biografía de las porras (7 Años de Gangsterismo, 1962–1969)," *Holguera*, 1969, FPJEP; and "Los intereses académicos del alemanismo," *César Vallejo*, no. 3, 1963, in "FR-U-IS, MS-P," Box 4, Exp. 288 in AH-UNAM.

7. For an excellent documentary on the mural, see Kamffer, *Mural efímero*.

8. See, for example, Marwick, *The Sixties*; Klimke, *The Other Alliance*; Horn, *The Spirit of '68*; and Varon, *Bringing the War Home*.

9. Gassert and Klimke, "1968 from Revolt to Research," 5.

10. Marwick, *The Sixties*; Klimke, *The Other Alliance*.

11. Sorensen, *A Turbulent Decade Remembered*, 1–14, 215 n. 2.

12. Ibid.; Gould, "Solidarity under Siege"; Spencer, ed., *Student Politics in Latin America*; Scott, "Student Political Activism"; Hennessy, "The New Radicalism."

13. See, for example, Zolov, "Expanding Our Conceptual Horizons"; Markarian, "'Ese héroe es el joven comunista'"; and Barbosa, "Insurgent Youth."

14. Pozas Horcasitas, ed., *Universidad Nacional y Sociedad*, 84.

15. "Editorial," *El Espectador*, no. 1 (May 1959).

16. See, for example, Gosse, *Rethinking the New Left*.

17. As Todd Gitlin explains, in the United States, the term "New Left" was "first used by SDS in 1963, which deliberately adapted it from the British New Left of the late fifties. 'New Left' meant both New (not Old, that is to say, neither Communist nor Social-Democratic) and Left (committed to social equality, opposed to militarism and racism, and loosely socialist." See Gitlin, *The Sixties*, 293. For two excellent revisions of Gitlin's work, see Goose, *Rethinking the New Left*; and Zolov, "Expanding Our Conceptual Horizons."

18. Its principal contributors included Enrique González Pedrero, professor of Political and Social Sciences (CPyS) and later director of that same school (1965–1970); Jaime García Terrés, director of *México en la Cultura*, *Revista de la Universidad de México*, and the Dirección de Difusión Cultural; Francisco López Camara, professor of CPyS and renowned writer; Luis Virollo, the one-time leader of the Communist Youth and later private secretary of the university rector; Víctor Flores Olea, professor of CPyS and director of the Centro de Estudios Latinoamericanos (1956–1969); and the rising intellectual Carlos Fuentes. See "Consejo Editorial," *El Espectador*, no. 1, May 1959, 2. Invited guests also included Demetrio Vallejo, Othón Salazar, Luis Cardoza y Aragón, Narciso Bassols, Silva Herzog, Enrique Florescano Mayet, Eli de Gortari, José Luis Balcárcel Ordoñez, Elena de la Souchere (from *France Observateur*), and Michel Bosquet (from *L'Express*).

19. Manuel Marcué Pardiñas, as noted earlier, served as the main editor of the journal *Problemas de Latinoamérica* in the 1950s. But his greatest accomplishment in journalism (and politics) came in 1960 with the creation of the weekly magazine *Política*.

20. See, for example, Víctor Flores Olea, "La Clase Trabajadora"; and Enrique

González Pedrero, "La Burguesía y la Revolución," *El Espectador*, nos. 6–7, October–November 1959, 12–14, 15–16, respectively.

21. Víctor Flores Olea, "La Clase Trabajadora," *El Espectador*, nos. 6–7, October–November 1959, 12–14.

22. Víctor Flores Olea, "Tiempos Nuevos,"*El Espectador*, no. 3, July 1959, 31.

23. "Atentado a el espectador," *El Espectador*, no. 4, August 1959, 15; Víctor Flores Olea, "Todavía sobre la izquierda," *El Espectador*, no. 5, September 1959, 32.

24. See "Presentación"; Víctor Flores Olea, "La Nación y los Sindicatos"; Enrique González Pedrero, "Crisis de la Izquierda"; Carlos Fuentes, "Un Trasfondo"; Luis Volloro, "Semana de Reflexión"; and Jaime García Terrés, "Libertad de Opinión," *El Espectador*, no. 1 (May 1959); "El Fin y los Medios"; Víctor Flores Olea, "Un Camino de la Democracia"; and Carlos Fuentes, "Dos Terribles Fantasmas," *El Espectador*, no. 2 (June 1959); "Disolución Social"; Francisco López Cámara, "El Común Denominador"; and Enrique González Pedrero, "Una Nueva Política," *El Espectador*, no. 3 (July 1959); Francisco López Cámara, "Bases Democráticas"; Jaime García Terrés, "Depuración del Periodismo"; and Luis Volloro, "La Máscara del Nacionalismo," *El Espectador*, no. 4 (August 1959); Jaime García Terrés, "Más allá del 'realismo'"; and Enrique González Pedrero, "La atmósfera reciente," *El Espectador*, no. 5 (September 1959); and "Las Condiciones de la Democracia"; Carlos Fuentes, "Un nuevo lenguaje"; Luis Villoro, "Socialismo democrático"; and Enrique González Pedrero, "Dos caminos," *El Espectador*, nos. 6–7 (October–November 1959).

25. "Un Ideario Común," *El Espectador*, no. 4, August 1959, 2–3. Carlos Fuentes described his enthusiasm for the Cuban Revolution as follows: "El destino de Hispanoamérica dependerá del éxito de la Revolución Cubana. No es esto una exageración. Lo que en Cuba se debate es la posibilidad de que nuestros países salgan, al fin, de la situación de dependencia económica y anacronismo político que, con ligeras variantes se mantiene desde la época de la Colonia." Carlos Fuentes, "Más allá de la guerra fría," *El Espectador*, no. 4, August 1959, 32.

26. *Política* continued to offer an important forum to promote the revolutionary nationalism endorsed by the writers of *El Espectador*, but it also opened up new opportunities for intellectuals and journalists that identified themselves with a more orthodox Marxism, as well as social activists who offered their political testimonies from prison. The most "radical" writers included Fernando Carmona, Alonso Aguilar, Jorge Carrión, Victor Rico Galán, Enrique Semo, Ramírez y Ramírez, Juan Noyola Vázquez, Rouset, Emilio Abreu Gómez, Boris Rosen, Dr. Cabrera, and Rosendo Gómez Lorenzo. Social activists who offered their political testimonies from prison included José Revueltas, Domicio Encinas, Valentín Campa, Demetrio Vallejo, Othón Salazar, David Alfaro Siqueiros, María Gloria Benavides, Paquita Calvo Zapata, and many others. In addition, *Política* also invited a number of intellectuals that did not express a defined political affiliation, including Salvador Novo, Pita Amor, Javier Alatorre, José Luis Martínez, Juan Buñuelos, Jaime Labastida, and many more. See Perzabal, *De las Memorias de Manuel Marcué*. In 1964 the majority of writers from *El Espectador* abandoned *Política*. "The reasons are disputed," as Camp argues, "but one

explanation is that *Política* had become overly critical of different intellectual beliefs and inquisitorial in tone." Camp, *Mexican Political Biographies*, 142.

27. The catalyst for forming the MLN was the Conference for National Sovereignty, Economic Emancipation, and Peace, held in Mexico City in March 1961 and organized by former president Lázaro Cárdenas. The Peace Conference, as Arthur Smith explains, emerged as "the external threat to survival of the Castro regime grew more intense." The conference, he further notes, was a direct effort on the Left throughout Latin America to "express their solidarity and render what assistance they could." The idea was first proposed by "General Lázaro Cárdenas of Mexico, in his capacity as one of three Latin American Presidents of the World Peace Council, [when he] announced plans in late December 1960 for a Hemispheric-wide Conference for National Sovereignty, Economic Emancipation and Peace." Smith, "Mexico and the Cuban Revolution," 87. See also Pellicer de Brody, *México y la Revolución Cubana*; Maciel, *El movimiento de liberación nacional*; and Paoli Bolio, *Conciencia y Poder*, 287–291.

28. Alonso Aguilar, "Movimiento de Liberación Nacional," *Política*, September 15, 1961; and MLN, "Al Sector Revolucionario," August 4, 1961, in DSDW, M-IA, 1960–1963, Desp. 250, August 24, 1961.

29. The Casa de Lago was founded in 1959 under the Dirección de Difusión Cultural (DDC), which had its heyday under the direction of Jaime García Terrés (1953–1965).

30. Cohn, "The Mexican Intelligentsia," 162–163.

31. A significant portion of this section was published earlier in Pensado, "Student Politics in Mexico."

32. Rodolfo Echeverría Martínez (member of the JCM), interview with the author, notes, Mexico City. See also Rousset, *La Izquierda cercada*, 271.

33. See, for example, "Manifiesto del Partido Estudiantil Socialista," 1961, in FRIIB, Vol. 3, Exp. 162, in AH-UNAM; and "Manifiesto a los Estudiantes del Grupo César Vallejo," 1963, in FRIIB, Vol. 4, Exp. 290, AH-UNAM.

34. "Hacia la Central Estudiantil Independiente," *La Voz de México*, June 15, 1963. The second and third congresses met in Mexico City in the School of Economics at UNAM in 1964 and in the IPN the following year. In 1966, CNED was officially recognized as a national student front composed of 800 delegates claiming to represent more than 160,000 students. See "La CNED, Nueva Fuerza de Lucha," *Política*, May 1, 1966.

35. "Declaración de Morelia," *Combate: Órgano Informativo del Partido Estudiantil Socialista de Economía*, no. 2, April 1964, FPJEP.

36. See, for example, "Protesta nacional por la agresión," *La Voz de México*, October 16, 1966; "Consejo de la CNED," *La Voz de México*, October 1, 1967; and "En solidaridad con los presos políticos," *La Voz de México*, December 24, 1967.

37. See, for example, Zermeño, *México*.

38. Other important student organizations representing the moderate New Left included Grupo en Defensa de la Constitución, Bloque Estudiantil Revolucionario (BER), Grupo Linterna, Partido de Reforma Universitaria Nacional (PRUN), Parti-

do Estudiantil Socialista de Economía (PESE), and Grupo Miguel Hernández. For a detailed discussion of these organizations, see Rivas Ontiveros, *La izquierda estudiantil*.

39. DSDW, M-IA, 1963–1966, Desp. A-1026; "Combativo acto de apoyo a Cuba," *La Voz de México*, March 7, 1961; "La grandiosa manifestación pro Vietnam," *Política*, April 1, 1966; "Firme defensa de la Revolución cubana," *La Voz de México*, July 19, 1966; and Bartra, "Tiempo de Jóvenes."

40. As referenced in multiple student magazines, newspapers, and manifestoes, over a dozen female activists participated in leading roles in the following student organizations: La Nueva Izquierda, the Grupo César Vallejo, the Partido Estudiantil Socialista, Nuevo Grupo, Grupo Linterna, Grupo Miguel Hernández, MIRE, Grupo Patricio Lumumba, and Grupo en Defensa de la Constitución. On the relationship between political consciousness and the appropriation of public (male) space, see Cohen and Frazier, "Talking Back to '68."

41. This was also true of those young women who joined the guerrilla movement. See, for example, Rayas, "Subjugating the Nation."

42. See, for example, Miller, *Latin American Women*.

43. Oscar González, interview with the author, notes, Mexico City; ADFS, "FEU," Exp. 63-1-960, L-9, H-237; "Opposition to Government's Teacher Assignment Plan Provokes Series of Demonstrations by Students and Teacher Groups," DSDW, M-IA, 1960–1963, Desp. A-1178, April 6, 1960; "La Guerra Fría en México," *Tiempo*, Vol. 37, no. 955, August 22, 1960; and "Mexican Students' Protest March," *New York Times*, August 2, 1960, 5. Besides collective beatings of the figure of "Uncle Sam," other examples rejecting American imperialism included the destruction of windows of American-owned stores, the daubing of American tourists, and a failed attempt to burn the American flag, which according to various testimonies was prevented by an "opportune intervention" of Mexican secret agents. Carlos Ortiz Tejeda, interview with the author, notes, Mexico City. See also DSDW, M-IA, 1960–1963, Desp. 9872, July 4, 1960; "Meeting at National University of Mexico in Protest against Visit of President Kennedy," CIA telegram, no. 16594, June 24, 1962; "5,000 Mexican Students March," *New York Times;* and esp. Carlos Ortiz Tejeda, "Lo de la Bandera de EU," *Política*, no. 1, May 1, 1960.

44. For a more detailed analysis of his writings, see Revueltas, *Ensayo de un proletario*. For a brief look at José Revueltas's life history of contestation against the PCM, see Crespi, "José Revueltas"; and Paolio Bolio, *Conciencia y poder*, 210–229.

45. Revueltas, *Ensayo de un proletario*. For early critiques of the Mexican Revolution, see the collection of essays in Ross, ed., *¿Ha muerto la revolución?*, esp. Cosío Villegas, "La crisis de México," 95–103.

46. According to an IPS document ("Breve análisis político/ideológico de la Escuela Nacional de Economía," n.d., in AIPS, Vol. 2011, Exp. 3, H-1-39), these student organizations were primarily active in the schools of Economics and Social and Political Sciences, including Movimiento de Izquierda Revolucionaria (MIRE), Alianza de Izquierda Revolucionaria de Economía (AIRE), Movimiento Estudiantil Revolucio-

nario (MER), Liga Obrero Estudiantil "23 de Marzo," Partido Estudiantil Socialista Revolucionario (PESR), and Partido de Acción Revolucionaria (PAR), among others. See also Rivas Ontiveros, *La izquierda estudiantil.*

47. See, for example, "Fracción Estudiantil del POR(t)," n.d., FR-U-IS, MS-P," Exp. 15; and "A la base de la Escuela Nacional de Ciencias Políticas y Sociales," n.d., in FRIIB, Vol. 9, Exp. 549, in AH-UNAM. On students incorporating the Maoist principles of "self-criticism" and the use of heated debates to "encourage political and emotional honesty and group bonding," see Fields, "French Maoism"; and Varon, *Bringing the War Home.*

48. AIRE, "Los Estudiantes dinamitaron la estatua de Miguel Alemán," *Praxis, Órgano Central de la Alianza de Izquierda Revolucionaria de Economía,* no. 1, July 1966, 11, in FRIIB, Vol. 8, Exp. 464, in AH-UNAM.

49. Oscar González, interview with the author, notes, Mexico City. On remarks relating to Díaz Ordaz, see ADFS, "UNAM," Exp. 63-1-60, L-11, H-88–90. See also ADFS, "UNAM," Exp. 63-1-966, L-38, H-166–167; and ADFS, "UNAM," Exp. 63-1-966, L-39, H-172–173.

50. AIRE, "Contra la confusión en el movimiento," February 13, 1967, in FRIIB, Vol. 9, Exp. 564, in AH-UNAM.

51. "¿Reforma o Revolución Universitaria?," March 1964, FPJEP.

52. Rodolfo Echeverría Martínez, interview with the author, notes, Mexico City; and "Dirección y Programa del FES," *La Chispa: Órgano Mensual del Frente Estudiantil Socialista,* no. 4, May 1966, in FRIIB, Vol. 9, Exp. 600, in AH-UNAM.

53. The most serious attempt to unite the different "R"evolutionary groups was promoted in 1967 by the Unión Nacional de Estudiantes Revolucionarios (UNER). See, for example, "Convocatoria al I. Congreso Nacional de Estudiantes Revolucionarios," FPJEP.

54. "Breve análisis político/ideológico de la Escuela Nacional de Economía," n.d., in AIPS, Vol. 2011, Exp. 3, H-1-39.

55. Among those who joined the guerrilla movement in the wake of the Tlatelolco massacre was Francisca (Paquita) Calvo Zapata. She enrolled in the UNAM's Law School in 1959. Here, she became a leading participant of the Grupo Patricio Lumumba and served as the director of the magazine *Combate* until she graduated in 1963. She then started working at the Instituto Mexicano-Cubano de Relaciones Culturales and six years later became one of the founders of the Zapatista Urban Front (FUZ). In 1971 she was sentenced to prison for thirty years after having participated in the kidnapping of the director of the Federal Airports, Julio Hirschfield Almada. See Pineda Ochoa, *En la profundidades del mar,* 91. See also Bellingeri, "La imposibilidad del odio," 49–73; Ulloa Bornemann, *Surviving Mexico's Dirty War*; Poo Hurtado, "Los protagonistas olvidados"; and essays by Oikión Solano, Cedillo, and Rayas in Herrera Calderón and Cedillo, *Challenging Authoritarianism,* 60–80, 148–166, 167–181.

56. "Editorial page," *Nueva Izquierda,* no. 1, 1963, 1, FPJEP.

57. See, for example, Revueltas, *México 68,* 38–39.

58. For the articulation of these student demands, see "Manifiesto a la Opinión Pública del Comité de 'Pro-defensa de la Constitución," n.d., FPJEP; "Al estudiantado universitario [informe del Bloque Estudiantil Revolucionario]," AH-UNAM-FR, Vol. 3, Exp. 172; "Que hay detrás de las elecciones," *Boletín Informativo del Movimiento II. Declaración de la Habana*, no. 4, 1962, in AH-UNAM-FR-U-IS, MS-P, Vol. 3, Exp. 224; Movimiento II. Declaración de la Habana, "Se ha perdido una batalla, pero no la guerra," 1965, in AH-UNAM-FR-U-IS, MS-P, Vol. 6, Exp. 374; and "Manifiesto del Grupo Nuevo," May 1966, in AH-UNAM-FR-U-IS, MS-P, Exp. 14.

59. For a complete list of the people appointed to the university by Ignacio Chávez, see DSDW, M-IA, 1960–1963, Desp. 1480, November 14, 1960.

60. Some examples of these provisionary courses included: Marx's "Critic of the Program of Gotha" and "Contribution to the Critic of the Political Economy"; Lenin's "What Is to Be Done? Burning Questions to Our Movement" and "Imperialism: The Highest Stage of Capitalism"; Mao Tse-Tung's "Against Liberalism"; Stalin's "Dialectic Materialism and Historical Materialism"; Ludwig Feuerbach's "Aim of the German Classic Philosophy"; and on a variety if themes that revolved around Mexican history, such as "Independence," "The Reform," and "The Revolution of 1910 and the Characterization of Today's Government." The issue of Marxism in the school curriculum, as noted in a Department of State document, was first "raised at a meeting of the [University] Council on December 20, 1962. At the time the issue had been focused on the question of whether the course on Marxism should continue to be obligatory. After three hours of angry debate, it was decided to postpone the discussion until January 17. The second session is reported to have been equally heated until Doctor Chavez broke the tie vote. Doctor Chavez explained his vote in terms of traditional academic freedom of expression and the need, in a university, to examine all points of view. Noting that half of the world was governed by principles emanating from Marxist philosophy, he said it was necessary to know this philosophy in order to be able to combat it." See "Increase in Marxist Instruction at the University of Mexico," DSDW, M-IA, 1963–1966, Desp. A-992, January 28, 1963.

61. Rivas Ontiveros, *La izquierda estudiantil*, 44.

62. Estrada Rodríguez, "Ciencias Políticas en los años sesenta," 100.

63. Careaga, "La vida cultural y política de los sesentas," 178.

64. The support by the DDC on cultural activities and infrastructure inside the university, as Deborah Cohn noted, lasted until 1966, when Gastón García Cantú replaced García Terrés. She explains: "The atmosphere on campus grew increasingly oppressive under the new leadership, which set out to purge the remainder of García Terrés's staff from the DDC. The situation reached a head in 1967, when Juan Vicente Melo was accused of a crime that he had not committed, and García Cantú obliged him to resign from his position as director of the Casa del Lago; his contemporaries defended him, and were forced to resign their positions at the University. This move effectively eliminated the outward-looking current from the University and marked the beginning of the end of the 'generación de la Casa del Lago' and its projects." See Cohn, "The Mexican Intelligentsia," 178–179.

65. Ibid., 167 n. 78. See also Careaga, "La vida cultural y política de los sesentas," 175.

66. Zolov, *Refried Elvis*, 12. See also Cabrera López, *Una inquietud de amanecer*, Chapter 3.

67. Other important magazines of less quality included *Renacimiento, La Piqueta, La Puya, La Chispa, Club Liberal, Cometa Universitario,* and *Hoja Universitaria*. For the impact of the weekly magazine on student politics, see also "Entrevista con Salvador Martínez de la Roca, de los herederos políticos" and "Entrevista con Oscar Levín Copel" in Perzabal, *De las Memorias*, 134–139, 142–145.

68. DSDW, M-IA, 1960–1963, Desp. 1414, June 8, 1961.

69. King Cobos, *Memorias de Radio UNAM*, 45.

70. Ibid., 39–102; "¿La Universidad Contra la Nación?," *Excélsior*, July 26, 1961; Semo, *¿Una oposición sin atributos?*, 31; Romo Medrano, *Un Relato Biográfico*, 350–351; and Pérez Rosas, "La radiofusión universitaria."

71. See, for example, Luis Villoro, "La Filosofia de la India" (September 1959); C. Wright Mills, "La última oportunidad de los intelectuales" (December 1959); Jean Paul Sartre, "Orfeo Negro" (April 1960); Victor Flores Olea, "El Marxismo es un Humanismo" (June 1960); C. Wright Mills, "El balance de la culpa" (December 1960); Ernesto Cardenal, "Misticismo beatnik" (April 1961); Miguel León Portilla, "Poesia Nahuatl" (June 1961); Herbert Marcuse, "Las implicaciones sociales del revisionismo Freudiano" (January 1963); Erich Fromm, "Las implicaciones humanas del radicalismo" (January 1963); Fernando Benitez, "Maria Sabina: La Santa de los Hongos" (September 1963); Herbert Marcuse, "Ideologia y sociedad industrializada" (January 1964); Victor Flores Olea, "La democracia socialista" (June 1964); Kazuya Sakai, "La vision Zen del mundo" (December 1965); Kazuya Sakai, "La Literatura Japonesa de Posguerra" (April 1966). Other important magazines that became influential inside UNAM during this period included *Pájaro Cascabel* (1962), *Busqueda* (1963), *TunAstral* (1964), *Punto y Partida* (1966), and *Xilote* (1967). See Cabrera López, *Una inquietud.*

72. Emilio García Riera, "Cine" (September 1959); Waldo Frank, "Llamado a América Hispana: La Verdad de Cuba" (December 1959); Gabriel García Marquez, "La siesta del martes" (March 1960); Rosario Castellanos, "Cuatro Poemas" (May 1960); Erich Fromm, "Un manifesto socialista" (September 1960); Elena Poniatowska, "Luis Buñuel" (January 1961); "Dibujos de José Luis Cuevas" (February 1961); Rosario Castellanos, "Tres nudos en la red" (April 1961); "Los Intelectuales Estadounidenses en contra de la invasión" (May 1961); Jaime Sabines, "Primeros pasos en la ciudad" (July 1961); Ricardo Pozas, "Reflexiones de un Mexicano" (December 1961); Luis Mario Schreder, "Sobre Juio Cortazar" (March 1963); Carlos Chávez, "El goce de la música" (April 1964); Carlos Monsiváis, "Notas sobre la Censura Mexicana" (October 1964); José Luis Cuevas, "Mis experiencias Kafkianas" (December 1964); "Jaime Sabines: sus poemas" (February 1966); Juan José Arreola, "Compañeros Estudiantes" (September 1966); Guilles Lapouge, "El drama de Vietnam" (September 1966); "Argentina: Universidad Avasallada" (October 1966); Sergio Pitol, "El Regreso" (November 1966); Gus-

tavo Sainz, "Treinta y nueve músculos en tensión" (November 1966); Ricardo Garibay, "Cuatro Capitulos en la Habana" (March 1967); and "Páginas del diario de José Luis Cuevas" (July 1967).

73. Marwick, *The Sixties*, 7, 1; italicized emphasis is in the original.

74. Oscar González, interview with the author, notes, Mexico City. On art as a revolutionary weapon, see Burton, "The Camera as Gun." On the importance of the *fusil*, or rifle, in launching a revolution, as understood by Guevara, see Deutschmann, ed., *Che Guevara*.

75. Oscar González, interview with the author, notes, Mexico City.

76. Díaz Ordaz in his September 1, 1968, presidential address, as cited in Braun, "Protest of Engagement," 531.

77. Zolov, *Refried Elvis*, 111; italicized emphasis is in the original.

78. Ibid., 101.

79. Dagrón, *Cine, censura y exilio*; and Mora, *Mexican Cinema*.

80. See, for example, Agnew, "¡Viva la Revolución!"; and Hinds and Tatum, *Not Just for Children*.

81. Ayala Blanco, "El movimiento estudiantil."

82. Other cartoonists who also began to take a more dissident approach were Abel Quezada and Jorge Carreño. See, for example, Camp, "The Cartoons of Abel Quezada"; and Zolov, "Jorge Carreño's Graphic Satire."

83. Rius, no title, *Política*, December 1, 1964. See also Carey, "Los Dueños de México."

84. Tatum, "Images of the United States"; and Rubenstein, *Bad Language, Naked Ladies*, 153.

85. Rius, "¡Auxilio! ¡Los Hippies!" *Los Agachados*, no. 24, 1969, 68.

86. Randall, "Lost and Found"; Willer, "El Corno Emplumado"; and Beltrán and Nielsen, *El Corno emplumado*.

87. See, for example, the editor's notes, *El Corno Emplumado*, from 1962 to 1968.

88. Padrón, "El Corno Emplumado."

89. On the impact of the Cuban Revolution on Randall's political and intellectual life, see Randall, *To Change the World*.

90. See, for example, *El Corno Emplumado*, no. 17, (January 1966), no. 20 (October 1966), and no. 25 (January 1968).

91. Beltrán and Nielsen, *El Corno emplumado*. See also Randall, *To Change the World*.

92. Willer, "El Corno Emplumado"; and Randall, *To Change the World*.

93. Anaya, "El corno . . . Revista de los poetas."

94. Crisp, *The Classic French Cinema*.

95. Other selected cineclubs included, Cuauhtémoc, Amigos de la Cultura, Juventud Israelita, Juventud Española, Bonampak, and Cine Club Ajef. See González Casanova, *¿Qué es un cine club?*, 17.

96. Rodríguez Álvarez, *Manuel González Casanova*.

97. González Casanova, *¿Qué es un cine club?*, 17.

98. The most influential of these were in the schools of Engineering, Law, Philosophy, Chemistry, Architecture, Plastic Arts, and Preparatorias nos. 2 and 5.

99. "Departamento de Actividades Cinematograficas," Dirección General de Difusión Cultural, *Anuario del Departamento de Actividades Cinematograficas, 1964* (UNAM, 1964).

100. Rashkin, *Women Filmmakers*; and Díaz Mendiburo, *Los hijos homoeróticos*.

101. For examples of these films, see the *Anuarios del Departamento de Actividades Cinematograficas.*

102. For an excellent study of these various movements, see Cowie, *Revolution.*

103. For a list other directors, see the *Anuarios del Departamento de Actividades Cinematograficas.*

104. Some examples include Enrique Rosas's *El Automovil Gris* (1919), Fernando de Fuentes's *El Compadre Mendoza* (1933), Juan Bustillo Oro's *Dos Monjes* (1934), and Emilio Gómez Muriel's *Redes* (1936). See ibid.

105. Some examples of these films include, Rossellini's *Roma, cittá aperta* (1945), Alejandro Galindo's *Espaldas Mojadas* (1953), Herbert J. Biderman's *Salt of the Earth* (1954), Karporaal's *El Brazo Fuerte* (1958), Julio Bracho's *La Sombra del Cuadillo* (1960), Roberto Gabaldón's *La Rosa Blanca* (1961), Luis Buñuel's *Viridiana* (1961), Stanley Kubrick's *Lolita* (1962), and Gillo Pontecorvo's *La Bataille d'Argel* (1966). See ibid.

106. Among some of these discussants were Eduardo Lizalde, Manuel Michel, Ricardo Vinos, Giamcarlo Zagni, Giovanni Karporaal, Armando Bartra, Nancy Cárdenas, Emilio Garcia Riera, Alberto Isaac, Eduardo Lizalde, Manuel Michel, José Revueltas, Paul Leduc, and Carlos Monsiváis. See ibid.

107. "Cine Debate Popular," Dirección General de Difusión Cultural, *Anuario 1966–7* (UNAM, 1967).

108. Some examples include González Casanova, "*¿Qué es un cine club?* (1961), Nancy Cárdenas, *El Cine Polaco* (primero de la colección de Cuadernos de Cine, 1962); Alfonso Reyes, Martin Luis Guzmán, and Federico de Onís, *Frente a la Pantalla, 1963;* Manuel Michel, *El Cine Frances, 1964;* and Francisco Pina, *Cine japonés* (1965).

109. González Casanova, *¿Qué es un cine club?*

110. "Manifiesto del Grupo Nuevo Cine," *Nuevo Cine*, no. 1, April 1961. Other people who belonged to this group included José de la Colina, Rafael Corkidi, Salvador Elizondo, J. M. García Ascot, Emilio García Riera, J. L. González de León, Heriberto Lafranchi, Julio Pliego, Gabriel Ramírez, José María Sbert, and Luis Vicens.

111. Ibid.

112. See, for example, Gil Olivo, *Cine y liberación.*

113. "Commemorative monuments," writes historian Benjamin Thomas, "have as their most obvious purpose the evocation and celebration of the past in the present. They are constructed to memorialize heroes and events for various, but not always clearly evident, reasons." In the case of postrevolutionary Mexico, the monuments served as a symbolic space to honor the heroes of the Mexican Revolution and celebrate the accomplishment of the state, but also as key sites for significant protest. Benjamin, *La Revolución*, 117, 161–162.

114. On the influence of these writers in the Southern Cone, see Brands, *Latin America's Cold War*.

115. On students becoming a "spectacle" in the long sixties, see Marwick, *The Sixties*.

116. See, for example, Brands, *Latin America's Cold War*; Liebman et al., eds., *Latin American University Students*; and Koonings and Kruijt, *Societies of Fear*.

Chapter 7

1. See, for example, "Next-door Neighbors," *New York Times*, June 8, 1958.

2. Ibid.; and Taylor, "The Mexican Election," 726.

3. Semo, "El ocaso de los mitos," 36.

4. "Next-door Neighbors," *New York Times*, June 8, 1958.

5. "Incoming Telegram to Secretary of State," June 29, 1961, in NSA, Doc. no. 3, in DSDW, M-IA, 1960–1963.

6. See, for example, Schmidt, "The Political and Economic Reverberations"; Smith, "Mexico and the Cuban Revolution"; and Pellicer de Brody, *México y la Revolución Cubana*.

7. DSDW, M-IA, 1960–1963, "Pressure of the Mexican Left," Desp. 175, August 11, 1960, 5.

8. Smith, "Mexico and the Cuban Revolution," 111.

9. "Implications of President Kennedy's Visit to Mexico," DSDW, M-IA, 1960–1963, Desp. 349, September 13, 1962.

10. DSDW, M-IA, 1960–1963, Desp. 762, December 26, 1961, 7–8.

11. The most salient of these included the nationalization of the Electric Company and the creation of the Institute of Social Security at the Service of Workers of the State (ISSSTE) in 1960. For additional examples, see Pozas Horcasitas, *La democracia en blanco*; and Krauze, *Mexico*, 625–664.

12. Semo, "El ocaso de los mitos," 66; "Por magnanimidad del Presidente," *Excélsior*, December 6, 1958; and Nicandro Mendoza, interview with the author, notes, Mexico City. On Mendoza's involvement in student activism in Morelia, see Zolov, "¡Cuba sí, yanquis no!"

13. See, for example, Knight, "Political violence"; Camp, *Mexico's Military*; and Hodges and Gandy, *Mexico under Siege*.

14. Condés Lara, *Represión y Rebelión*; and Krauze, *Mexico*, 629–652.

15. Compare, for example, the descriptions of Díaz Ordaz in Loaeza, "Gustavo Díaz Ordaz"; and Krauze, *Mexico*. See also Lomnitz, "An Intellectual's Stock."

16. On Mexico's "exceptionality," see Chapter 8.

17. ADFS, "INJM," Exp. 63-7-959, L-1, H-29.

18. These brigades and the staff of the provincial headquarters were composed of volunteer students from the Law, Medicine, Dental, and Veterinary schools from UNAM and the IPN, as well as other young people who chose to enroll in order to fulfill the requirement of eight hours a week of service that were required of all

eighteen-year-old males as part of their military service. The brigades completed "Peace Corps–type projects" such as school restoration, reforestation, slum clean-up, anti-illiteracy work, vaccinations, marriages, and civic registration. See DSDW, M-PGNDA, 1963–1966, Desp. A-1064, May 15, 1965; and Sáenz de Miera, *El Instituto Nacional de la Juventud*. In addition, the institute also offered manual labor training programs, championed the importance of sports and citizenship training, and created new International Relations and Social Welfare departments to acquaint its members with life in other countries and foster healthier practices in rural Mexico, respectively. See Instituto Nacional de la Juventud Mexicana, *Casas de la Juventud*, 4.

19. See, for example, ADFS, "PCM," Exp. 11-4-65, L-14, H-131.

20. "Youth Organization of the Partido Revolucionario Institucional (PRI)," DSDW, M-IA, 1963–1966, Desp. A-269, September 10, 1965.

21. On Carlos Madrazo, see Hernández Rodríguez, *La formación del político mexicano*.

22. As a young leftist student, Carlos Madrazo had played a key role in the creation of the Confederación de Jóvenes Mexicanos (CJM). From 1959 to 1964 he was governor of his native state of Tabasco. In 1969 he died in an airplane crash that many people believed was directly linked to his political efforts of trying to democratize the PRI by modernizing its electoral base and instituting party elections "from the bottom up." See, for example, Krauze, *Mexico*, 685.

23. Some of the topics discussed in the seminars and workshops included "National Policy of the Regime of the Mexican Revolution," "Biographies of Mexico's Heroes," "Furthering the Goals of the PRI Youth," "PRI Youth in Its Fight against Regressive Forces of the Country," among many others. See DSDW, M-IA, 1963–1966, Desp. A-269, September 10, 1965.

24. According to the director of the PRI Juvenil, Rodolfo Echeverría, its official membership in 1965 was approximately 60,000. But as the document by the Department of State cited above notes, "Estimates from other sources put the total as high as 200,000." See DSDW, M-IA, 1963–1966, Desp. A-269, September 10, 1965.

25. In a conversation with an agent of the American embassy, the director of the PRI Juvenil, Rodolfo Echeverría, speaks on this issue: "[B]ecause of the prohibition against activities by political parties on campus," they were not allowed to establish student organizations "openly. [But] whenever possible [our] youth members naturally tried to influence university groups along the lines of PRI principles." DSDW, M-IA, 1963–1966, Desp. A-269, September 10, 1965, 13.

26. ADFS, "UNAM," Exp. 63-1-68, L-58, H-139–186.

27. See, for example, Arroyo Villalobos, "*¿Qué hay de cierto?*" *El Político: Órgano de la Escuela nacional de Ciencias Políticas y Sociales editado por el Partido Revolucionario Estudiantil*, no. 1, April 1964, in FRIIB, Vol. 5, Exp. 303, in AH-UNAM; and "A los estudiantes de ENCPS: ¿Qué es el PEFI?," April 7, 1967, and "A la base estudiantil de la Escuela de Ciencias Políticas y Sociales," November 7, 1967, in FRIBB, Vol. 9, Exps. 538, 546, respectively, in AH-UNAM.

28. Or "ghost organizations." David Vega, interview with the author, notes, Mexico City.

29. El Angel, interview with the author, notes, Mexico City.

30. See, for example, AIPS, Vol. "Universidad Nacional Autónoma de México," June 7, 1966, Vol. 1618 (C), Exp. 826, H-1-22; ADFS, "ENP #9," Exp. 63-1-68, L-58, H-142; ADFS, "UNAM," Exp. 63-1-70, L-161, H-242; ADFS, "Facultad de Derecho," Exp. 11-4-71, L-149, H-21; and ADFS, "Panorama Político de la Universidad," June 8, 1968, Exp. 63-1-68, L-58, H-139–186.

31. Ibid.

32. "Plan to be carried out inside the schools to offset the communist agitations during the month of March of 1966," AIPS, Vol. 2946.

33. The report explains why the agents chose this name as follows: "Se escogió el nombre de Van Troi porque este guerrillero del Vietcong que fue fusilado por haber intentado asesinar al Secretario Norteamericano de la Defensa, ha sido hecho martir por los comunistas. Su retrato juntamente con el de Sandino y Lumumba presidió la conferencia tricontinental." Ibid.

34. Ibid.

35. See, for example, ADFS, "Panorama Político de la Universidad," June 8, 1968, Exp. 63-1-68, L-58, H-139–186; ADFS, "Porra Universitaria," Exp. 11-4-69, L-72, H-154; "Problema de las Llamadas 'Porras Preparatorianas'"; ADFS, "Porra Universitaria," Exp. 11-4-69, L-72, H-153; and Cabecilla, "Biografía de las porras."

36. El Gato, interviews with the author, notes, Mexico City.

37. El Angel and David Vega, interviews with the author, notes, Mexico City; Guitán Berniser, "Las porras"; "Denuncian a la porra de Ingeniería," *Boletín Comité Coordinador*, no. 4, May 12, 1971, FR-U-IS, MS-P, Vol. 5; "Acción estudiantil contra las porras," *Lucha Popular. Órgano de Información y Orientación de las Luchas del Pueblo Mexicano*, no. 36, April 16, 1971, FR-U-IS, MS-P, Vol. 27; and Cabecilla, "Biografía de las porras."

38. See Lomnitz, "The Uses of Fear," 18–19.

39. El Angel, interviews with the author, notes, Mexico City. See also "Problema de las Llamadas 'Porras Preparatorianas,'" ADFS, Exp. 11-4-69, L-72, H-153.

40. As noted in Chapter 8, the Ciudadelos were also involved in the street fight that sparked the rise of the 1968 student movement. See also Carey, *Plaza of Sacrifices*, 39–40.

41. Marin, "Canta 'El Johnny,'" "Soy El Johny, soy leyenda"; Homero Campa, "Porro, pero institucional," *Proceso*, November 21, 1987; Evaristo Corona Chávez, "Echeverría madrugó a Corona del Rosal," *Mercurio*, no. 137, August, 2002; and Jesús Flores Palafox (student of the IPN, 1952–1958, and teacher of El Johnny in the 1960s), interview with the author, notes, Mexico City.

42. El Angel, El Gato, and David Vega, interviews with the author, notes, Mexico City; and Guitán Berniser, "Las porras."

43. The first references to porros in DFS and IPS archives start to appear in 1966 and 1967; but it will not be until 1968–1969 and, especially, the early 1970s that the term "porro" replaces "porrista."

44. El Angel, interview with the author, notes, Mexico City.

45. See also Cabecilla, "Biografía de las porras"; ADFS, "ENP #3," Exp. 63-1-62, L-17, H-42; ADFS, "ENP #5," Exp. 63-1-65, L-9, H-31.

46. ADFS, "Porra Universitaria," Exp. 11-4-69, L-72, H-154.

47. Born in Peru, Marino Sagástegui Córdova started working as an editorial cartoonist with *Excélsior* in 1963. See Sagástegui, *El humor, la Guerra y la paz.*

48. Despite ample evidence against him, Méndez Rostro repeatedly insisted in the press that he had nothing to do with the problem of the porras and pledged on numerous occasions that he would do everything in his power to put an end to such "social and political vice." See, for example, Ramón H. Cosío, "Méndez Rostro dice que no protege a las 'porras,'" *El Heraldo*, March 25, 1969, in Fondo Movimiento Estudiantil en la Escuela Nacional Preparatoria (hereafter FMEENP), Box 61, Exp. 334, f 94 in Centro de Estudios Sobre la Universidad (hereafter CESU); "Control de Jóvenes Adictos," *Novedades*, March 26, 1969, in FMEENP Box 61, Exp. 334, f 115 in CESU; "Se llegó la hora," *La Prensa*, March 26, 1969, in FMEENP Box 61, Exp. 334, f 121 in CESU; "Fin al Régimen de las 'Porras,'" *Excélsior*, April 17, 1969; and "Baile de Preparatorianos," *El Sol de México*, December 18, 1969, in FMEENP Box 61, Exp. 337, f 53 in CESU. As examined later on, other important figures surrounding Díaz Ordaz included Miguel Osorio Marban, Alfredo Rios Camarena, Lauro Ortega, and Alfonso Corona del Rosal.

49. For similar and more detailed cartoons on porros, see Rius, "Toda la verdad."

50. Lomnitz, "The Uses of Fear," 15. See also Durón, *Yo Porro*; and Sánchez Gudiño, *Génesis, desarrollo, y consolidación.*

51. *La Voz de México*, February 19, 1967.

52. AIPS, "Porras," Vol. 2944 (A), n.d.; "Secuestro de camiones," ADFS, 1963–1970.

53. El Angel, interview with the author, notes, Mexico City.

54. Guitán Berniser, "Las porras"; Durón, *Yo Porro*; Lomnitz, "The Uses of Fear"; Monsiváis, "Los porros van dejando de ser impunes, perdida ya su eficacia como instrumentos de control," *Proceso*, no. 561, August 1, 1987, 15–16; and Sánchez Gudiño, *Génesis, desarrollo, y consolidación.*

55. For an exhaustive list of the various "leaders" involved in this violent event and their alleged affiliation to the Left, see Chávez de la Lama, *La madre de todas las "huelgas."* On the Sinaloa Group, see Romo Medrano, *Un relato biográfico.*

56. For a detailed history of MURO's campaign against Chávez, see González Ruiz, *MURO*. See also the attacks launched against the rector in the ultraconservative newspapers *El Gallo Universitario: Órgano de acción de reconquista universitaria* and *Puño: Órgano Informativo del MURO "¡Para Golpear con la Verdad!"* On the 1966 student strike, see Segovia, "Mexican Politics"; Rivas Ontiveros, *La izquierda estudiantil*, 451–500; and the particularly sympathetic account of the administration of Ignacio Chávez by his grandson, Chávez de la Lama, *La madre de todas las "huelgas."*

57. Rivas Ontiveros, *La izquierda estudiantil*, 451–500.

58. "Universidad. Normalidad o Crisis," *Tiempo*, April 25, 1966.

59. Segovia, "Mexican Politics"; and Rivas Ontiveros, *La izquierda estudiantil*, 451–500.

60. Like the schools of Dentistry, Social Work, Veterinary, Music, Nursing, and Architecture, the School of Chemistry was rather characterized for its moderate, conservative student body.

61. Jorge Maza Reducinco, interview with the author, notes, Mexico City.

62. Oscar González, interview with the author, notes, Mexico City.

63. Fernando Gutiérrez Barrios, "Situación actual que prevalece en la UNAM," ADFS, "UNAM," Exp. 63-1-65, L-27, H-286–293.

64. González Ruiz, *MURO*; and ADFS, "FCMAR," Exp. 63-1-65, L-27, H-266.

65. Fernando Gutiérrez Barrios, "Situación actual que prevalece en la UNAM," ADFS, "UNAM," Exp. 63-1-65, L-27, H-286–293.

66. See, for example, "Lucha contra todo sectarismo," *Excélsior*, August 8, 1961; "Los universitarios unidos," *Excélsior*, October 26, 1961; and "Unificación estudiantil," *Gaceta de la Universidad*, no. 377, November 6, 1961.

67. ADFS, "UNAM," Exp. 63-1-65, L27, H-197; and AIPS, "Breve análisis de la actual situación universitaria," April 26, 1966, Vol. 2946.

68. Fernando Gutiérrez Barrios, "Panorama Político de la Universidad Nacional Autónoma de México," ADFS, "UNAM," Exp. 63-1-68, L58, H-139–186; and ADFS, "MURO," Exp. 63-1-62, L18, H-90; DFS, "UNAM," Exp. 63-1-64, L-25, H-53; and ADFS, "UNAM," Exp. 63-1-65, L-27, H-290.

69. ADFS, "UNAM," Exp. 63-1-65, L27, H-197; and ADFS, "UNAM," Exp. 63-1-65, L27, H-290.

70. Another key contact for El Fish was Lauro Ortega, general secretary of the National Executive Committee (CNE) of the PRI (1964–1965) and interim president of the CNE (1965–1968). The principal contact between Ortega and El Fish was Miguel Osorio Narván. A one-time secretary general of the FEU (1955–1956), Osorio Narván was the director of the PRI Juvenil (1959–1964) and private secretary of Lauro Ortega. Having become friends with Osorio Narván and Rios Camarena, El Fish left behind his affiliations with the alemanistas. "Problema de las Llamadas 'Porras Preparatorianas,'" ADFS, "Porra Universitaria," Exp. 11-4-69, L-72, H-153; DFS, "UNAM," Exp. 63-1-966, L-38, H-80; Fiscalía Especial para Movimientos Sociales y Políticos del Pasado, "Informe Histórico," Chapters 3 and 4; and Camp, *Mexican Political Biographies*, 523–524, 532–533.

71. By 1966, the FUSA had already split into different factions. At the same time, the different FEUs had returned to the university.

72. Gutiérrez Barrios, "Panorama Político"; and Fiscalía Especial para Movimientos Sociales y Políticos del Pasado, "Informe Histórico," chs. 3, 4.

73. See Chapter 4.

74. See, for example, "Los funerales de Simpson," *Oposición*, November 2, 1970; and "Será entregado el que asesinó al estudiante," *Novedades*, October 23, 1969, in "Fondo Movimiento Estudiantil en la Escuela Nacional Preparatoria," FMEENP, Box 62, Exp. 337, f 24 in CESU. On the killings of porros between 1969 and 1972, see ADFS, "P5," Exp.

11-4-68, L-59, H-1; ADFS, "P5," Exp. 11-4-69, L-72, H-1; ADFS, "UNAM," Exp. 11-4-69, L-99, H-54; ADFS, "P9," Exp. 11-4-69, L-72, H-194; "El superman resulta ser un peligroso delincuente," *Novedades*, March 22, 1969, in FMEENP, Box 61, Exp. 334, f 79 in CESU; "Los Intocables," *Diario de la Tarde*, March 29, 1969, in FMEENP, Box 31, Exp. 159, f 27 in CESU; "El choque ocurrió," *El Día*, July 24, 1969, in FMEENP, Box 61, Exp. 336, f-4 in CESU; "Se planeaba otro Tlatelolco," *Por qué?*, no. 41, April 11, 1969, 6–9; ADFS, "P5," Exp. 63-1-70, L-67, H-191; ADFS, "P5," Exp. 11-4-70, L-105, H-34; "Crónica Nacional," *Punto Crítico*, no. 7, July 1972; and "UNAM. Martes 13," *Oposición*, June 15–30, 1972.

75. See the Conclusion.

76. El Angel, interview with the author, notes, Mexico City.

77. "Las porras y el cuento de las dos pesas," *Por que?*, no. 166, September 2, 1971; "Adelante vs. los porristas," *Excélsior*, August 12, 1971; "11 porristas más presos, 30 denuncias," *Excélsior*, August 13, 1971; "No pacto con hampones," *Excélsior*, August 14, 1971; "Ataques de porristas," *Excélsior*, August 15, 1971; "Maestros propiciadores," *Excélsior*, August 16, 1971; "Batalla total," *Excélsior*, August 17, 1971; and ADFS, "ENP #8," Exp. 11-4-71, L-141, H-231.

78. DSDW, M-IA, "Anti-Porra Campaign," A-453, August 20, 1971; "Declaración del Rector," *Gaceta de la Universidad*, Vol. 1, no. 6, September 2, 1970; and "Boletín Informativo del Comité de Lucha de la ENE," no. 2, April 1, 1971, FR-U-IS, MS-P, Vol. 17. See also "Porras asesinas," *Por qué?*, no. 117, September 24, 1970; "Porristas por Méndez Rostro," *Excélsior*, June 11, 1970, in FMEENP, Vol. 61, Exp-338, H-87, in CESU; "Ni porristas ni viciosos," *El Sol de Medio Día*, July 18, 1970, in FMEENP, Vol. 61, Exp-339, H-35; "Los Porristas Profesionales," *Revista de América*, July 25, 1970, in FMEENP, Vol. 61, Exp-339, H-57 in CESU; "Huelga de Maestros," *El Heraldo de México*, August 26, 1970, in FMEENP, Vol. 61, Exp-340, H-40 in CESU; and "Brigadas de Paterfamilias," *Excélsior*, August 28, 1970, in FMEENP, Vol. 61, Exp-340, H-73 in CESU.

79. This and similar sentiments were expressed to the author by El Angel, El Negro, and Oscar González.

80. "Crisis y Educación Superior," *Manifiesto del Grupo Comunista Internacionalista*, September 1970, FR-U-IS, MS-P, Vol. 25; and "La policía no puede ser salvadora de la Universidad," ADFS, "Porra Universitaria," Exp. 63-1-70, L-68, H-229.

81. El Angel, interview with the author, notes, Mexico City.

82. "Declaración del Comité de Lucha de las Facultad de Ciencias Políticas y Sociales frente a la situación actual del movimiento y en concreto ante el problema de las porras y el dialogo planteado por las autoridades," n.d., FR-U-IS, MS-P, Vol. 25. See also "Los Porristas Asesinan en la UNAM," *El Mexicano*, no. 10, July 1972, FPJEP.

83. Palillo, interview with the author, notes, Mexico City.

84. Rivas Ontiveros, *La izquierda estudiantil*, 498.

Chapter 8

1. "Dramática Carta de Helena Paz," *El Universal*, October 23, 1968.

2. See, for example, the 1968 public opinion poll referenced by Sergio Aguayo in

which it was estimated that as many as 80 percent of the people who participated in the questionnaire believed that "foreigners" were involved in the student movement. Some 40 percent of them specifically blamed the United States; 30 percent accused the "communists." And 20 percent rather pointed the finger at the Opus Dei. See Aguayo, 1968, 91. See also Rodríguez Kuri, "El lado oscuro de la luna."

3. As a number of scholars of U.S. and Latin American history have recently pointed out, the Right also expanded its influence on the international scene during the 1960s. Yet its mobilization at the grassroots levels has been overshadowed by an immense scholarship of leftist and countercultural movements. See, for example, McGirr, *Suburban Warriors*; Andrew III, *The Other Side of the Sixties*; McLeod, *The Religious Crisis of the 1960s*; Rodríguez Kuri, "El lado oscuro de la luna"; and Power, *Right Wing Women in Chile*. For an earlier work stressing the lack of popular support of the Mexican student movement, see Zolov, "La juventud se impone."

4. Similar accusations were published in various newspapers by Helena's mother, Elena Garro, one of Mexico's most influential intellectuals and key public supporter of Rubén Jaramillo and Carlos A. Madrazo. According to Garro's biographers, Elena's "puzzling" accusations against leftist intellectuals could only be explained by the intimidating threats she had received from the government during the 1968 movement. Prior to the student uprising Garro not only had achieved a reputation of criticizing the government for having "corrupted" the ideals of the Mexican Revolution, but also had become an outspoken critic of her former husband, Octavio Paz. In particular, she accused Paz, his circle of leftist intellectuals, and key members of the state of hiding behind progressive ideals of the Constitution without ever truly committing themselves to improving the lives of the poorest sectors of society. Her accusations against the government of López Mateos in support of the 1958 railroad strikers forced her to go into exile in 1959. Nine years later the administration of Díaz Ordaz accused Elena Garro (who had returned to Mexico in 1963 and who had subsequently participated in the radical magazines *Sucesos* and *Porqué?*) of instigating the student movement with the ultimate goal of bringing her friend Carlos A. Madrazo into power. Throughout the 1960s she was kept under close surveillance by the state, and in 1968 she was allegedly asked to collaborate with the government by selling information to the DFS. In 1972, both Elena and her daughter were forced to leave Mexico, first to Spain and then to France, where they lived until 1997. A year later Elena died of throat cancer in Cuernavaca in relatively poor living conditions. Today Elena and her daughter continue to be remembered by the Left as "enemies" of Mexico who "betrayed" the democratic principles of the 1968 student movement. By contrast, Elena Garro—who had always identified herself as a devout Catholic and an anticommunist admirer of Zapata, Villa, and Madero, and who in the 1960s had become an outspoken critic of Fidel Castro and the Cuban Revolution—insisted until her death that the students of 1968 had been manipulated by a group of leftist opportunists who orchestrated the CHN strike only to improve their political careers and bring instability to Mexico. For her, 1968 represented an international threat to the nation and its revolutionary legacy. See Elena's testimonies in Ramírez, *La*

ingobernable; and Rosas Lopátegui, *El asesinato de Elena*. See also Messinger Cypess, *Uncivil Wars*, 115–149.

5. For an excellent discussion of "wound," as a metaphor to describe a fractured or divided nation/state, see Nelson, *A Finger in the Wound*.

6. Often conservatives were not so tidily ordered in their critiques, which often appeared as wholesale grab-bags of complaints of everything from Altusser to Zen, so the organization of this chapter is somewhat heuristic.

7. See, for example, Aguayo Quezada, *1968*; and Witherspoon, *Before the Eyes of the World*.

8. Unless otherwise noted, for this brief chronology of the 1968 student movement that follows I have relied on Ramírez, *El Movimiento, I and II*; Poniatowska, *La Noche de Tlatelolco;* López Aretche, *El Grito*; and Cano Andaluz, *1968*.

9. Perhaps it is true—as many who participated in the movement have argued—that it was, in fact, the government that orchestrated the involvement of these two neighboring gangs. It was done as an excuse to send the granaderos inside the schools and, thus, violently warn the students that the administration of Díaz Ordaz would not tolerate any form of youthful political activism during the preliminary celebrations of the Olympic Games (which were scheduled to begin at the end of the summer). Regardless of the government's motives, however, what does seem clear, as will be shown in this chapter, is that porros and granaderos would both fail miserably at containing the student movement and, consequently, their involvement would only entice the students to adopt a more militant stance. For an extensive look at the use of provocateurs during the movement, see Guevara Niebla, *La Libertad nunca se olvida*.

10. On the role of porros during the movement, see the testimonies of "El Buho" in Jardón, *1968*, 228–232; "El Pelícano" in Durón, *Yo Porro*; and Poo Hurtado, "Los protagonistas olvidados." See also Rodriguez Kuri, "Los primeros días"; Guitán Berniser, "Las porras," 39–46; and Sánchez Gudiño, *Génesis, desarrollo, y consolidación*, 254–261.

11. Accusations against "foreign elements" continued to be made even after the movement. See, for example, Urrutia Castro, *Trampa en Tlatelolco*; Corona del Rosal, *Mis memorias políticas*; and General Marcelino García Barragán, as cited in Scherer García and Monsiváis, *Parte de Guerra*.

12. For an excellent discussion of the "public dialogue" and its consequences, see Braun, "Protest of Engagement."

13. The best descriptions of these meetings include Monsiváis, *Dias de Guardar;* and González de Alba, *Los Días y los Años*.

14. Gilabert, *El hábito de la utopía*; and Carey, "Los Dueños de México."

15. Carey, *Plaza of Sacrifices*; and Cohen and Frazier, "Mexico '68."

16. López Aretche, *El Grito*.

17. "Cuarto Informe de Gobierno del Presidente Gustavo Díaz Ordaz," September 1, 1968, in Ramírez, *El movimiento*.

18. Braun, "Protest of Engagement."

19. Taibo II, *'68*, 41.

20. Between August 29 and August 31, several gangs of porros attempted to undermine the movement by calling for students to return to classes, by suggesting that the strike had been commandeered by "international communist forces," by distributing apocryphal propaganda, and by creating antagonistic pseudo-student organizations. However, when these strategies failed, the gangs then proceeded to loot stores, classrooms, cafeterias, laboratories, and libraries during political rallies and throughout the city in an effort to further discredit the movement. More violently, they kidnapped and beat up members of the comités, organized strategic attacks that involved Molotov cocktails, and even went so far as to open fire with machine guns on the preparatorias and the vocacionales on numerous occasions. Yet students fought back and successfully kicked the provocateurs out the schools. El Chaparro, interview with the author, notes, Mexico City. See also ADFS, "P5," Exp. 11-4-68, L1, H-59; "Los Motivos del Porro," Sucesos, no. 2030, 1972; and Durón, Yo Porro.

21. Braun, "Protest of Engagement."

22. Ibid.; and Guevara Niebla, La libertad nunca se olvida.

23. García Reyes, Hernández Zárate, and Vega, "Las batallas en el Politécnico," 81–90; and León, La noche de Santo Tomás.

24. Aguayo Quezada, 1968; Álvarez Garín, La Estela de Tlatelolco; and Scherer García and Monsiváis, Parte de Guerra.

25. Aguayo Quezada, 1968, 226–227.

26. For a detailed discussion of the difficulties that exist in identifying the exact number of people killed during the student massacre of 1968, see Doyle, "The Dead of Tlatelolco"; Rodda, "Prensa, Pensa"; and Fournier and Martínez Herrera, "Mexico, 1968."

27. On the challenges to these figures as reported in the French press, see Arriola, El Movimiento estudiantil mexicano.

28. Aktuelt, October 13, 1968, in AHGE, DGAD, III 664 (72), Exp. 489-0/870 "68"; no. 568, October 14, 1968.

29. Le Monde, October 7, in AHGE, DGAD, III 664 (72), Exp. 44-0/510/; no. 2529, October 7, 1968; "Protest gegen das Blutvergiefsen in Mexiko," AHGE, DGAD, III 664 (72), Exp (43–47)/870/"68"; no. 1508, October 10, 1968; and Helsingin Sonomat, October 4, 1968, in AHGE, DGAD, III 664 (72), Exp. 34490, no. 1728.

30. AHGE, DGAD, III 664 (72), Exp. 728.5-0/510 "68"; no. 1777, October 4, 1968.

31. AHGE, DGAD, III 664 (72), Exp. 1797, October 9, 1968.

32. AHGE, DGAD, III 664 (72), Exp. 861.0/510 "68," no. 1048, October 5, 1968; and "El Festival de los Estudiantes," AHGE, DGAD, III 664 (72), Exp. 891.0/823.1 "68," no. 911, October 5–November 3, 1968.

33. AHGE, DGAD, III 664 (72), Exp. 73.0/515(72)/1–35, no. 1421, October 14, 1968.

34. Police brutality and xenophobic sentiments, they argued, "had reached alarming proportions" in Mexico. The government authorities not only had repressed local radical students but also had gathered up as many as three hundred foreigners and sent them back to their respective countries of origin simply because "they wore the

wrong clothes" or sported "long hair." Another journalist similarly noted, "Are you one of the 2,000 Swedish traveling to Mexico this summer? Then, get ready to witness violent student uprisings, barricades, and teargas . . . . The authorities continue to blame these events on 'foreign hands' supposedly financed by Fidel Castro." But the world "has yet to see the evidence" of these allegations. See AHGE, DGAD, III 664 (72), Exp. 485-0/870; no. 1647. Ulf Nilsson, "Violentos tumultos amenazan las Olimpiadas," *Expressen*, August 30, 1968.

35. AHGE, DGAD, III 664 (72), Exp. 436-0/821.7(XIX)/"68"; no. 1341, October 13, 1968. See also AHGE, DGAD, III 664 (72), Exp. 436-0/820/"68"; no. 1242, "Memorandum, Vienna," October 14, 1968; and AHGE, DGAD, III 664 (72), Exp. (43–47)/870/"68"; no. 1574, "Consigna Batallón Olímpico," *Zeit*, October 21, 1968.

36. See, among other examples, "Olympics Mexican Style," *Times of India*, October 6, 1968; and "La Flamme Olympique," *Le Figaro* (France), October 7, 1968, in AHGE, DGAD, III 664 (72). For detailed studies of the 1968 Olympic Games and the pressures they created on the Mexican government, see Rodríguez Kuri, "Hacia México 68"; Zolov, "Showcasing the 'Land of Tomorrow'"; and Witherspoon, *Before the Eyes of the World*. On early representations of Mexico as negatively depicted in Hollywood and challenged in Mexico's film industry, see Pick, *Constructing the Image of the Mexican Revolution*.

37. See, for example, "Rivales absurdos," *El Siglo* (Bogotá, Colombia), October 4, 1968; "Rivales absurdos," "Méjico," *El Espectador* (Bogotá, Colombia), October 4, 1968; "México, México, México," *La Prensa* (Managua, Nicaragua), October 7, 1968; and "Oito segundos e três décimos, e nem sequer foi seleccionado!," *Primeiro de Janeiro* (Porto, Brazil), October 10, 1968; in AHGE, DGAD, III 664 (72).

38. AHGE, DGAD, III 664 (72), Exp. 728.4-0/210 "68"/1; no. 737, October 5, 1968.

39. See, for example, the collection of articles in Medina Valdés, *El 68*; Martínez Fisher, "La postura del Partido"; and Centro de Estudios, Documentación e Información sobre el Partido Acción Nacional (hereafter CEDISPAN), "El PAN y el Movimiento Estudiantil."

40. For the use of photographs employed by newspapers to critique the over-reaction of the government, see Castillo del Troncoso, "El movimiento estudiantil."

41. "Los disturbios," *La Nación*, August 15, 1968; and "La ocupación militar," *La Nación*, October 1, 1968.

42. CEDISPAN, José Angel Conchello, "La conjura y la inquietud," August 30, 1968; and José Angel Conchello, "La calidad humana," September 20, 1968.

43. AHGE, DGAD, III 664 (72), Exp. III/664(12)34420, no. 51928, September 3, 1968.

44. AHGE, DGAD, III 664 (72), no. 1504, September 5, 1968.

45. AHGE, DGAD, III 664 (72), Exp. 84-01/"68," no. 597, September 6, 1968; AHGE, DGAD, III 664 (72), no. 1526, September 6, 1968; AHGE, DGAD, III 664 (72), Exp. 866-0/510(04)/1, no. 1471, September 6, 1968; AHGE, DGAD, III 664 (72), Exp. 85-0, no. 1285, September 9, 1968; AHGE, DGAD, III 664 (72), Exp. 53.1/210/"68," no. 576, September 10, 1968; AHGE, DGAD, III 664 (72), Exp. 45-0/510/"68," no. 1522, September 12, 1968; AHGE, DGAD, III 664 (72), Exp. 729.3-0/510/1, no. 923, September 18, 1968; AHGE,

DGAD, III 664 (72), Exp. 210(131.10)/"68," no. 1735, September 20, 1968; and AHGE, DGAD, III 664 (72), Exp. (43.0)/510, no. 1163, October 3, 1968.

46. AHGE, DGAD, III 664 (72), Exp. 53.1/210/"68," no. 576, September 10, 1968; AHGE, DGAD, III 664 (72), Exp. 45-0/510/"68," no. 1522, September 12, 1968; AHGE, DGAD, III 664 (72), Exp. 729.3-0/510/1, no. 923, September 18, 1968; AHGE, DGAD, III 664 (72), Exp. 84-0/510/"68," no. 629, September 19, 1968; and AHGE, DGAD, III 664 (72), Exp. 210(131.10)/"68," no. 1735, September 20, 1968.

47. Letter to Luis Echeverría by Antonio Carrillo Flores, September 25, 1968, in AHGE, DGAD, III 664 (72)/34490; no. 569076.

48. Daniel Cohn Bendit was apprehended at the Miquetia Airport on September 10. According to the report, he was planning to attend the Latin American Student Conference to be held in Merida. See AHGE, DGAD, III 664 (72), Exp. 87-0/510; no. 810, September 13.

49. AHGE, DGAD, III 664 (72), Exp. 34490; no. 52051, September 19, 1968.

50. Scherer García and Monsiváis, *Tiempo de Saber*, 67–97.

51. Mondrigo, *¡El Móndrigo!*

52. The book was distributed in 1969. According to Juan Miguel de Mora and Gonzalo Martré, Jorge Joseph (a journalist who later became the mayor of Acapulco, Guerrero) was the author of *¡El Móndrigo!* See Mora de, *Tlatelolco 1968*; and Martré, *El movimiento popular*.

53. The reference to "Raúl" appears to be a direct attack on Raúl Álvarez Garín, one of the most outspoken leaders of the CNH.

54. Mondrigo, *¡El Móndrigo!*, 183–184.

55. The most influential of these testimonies came from Sócrates Campos Lemus, whom many labeled a "government-sponsored provocateur." For two opposing views of these testimonies, see Campos Lemus, *El otoño*; and Guevara Niebla, *La libertad nunca se olvida*.

56. Rodríguez Lozano, *El gran chantaje*.

57. See, for example, Parra, "The Revolution Begins a New Era."

58. Many in Mexico's Olympic Committee made similar arguments. See, for example, Rodríguez Kuri, "Hacia México 68"; and Zolov, "Showcasing the 'Land of Tomorrow.'"

59. Rodríguez Lozano's concerns over the crisis of Mexico's youth and sympathetic views of the president's fight against communism were also voiced in his *Balance de la Revolución Mexicana* (1960), *El INJM: su obra patriótica y su proyección nacional* (1961), *Síntesis de la obra educativa de la Revolución Mexicana, 1910–1960* (1961), *Maestros revolucionarios* (1963), *Ideario político del Lic. Gustavo Díaz Ordaz* (1964), *Los gobiernos de la revolución contra la ignorancia* (coauthored with Gustavo Díaz Ordaz, 1965), *Nueva etapa de Instituto Nacional de la Juventud* (1966), and *Vida y obra del Dr. Gabino Barreda* (1968).

60. Rodríguez Lozano, *El gran chantaje*, 60.

61. Blanco Moheno, *Tlatelolco*.

62. On Roberto Blanco Moheno's sympathetic views of the Mexican Revolution,

see his *Crónica de la Revolución Mexicana* (1958, 1961, 1967, and 1968), *El Cardenismo* (1963), *Pancho Villa, que es su padre* (1969), *Zapata* (1970), *Cuando Cárdenas nos dio la tierra: la novela de la reforma agraria* (1970), and *Tata Lázaro: vida, obra y muerte de Cárdenas, Múgica y Carrillo Puerto* (1972).

63. He also includes a detailed critique of José Revueltas, *Los Errores* (1964).

64. Anda de, *Maquina Infernal*; Urrutia Castro, *Trampa en Tlatelolco*; Solana, *Juegos de Invierno*; Spota, *La Plaza*; Martínez, *Tlatelolco: tres instantáneas*; and Flores Zavala, *El Estudiante Inquieto.*

65. Monsiváis, *Salvador Novo*, 205–207; Volpi, *La Imaginación*, 411–413; Lombardo Toledano, *La Juventud;* and Krauze, *Daniel Cosío Villegas.*

66. See, for example, his weekly entries in *Tiempo*, from 1968 to 1970.

67. Borrego Escalante, *México*; and Magaña Contreras, *Troya Juvenil.*

68. Manuel Magaña Contreras was also the author of *Poder laico* (1970) and *Marx en Sotana* (1974).

69. On the progressive politics of Bishop Méndez Arceo, see Fazio, *La Cruz y el Martillo.*

70. Also feminized by Magaña Contreras and Borrego (in relation to communism) are the priests and laymen in charge of the Centro Nacional de Comunicación Social (CENCOS), the Juventud Obrera Católica (JOC), and the Secretariado Social Mexicano (SSM).

71. Borrego's invocations and conflation of religion and politics should also be noted. In his highly anti-Semitic books *Derrota Mundial* (*Global Defeat*, 1953) and *América Peligra* (*America under Danger*, 1964), he targets "Jewish" and "Mason" forces of a global communist revolution who had infiltrated European as well as North and South American schools. As González Ruiz has pointed out in *MURO*, these works were widely read among ultraconservative students organizations.

72. On Iván Illich's role in creating CIDOC, see Francine Du Plessix Gray, "The Rules of the Game," *New Yorker*, April 25, 1970. On the influential role of Grégoire Lemrecier in Cuernavaca, see Gallo, *Freud's Mexico*, 117–151; and González, *Crisis de Fe.*

73. Ivan Illich, "To Hell with Good Intentions," address to the Conference on InterAmerican Student Projects (CIASP) in Cuernavaca, April 20, 1968; in http://www.swaraj.org/illich_hell.htm; accessed April 5, 2012.

74. See, for example, Felipe Pardinas, S. J., "Carta del Editor," *Comunidad*, Vol. 1, no. 1, March 1966, 3–8.

75. Founded in 1964 by Felipe Pardinas Illanes, *Comunidad* became an important forum for analyzing social problems and promoting an open dialogue between Christians and non-Christians. In this effort, students were introduced not only to different and more progressive (and even radical) interpretations of Christianity as envisioned, among many others, by Ernesto Cardenal, Thomas Merton, Lemercier, Gustavo Gutiérrez, Camilo Torres, and Enrique Maza (one of the few Mexican priests who voiced his support of the 1968 student movement and offered a harsh critique of the church for failing to side with the students) but also to a broad range of New Left

intellectuals and Orthodox Marxists, such as Roger Garaudy (author of *De l'anatheme au dialogue: Un Marxiste tire les conclusions du Concile,* 1965), Herbert Marcuse, Althuser, Debray, Gunder Frank, C. Wright Mills, and Arnoldo Córdova.

76. CEDISPAN, Adolfo Chistlieb, "Orígenes del Movimiento," August 30, 1968; "Por el bien de México," *La Nación,* September 15, 1968; CEDISPAN, José Angel Conchello, "Las críticas al movimiento," September 20, 1968; and CEDISPAN, Gerardo Medina Valdés, "La violencia," October 4, 1968.

77. "El conflicto tiene solución," *La Nación,* September 1, 1968; "Por el bien de México," *La Nación,* September 15, 1968; "El puño cerrado," *La Nación,* September 15, 1968; and "El PRI coloca a la Cámara como cómplice," *La Nación,* October 15, 1968.

78. Blanco Moheno, *Tlatelolco;* and Borrego Escalante, *México.*

79. The author of more than thirty books, Salvador Borrego (1915–) is Mexico's most prolific anti-Semitic writer. He worked for *Excélsior* and *Últimas Noticias* from 1936 to 1965. In the following decade he founded dozens of new ultraconservative newspapers, including *El Sol de México* and *El Sol de Guadalajara.*

80. In 1965, Borrego argues, the once conservative pages of this newspaper fell under the "communist" hands of Julio Scherer—a "Jew"—who not only became increasingly sympathetic to the Marxist movements that had exploded throughout the continent but also had contributed to the transformation of the global counterculture into an "acceptable" product of consumption. He attests that the global liberal media—interested in expanding its readership within the leftist market—had "dangerously" depicted the fashion of hippies, the consumption of drugs, the youthful practice of extramarital sex, and the images of Che Guevara as iconic "symbols of rebellion." In so doing, he further contends, it has "normalized" and even "nationalized" these illicit acts, turned subversive symbols into fashionable slogans, and minimized their connection to communism. Borrego Escalante, *México.*

81. Examples of the "true" intellectuals (who came in support of the government) included Martín Luis Guzmán, Salvador Novo, and Agustín Yañez, as well as the more reactionary René Capistran and Jorge Prieto Laurens.

82. Zolov, "Toward an Analytical Framework."

83. Ibid., 53.

84. Ibid.

85. DSDW, M-IA, 1960–1963, "The Attitude of Many Latin American Intellectuals," Desp. 75, July 18, 1960, 4.

86. DSDW, M-IA, 1960–1963, Desp. 1480, June 20, 1962, 29.

87. DSDW, M-IA, 1960–1963, "The Attitude of Many Latin American Intellectuals," Desp. 75, July 18, 1960.

88. AHGE, DGAD, III 664 (72), Exp. 73-01515 (72)/1, "Letter to the Mexican Embassy by R. G. Martin," October 7, 1968.

89. AHGE, DGAD, III 664 (72), Exp. 73-01515 (72)/1, "Letter to the Mexican Embassy by Andrew H. Passmore," October 7, 1968.

90. See, for example, Zolov, "Showcasing the 'Land of Tomorrow'"; and Rodríguez Kuri, "El lado oscuro de la luna."

91. Zolov, "Toward an Analytical Framework"; and Aguayo Quezada, *1968.*
92. Rodríguez Lozano, *El gran chantaje,* 225.
93. Aguayo Quezada, *1968.*
94. On the literary and political life of Guzmán, see Ramírez Garrido, *Axkaná.*
95. Founded in 1909, the group emerged as a cultural rebellion against the positivist philosophy that had been endorsed during the Porfiriato (1876–1910). Other key intellectuals who participated in the Athenaeum were José Vasconcelos, Alfonso Reyes, Antonio Caso, Pedro Henríquez Ureña, and Julio Torri (among others). See Garciadiego Dantan, *Rudos contra científicos.*
96. As documented by Pablo González Casanova, of these three magazines, *Siempre!* sold the most copies: 54,200 in 1961 and 70,000 in 1964. By comparison, *Tiempo* and *Política* sold 17,421 and 21,000 in 1961 and 18,030 and 25,000 in 1964, respectively. See González Casanova, *Democracy in Mexico,* 216.
97. See, for example, *Tiempo:* "¿Nadie lo puede detener?," July 29, 1968, "El Estado y la Universidad," August 5, 1968, "Granaderos y orden público," August 12 and 19, 1968, "Los agitadores y el orden público," September 2, 9, 16, 23, and 30, and October 7 and 14, 1968, "La voluntad de no salvarse," September 30, 1968, "Fuego y subversión" and "Operación guerrilla," October 7, 1968, and "El movimiento subversivo," October 14, 1968.
98. See, for example, *Tiempo:* "Quetzquemetl y transparencia," June 3, 1968, "Juegos olímpicos: La vista de posa en los atletas," July 29, 1968, and "Edecanes y relaciones públicas," September 30, 1968. On the edecanes, see also Zolov, "Showcasing the 'Land of Tomorrow.'"
99. See, for example, *Tiempo:* "La UNAM y la violencia," May 6, 1968, "La rebeldía juvenil," June 24, 1968, "Acerca de la violencia," July 1, 1968, "El mundo comunista," July 8, 1968, "El 'Che' y el fracaso," July 29, 1968, "¿De quién es la culpa?," August 5, 1968, "Ciudadania y disturbios," August 12, 1968, "Los muertos" and "La autonomía," August 19, 1968, "Contradicciones," September 2, 1968, "Un padre preocupado," September 16 and 23, 1968, "La Universidad," September 30, 1968, "Agitadores extranjeros," September 30, 1968, "Los verdaderos criminals," October 7, 1968, "Los muertos," October 14, 1968, and "De democracia a democracia," October 21, 1968.
100. See, for example, *Tiempo:* "Alemania: locura criminal" and "Tabasco: Agitación estudiantil," May 6, 1968, "¿Disconformidad magisterial?," May 13, 1968, "Francia: Ofensiva contra la república," May 27, 1968, "Agitación mundial," June 3, 1968, "Francia: Imperio de la Ley" and "Agitación en Europa," June 10, 1968, "Agitación Impecable," June 17, 1968, "Brasil: los estudiantes," July 8, 1968, "Peru: violencia estudiantil" and "La Pantera Negra," August 5, 1968, and "La juventud del campo con GDO," August 19, 1968. On Siqueiros appearing on European television, see ARE, Exp. 485-0/510(72); no. 1895, "Programas sobre México difundidos po la Televisión Sueca," October 22, 1968.
101. Aguayo Quezada, *1968.*
102. Braun, "Protest of Engagement."
103. See, for example, Guevara Niebla, *La libertad nunca se olvida.*

104. A number of the more radical students continued to make efforts to sustain the movement throughout 1969. See, for example, Jardón, *Travesía a Ítaca.*

105. See, for example, the list of sources in Sánchez Saénz, "Bibliografía sobre el movimiento."

106. Some recent and excellent exceptions include, Braun, "Protest of Engagement"; Soltenko, "México '68"; Cohen and Frazier, "Mexico '68"; Rodríguez Kuri, "El lado oscuro de la luna," "Los primeros días"; Carey, *Plaza of Sacrifices*; Aguayo Quezada, *1968*; González Bustamante, "1968 Olympic"; Castillo del Troncoso, "El movimiento estudiantil"; and Marsh, "Writing Our History in Songs."

107. On the influential role of this "Tlatelolco literature," see Young, "Mexican Literary Reactions"; Brewster, *Responding to Crisis*; Volpi, *La imaginación*; Harris, "Luis González de Alba's *Los días;* and Poniatowska's *La noche de Tlatelolco* (1971)"; Martré, *El movimiento popular*; Sorensen, *A Turbulent Decade Remembered*, 54–77; and King, *The Role of Mexico's* Plural.

108. The exception in this case is Rodríguez Kuri, "El lado oscuro de la luna."

109. Rodriguez Kuri, "Los primeros días," 182.

110. On the lack of historical attention to the "messiness" of the movement, see Zolov, "Protest and Counterculture."

111. Carr, "The Many Meanings of 1968."

Conclusion

1. The attack on the demonstrators can be seen in Mendoza, *Halcones: Terrorismo de Estado.*

2. The educational reforms threatened to reduce student/faculty control of the University of Nuevo León (UAULN) in Monterrey. For detailed studies of the students' demands and government reaction, see Ortíz, *Jueves de Corpus*; Medina Valdés, *Operación 10 de Junio*; Condés Lara, *El 10 de Junio*; and Ortega Juárez, *10 de Junio.*

3. King, *The Role of Mexico's* Plural, 58–60; Brewster, *Responding to Crisis*, 78–79; Carey, *Plaza of Sacrifices*, 164–169; and Schmidt, *The Deterioration of the Mexican Presidency.*

4. Solis Mimendi, *Jueves de Corpus Sangriento.*

5. See, for example, the collection of government documents in Doyle, "The Corpus Christi Massacre"; Fiscalía Especial para Movimientos Sociales y Políticos del Pasado, "Informe Histórico," ch. 4; and Condés Lara, *Los Papeles Secretos.*

6. Loaeza, "Gustavo Díaz Ordaz."

7. On MURO's "crusade" against Chávez, see Chávez de la Lama, *La madre de todas las "huelgas"*; and González Ruiz, *MURO.*

8. Among those accused by Solis Mimendi is the founder of the University Parish, Agustín Desobry.

9. In the view of Solis Mimendi, therefore, there was no real difference between the leaders of the student movement, members of the ultraconservative MURO, provocateurs, and *golpeadores* (hit men) like himself: "We were all cut from the same

cloth" (63). In other words, in this environment of the Cold War, they were all equally "opportunistic," in that they were willing to sell their ideologies to the highest bidder. They were all equally violent as well.

10. Waters, "1968 in Memory and Place."

11. Álvaro Delgado, "El Fish se confiesa," *Proceso*, no. 1405, October 5, 2003.

12. See similar statements made by El Johnny in Homero Campa, "Porro, pero institucional," *Proceso*, November 21, 1987.

13. See, for example, "Declaración del Comité de Lucha de las Facultad de Ciencias Políticas y Sociales frente a la situación actual del movimiento y en concreto ante el problema de las porras y el dialogo planteado por las autoridades," n.d., FR-U-IS, MS-P, Vol. 25.

14. DSDW, M-IA, "Anti-Porra Campaign," A-453, August 20, 1971.

15. James C. Mckinley Jr., "Federal Judge Overturns Ruling against Mexico's Former President," *New York Times*, July 13, 2007.

16. El Negro, interview with the author, notes, Mexico City.

17. On Echeverría's "democratic aperture," see Schmidt, *The Deterioration of the Mexican Presidency*; and the collection of essays in Kiddle and Muñoz, eds., *Mexico*. On Fuentes's support of the Echeverría administration, see Volpi, *La imaginación*.

18. "El Larita" was a porro leader from the ENP #2 who in 1969 began to distance himself from both El Fish and the general director of the Preparatorias, Méndez Rostro. His goal was to create new political networks with padrinos associated with the new president, including Luis Gómez Zepeda, the general director of the National Railroads of Mexico (1970–1982), who provided him and other porros with financial backing to create one of the most violent groups to emerge inside UNAM during this period. This new group of porros was named Grupo Cultural Francisco Villa, and it became known inside the schools as Los Pancho Villa. To give legitimacy to their new organization, the leaders of Los Pancho Villa organized "Anti-Drugs" and "Liberation of Political Prisoners" campaigns. Self-described as "moderate conservative and revolutionary," they voiced their support for the "progressive" administration of Luis Echeverría. They coordinated student assemblies to address the "problem of violence" inside the schools and put out pamphlets that "exposed" the ill intentions of all those "false leaders" who "hid behind" the leftist rhetoric of the comités de lucha. See Grupo Francisco Villa," Exp. 63-1-70, L-113, H-245; ADFS, "Grupo Francisco Villa," Exp. 63-1-70, L-67, H-104; ADFS, "UNAM," Exp. 63-1-68, L-58, H-155; and "Curriculum Vitae de la Asociación Universitaria Francisco Villa," ADFS, "Grupo Francisco Villa," Exp. 11-4-72, L-189, H-189–190.

19. ADFS, "IPN" Exp. 63-3-66, L-23, H-257; "En el IPN . . . todo se pospone" *Punto Crítico*, no. 6, June 1972.

20. See, for example, Jardón, *Travesía a Ítaca*.

21. For three excellent examples of these films, see Joskowicz, *Crates; El Cambio* (1971); and Federico Weingarshofer, *Quiza siempre si me muera* (1971). On the "lumpen" phase of porrismo during the administration of Echeverría, see Rius, "Toda la verdad."

22. For a recent example, see Trevizo, *Rural Protest*.

23. See, among other examples, Preston and Dillon, *Opening Mexico*; and Krauze, *Mexico*.

24. Pensado, "The (Forgotten) Sixties in Mexico."

25. Ruisánchez Serra, "Reading '68," 181.

26. Arroyo, "Mexico," 51–52.

27. See, for example, "El 68 debe estar en los libros," *El Universal*, May 13, 2008; and Brewster, *Responding to Crisis*, 168.

28. These testimonies can be read and heard in Vázquez Mantecón and Arroyo, *Memorial del 68*; and Echeverría, *Memorial del 68*. See also the museum's virtual tour, "Memorial del 68," Centro Cultural Universitario Tlatelolco, http://www.tlatelolco. unam.mx/museos1.html; accessed April 1, 2012.

29. Yet, in hoping to provide the experience at the Colegio de México (which played a minimal role in the movement), the *Memorial* includes several vignettes by Guillermo Palacios.

30. De Groot, *The Sixties Unplugged*, 3.

Bibliography

Archives

AGG: Archivo General de la Nación
    ADFS: Archivo de la Dirección Federal de Seguridad.
    AIPS: Archivo de la Dirección General de Investigaciones Políticas y Sociales.
    FARC: Fondo Adolfo Ruiz Cortinez.
    FED: Fondo Enrique Díaz.
    FGDO: Fondo Gustavo Díaz Ordaz.
    FHM: Fondo Hermanos Mayo.
    FMAC: Fondo Manuel Ávila Camacho.
AH-UNAM: Archivo Histórico de la UNAM
    FRIIB: Fondo Reservado del Instituto de Investigaciones Bibliográficas.
    FR-U-IS, MS-P: Fondo Reservado de la UNAM—Impresos Sueltos, Movimientos Socio-Políticos.
AHGE, DGAD: Archivo Histórico Genaro Estrada, Dirección General de Asuntos Diplomáticos
AHP: Archivo Histórico del Politécnico.
APLL: Archivo Personal de Larissa Lomnitz
CEDISPAN: Centro de Estudios de Documentación e Información sobre el Partido Acción Nacional.
CESU: Centro de Estudios Sobre la Universidad
    CEM: Colección Esther Montero.
    FMEENP: Fondo Movimiento Estudiantil en la Escuela Nacional Preparatoria.
FPJEP: Fondo Personal de José Enrique Pérez
HL: Hesburgh Library, University of Notre Dame
RL: Regenstein Library, University of Chicago

DSDW, M-IA: Department of State Washington, Mexico—Internal Affairs Department.

DSDW, M-PGNDA: Department of State Washington, Mexico—Politics, Government and National Defense Affairs.

Student Newspapers and Bulletins

Boletín César Vallejo.

Boletín Comité Coordinador.

Boletín Informativo del Movimiento II. Declaración de la Habana.

Chispa, La: Órgano Mensual del Frente Estudiantil Socialista.

Combate: Órgano del Grupo de Acción Política "Patricio Lumumba."

Combate: Órgano Informativo del Partido Estudiantil Socialista de Economía.

Cometa Universitario, El.

Controversia: Revista de temas sociales y políticos de la UNAM.

Diálogo, Revista de Estudiantes.

Fuerza de la ESIME.

Gaceta, de la ENP (Escuela Nacional Preparatoria).

Gaceta de la Universidad.

Gallo Universitario, El: Órgano de acción de reconquista universitaria.

Goya.

Holguera, La (Órgano del CoCo de la UNAM e IPN).

Lucha Popular: Órgano de Información y Orientación de las Luchas del Pueblo Mexicano.

Mexicano, El.

Mundo Universitario, El.

Nigromante, El.

Nueva Izquierda.

Palabras.

Perspectiva. Órgano del Movimiento Estudiantil Independiente.

Político, El: Órgano de la Escuela Nacional de Ciencias Políticas y Sociales.

Praxis: Órgano Central de la Alianza de Izquierda Revolucionaria de Economía.

Puño: Órgano Informativo del MURO "¡Para Golpear con la Verdad!"

Técnica y Patria.

Testimonios (Periódico de la F. U. S. A.).

Universitario, El: Voz y expresión de la FUSA.

Virus Rojo. Juventud Marxista Revolucionaria.

National Newspapers and Magazines

Agachados, Los.

Anuarios del Departamento de Actividades Cinematograficas.

Atisbos.
Cine Mundial.
Comunidad.
Contenido.
Corno Emplumado/The Plumed Horn.
Día, El.
Espectador, El.
Excélsior.
Extra, La.
Hispanic American Report.
Imparcial, El.
Mundo Mejor.
Nación, La.
Nacional, El.
New York Times, The.
Novedades.
Nuevo Cine.
Oposición.
Política.
Popular, El.
Porque?
Prensa, La.
Punto Crítico.
Revista de Revistas.
Siempre!
Sol de México, El.
Supermachos, Los.
Tiempo (Seminario de la Vida y la Verdad Hispano Americano).
Últimas Noticias.
Universal, El.
Verdad.
Voz de México, La.
Washington Post.

Films and Documentaries Consulted

Al compass del rock and roll (José Díaz Morales, 1957).
Comunicados Cinematográficos del CNH (CUEC, 1968).
Crates (Alfredo Joskowicz, 1970).
El Brazo Fuerte (Giovanni Korporaal, 1958).
El Cambio (Alfredo Joskowicz, 1971).
El Corno emplumado. Una historia de los Sesentas (Nicolenka Beltrán and Anne Mette
    W. Nielsen, 2005).

El Grito (Leobardo López Aretche, 1968).
El Topo (Alejandro Jodorowsky, 1970).
Fando y Lis (Alejandro Jodorowsky, 1968).
Halcones: Terrorismo de Estado (Carlos Mendoza, 2006).
Historia de un document/Historie d'un document (Oscar Menéndez, 1970).
Los Caifanes (Juan Ibañez, 1966).
Los Olvidados (Luis Buñuel, 1953).
Memorial del 68 (Nicolás Echeverría, 2008).
Mural efímero (Raúl Kamffer, 1968).
Quiza siempre si me muera (Federico Weingarshofer, 1971).
Serenata en Acapulco (Chano Urueta, 1951).
The Wild One (Laslo Benedek, 1953).
Viva la Juventud (Fernando Cortes, 1956).
Viridiana (Luis Buñuel, 1961).

Published Sources

Acevedo-Muñoz, Ernesto R. *Buñuel and Mexico: The Crisis of National Cinema.* Berkeley: University of California Press, 2003.

Agnew, Bob. "¡Viva la Revolución! *Los Agachados* and the Worldview of Eduardo del Río (Rius)." *Studies in Latin American Popular Culture* 23 (2004), 1–20.

Aguayo Quezada, Sergio. *1968: Los archivos de la violencia.* Mexico City: Grijalbo, 1998.

———. *La Charola: Una historia de los servicios de inteligencia en México.* Mexico City: Grijalbo, 2001.

Aguilar Camín, Héctor, and Lorenzo Meyer. *In the Shadow of the Mexican Revolution: Contemporary Mexican History, 1910–1989.* Translations from Latin America series. Austin: University of Texas Press, 1993.

Agustín, José. *La tragicomedia mexicana, Vol. 1: La vida en México de 1940 a 1970.* Mexico City: Planeta, 1990.

Alegre, Robert F. "Las Rieleras: Gender, Politics, and Power in the Mexican Railway Movement, 1958–1959." *Journal of Women's History* 23, no. 2 (Summer 2011), 162–186.

Alejo Montes, Javier. *La Universidad de Salamanca bajo Felipe II: 1575–1598.* Salamanca, Spain: Aldecea, 1998.

Alonso, Antonio. *El movimiento ferrocarrilero en México: 1958/1959.* Mexico City: Era, 1975.

Altbach, Philip G. *Student Politics in America: A Historical Analysis.* New York: McGraw Hill, 1974.

Álvarez Garín, Raúl. *La Estela de Tlatelolco: Una reconstrucción histórica del movimiento estudiantil del 68.* Mexico City: Itaca, 2002.

Amador de Gama, Luis. *Historia gráfica del fútbol americano en México.* Mexico City: IPN, 1982.

Anaya, José Vicente. "El corno . . . Revista de los poetas que sueñan demasiado," *Revista electronica de literatura* (January 2011), http://circulodepoesia.com/ nueva/2011/01/el-corno-revista-de-los-poetas-que-suenan-demasiado/, accessed October 2, 2012.

Anda de, Gustavo. *Maquina Infernal, 1968.* Mexico City: Anda, 1975.

Anderson, Bo, and James D. Cockcroft. "Control and Co-optation in Mexican Politics." In James D. Cockcroft, André Gunder Frank, and Dale L. Johnson, eds. *Dependence and Underdevelopment: Latin America's Political Economy.* New York: Anchor Books, 1972.

Andrew III, John A. *The Other Side of the Sixties: Young Americans for Freedom and the Rise of Conservative Politics.* New Brunswick, NJ: Rutgers University Press, 1997.

Appendini, Guadalupe. *Historia de la Universidad Nacional Autónoma de México.* Mexico City: Porrúa, 1981.

Aquino Casas, Arnulfo, and Jorge Perezvega. *Imágenes y símbolos del 68: fotografía y gráfica del movimiento estudiantil.* Mexico City: UNAM, 2004.

Arana, Federico. *Guaraches de ante azul. I.* Mexico City: Editoriales Posada, 1985.

Arbena, Joseph L. "Sport, Development, and Mexican Nationalism, 1920–1970." *Journal of Sport History* 18, no. 3 (Winter 1991), 350–364.

Arenas, Francisco Javier. *La Flota. Cuadros Universitarios.* Mexico City: AUM, 1963.

Arriola, Carlos. *El Movimiento estudiantil mexicano en la prensa francesa.* Mexico City: Colegio de México, 1979.

Arroyo, Sergio Raúl. "Mexico: The Power of Memory." In Phillip Gassert and Martin Klimke, eds. "1968: Memories and Legacies of a Global Revolt." *Bulletin of the German Historical Institute,* Supplement 6 (2009), 51–55.

Aviña, Alexander. "Seizing Hold of Memories in Moments of Danger: Guerrillas and Revolution in Guerrero, Mexico." In Fernando Herrera Calderón and Adéla Cedillo, eds. *Challenging Authoritarianism in Mexico: Revolutionary Struggles and the Dirty War, 1964–1982.* London: Routledge, 2012, 40–59.

Ayala Blanco, Jorge. "El movimiento estudiantil." In *La Busqueda del cine mexicano, 1968–1972.* Mexico City: UNAM, 1974.

Azaola, Elena. *La institución correccional en México. Una mirada extraviada.* Mexico City: Siglo XXI, 1990.

Barbosa, Francisco. "Insurgent Youth: Culture and Memory in the Sandinista Student Movement." Ph.D. dissertation, Indiana University, 2006.

Bartra, Armando. "Tiempo de Jóvenes." In Salvador Martínez della Rocca, ed. *Voces y Ecos del 68.* Mexico City: Porrúa, 2009, 63–84.

Bartra, Roger. "La crisis del nacionalismo en México." *Revista Mexicana de Sociología* 51, no. 3 (July–September 1989), 191–220.

———. *The Cage of Melancholy: Identity and Metamorphosis in the Mexican.* Translated by Christopher J. Hall. New Brunswick, NJ: Rutgers University Press, 1992.

Becker, Howard. *Outsiders: Studies in the Sociology of Deviance.* New York: Free Press, 1991.

Beezley, William H. *Judas at the Jockey Club and Other Episodes of Porfirian Mexico.* Lincoln: University of Nebraska Press, 1989.

Bellingeri, Marco. "La imposibilidad del odio: la guerrilla y el movimiento estudiantil en México, 1960–1974." In Ilán Semo et al., eds. *La transición interrumpida: México, 1968–1988.* Mexico City: Nueva Imágen, 1993, 49–74.

Benjamin, Thomas. *La Revolución: Mexico's Great Revolution as Memory, Myth, and History.* Austin: University of Texas Press, 2000.

Blacker-Hanson, O'Neill. "Cold War in the Countryside: Conflict in Guerrero, Mexico." *The Americas* (September 2009), 181–210.

Blanco Moheno, Roberto. *Tlatelolco: historia de una infamia.* Mexico City: Editorial Diana, 1969.

Borrego Escalante, Salvador. *México: Futuro.* Mexico City: N/P, 1972.

Bortz, Jeffrey. "Wages and Economic Crisis in Mexico." In Barry Carr and Ricardo Anzaldúa Montoya, eds. *The Mexican Left, the Popular Movements, and the Politics of Austerity.* San Diego, CA: Center for U.S.-Mexican Studies, 1986.

Brachet-Márquez, Viviane. *El pacto de dominación. Estado, clase y reforma social (1910–1995).* Mexico City: El Colegio de México, 2001.

Brands, Hal. *Latin America's Cold War.* Cambridge: Harvard University Press, 2010.

Braun, Herbert. "Protest of Engagement: Dignity, False Love, and Self-Love in Mexico during 1968." *Comparative Studies in Sociology and History* 39, no. 3 (July 1997), 511–549.

Brewster, Claire. *Responding to Crisis in Contemporary Mexico.* Tucson: University of Arizona Press, 2005.

Brito Lemus, Roberto. "Cambio generacional y participación juvenil durante el cardenismo." In José A. Pérez, et al., eds. *Historias de los jóvenes en México. Su presencia en el siglo XX.* Mexico City: IMJ, 2004.

Britton, John. "Urban Education and Social Change in the Mexican Revolution, 1931–1940." *Journal of Latin American Studies* 5, no. 2 (November 1973), 233–245.

Burke, Michael E. "University of Mexico and the Revolution, 1910–1940." *Americas* 34, no. 2 (October 1977), 252–273.

Burton, Julianne. "'The Camera as Gun': Two Decades of Culture and Resistance in Latin America." *Latin American Perspectives* 5, no. 1 (Winter 1978), 49–76.

Cabrera López, Patricia. *Una inquietud de amanecer. Literatura y política en México, 1962–1987.* Mexico City: Porrúa, 2006.

Camp, Roderic Ai. "Education and Political Recruitment in Mexico: The Alemán Generation." *Journal of Interamerican Studies and World Affairs* 18, no. 3 (August 1976), 295–321.

———. *Intellectuals and the State in Twentieth-Century Mexico.* Austin: University of Texas Press, 1985.

———. "The Cartoons of Abel Quezada." *Journal of Popular Culture* 4 (1985), 125–138.

———. *Mexican Political Biographies 1935–1993.* Third Edition. Austin: University of Texas Press, 1995.

———. *Mexico's Military on the Democratic Stage.* London: Praeger Security International, 2005.

Campos Lemus, Sócrates A. *El otoño de la revolución (octubre).* Mexico City: Costa-Amic, 1973.

Cano Andaluz, Aurora, *1968: antología periodística*. Mexico City: UNAM, 1993.

Careaga, Gabriel. "La vida cultural y política de los sesentas." *Revista Mexicana de Ciencias Políticas y Sociales*, no. 108 (October–December 1994), 171–182.

Carey, Elaine. *Plaza of Sacrifices: Gender, Power and Terror in 1968 Mexico*. Albuquerque: University of New Mexico Press, 2005.

———. "Los Dueños de México: Power and Masculinity in '68." In Lessie Jo Frazier and Deborah Cohen, eds. *Gender and Sexuality in 1968: Transformative Politics in the Cultural Imagination*. New York: Palgrave Macmillan, 2009, 59–83.

Carlos, Manuel L. "Fictive Kinship and Modernization in Mexico: A Comparative Analysis." *Anthropological Quarterly* 46, no. 2 (April 1973), 75–91.

Carr, Barry. *La izquierda mexicana a través del siglo xx*. Mexico City: Era, 1996.

———. "The Many Meanings of 1968." *Enfoque* (Fall–Winter 1998).

Carr, Barry, and Ricardo Anzaldúa Montoya, eds. *The Mexican Left, the Popular Movements, and the Politics of Austerity*. San Diego, CA: Center for U.S.-Mexican Studies, 1986.

Casanova, Rosa, and Adriana Konzevik. *Luces sobre México. Catálogo selectivo de la Fototeca Nacional del INAH*. Mexico City: Consejo Nacional para la Cultura y las Letras, 2006.

Caso y Andrade, Alfonso. "Ley Orgánica de la Universidad Nacional Autónoma de México." In Xavier Cortés Rocha and Adoldo Rodríguez Gallardo, eds. *Visión de la Universidad. Una visión plural*. Mexico City: UNAM, 1999.

Castillo del Troncoso, Alberto. "El movimiento estudiantil de 1968 narrado en imagines." *Sociológica* 23, no. 68 (September–December 2008), 63–114.

Chávez de la Lama, Ignacio. *La madre de todas las "huelgas." La UNAM en 1966*. Nuevo León, Mexico: Universidad Autónoma de Nuevo León, 2011.

Cline, Howard F. *Mexico: Revolution to Evolution, 1940–1960*. New York: Oxford University Press, 1962.

Cockcroft, James. *Mexico's Hope: An Encounter with Politics and History*. New York: Monthly Review Press, 1998.

Cohen, Albert K. *Delinquent Boys: The Culture of the Gang* [1955]. New York: Free Press, 1963.

Cohen, Deborah, and Lessie Jo Frazier, "'No sólo cocinábamos . . .' Historia inédita de la otra mitad del 68." In Ilán Semo et al., eds. *La Transición interrumpida: México, 1968–1988*. Mexico City: Nueva Imágen, 1993, 75–109.

———. "Mexico '68: Defining the Space of the Movement, Heroic Masculinity in the Prison, and 'Women' in the Streets." *Hispanic American Historical Review* 84, no. 4 (November 2003), 617–660.

———. "Talking Back to '68: Gendered Narratives, Participatory Spaces, and Political Cultures." In Lessie Jo Frazier and Deborah Cohen, eds. *Gender and Sexuality in 1968: Transformative Politics in the Cultural Imagination*. New York: Palgrave Macmillan, 2009, 145–172.

Cohen, Phil. *Rethinking the Youth Question: Education, Labor, and Cultural Studies*. Durham, NC: Duke University Press, 1999.

Cohen, Stanley. *Folk Devils and Moral Panics: The Creation of the Mods and the Rockers*. Oxford: Blackwell, 1990.

Cohn, Deborah. "The Mexican Intelligentsia, 1950–1968: Cosmopolitanism, National Identity, and the State." *Mexican Studies/Estudios Mexicanos* 21, no. 1 (Winter 2006), 141–182.

Condés Lara, Enrique. *10 de Junio. No se olvida!* Puebla, Mexico: Benemérita Universidad Autónoma de Puebla, 2001.

———. *Los papeles secretos del 10 de Junio*. Mexico City: Reflexión Abierta, 2002.

———. *Represión y rebelión en México (1959–1985), Vols. I–III*. Mexico City: Porrúa, 2007–2009.

Confederación Deportiva Mexicana, *60 Aniversario. Confederación Deportiva Mexicana, 1933–1993*. Mexico City: CODEME, 1993.

Consejo Nacional para la Cultura y las Artes. *1968. Un archivo inédito*. Mexico City: CNCA, 2008.

Contreras Pérez, Gabriela. *Los grupos católicos en la Universidad Autónoma de México (1933–1944)*. Mexico City: Universidad Autónoma Metropolitana, 2002.

Córdova, Arnaldo. *La política de masas del cardenismo*. Mexico City: Serie Popular Era, 1974.

Corona del Rosal, Alfonso. *Mis memorias políticas*. Mexico City: Grijalbo, 1995.

Cosío Villegas, Daniel. "La crisis de México." In Stanley R. Ross, ed. *¿Ha muerto la revolución?* Mexico City: Red de Jonás, 1979.

Covo, Milena. "La composición social de la población estudiantil de la UNAM: 1960–1985." In Ricardo Pozas H., ed. *Universidad Nacional y Sociedad*. Mexico City: Porrúa, 1990, 29–136.

Cowie, Peter. *Revolution: The Explosion of World Cinema in the 1960s*. New York: Faber and Faber, 2004.

Crespi, Roberto Simón. "José Revueltas (1914–1976): A Political Biography." *Latin American Perspectives* 6, no. 3 (1979), 93–113.

Crisp, Colin. *The Classic French Cinema, 1930–1960*. Bloomington: Indiana University Press, 1997.

Cuevas Díaz, Aurelio. *El Partido Comunista Mexicano, 1963–1973*. Guerrero, Mexico: Universidad Autónoma de Guerrero, 1984.

Dagrón, Alfonso Dumucio. *Cine, censura y exilio en América Latina*. Mexico City: CIMCA, 1984.

Davis, Diane E. *Urban Leviathan: Mexico City in the Twentieth Century*. Philadelphia: Temple University Press, 1994.

De Groot, Gerard J. "The Culture of Protest: An Introductory Essay." In Gerard J. Degroot, ed. *Student Protest: The Sixties and After*. London: Longman, 1997.

———. *The Sixties Unplugged: A Kaleidoscopic History of a Disorderly Decade*. Cambridge: Harvard University Press, 2008.

Deutschmann, David, ed. *Che Guevara and the Cuban Revolution: Writings and Speeches or Ernesto Che Guevara*. New York: Pathfinder, 1987.

Díaz y de Ovando, Clementina, ed. *La Ciudad Universitaria de México. Volumen X. Tomo I: Reseña histórica 1929–1955*. Mexico City: UNAM, 1979.

Díaz Mendiburo, Aarón. *Los hijos homoeróticos de Jaime Humberto Hermosillo*. Mexico City: Plaza y Valdés, 2004.

Domínguez, Raúl. "El perfil político de las organizaciones estudiantiles durante la década de 1950." In Renate Marsiske et al., eds. *Los estudiantes. Trabajos de historia y sociología*. Mexico City: UNAM, 1989.

Doyle, Kate. "The Dead of Tlatelolco." In The National Security Archive, http://www.gwu.edu/~nsarchiv/NSAEBB/NSAEBB201/index.htm#article, accessed April 17, 2012.

———. "The Corpus Christi Massacre. Mexico's Attack on Its Student Movement, June 10, 1971." In the National Security Archive, http://www.gwu.edu/~nsarchiv/NSAEBB/NSAEBB91/, accessed September 10, 2012.

———. "Human Rights and the Dirty War in Mexico." In the National Security Archive Project, http://www.gwu.edu/~nsarchiv/NSAEBB/NSAEBB99/, accessed August 15, 2012.

Durón, Olga. *Yo Porro (Retrato hablado)*. Mexico City: Editorial Posada, 1984.

Elizondo Alceraz, Carlos. *Universidad. Novela*. Mexico City: EDIA SA, 1953.

Espinosa, David. "Student Politics, National Politics: Mexico's National Student Union, 1926–1943." *Americas* 62, no. 4 (April 2006), 533–562.

Estrada Rodríguez, Gerardo. "Ciencias Políticas en los años sesenta." *Revista Mexicana de Ciencias Políticas y Sociales*, no. 115–116 (January–June 1984), 95–102.

———. *1968, estado y universidad: orígenes de la transición política en México*. Mexico City: Plaza Janés, 2004.

Fazio, Carlos. *La Cruz y el Martillo. Pensamiento y Acción de Sergio Méndez Arceo*. Mexico City: J. Mortiz, 1987.

Feixa, Carles. *El reloj de arena. Culturas juveniles en México*. Mexico City: Jóvenes, 1988.

Fernández de Lizardi, José Joaquín. *The Mangy Parrot: The Life and Times of Periquillo Sarniento, Written by Himself for His Children*. Translated by David Frye. Indianapolis, IN: Hackett Publishing Company, 2004.

Fields, Belden. "French Maoism." *Social Text*, no. 9/10 (Summer 1984), 148–177.

Fiscalía Especial para Movimientos Sociales y Políticos del Pasado. "Informe Histórico a la Sociedad Mexicana, 2006." In the National Security Archive, http://www.gwu.edu/~nsarchiv/NSAEBB/NSAEBB209/index.htm, accessed September 20, 2012.

Flores Zavala, Ernesto. *El estudiante inquieto. Los movimientos estudiantiles, 1966–1970*. Mexico City: UNAM, 1988.

Foucault, Michel. *Power/Knowledge: Selected Interviews and Other Writings, 1972–1977*. New York: Pantheon, 1980.

Fournier, Patricia, and Jorge Martínez Herrera. "'Mexico, 1968': Among Olympic Fanfares, Government Repression and Genocide." In P. Funari et al., eds. *Memories from Darkness: Archaeology of Repression and Resistance in Latin America* (Spring 2009), 145–174.

Foweraker, Joe. "Popular Organization and Institutional Change." In Joe Foweraker and Ann L. Craig, eds. *Popular Movements and Political Change in Mexico*. Boulder, CO: Lynne Rienner Publishers, 1990, 3–21.

Freyre, Rafael. *Mira lo que me encontré.* Mexico City: NP, 1958.

Fuentes, Carlos. *La Región mas transparente.* Mexico City: Fondo de Cultura Económica, 1958.

————. *La muerte de Artemio Cruz.* Mexico City: Fondo de Cultura Económica, 1962.

Gallo, Rubén. *Freud's Mexico: Into the Wilds of Psychoanalysis.* Cambridge: MIT Press, 2010.

García Barragán, Elisa, ed. *La Ciudad Universitaria de México. Volumen X. Tomo II: Reseña histórica 1956–1979.* Mexico City: UNAM, 1979.

García Reyes, Jaime, Fernando Hernández Zárate, and David Vega. "Las batallas en el Politécnico." In Gilberto Guevara Niebla and Raúl Álvarez Garín, eds. *Pensar el 68.* Mexico City: Ediciones Cal y Arena, 2008, 81–90.

García Riera, Emilio. *Historia documental del cine mexicano,* Vol. 9, 1957–1958. Jalisco, Mexico: Universidad de Guadalajara, 1994.

García Saldaña, Parmenides. *En ruta de la onda.* Mexico City: Editorial Diógenes, S. A., 1972.

————. *El Rey criollo* [1970]. Mexico City: J. Mortiz, 2003.

Garciadiego Dantan, Javier. *Rudos contra científicos. La Universidad Nacional durante la Revolución Mexicana.* Mexico City: El Colegio de México, 1996.

Garza, Enrique de la, Tomás Ejea León, and Luis Fernando Macias. *El otro movimiento estudiantil.* Mexico City: Extemporáneos, 1986.

Gassert, Phillip, and Martin Klimke. "1968 from Revolt to Research." *Bulletin of the German Historical Institute* 6 (2009), 5–24.

Ghosh, S. K. *Ragging: Unquiet Campus.* Delhi, India: Ashish Publishing House, 1993.

Gil, Mario. *Los ferrocarrileros.* Mexico City: Extemporáneos, 1971.

Gil Olivo, Ramón. *Cine y liberación. El Nuevo cine latinoamericano (1954–1973). Fuentes para un lenguaje.* Mexico City: CUAAD, 2009.

Gilabert, César. *El hábito de la utopía. Análisis del imaginario sociopolítico en el movimiento estudiantil de México, 1968.* Mexico City: Porrúa, 1993.

Gitlin, Todd. *The Whole World Is Watching: Mass Media in the Making and Unmaking of the New Left.* Berkeley: University of California Press, 1981.

————. *The Sixties: Years of Hope, Days of Rage.* New York: Bantam Books, 1987.

Gómez Nashiki, Antonio. "El movimiento y la violencia institucional. La Universidad Michoacana de San Nicolás de Hidalgo, 1956–1966." *Revista de Investigaciones Educativa* 12, no. 35 (October–December 2007), 1179–1208.

Gómez, Pablo. *1968: la historia también está hecha de derrotas.* Mexico City: Porrúa, 2008.

Gomezjara, Francisco A. "Juventud ¿Y la banda que?" In F. A. Gomezjara et al. *Las bandas en tiempos de crisis.* Mexico City: Ediciones Nueva Sociología, 1987.

González de Alba, Luis. *Los días y los años.* Mexico City: Era, 1971.

González Bustamante, Celeste. "1968 Olympic, Dreams and Tlatelolco Nightmares: Imagining and Imaging Modernity on Television." *Mexican Studies/Estudios Mexicanos* 26, no. 1 (Winter 2010), 1–30.

González Casanova, Manuel. *¿Qué es un cine club?* Mexico City: UNAM, 1962.

González Casanova, Pablo. *Democracy in Mexico*. Translated by Danielle Salti. New York: Oxford University Press, 1970.

González Cosío, Arturo. *Historia estadística de la universidad, 1910–1967.* Mexico City: UNAM, Instituto de Investigaciones Sociales, 1968.

González, Fernando M. *Crisis de fe: Psicoanálisis en el Monasterio de Santa María de la Resurección, 1961–1968.* Mexico City: Tusquets, 2011.

González Ruiz, Edgar. *MURO, memorias y testimonios, 1961–2002.* Puebla, Mexico: Benemérita Universidad Autónoma de Puebla, 2004.

Gosse, Van. *Rethinking the New Left: An Interpretative History.* New York: Palgrave Macmillan, 2005.

Gould, Jeffrey L. "Solidarity under Siege: The Latin American Left, 1968." *American Historical Review* 114, no. 2 (April 2009), 348–375.

Guevara Niebla, Gilberto. *La libertad nunca se olvida: Memoria del 68.* Mexico City: Cal y arena, 2004.

Guitán Berniser, Carmen. "Las porras: Estudio de caso de un grupo de presión Universitaria." Thesis, UNAM, 1975.

Hansen, Roger D. *The Politics of Mexican Development.* Baltimore, MD: Johns Hopkins Press, 1971.

Hanson, Mary Ellen. *Go! Fight! Win! Cheerleading in American Culture.* Bowling Green, OH: Bowling Green State University Popular Press, 1995.

Harris, Chris. "Luis González de Alba's *Los días y los años* (1971) and Elena Poniatowska's *La noche de Tlatelolco* (1971): Foundational Representations of Mexico '68." *Bulletin of Latin American Research* 29 (March 2010), 107–127.

Hart, John Mason. *Empire and Revolution: The Americans in Mexico since the Civil War.* Berkeley: University of California Press, 2002.

Hennessy, Alistair. "The New Radicalism in Latin America." *Contemporary History* 7, no. 1 (January 1972), 1–26.

Henson, Elizabeth. "Madera 1965: Primeros Vientos." In Fernando Herrera Calderón and Adéla Cedillo, eds. *Challenging Authoritarianism in Mexico: Revolutionary Struggles and the Dirty War, 1964–1982.* London: Routledge, 2012, 19–39.

Hernández Rodríguez, Rogelio. *La formación del político mexicano: El caso de Carlos A. Madrazo.* Mexico City: Colegio de México, 1998.

———. "Challenging Caciquismo. An Analysis of the Leadership of Carlos Hank González." In Alan Knight and Wil Pansters, eds. *Caciquismo in Twentieth Century Mexico.* London: Institute for the Studies of the Americas, 2005, 249–271.

Herrera Calderón, Fernando. "From Books to Bullets: Youth Radicalism and Urban Guerrilla in Guadalajara." In Fernando Herrera Calderón and Adéla Cedillo, eds. *Challenging Authoritarianism in Mexico: Revolutionary Struggles and the Dirty War, 1964–1982.* London: Routledge, 2012, 105–128.

Herrera Calderón, Felipe, and Adéla Cedillo, eds. *Challenging Authoritarianism in Mexico: Revolutionary Struggles and the Dirty War, 1964–1982.* London: Routledge, 2012.

Hinds, Harold E., and Charles M. Tatum. *Not Just for Children: The Mexican Comic Book in the Late 1960s and 1970s.* Westpoint, CT: Greenwood Press, 1992.

Hodges, Donald, and Ross Gandy. *Mexico under Siege: Popular Resistance to Presidential Despotism.* London: Long House, 2002.

Hofstadter, Dan. *Mexico, 1946–73.* New York: Facts on File, 1974.

Horn, Gerd-Rainer. *The Spirit of '68: Rebellion in Western Europe and North America, 1956–1976.* New York: Oxford University Press, 2007.

Human Rights Watch. *Lost in Transition: Bold Ambitions, Limited Results for Human Rights under Fox.* May 2006 report, http://hrw.org/reports/2006/mexico0506/, accessed June 17, 2012.

Instituto Nacional de la Juventud Mexicana. *Instituto Nacional de la Juventud Mexicana: Objetivos y realizaciones.* Mexico City: INJM, 1953.

———. *Casas de la Juventud: Proyección de la obra del INJM a la provincia.* Mexico City: INJM, 1960.

Instituto Politécnico Nacional. *50 años en la historia de la educación tecnológica.* Mexico City: IPN, 1988.

Jardón, Raúl. *1968: El fuego de la esperanza.* Mexico City: Siglo XXI, 1998.

———. *El espionaje contra el movimiento estudiantil. Los documentos de la Dirección Federal de Seguridad y las agencias de inteligencia estadounidense en 1968.* Mexico City: Itaca, 2003.

———. *Travesía a Ítaca. Recuerdos de un militante de izquierda (del comunismo al zapatismo, 1965–2001).* Mexico City: Cenzontle, 2008.

Joseph, Gilbert M. "What We Now Know and Should Know: Bringing Latin America More Meaningfully into Cold War Studies." In Gilbert M. Joseph and Daniela Spenser, eds. *In from the Cold: Latin America's New Encounter with the Cold War.* Durham, NC: Duke University Press, 2008, 3–46.

Joseph, Gilbert M., Anne Rubenstein, and Eric Zolov, eds. *Fragments of a Golden Age: The Politics of Culture in Mexico since 1940.* Durham, NC: Duke University Press, 2001.

Joseph, Gilbert M., and Daniela Spenser, eds. *In from the Cold: Latin America's New Encounter with the Cold War.* Durham, NC: Duke University Press, 2008.

Kemper, Robert V. "The Compadrazgo in Urban Mexico." *Anthropological Quarterly* 55, no. 1 (January 1982), 17–30.

Kiddle, Amelia M., and María L. O. Muñoz, eds. *Mexico: The Presidencies of Lázaro Cárdenas and Luis Echeverría.* Tucson: University of Arizona Press, 2010.

King Cobos, Josefina. *Memorias de Radio UNAM, 1937–2007.* Mexico City: UNAM, 2007.

King, John. *The Role of Mexico's Plural in Latin American Literary and Political Culture: From Tlatelolco to the "Philanthropic Ogre."* New York: Palgrave Macmillan, 2007.

Klimke, Martin. *The Other Alliance: Student Protest in West Germany and the United States in the Global Sixties.* Princeton: Princeton University Press, 2010.

Knight, Alan. "Political Violence in Post-revolutionary Mexico." In Kees Kooning and Dirk Kruijt, eds. *Societies of Fear: The Legacy of Civil War, Violence and Terror in Latin America.* New York: Zed Books, 1999.

———. "The Modern Mexican State: Theory and Practice." In Miguel Ángel Centeno and Fernando López-Alvez, eds. *The Other Mirror: Grand Theory through the Lens of Latin America*. Princeton: Princeton University Press, 2001, 177–218.

———. "The Weight of the State in Modern Mexico." In James Dunkerley, ed. *Studies in the Formation of the Nation-State in Latin America*. London: Institute of Latin American Studies, 2002, 212–253.

Knight, Alan, and Wil Pansters, eds. *Caciquismo in Twentieth Century Mexico*. London: Institute for the Studies of the Americas, 2005.

Koonings, Kees, and Dirk Kruijt, eds. *Societies of Fear: The Legacy of Civil War, Violence and Terror in Latin America*. New York: Zed Books, 1999.

Kruaze, Enrique. *Daniel Cosío Villegas: Una biografía intellectual*. Mexico City: Fondo de Cultura Económica, 1991.

———. *La presidencia imperial: Ascenso y caída del sistema político mexicano (1940–1996)*. Mexico City: Tusquets, 1997a.

———. *Mexico: Biography of Power: A History of Modern Mexico, 1810–1996*. Translated by Hank Heifetz. New York: Harper Collins Publishers, 1997b.

Lechuga, Graciela, ed. *Ideología de la Revolución Mexicana*. Mexico City: UAM, 1984.

León, Igor de. *La noche de Santo Tomás*. Mexico City: Ediciones de Cultura Popular, 1988.

Levinson, Bradley A. "'Una etapa siempre difícil': Concepts of Adolescence and Secondary Education in Mexico." *Comparative Education Review* 43, no. 2. (May 1999), 129–161.

Levy, Daniel C. *University and Government in Mexico: Autonomy in an Authoritarian System*. New York: Praeger, 1980.

Liebman, Arthur, et al., eds. *Latin American University Students: A Six Nation Study*. Cambridge: Harvard University Press, 1972.

Lira, Luis Fernando, ed. *Diccionario del Español usual en México*. Mexico City: Colegio de México, 1996.

Loaeza, Soledad. *Clases medias y política en México: La querella escolar, 1959–1963*. Mexico City: El Colegio de México, 1999.

———. "Gustavo Díaz Ordaz: Las insuficiencias de la presidencia autoritaria." In Will Fowler, ed. *Gobernantes mexicanos*. Mexico City: Fondo de Cultura Económica, 2008, 287–336.

Lombardo Toledano, Vicente. *La Juventud en el mundo y en México*. Mexico City: Partido Popular Socialista, 1968.

Lomnitz, Claudio. "An Intellectual's Stock in the Factor of Mexico's Ruins (Mexico: Biography of Power by Enrique Krauze)." *American Journal of Sociology* 103, no. 4 (January 1998), 1052–1065.

———. *Deep Mexico, Silent Mexico: An Anthropology of Nationalism*. Minneapolis: University of Minnesota Press, 2001.

Lomnitz, Larissa. "Carreras de vida en la UNAM." *Plural* (March 1976), 18–22.

———. "Conflict and Mediation in a Latin American University." *Journal of Latin America and World Affairs* 19, no. 3 (1977), 315–338.

————."Horizontal and Vertical Relations and the Social Structure of Urban Mexico." *Latin American Research Review* 17, no. 2 (1982), 51–74.

————. "The Uses of Fear: Porro Gangs in Mexico." In Mary LeCron Foster and Robert A. Rubinstein, eds. *Peace and War: Cross-Cultural Perspectives*. New Brunswick, NJ: Transaction Books, 1986.

López Cabrera, Luis, et al. "Ensayo histórico de la educación física en México." *Geschichte der Leibesubungen* 6 (1989), 1095–1112.

Lorey, David E. *The University System & Economic Development in Mexico since 1929*. Stanford: Stanford University Press, 1993.

Loyo Brambila, Aurora. "El marco socio-económico de la crisis política de 1958–1959 en México." *Revista Mexicana de Sociología* 37, no. 2 (April–June 1975), 249–362.

————. *El movimiento magisterial de 1958 en México*. Mexico City: Ediciones Era, 1979.

Loyo Brambila, Aurora, and Ricardo Pozas Horcasitas. "La crisis política de 1958 (notas en torno a los mecanismos de control ejercidos por el estado mexicano sobe la clase obrera organizada)." *Revista Mexicana de Ciencias Políticas y Sociales*, no. 89 (July–September 1977), 77–118.

Mabry, Donald. *The Mexican University and the State. Student Conflicts, 1910–1971*. Texas: A & M University Press, 1982.

Maciel, Carlos. *El movimiento de liberación nacional. Vicisitudes y aspiraciones*. Sinaloa, Mexico: Universiad Autónoma de Sinaloa, 1990.

Magaña Contreras, Manuel. *Troya Juvenil*. Mexico City: Ideal, 1971.

Maldonado Aranda, Salvador. "Between Law and Arbitrariness: Labour Union Caciques in Mexico." In Alan Knight and Wil Pansters, eds. *Caciquismo in Twentieth Century Mexico*. London: Institute for the Studies of the Americas, 2005, 227–248.

Manzano, Valeria. "The Making of Youth in Argentina: Culture, Politics, and Sexuality, 1956–1976." Ph.D. dissertation, Indiana University, 2009.

Marcúe Padiñas, Manuel, et al. "La crisis de la educación en México. La ocupación del Instituto Politécnico Nacional." *Problemas de Latinoamérica* 3, no. 13 (November 1956).

Markarian, Vania. "El movimiento estudiantil mexicano de 1968. Treinta años de debates públicos." In *Anuario de Espacios Urbanos, Historia, Cultura, Diseño* (2001), 240–264.

————. " 'Ese héroe es el joven comunista': Violencia, heroísmo y cultura juvenil entre los comunistas uruguayos de los sesenta." *Estudios Interdisciplinario de América Latina* 21, no. 2 (July–December 2010), 7–32.

Marsh, Hazel. " 'Writing Our History in Songs': Judith Reyes, Popular Music and the Student Movement of 1968." *Bulletin of Latin American Research* 29 (March 2010), 144–159.

Marsh, Peter, Elizabeth Rosser, and Ron Harré, "Life on the Terraces." In Ken Gelder and Sarah Thornton, eds. *The Subcultures Reader*. London: Routledge, 1997, 327–339.

Martínez Assad, Carlos, and Alicia Ziccardi, eds. *1910: La Universidad Nacional y el Barrio Universitario*. Mexico City: UNAM, 2010.

Martínez, Carlos. *Tlatelolco: tres instantáneas: violencia azteca, violencia al nacer la colonia, violencia en pleno siglo xx.* Mexico City: Editorial Jus, 1972.

Martínez Della Rocca, Salvador. *Estado y Universidad en México, 1920–1968: Historia de los movimientos estudiantiles en la UNAM.* Mexico City: Joan Boildi I Clement, 1986.

Martínez Fisher, Margarita. "La postura del Partido Acción Nacional ante el movimiento estudiantil de 1968." In Salvador Martínez della Rocca, ed. *Voces y Ecos del 68.* Mexico City: Porrúa, 2009, 233–253.

Martínez Nateras, Arturo. "La ruta de la rebeldía." *Revista de la Universidad de México* 34, no. 5 (January 1980), 6–12.

Martré, Gonzalo. *El movimiento popular estudiantil de 1968 en la novela mexicana.* Mexico City: UNAM, 1998.

Marwick, Arthur. *The Sixties: Cultural Revolution in Britain, France, Italy, and the United States, c. 1958–c.1974.* New York: Oxford University Press, 1998.

Marx, Gary T. "Thoughts on a Neglected Category of Social Movement Participant: The Agent Provocateur and the Informant." *American Journal of Sociology* 80, no. 2 (September 1974), 402–442.

Mayo, Sebastián. *La Educación socialista en México. El Asalto a la Universidad Nacional.* Rosario, Argentina: Bear, 1964.

McGirr, Lisa. *Suburban Warriors: The Origins of the New American Right.* Princeton: Princeton University Press, 2001.

McLeod, Hugh. *The Religious Crisis of the 1960s.* New York: Oxford University Press, 2007.

McMillian, John. *Smoking Typewriters: The Sixties Underground Press and the Rise of Alternative Media in America.* New York: Oxford University Press, 2011.

Medina, Luis. *Del cardenismo al avilacamachismo.* Mexico City: El Colegio de México, 1978.

Medina C., Manuel. *EE. UU, y a independencia de América Latina: La soberanía en la constitucion ecuatoriana.* Ecuador: Artes Gráficas Senefelder, 1947.

Medina Valdés, Gerardo. *Operación 10 de Junio.* Mexico City: Ediciones, Universo, 1972.

———. *El 68, Tlatelolco, y el PAN.* Mexico City, PAN, 1990.

Mejía Prieto, Jorge. *Así se habla el mexicano. Diccionario básico de mexicanismos.* Mexico City: Panorama, 1997.

Mendieta y Nuñez, Lucio. "La clase media en México." *Revista Mexicana de Sociología* 17, no. 2/3 (May–December 1955), 517–531.

Mendoza, Nicandro. "Relaciones Estado-IPN, en 1956." In Oscar Mohar, ed. *Crisis y contradicciones en la educación técnica de México.* Mexico City: Edición Gaceta, 1984, 73–96.

Mendoza Rojas, Javier. *Los conflictos de la UNAM en el siglo XX.* Mexico City: UNAM, 2001.

Messinger Cypess, Sandra. *Uncivil Wars: Elena Garro, Octavio Paz, and the Battle for Cultural Memory.* Austin: University of Texas Press, 2012.

Meyer, Lorenzo. "La guerra fría en el mundo periférico: el caso del régimen autoritario mexicano. La utilidad del anticomunismo discreto." In Daniela Spenser, ed. *Espejos de la guerra fría: México, América Central y el Caribe*. Mexico City: CIESAS, 2004, 95–117.

Middlebrook, Kevin J. *The Paradox of Revolution: Labor, the State, and Authoritarianism in Mexico*. Baltimore: Johns Hopkins University Press, 1995.

Miller, Francesca. *Latin American Women and the Search for Social Justice*. New England: University Press of New England, 1991.

Móndrigo, El. *¡El Móndrigo! Bitácora del Consejo Nacional de Huelga*. Mexico City: Editorial Alba Roja, S. C. L., n.d.

Monsiváis, Carlos. *Carlos Monsiváis*. Mexico City: Empresas Editoriales, 1966.

———. *Dias de guardar*. Mexico City: Era, 1970.

———. "Sociedad y cultura." In Rafael Loyola, ed. *Entre la guerra y la estabilidad política. El México de los 40*. Mexico City: Grijalbo, 1990, 259–280.

———. *Salvador Novo: Lo marginal en el centro*. Mexico City: Era, 2000.

———. *El 68: La tradición de la resistencia*. Mexico City: Ediciones Era, 2008.

Mora, Carl. *Mexican Cinema: Reflections of a Society, 1896–1980*. Berkeley: California University Press, 1982.

Moore, Robin D. *Music and Revolution: Cultural Change in Socialist Cuba*. Berkeley: University of California Press, 2006.

Mora de, Juan Miguel. *Tlatelolco 1968: Por fin toda la verdad*. Mexico City: Idamex, 1980.

Moreno, Julio. *Yankee Don't Go Home! Mexican Nationalism, American Business Culture, and the Shaping of Modern Mexico, 1920–1950*. Chapel Hill: University of North Carolina Press, 2003.

Morlet de Varela, Claudia. *Yo dirigí la porra Universitaria*. Mexico City: Imprenta Carma, 1976.

Mraz, John. *Nacho López: Mexican Photographer*. Minneapolis: University of Minnesota Press, 2003.

———. *Looking for Mexico: Modern Visual Culture and National Identity*. Durham, NC: Duke University Press, 2009.

Navarro, Aaron William. "Political Intelligence: Opposition, Parties and the Military." Ph.D. dissertation, Harvard University, 2004.

———. *Political Intelligence and the Creation of Modern Mexico, 1938–1954*. University Park: Pennsylvania State University Press, 2010.

Navarro Palacios, Enrique. "La Reforma Universitaria en México (Ley Caso)." Master's thesis, UNAM, 1949.

Nelson, Diane M. *A Finger in the Wound: Body Politics in Quincentennial Guatemala*. Berkeley: University of California Press, 1999.

Niblo, Stephen. *Mexico in the 1940s: Modernity Politics and Corruption*. New York: SR Books, 1999.

Noguez Quintanar, Jesus. *Primero y diez. 104 años del fútbol americano en México (1890–1994)*. Mexico City: SEESIME, 1994.

Nuwer, Hank. *Wrongs of Passage: Fraternities, Sororities, Hazing, and Binge Drinking*. Bloomington: Indiana University Press, 1999.

Ochoa, Enrique. *Feeding Mexico: The Political Uses of Food since 1910.* New York: SR Books, 2010.

Ornelas Navarro, Carlos. "La Educación técnica y la ideología de la revolución mexicana." In Graciela Lechuga, ed. *Ideología de la revolución mexicana.* Mexico City: Universidad Autónoma Metropolitana, 1984.

Ortega Juárez, Joel. *10 de Junio: ¡Ganámos la calle!* Mexico City: Siglo XXI, 2011.

Ortíz, Orlando. *Jueves de corpus.* Mexico City: Diógenes, 1971.

Ortiz Tovar, Walter. "Informe político del comité ejecutivo de la Asociación de Alumnos de la Escuela Nacional de Ciencias Políticas y Sociales sobre su actividad en FUSA." *Controversia,* no. 2 (January–February, 1968), 40–50.

Padilla, Tanalis. *Rural Resistance in the Land of Zapata: The Jaramillista Movement and the Myth of the Pax Priísta, 1940–1962.* Durham, NC: Duke University Press, 2008.

Padrón, Juan Nocolás. "'El corno emplumado': Un verdadero proyecto de globalización de la cultura." In *La Ventana,* http://laventana.casa.cult.cu/, accessed September 20, 2012.

Palacios, Julia E. "Yo no soy un rebelde sin causa . . . o de cómo el rock & roll llegó a *México.*" In José A. Pérez Islas et al., eds. *Historias de los jóvenes en México: Su presencia en el siglo XX.* Mexico City: IMJ, 2004.

Pansters, Wil. *Politics and Power in Puebla: The Political History of a Mexican State, 1937–1987.* Amsterdam: CEDLA, 1987.

———. "Theorizing Political Culture in Modern Mexico." In Wil Pansters, ed. *Citizens of the Pyramid: Essays on Mexican Political Culture.* Amsterdam: Thela Publishers, 1997, 1–37.

———. "The Transition under Fire: Rethinking Contemporary Mexican Politics." In Kees Kooning and Dirk Kruijt, eds. *Societies of Fear: The Legacy of Civil War, Violence and Terror in Latin America.* New York: Zed Books, 1999, 235–263.

Paoli Bolio, Francisco José. *Conciencia y poder en México. Siglos XIX y XX.* Mexico City: Porrúa, 2002.

Parra, Manuel Germán. "The Revolution Begins a New Era." In Stanley R. Ross, *Is the Mexican Revolution Dead?* Philadelphia: Temple University Press, 1975, 156–160.

Passerini, Luisa. "Youth as a Metaphor for Social Change: Fascist Italy and America in the 1950s." In Giovanni Levi and Jean-Claude Schmitt, eds. *A History of Young People in the West.* Translated by Camille Naish. Cambridge: Belknap Press, 1997, 281–342.

Pellicer de Brody, Olga. *México y la Revolución Cubana.* Mexico City: El Colegio de México, 1972.

Pensado, Jaime. "The (Forgotten) Sixties in Mexico." *The Sixties: A Journal of History, Politics and Culture* 1, no. 1 (June 2008), 83–90.

———. "Student Politics in Mexico in the Wake of the Cuban Revolution." In Karen Dubinsky, Catherine Krull, Susan Mills, and Scott Rutherford, eds. *New World Coming: The Sixties and the Shaping of Global Consciousness.* Toronto: Between the Lines, 2009, 330–338.

———. "Between Cultured Young Men and Mischievous Children: Youth, Transgression, and Protest in Late Nineteenth-Century Mexico." *Journal of the History of Childhood and Youth* 4, no. 1 (2011), 26–57.

Pérez Islas, José A., et al., eds. *Historias de los Jóvenes en México: Su presencia en el siglo XX.* Mexico City: Instituto Mexicano de la Juventud, 2004.

Pérez Rosas, Luís David. "La radiofusión universitaria y los circuitos cerrados de radio en las instituciones de educación superior: una propuesta para la expresión de los estudios." *Revista Mexicana de Ciencias Políticas y Sociales,* no. 192 (September–December 2004), 153–188.

Perlstein, Rick. "Who Owns the Sixties?" *Lingua Franca* 6, no. 4 (1996), 30–37.

Perzabal, Carlos. *De las Memorias de Manuel Marcué Pardiñas.* Mexico City: Rino, 1997.

Pick, Zuzana M. *Constructing the Image of the Mexican Revolution.* Austin: University of Texas Press, 2010.

Pineda Ochoa, Fernando. *En la profundidades del mar (el oro no llegó de Moscú).* Mexico City: Plaza y Valdés, 2003.

Poniatowska, Elena. *La Noche de Tlatelolco.* Mexico City: Era, 1971.

Poo Hurtado, Jorge. "Los protagonistas olvidados." In Rubén Aréchiga Robles et.al., eds. *Asalto al cielo. Lo que no se ha dicho del 68.* Mexico City: Océano, 1998, 121–130.

Porte Petit, Celestino. *El Instituto de la Juventud Mexicana.* Mexico City: Editorial Ruta, 1950.

Portilla, Jorge. *Fenomenología del relajo y otros ensayos* [1962]. Mexico City: Era, 1987.

Power, Margaret. *Right Wing Women in Chile: Feminine Power and the Struggle against Allende, 1964–1973.* University Park: Pennsylvania State University Press, 2002.

Pozas Horcasitas, Ricardo. *La democracia en blanco. El movimiento médico en México, 1964–65.* Mexico City: Siglo XXI, 1993.

———, ed. *Universidad Nacional y Sociedad.* Mexico City: Porrúa, 1990.

Preston, Julia, and Samuel Dillon. *Opening Mexico: The Making of a Democracy.* New York: Farrar, Straus and Giroux, 2004.

Prieto Laurens, Jorge. *Llamado a la América Latina.* Mexico City: FPAC de M, 1954.

Ramírez Garrido, Jaime. *Axkaná: Martin Luis Guzmán.* Mexico City: Conaculta, 2003.

Ramírez, Luis Enrique. *La ingobernable: Encuentros y desencuentros con Elena Garro.* Mexico City: Raya en el Agua, 2000.

Ramírez, Ramón. *El Movimiento Estudiantil de México: Julio-Diciembre de 1968. Tomo I: Análisis Cronología.* Mexico City: Era, 1969a.

———. *El Movimiento Estudiantil de México. Julio-Diciembre de 1968. Tomo II: Documentos.* Mexico City: Era, 1969b.

Randall, Margaret. *To Change the World: My Years in Cuba.* Brunswick, NJ: Rutgers University Press, 2009.

———. "Lost and Found: Pages from El Corno Emplumado/The Plumed Horn," http://www.margaretrandall.org/LOST-FOUND-Selections-from-EL, accessed September 20, 2012.

Rangel Hernández, Lucio. *La Universidad de Michoacana y el movimiento estudiantil, 1966–1989.* Mexico City: Instituto de Investigaciones Históricas, 2009.

Rankin, Monica A. *¡México, la patria! Propaganda and Production during World War II.* Lincoln: University of Nebraska Press, 2009.

Rashkin, Elissa J. *Women Filmmakers in Mexico: The Country of Which We Dream.* Austin: University of Texas Press, 2001.

Rayas, Lucía. "Subjugating the Nation: Women and the Guerrilla Experience." In Fernando Herrera Calderón and Adéla Cedillo, eds. *Challenging Authoritarianism in Mexico: Revolutionary Struggles and the Dirty War, 1964–1982.* London: Routledge, 2012, 167–181.

Reich, Peter L. "The Mexican Catholic Church and Constitutional Change since 1929." *Historian* (September 1997), 77–86.

Revueltas, José. *Ensayo de un proletario sin cabeza.* Mexico City: Era, 1962.

———. *México 68: Juventud y revolución.* Mexico City: Era, 1978.

Rius. "Toda la verdad acerca de los porros." *Supermachos*, no. 596 (June 1977).

———. *Un siglo de caricatura en México.* Mexico City: Grijalbo, 1984.

Rivas Hernández, Eulalio. *Grillos y Gandallas. Lecciones de política "a la Mexicana."* Mexico City: Costa-Amic Editores, 1984.

Rivas Ontiveros, José René. *La izquierda estudiantil en la UNAM: Organizaciones, movilizaciones y liderazgos (1958–1972).* Mexico City: UNAM, 2007.

Robles, Martha. *Educación y sociedad en la historia de México.* Mexico City: Siglo XXI, 1981.

Rock, Paul, and Stanley Cohen. "The Teddy Boy." In V. Bugdano and R. Skidelsky, eds. *The Age of Affluence: 1951–1964.* London: Macmillan, 1970.

Rodda, John. "'Prensa, Pensa': A Journalist's Reflections on Mexico '68." *Bulletin of Latin American Research* 29 (March 2010), 11–22.

Rodríguez Álvarez, Gabriel. *Manuel González Casanova: Pionero del cine universitario.* Jalisco, Mexico: Universidad de Guadalajara, 2009.

Rodríguez Araujo, Octavio. "El henriquismo: Última disidencia política organizada en México." In Carlos Martínez Assad, ed. *La sucesión presidencial en México (Coyuntura electoral y cambio político).* Mexico City: Nueva Imagen, 1981, 139–173.

Rodríguez Kuri, Ariel. "Los primeros días: Una explicación de los orígenes inmediatos del movimiento estudiantil de 1968." *Historia Mexicana* 53, no. 1 (July–September 2003), 179–228.

———. "Hacia México 68: Pedro Ramírez Vázquez y el proyecto olímpico." *Secuencia* 56 (May–August 2003), 37–73.

———. "El lado oscuro de la luna. El momento conservador en 1968." In Erika Pani, ed. *Conservadurismo y derechas en la historia de México.* Mexico City: Fondo de Cultura Económica, 2009, 512–559.

Rodríguez Lozano, Rubén. *El gran chantaje.* Mexico City: Fomento de la Cultura, 1968.

Rojas Bernal, José Enrique. "Por la Federación Estudiantil Universitaria a la organización universitaria del movimiento estudiantil de la Universidad." *Controversia*, no. 2 (January–February 1968), 30–34.

Romero, Laura. "El movimiento fascista en Guadalajara." In Jaime Tamayo, ed. *Perspectivas de los movimientos sociales en la región centro-occidente.* Mexico City: Línea, 1986.

Romo Medrano, Lilia Estela. *Un relato biográfico: Ignacio Chávez rector de la UNAM.* Mexico City: El Colegio Nacional, 1997.

Rosas Lopátegui, Patricia. *El asesinato de Elena Garro.* Mexico City: Porrúa, 2005.

Ross, Stanley R. ed. *¿Ha muerto la revolución?* Mexico City: Red de Jonás, 1979.

Rousset, Antonio. *La Izquierda cercada. El Partido Comunista y el poder durante las coyunturas de 1955 a 1960.* Baja California, Mexico: Universidad Autónoma de Ciudad Juárez, 2000.

Rubenstein, Anne. *Bad Language, Naked Ladies, & Other Threats to the Nation: A Political History of Comic Books in Mexico.* Durham, NC: Duke University Press, 1998.

Rubin Jeffrey W. *Decentering the Regime: Ethnicity, Radicalism and Democracy in Juchitán, México.* Durham, NC: Duke University Press, 1997.

Ruisánchez Serra, José Ramón. "Reading '68: The Tlatelolco Memorial and Gentrification in Mexico City." In Ksenija Bilbija and Leigh A. Payne, eds. *Accounting for Violence: Marketing Memory in Latin America.* Durham, NC: Duke University Press, 2011, 179–206.

Russell Morris, Donald. "Political Violence and Political Modernization in Mexico: 1952–1964." Ph.D. dissertation, University of Wisconsin, 1971.

Sáenz de Miera, Alejandro. *El Instituto Nacional de la Juventud Mexicana visto por un Periodista.* Mexico City: INJM, 1964.

Sagástegui, Marino. *El humor, la guerra y la paz.* Mexico City: Rhumor, 1993.

Sánchez Gudiño, Hugo. *Génesis, desarrollo, y consolidación de los grupos estudiantiles de choque en la UNAM, 1930–1990.* Mexico City: UNAM, 2006.

Sánchez Hidalgo B., Joaquín. *Trazos y mitos de una utopía: La institución Politécnica.* Mexico City: SAIPN, 2000.

Sánchez Saénz, Ana Maria. "Bibliografía sobre el movimiento estudiantil Mexicano de 1968." In Silvia González Marín, ed. *Diálogos sobre el 68.* Mexico City: UNAM, 2003.

Scherer García, Julio, and Carlos Monsiváis. *Parte de Guerra. Tlatelolco 1968, documentos del general Marcelino García Barragán: los hechos y la historia.* Mexico City: Aguilar, 1999.

———. *Tiempo de Saber: Prensa y poder en México* Mexico City: Aguilar, 2003.

Schmidt, Arthur. "Making It Real Compared to What? Reconceptualizing Mexican History since 1940." In Gilbert Joseph, Anne Rubenstein, and Eric Zolov, eds. *Fragments of a Golden Age: The Politics of Culture in Mexico since 1940.* Durham, NC: Duke University Press, 2001.

———. "The Political and Economic Reverberations of the Cuban Revolution in Mexico." *History Compass* 6, no. 4 (July 2008), 1140–1163.

Schmidt, Samuel. *The Deterioration of the Mexican Presidency: The Years of Luis Echeverría.* Edited and translated by Dan A. Cothran. Tucson: University of Arizona Press, 1991.

Schmitt, Karl M. *Communism in Mexico: A Study in Political Frustration.* Austin: University of Texas Press, 1965.

Schmitter, Philippe C. "Still the Century of Corporatism?" *Review of Politics* 36, no. 1 (January 1974).

Scott, Robert E. "Student Political Activism in Latin America." *Daedalus* 97, no. 1 (Winter 1968), 70–98.

Secretaría de Educación Pública, *Memoria de los juegos deportivos nacionales de la revolución*. Mexico City, SEP, 1941.

Segovia, Rafael. "Mexican Politics and the University Crisis." In Richard Fagen and Wayne Cornelius, eds. *Political Power in Latin America: Seven Confrontations*. New Jersey: Prentice Hall, 1970.

Semo, Ilán. *¿Una oposición sin atributos? (Visiones y revisiones sobre la oposición estudiantil.)* Mexico City: CEC-ICUAP, 1981.

———. "El ocaso de los mitos (1958–1968)." In Enrique Semo, ed. *México: Un pueblo en la historia*, vol. 6. Mexico City: Alianza, 1989.

Servín, Elisa. *Ruptura y oposición. El movimiento henriquista, 1945–1954*. Mexico City: Cal y Arena, 2001.

———. "Propaganda y guerra fría: la campaña anticomunista en la prensa mexicana del medio siglo." *Signos Históricos*, no. 11 (January–June 2004), 9–39.

Silva Herzog, Jesús. *Una historia de la Universidad de México y sus problemas*. Mexico City: Siglo XXI, 1974.

Skidmore, Thomas E., and Peter H. Smith. *Modern Latin America*. 6th ed. New York: Oxford University Press, 2005.

Smith, Arthur K., Jr. "Mexico and the Cuban Revolution: Foreign Policy-Making in Mexico under Adolfo López Mateos (1958–1964)." Ph.D. dissertation, Cornell University, 1970.

Smith, Peter H. *Labyrinths of Power: Political Recruitment in Twentieth Century Mexico*. Princeton: Princeton University Press, 1979.

———. "Mexico since 1946." In *The Cambridge History of Latin America*, Vol. VII, 1990.

Solana, Rafael. *Juegos de Invierno*. Mexico City: Ediciones Oasis, 1970.

Solis Mimendi, Antonio. *Jueves de Corpus Sangriento (Revelaciones de un Halcón)*. Mexico City: Offset Alfaro Hnos., S. A., 1975.

Soltenko, Michael. "*México '68*: Power to the Imagination!" *Latin American Perspectives* 32, no. 4 (July 2005), 111–132.

Sorensen, Diana. *A Turbulent Decade Remembered: Scenes from the Latin American Sixties*. Stanford: Stanford University Press, 2007.

Spenser, Daniela, ed. *Espejos de la guerra fría: México, América Central y el Caribe*. Mexico City: SRE, 2004.

Spencer, David. "The Impact of the Cuban Revolution on Latin American Student Politics." In David Spencer, ed. *Student Politics in Latin America*. Philadelphia: USNSA, 1965.

Spota, Luis. *La Plaza*. Mexico City: J. Mortiz, 1972.

Stevens, Evelyn P. "Legality and Extra-legality in Mexico." *Journal of Inter-American Studies and World Affairs* 12, no. 1 (January 1970), 62–75.

————. *Protest and Response in Mexico.* Cambridge: MIT Press, 1974.

Suárez, Luis. *Alejo Peralta, un patrón sin patrones.* Mexico City: Grijalbo, 1992.

Taibo II, Paco Ignacio. *'68.* New York: Seven Stories Press, 2004.

Tatum, Charles. "Images of the United States in Selected Mexican Books." In Roger Rollin, ed. *The Americanization of the Global Village: Essays in Contemporary Popular Culture.* Bowling Green, OH: Bowling Green State University Popular Press, 1989, 33–60.

Taylor, Philip B. "The Mexican Election of 1958: Affirmation of Authoritarianism?" *Western Political Quarterly* 13, no. 3 (September 1960), 722–744.

Teichman, Judith A. *The Politics of Freeing Markets in Latin America: Chile, Argentina, and Mexico.* Chapel Hill, NC: University of North Carolina Press, 2001.

Tirado Villegas, Gloria. *La otra historia. Voces de mujeres del 68, Puebla.* Puebla, Mexico: Benemérita Universidad Autónoma de Puebla, 2004.

Torremocha, Margarita. *La vida estudiantil en el Antiguo Régimen.* Madrid, Spain: Alianza, 1998.

Trevizo, Dolores. *Rural Protest and the Making of Democracy in Mexico, 1968–2000.* University Park: Pennsylvania State University Press, 2011.

Ulloa Bornemann, Alberto. *Surviving Mexico's Dirty War: A Political Prisoner's Memoir.* Edited and translated by Arthur Schmidt and Aurora Camacho de Schmidt. Philadelphia: Temple University Press, 2007.

Urrutia Castro, Manuel. *Trampa en Tlatelolco. Sintesis de una felonía contra México.* Mexico City: n/p, 1969.

Valle, Eduardo. *El año de la rebelión por la democracia. Con una cierta mirada.* Mexico City: Oceano, 2008.

Varon, Jeremy. *Bringing the War Home: The Weather Underground, the Red Army Faction, and Revolutionary Violence in the Sixties and Seventies.* Berkeley: University of California Press, 2004.

Vaughan, Mary Kay. *Cultural Politics in Revolution: Teachers, Peasants, and Schools in Mexico, 1930–1940.* Tucson: University of Arizona Press, 1997.

Vázquez Mantecón, Alvaro, and Sergio R. Arroyo. *Memorial del 68.* Mexico City: UNAM, Dirección General de Publicaciones y Fomento Editorial, 2007.

Vélez-Ibañez, Carlos G. *Rituals of Marginality: Politics, Process, and Culture Change in Urban Central Mexico, 1969–1974.* Berkeley: University of California Press, 1983.

Verkaaik, Oskar. *Migrants and Militants: Fun and Urban Violence in Pakistan.* Princeton: Princeton University Press, 2004.

Vila, Pablo. "Rock Nacional and Dictatorship in Argentina." *Popular Music* 6, no. 2 (May 1987), 129–148.

Villaseñor y Villaseñor, Alejandro. *Guillermo: Memorias de un estudiante.* Mexico City: El Tiempo, 1897.

Viqueira Albán, Juan Pedro. *Propriety and Permissiveness in Bourbon Mexico.* Translated by Sonya Lipsett-Rivera and Sergio Rivera Ayala. New York: Scholarly Resources, 1999.

Vogeley, Nancy. *Lizardi and the Birth of the Novel in Spanish America.* Miami: University Press of Florida, 2001.

Volpi Escalante, Jorge. *La imaginación y el poder: Una historia intelectual de 1968.* Mexico City, Era, 1998.

Ward, Peter. *Mexico City: The Production and Reproduction of an Urban Environment.* New York: G. K. Hall and Co., 1990.

Waters, Sarah. "1968 in Memory and Place." In Ingo Cornils and Sarah Waters, eds. *Memories of 1968: International Perspectives, Vol. 16 of Cultural History and Literary Imagination.* Bern: Peter Lang, 2010, 1–22.

Willer, Claudio. "El corno emplumado e eco contemporáneo, grandes momentos da história da cultura Ibero-Americana: Sergio Mondragón e Miguel Grinberg." *Revista de Cultura,* no. 32 (2003), http://www.revista.agulha.nom.br/ag32willer.htm, accessed October 2, 2012.

Witherspoon, Kevin B. *Before the Eyes of the World: Mexico and the 1968 Olympic Games.* DeKalb: Northern Illinois University Press, 2008.

Whyte, William F. *Street Corner Society.* Chicago: University of Chicago Press, 1943.

Wolf, Eric R. "Aspects of Group Relations in a Complex Society: Mexico." *American Anthropologist,* no. 58 (1956), 1065–1078.

Wright, Thomas C. *Latin America in the Era of the Cuban Revolution.* Westport, CT: Praeger, 1991.

Yáñez Delgado, Alfonso. *La manipulación de la fe: Fúas contra Carolinos en la Universidad Poblana.* Puebla, Mexico: Benemérita Universidad Autónoma de Puebla, 1996.

Young, Dolly J. "Mexican Literary Reactions to Tlatelelco 1968." *Latin American Research Review* 20, no. 2 (1985), 71–85.

Young, Jock. "The Subterranean World of Play." In Ken Gelder and Sarah Thornton, eds. *The Subcultures Reader.* London: Routledge, 1997.

Zermeño, Sergio. *México: Una democracia utópica.* Mexico City: Siglo XXI, 1978.

Zirión, Antonio Q. "Phenomenology in Mexico: A Historical Profile." *Continental Philosophy Review,* no. 33 (2000), 75–92.

Zolov, Eric. "Protest and Counterculture in the 1968 Student Movement in Mexico." In Gerard J. De Groot, ed. *Student Protest: The Sixties and After.* London: Longman, 1998, 70–84.

———. *Refried Elvis: The Rise of the Mexican Counterculture.* Berkeley: University of California Press, 1999.

———. "Toward an Analytical Framework for Assessing the Impact of the 1968 Student Movement on U.S.-Mexican Relations." *Journal of Iberian and Latin American Studies* 9, no. 2 (December 2003), 41–68.

———. "Showcasing the 'Land of Tomorrow': Mexico and the 1968 Olympics." *Americas* 61, no. 2 (October 2004), 159–188.

———. "Jorge Carreño's Graphic Satire and the Politics of 'Presidentialism' in Mexico during the 1960s." *Estudios Interdisciplinarios de América Latina y el Caribe* 17, no. 1 (January–June 2006), 13–38.

———. "¡Cuba sí, yanquis no!: The Sacking of the Instituto Cultural México-Norteamericano in Morelia, Michoacán, 1961." In Gilbert M. Joseph and Daniela

Spenser, eds. *In from the Cold: Latin America's New Encounter with the Cold War.* Durham, NC: Duke University Press, 2008, 214–252.

———. "Expanding Our Conceptual Horizons: The Shift from an Old to a New Left in Latin America." *Contra-corriente: A Journal on Social History and Literature in Latin America* 5, no. 2 (Winter 2008), 47–73.

———. "La juventud se impone: Rebelión cultural y los temores de los mayors en México 1968." *De/RotaR* I, no. 2 (2009), 102–107.

Index

CPSIA information can be obtained
at www.ICGtesting.com
Printed in the USA
JSHW032238250821
18178JS00001B/12